FAVORITE RECIPES®
OF HOME ECONOMICS TEACHERS

REVISED EDITION

Quick & Easy Dishes

© Favorite Recipes Press/Nashville EMS MCMLXXVIII
Post Office Box 77, Nashville, Tennessee 37202
Library of Congress Cataloging in Publication Data
Main entry under title:
Quick and easy dishes.
    Includes index.
    1. Cookery. 2. Low-calorie diet. I. Favorite
Recipes Press. II. Title: Favorite recipes of home
economics teachers.
TX715.Q6   1978   641.5'55   78-23575
ISBN 0-87197-124-0

1 2 3 4 5 6 7 8 9 0

DEAR HOMEMAKER,

Lifestyles change, demands change, but good recipes don't need changing! Working couples, single women and men and just the average homemaker with a family, must find economical ways to provide that much needed "extra time" for pleasure and relaxation. So, frequently seeking an *"easy out,"* they turn to the *packaged food* or "quickie-food shop" — an unhealthy habit in either case!

QUICK AND EASY DISHES from Home Economics Teachers, is the *best answer and the best "out"* for all homemakers who want more free time without sacrificing good nutrition. My first rule of thumb is, "if it is good enough for the experts, it's good enough for me!" That's why I have always loved the Home Economics Teachers' Cookbooks for myself and why I can recommend them to all my friends without a twinge of uncertainty! They are so reliable, many homemakers say they just *can't cook* without them.

NEVER OUT OF STYLE

So, after years of hard, daily use, cookbooks begin to simply wear out — but the demand and popularity of the oldest editions *never wears out!* That's why we have reprinted this very outstanding cookbook, *QUICK AND EASY DISHES* . . . to fill the demands of long-time customers who are reordering.

If you have never *"experienced"* a Home Economics Teachers' Cookbook, then I'll tell you it's time for a new beginning of cooking pleasure for you with *QUICK AND EASY DISHES.* Your support of the Home Economics Clubs and FHA Clubs through the purchase of these cookbooks, will be worth your investment many times over!

Thank you, *dear homemaker,* and after you have tried *QUICK AND EASY DISHES,* you may order more Home Economics Teachers' Cookbooks, listed in the back pages of this book. Very soon, *"our favorite recipes"* will be *your favorites too!*

> Nicky Beaulieu
> Home Economist

BOARD OF ADVISORS

RUTH STOVALL, *Chairman*
Branch Director, Program Services Branch
Division of Vocational-Technical
    and Higher Education
Alabama Department of Education

CATHERINE A. CARTER
Consultant, Consumer Homemaking
    Education
Illinois Division of Vocational
    and Technical Education

ANNE G. EIFLER (Retired)
Senior Program Specialist
Home Economics Education
Pennsylvania Department of Education

BARBARA GAYLOR
Supervisor, Consumer and Homemaking
    Education
Michigan Department of Education

JANET LATHAM
Supervisor, Home Economics Education
Idaho State Board of Vocational Education

BETTY ROMANS
State Advisor, Texas Association
    Future Homemakers of America
Consultant, Homemaking Education
Texas Education Agency

FRANCES RUDD
Supervisor, Home Economics Education
Arkansas Department of Education

ODESSA N. SMITH (Retired)
State Supervisor, Home Economics Education
Louisiana Department of Education

3

Contents

Timesaving Tips For Easy Cooking

Creative homemakers take self-rewarding satisfaction in being the inventive force behind the comfortable atmosphere and smooth operation of a happy household. They find that it is always time well spent when they personally create "from scratch," so to speak — especially when the result is a memorable meal. But, even the most creative homemakers know from experience that there is just no avoiding those occasions when the time is just not there to spend — wisely or unwisely.

The average American family is a busy bunch! In addition to work, school and household chores, most families also enjoy sports, bridge or bowling nights, choir practice, art classes, volunteer work, movies, concerts, and Sunday drives — just to name a few! This often puts meals on a very tight time schedule. Then, there are the unscheduled hurry-up meals, too. It usually happens when Mom has decided it is a good night to eat out: Dad comes hungry and loaded down with an evening full of work; the kids are even hungrier and headed for a last-minute library trip or a forgotten play rehearsal. So, dinner has to be something that is both quick to fix and easy to clean up.

Scheduled or unscheduled, the only answer to times like these is to be ready in advance. But, even if you don't always know WHEN you will need a quick and easy menu, you can be sure that you WILL need one at some time or another. So, be prepared! There are a variety of ways to make cooking faster and more efficient. Some you will use only on occasion, others you will find helpful all the time. Moreover, your meals will be as delicious as ever, and you may even find you want to use quick and easy menu plans most of the time!

Even if a homemaker could always be assured of having plenty of time to do all that she needs to do, she still needs an organized and uncluttered cooking and serving area. The busier you and your family are, the more important an easy-to-use kitchen becomes. Anyone who spends a lot of time cooking almost instinctively has the most-used pots and pans, foods, dishes, utensils, and appliances within easy reach. But, if you have drawers cluttered with duplicate or unused utensils, or cabinets containing pans, plates, or other equipment you haven't used in a year, clean out! You will save time rummaging through needless things when you are in a hurry — and when you are *not* in a hurry. Timesaving *additions* to your kitchen might include either a pressure cooker, a blender, a food processor, or a microwave, a slow-cooker, a toaster oven — or even such simple items as a hand mixer, a pair of kitchen scissors, or a chopping board.

When planning meals, include several dishes that may be baked at the same time in order to save time and money.

To keep parsley from spoiling, place in ice cube tray. Fill tray with water and freeze. Place frozen cubes, as needed, in small amount of warm water to thaw.

A surprising amount of time can be saved just by using a few tricks when unloading and putting up the groceries. Before putting foods into the cabinets, freezer or refrigerator, remove unnecessary "window dress" packaging on food items, leaving only that wrapping which is needed to keep the product fresh. Freeze ground meat, chicken pieces, chops, rolls, and other foods in small, serving-size packages. These thaw quickly and you prepare only as much as is needed, whether it's for one person or for five. Buy an extra block of cheese. Grate the entire block, and store, tightly covered, in the refrigerator. You will save *lots* of time every time you use a recipe calling for grated cheese. Slice, butter and season French bread before freezing. Store in serving-size packages for instant oven-to-table use. Buy large (economical, also!) packages of ground meat. Before storing in freezer, make hamburger patties out of one portion, meat loaf mix out of another, and meatballs from the rest. You will have meals that are quick to thaw and quick to eat!

Purchase onions, green peppers, parsley, celery, and similar foods in quantity, when prices are low and they taste their best. Chop and store in freezer for instant use. Purchase lemons and other citrus fruits in the same way; squeeze as usual and freeze the juice in ice cube trays. Remove the frozen cubes to plastic bags and store in freezer for use as needed. Don't throw away the peel, either! Grate it, refrigerate it in small plastic bags for citrus peel flavoring whenever you need it — in an instant.

Use these hints, and invent your own, as your cooking and shopping habits allow. You have to set aside time for grocery shopping each week or two, anyway. The extra time it takes right then to practice these hints will save you double the time and energy it will take to do the same things later. And, if you need to fix something in a hurry, the time you will have saved will seem invaluable.

In addition to freezing meat loaf and casserole mixes, and individual portions of entrees and vegetables, there is another timesaving way to use your freezer. Set aside a time each week or every few weeks to mix, bake, and freeze. If you spend time each day or two preparing fresh quick breads and homemade desserts for your family, this will save you lots of time without sacrificing any of the quality you want in your menu plans. Bake several cake layers and freeze them; all you will have to do after that is thaw, frost, and serve. You can also do the same for quick and sweet breads, brownies, cookies and cookie dough, corn muffins, and other baked goods. This is a quick and easy trick the whole family can join in on, so you can have fun while saving time and energy.

Pack cookie dough firmly into juice cans. Cover and freeze. Open other end of can and push dough out gently. Slice and bake. Dough need not be thawed before slicing.

Place 2 tablespoons cornstarch in 1-cup measuring cup. Fill cup with all-purpose flour and sift 3 times. Mixture is equal to 1 cup of sifted cake flour.

As the information in this section indicates, a freezer is invaluable to quick and easy cooking. You can prepare everything from simple garnishes and single recipes to complete meals, in advance, and have them ready-to-use, right in your freezer. But, there are some important things to remember in using your freezer to assure your foods will stay fresh and flavorful until you are ready to use them. Most importantly, the foods should be properly wrapped and protected from freezer burn, which occurs when the very cold air of the freezer draws moisture from the food, drying and discoloring it, and making it inedible.

Timesaving Tips

Pour leftover coffee into ice cube trays; freeze; Remove cubes from trays; store in plastic bag in freezer. Serve as needed in iced coffee.

When preparing a casserole, double the amount of ingredients. Line 1 baking dish with foil and fill with casserole mixture. Freeze until firm. Remove the frozen block from the dish and wrap for storage, freeing the dish for use. Return the frozen block to the same dish to bake.

Collect vegetables and meats left in pans at close of each meal; chop meats. Place in plastic container; cover. Place in freezer. Combine contents of container and tomato juice or broth; season and heat when nutritious hot soup is needed.

Whenever you make waffles, prepare an extra recipe and freeze the extra waffles. Frozen waffles can be placed unthawed in a hot oven and be ready to eat in a very few minutes, fresh and delicious.

Make whipped cream swirls on cookie sheet using leftover whipping cream. Place cookie sheet in freezer until swirls are firm. Remove from cookie sheet; wrap in plastic wrap. Store in freezer until needed.

When making meat loaf, casseroles or other items that may be frozen, make more than one and freeze the extras. This utilizes the freezer, saves time, energy and cleaning as well as giving homemade convenient foods. Party foods may be readied for guests in minutes.

Freeze chili in ice cube trays; transfer cubes to plastic bag for storage. Select needed number of cubes; thaw. Heat in saucepan. Chili cubes thaw faster than a larger frozen block.

Prepare sandwiches from leftover meats. Freeze. Sandwiches are ready as needed for packed lunches, or for surprise lunch company.

Plastic wrap and aluminum foil are adequate only for small freezer compartments (which will hold food at 32°F. or lower), especially when the food will only be frozen for a short period of time. But, if you store foods in a colder freezer unit (which holds the food at 0°F. or less), you must protect the food with one or more layers of freezer paper. This paper is readily available in grocery stores.

Also, you should always *date* any packages you place in the freezer, even if you plan to store it for a short period of time. You might even want to be very specific, such as "Best When Used Before ___(date)___." Be sure, as well, to clearly mark what the package contains so that you won't thaw cupcakes when you were planning to serve chicken. Most foods keep in a deep freeze from six months to one year, and up to three months in the freezing compartment of a refrigerator.

QUICK TRICKS WITH MASTER MIXES

Save yourself numerous individual mixing times by using Master Mixes such as the following. They are cheaper and fresher than the ones purchased in the grocery store. And, the results will be quick and easy foods that taste homemade because they are homemade!

Master Mix for Biscuits and Muffins:

9 c. all-purpose flour, sifted
1/3 c. double-acting baking powder
1 tbsp. salt

2 tsp. cream of tartar
1/4 c. sugar
2 c. all-vegetable shortening

Sift dry ingredients together three times in large mixing bowl. Cut in shortening with two knives or pastry blender until mixture resembles coarse meal. Store, tightly covered, at room temperature.

To Make Biscuits from Master Mix:

3 c. Master Mix
2/3 to 1 c. milk

Stir together about 25 strokes. Knead several times on floured surface. Roll out and cut in rounds. Place on baking sheet. Bake at 425 degrees for 12 to 15 minutes, or until biscuits are golden brown. Yield: 12-15 biscuits.

To Make Muffins from Master Mix:

2 tbsp. sugar
3 c. Master Mix
1 egg
1 c. milk

Add sugar to mix. Combine egg and milk. Add to mix; stir just until moistened. Place in greased muffin tins. Bake at 425 degrees for about 20 minutes. Yield: 12 medium muffins.

Master Mix for Pudding:

1 1/2 c. sugar
2 1/2 c. instant nonfat dry milk
1 1/4 c. flour
1 tsp. salt

Combine sugar, dry milk, flour and salt in bowl; stir until thoroughly mixed. Store, tightly covered, at room temperature.

To Make Vanilla Pudding from Master Pudding Mix:

1 1/4 c. Master Pudding Mix
2 1/2 c. warm water
1 tbsp. butter or margarine
1 egg, beaten
3/4 tsp. vanilla extract

Combine mix with water in saucepan. Cook over low heat until thick, stirring constantly. Stir in butter, beaten egg and vanilla. Cool, then chill. Yield: 6 servings.

Master Mix for Pie Pastry:

2 tbsp. salt
6 c. flour
4 c. all-vegetable shortening

Stir salt into flour thoroughly. Cut shortening into flour until mixture resembles coarse meal. Separate into six equal portions and store in small plastic bags. When ready to use, add ice water until pastry mix is moistened. Roll out thin, and use as directed for pie recipe. Yield: Dough for 3 double-crust pies.

Master Mix for Hot Chocolate:

1 c. instant cocoa
1/2 c. powdered sugar
1/4 tsp. salt
1/2 c. nondairy creamer
4 c. instant nonfat dry milk

Combine all ingredients thoroughly. Store, tightly covered, at room temperature. To Make Hot Cocoa: Place 6 tablespoons of mix in cup or mug. Add 3/4 cup very hot water, and stir until mix is dissolved. Add more or less mix, according to taste. Yield: Mix for 15 servings.

BE PREPARED FOR SURPRISES

You can never predict when you might find yourself unprepared for a meal — surprise guests *do* show up at times, you *do* forget to thaw out meat every now and then, and grocery shopping trips *do* get delayed, sometimes. So, keep yourself an "emergency shelf" stocked, and DO NOT use the items you put there, unless you are truly caught off guard. Then, always immediately replace what you use from your supply. Concentrate on stocking the shelf with canned, dry, and instant foods, even if you do not normally use these foods. As a rule, they have a very long shelf life. Of course, even these foods can stay on the shelf only so long. So, date each can or container and make a habit of replacing them regularly. For example, every three to six months, take one of the emergency shelf items, replace it with an item from your everyday shelf (date the replacement), and use the older item in that night's menu.

There is no reason to overstock the shelf with every single item you think you might need. Just keep a variety of things on hand from which you could prepare one, three, or even more meals. Gear the contents of the shelf to your lifestyle, and it won't be overstocked. Some examples of the foods you might choose for your emergency shelf include:

CANNED GOODS: Ham, tuna, or seafood; corn, carrots, green beans or peas, potatoes, tomatoes; creamed soups, tomato soup; fruit and fruit pie filling; tomato paste, mushroom pieces, pickles or relish; jelly or preserves; brown bread; cocktail nuts; bouillon cubes.

DRY GOODS: Pasta and/or rice; dry mixes for soups and various sauces; dry milk; instant soft drink mixes, instant tea, coffee, nondairy creamer; cake and frosting mix, pancake mix; dried fruits.

Finally, do not neglect keeping your Master Mixes ready for use, and do not let your staple foods and seasonings run out. With these foods on hand, you should never be without ingredients to create a meal you can be proud of. And, no one ever has to know that you were "caught off guard."

MORE QUICK TRICKS WITH FOOD

There are times when you are preparing a meal in a hurry, or at a moment's notice that you wish you had this ingredient or that garnish, or just a few extra minutes of time to cook something extra special — and it helps when you can save on clean up time, as well. Many of the suggestions that follow may be just what you are looking for!

Beat equal amounts of instant nonfat dry milk and cold liquid into stiff peaks. Use for topping for desserts and salads or in fluffy fruit dressings. Lemon juice may be added at soft-peak stage to stabilize whip and accent flavor.

Grind leftover roast pork or other meat in food grinder. Add salad dressing, garlic salt and onion salt to taste. Store in freezer or in glass jar in refrigerator. A welcome change from cold cuts for sandwiches.

Many Chinese dishes such as chop suey and chow mein call for water chestnuts. Substitute an equal quantity of peeled sliced radishes for water chestnuts. Add to Chinese dish about 5 minutes before removing from heat. Radishes remain crisp.

A tasty substitute for sour cream may be prepared by combining 1/4 cup water and 1 cup cottage cheese in blender container. Blend on high speed for 20 seconds, until cottage cheese is liquified. Add 1 teaspoon lemon juice, 1/2 teaspoon salt and onion salt, garlic salt or chives to taste.

Leftover gravy may be used in place of soup in casserole dishes such as green beans and mushroom soup.

Cook vegetables in bottom of double boiler while preparing cheese sauce or other recipe in top of double boiler. This saves both time and fuel.

Cut thin slice from each end of potatoes; cut deep slash in each side. Bake at usual temperature for shorter than usual baking time.

Use the divider from an ice tray to cut biscuits in a hurry. Shape dough to conform with size of divider and cut, biscuits will separate at dividing lines.

Combine 1 cup confectioners' sugar and 2 tablespoons frozen lemonade and mix until smooth. Use as dessert topping on cakes, puddings or custards. Topping may be stored in refrigerator or freezer.

Timesaving Miscellany

Aluminum foil is a time and mess saver almost without equal. Not only does it seal in flavor and moistness, it seals in the mess! Foods can be cooked in it, over the coals or in the oven, to save time that would be spent in cleaning and scrubbing pans. Casseroles, broiler pans, baking sheets, and other cooking pans can be lined with foil and the mess "thrown away" after the cooking is done.

Be careful not to use too much foil wrap for your cooking packages, or it will serve to slow down the cooking process. Use only enough to fully cover and tightly seal the food. Don't just crumple the foil around the food; fold it neatly with even creases and firm crimps. For a more stable cooking package when needed, set the food bundle into a pan — the pan will remain clean. Leftover food portions can be rewrapped in the original cooking foil and refrigerated for later use.

Aluminum foil is a virtual necessity if you make a habit of cooking double recipes of meat loaf, casseroles, poultry stuffing, and so forth. The extra recipe can be cooked, cooled, and put directly into the freezer to be thawed, warmed and eaten later. Or, the recipe mixture can be readied and frozen for later cooking. Aluminum foil is also an excellent surface for sifting, grating, squeezing, crushing cracker crumbs, and so forth. Tomato juice, lemon juice, vinegar, and similar foods may cause the aluminum foil to darken slightly, but it is not at all harmful. If foods tend to stick to the foil during cooking, feel free to lightly grease the foil before wrapping it around the food.

FABULOUS "FAST FOODS"

As homemakers everywhere already know, it's the care and attention put into food preparation that makes for memorable mealtimes — and not the hours spent "slaving in a hot kitchen." You can make any mealtime quick and easy without making it look and taste like the "fast foods" you can carry home in a sack. The time you save in using quick and easy cooking and clean up ideas can be added to so many of the other things you do — the time you spend with your family after a meal, or in sewing, jogging, writing letters, or anything! Whether you save quick and easy cooking for only those times when you need it, or whether you always think quick and easy, you can be sure that your meals will never fail to be perfectly delicious.

Quick Meat & Poultry Dishes

On most tables, the meal is built around the meat — whether it is beef, pork, poultry, lamb or veal. But, creating a quick and easy meat entree that is appealing as it is full of flavor poses a real problem for the hurried homemaker. Never fear! Innovative cooks have created delicious ways around this problem that please the palate as easily as they challenge the clock.

There is always a speedy way to prepare ground meat — such as having the makings for a meat loaf or meatballs on hand in the freezer, ready to cook. Or, it can be mixed quickly into a hearty chili, a family-style skillet meal, or into savory patties to be broiled and dressed up with seasonings and sauces, in a snap! Stir-fry dishes, cooked quickly Oriental style, can feature beef, pork, or chicken, complemented with an array of exciting flavors. Here's a quick way with chicken: Drop freshly-bought chicken into boiling, seasoned water as soon as you get it home. When it is done, pull the meat from the bone (separate it into packages of dark and light meat, if you wish). Wrap it securely and freeze it. You'll have cooked chicken on hand whenever you need it for casseroles, soups, sandwiches, chicken pie, and other favorite poultry dishes.

The age-old way of preparing lamb is also one of the quickets — chunks of lamb, alternated on a skewer with pieces of onion and other vegetables, known as shish kabob. You can have this Middle-Eastern treat ready within minutes under the broiler, and lamb chops, too. Veal, because it is such a delicate and lean meat, requires short cooking time. So, even gourmet favorites like breaded veal cutlets browned in butter can be on the table in less than an hour.

It seems that the modern approach to cooking is "the quicker the better." Good cooks know the secret to successful quick and easy cookery. If the food looks and tastes as if it took hours to prepare, then it will bring compliments — even if the dish took only a short time. You can depend on these quick and easy recipes for your favorite meats to bring you those compliments, Home Economics Teachers wouldn't have it any other way!

Meats

BARBECUED CORNED BEEF

3 or 4 med. onions, chopped
1 c. catsup
1/4 c. Worcestershire sauce
1 tsp. vinegar
1 tsp. sugar
1 tsp. salt
1 tsp. chili powder
1 can corned beef

Brown onions in fat. Add remaining ingredients with 2 cups water. Simmer for 2 hours or until thick. Yield: 8 servings.

Stephanie Preston Heatwell
Mark Twain Intermediate School
Alexandria, Virginia

TASTY CORNED BEEF AND CABBAGE

1 med. cabbage
1 No. 303 can tomatoes
1 can corned beef
1 tsp. salt

Wash cabbage; chop medium fine. Heat tomatoes, corned beef and salt in medium saucepan to boiling point. Add cabbage; cover. Cook for 5 to 10 minutes or until cabbage is tender. Yield: 4 servings.

Marilyn B. Newton, Cobb Jr. H.S.
Tallahassee, Florida

CORNED BEEF-CORN PATTIES

1   15 1/2-oz. can corned beef hash
1 tbsp. prepared mustard
1   7-oz. can whole kernel corn,
     drained
1 egg, beaten
1/4 c. sifted flour
1/4 tsp. salt
1/2 tsp. baking powder
4 tbsp. margarine

Combine corned beef hash, mustard and corn with egg. Sift flour with salt and baking powder. Add to hash mixture. Shape mixture into 8 patties. Fry in hot margarine until brown. Yield: 8 servings.

Ilene Ridgely, East Richland H.S.
Olney, Illinois

CORNED BEEF CHEESEBURGERS

1   15-oz. can corned beef hash
1/4 c. chili sauce

1/4 c. sweet pickle relish
1 tbsp. prepared mustard
8 buns
8 slices process American cheese

Mix hash, chili sauce, relish and mustard together. Split buns; spread hash mixture on each half of bun. Broil 6 minutes. Cut cheese slices in half; place on buns. Broil 1 to 3 minutes more until cheese melts. Yield: 8 servings.

Mrs. Ann Holt, Ousley Jr. H.S.
Arlington, Texas

BAKED EGGS-CORNED BEEF AND BANANAS

1   15 1/2-oz. can corned beef hash
2 firm bananas, halved crosswise
2 tsp. butter or margarine, melted
4 eggs

Spread corned beef hash over bottom and side of 9-inch pie pan. Press bananas into corned beef hash spoke-fashion or at right angles, making a cross. Brush with melted butter. Bake in 400-degree oven for 15 minutes. Make a depression in each corned beef area; break an egg into each depression. Reduce oven temperature to 350 degrees. Bake 8 to 10 minutes or until egg is set. Yield: 4 servings.

Photograph for this recipe on page 136.

PICNIC BARBECUE

4 med. yellow onions, chopped
2 stalks celery, chopped
1 can corned beef, chopped
1 c. drained canned tomatoes
1 tbsp. chili powder
1 tbsp. vinegar
3 tbsp. Worcestershire sauce
1/4 c. chili sauce

Saute onions and celery in small amount of oil until glossy. Add remaining ingredients with 1 1/2 cups water. Simmer slowly, uncovered, 1 hour to 1 hour and 30 minutes. Add more water if mixture becomes too dry. Reheat when needed. Serve in warm hamburger buns. Yield: 6 servings.

Blanche Knott, Lawrence Co. H.S.
Lawrenceburg, Tennessee

CORNED BEEF AND CABBAGE ROLLS

1   16-oz. can corned beef hash
1 tbsp. onion, chopped

8 lg. cabbage leaves
Salt and pepper to taste
Butter
1 beef bouillon cube

Combine hash and onion. Form into eight 3-inch rolls. Pour boiling water over cabbage leaves. Cook 2 minutes; drain. Sprinkle with salt and pepper. Place corned beef roll on each leaf. Roll up and fasten with toothpicks. Place in baking dish; dot with butter. Dissolve bouillon cube in 3/4 cup hot water. Pour over cabbage rolls; cover. Bake in 350-degree oven for 20 minutes. Yield: 8 servings.

Mrs. Leona Vaughn, Ferndale H.S.
Ferndale, Washington

SHORT CUT BEEF STEW

2 med. cooked potatoes, diced
2 cooked carrots, chopped
1 can corned beef
1 can stewed tomatoes
1 med. onion, chopped
1 beef bouillon cube
Celery and garlic salt to taste

Combine all ingredients; mix well. Simmer until flavors are blended. Yield: 4 servings.

Mrs. Judy Elmore, Mowat Jr. H.S.
Lynn Haven, Florida

CHIPPED BEEF ON TOAST

1 box frozen creamed peas
3 to 4 oz. dried beef
Toast

Prepare peas according to package directions. Add dried beef and heat. Milk may be added if mixture is too thick. Serve on toast. Yield: 4-5 servings.

Suzanne Blue, Deerfield School
Deerfield, Michigan

DRIED BEEF-MACARONI MIX-UP

1 pkg. macaroni and Cheddar cheese dinner
1 can cream of celery or mushroom soup
1 4-oz. can or jar dried beef, torn
  into bite-sized pieces

Cook macaroni according to package directions; drain. Add 1 1/2 cups hot water, soup, dried beef

and cheese sauce mix. Bring to a boil. Simmer until thick, about 2 minutes. Yield: 4 servings.

Mrs. Lou Penton, Sherman H.S.
Sherman, Texas

BEEF WITH BAKED BEANS

1 sm. jar or pkg. dried beef
1 tbsp. butter
1 med. can baked beans
2 tbsp. catsup
1 tbsp. sugar

Break dried beef into small pieces; brown in butter. Add beans, catsup and sugar. Heat thoroughly. Serve on pieces of brown toast.

Byrdella I. Pawlowski, Lane Indep. School
Lane, South Dakota

SKILLET BEEF AND CORN

2 1/2 oz. shredded dried beef
2 tbsp. minced onion
2 tbsp. butter
1 tbsp. flour
3/4 c. milk
1 No. 303 can cream-style corn
1/2 c. shredded Cheddar cheese
2 tbsp. minced green pepper or pimento

Fry beef and onions in butter until beef begins to curl. Stir in flour. Add milk; stir until thickened. Add corn; heat until hot. Add cheese and green pepper; stir over low heat until cheese melts. Serve on buttered toast cups or triangles. Yield: 4 servings.

Viola Gracey, Travis Jr. H.S.
Snyder, Texas

EASY ROAST BEEF AND GRAVY

1 3 to 5-lb. beef roast
1 env. dry onion soup mix
1 can cream of mushroom soup

Place roast in large piece of heavy aluminum foil. Sprinkle soup mix over roast; add soup. Close foil so steam does not escape but leave an air pocket above roast. Bake at 300 to 350 degrees about 45 minutes per pound. Yield: 8 servings.

Mrs. Mary Menking, Gonzales H.S.
Gonzales, Texas

Meats

REPEAT MEAT PIE

Leftover roast beef
Leftover roast beef gravy
Leftover potatoes, diced
Leftover carrots, diced
1 can refrigerator biscuits

Cut beef into cubes. Thin gravy with water. Combine all ingredients except biscuits; place in greased casserole. Top with biscuits. Bake at 400 degrees for 15 or 20 minutes until brown. Serve hot.

Mrs. Dony R. Baker, McLean H.S.
McLean, Texas

SKILLET BEEF WITH CABBAGE

1   1 1/2-lb. head of cabbage
1 onion, sliced
4 tbsp. butter or margarine
1/2 tsp. salt
Dash of pepper
4 servings of thinly sliced cooked roast beef

Cut cabbage into quarters; wash, dry and chop fine. Cook, covered, in salted water until almost tender; drain. Saute with onion in 3 tablespoons butter until tender. Season with salt and pepper. Saute beef gently in remaining butter until very hot. Place on serving platter; top with cabbage and drippings. Yield: 4 servings.
Cabbage is a boon to the budget-wise cook and is enjoyed by weight watchers.

Mrs. Esther Williams, Pocatello H.S.
Pocatello, Idaho

SOUPER LEFTOVERS

1 c. leftover roast, steak or chicken,
   chopped
1 c. leftover vegetables
1   10 1/2-oz. can cream of celery soup
4 crisp toast slices

Combine all ingredients except toast. Heat thoroughly. Serve on toast. Thin with milk or water if needed. Yield: 4 servings.

Gail P. Corbett, Murfreesboro H.S.
Murfreesboro, North Carolina

SKILLET HASH

1   10 3/4-oz. can beef gravy
2 c. finely chopped leftover beef
2 c. finely diced cooked potatoes
1/2 c. chopped onion
1 tsp. salt
Dash of pepper
2 tbsp. margarine

Combine gravy, beef, potatoes, onion, salt and pepper. Cook hash in margarine for 15 minutes on one side; turn and cook 15 minutes more or until browned. Yield: 4-6 servings.

Mrs. William Hamlet, East Lake Jr. H.S.
Chattanooga, Tennessee

SLOW AND EASY CASSEROLE

1 lb. beef stew meat
1 can cream of mushroom soup

Place beef in buttered casserole. Add soup and 1/4 cup water. Cover. Bake at 250 degrees for 2 hours to 2 hours and 30 minutes. Yield: 4 servings.

Mrs. Adelaide N. Cairns, Oxford Hills H.S.
South Paris, Maine

MEXICAN STEW

2 c. cooked beef, cut into 1-in. cubes
1 med. onion, chopped
1 med. green pepper, chopped
1/4 c. chopped celery
1 clove of garlic, chopped
5 med. tomatoes, peeled and chopped
1 1/4 tsp. salt
1 tsp. Worcestershire sauce
1 tbsp. chili powder

Fry cubed beef in hot fat in skillet until browned. Add onion, green pepper, celery and garlic; cook until tender. Add remaining ingredients and 1/4 cup water. Reduce to low heat and simmer for 20 minutes. Pour into serving dish; top with mashed potatoes if desired. Yield: 4 servings.

Mrs. Fred Liggett, Azle H.S.
Azle, Texas

OVEN BEEF STEW

1 lb. lean stew beef
1 can mushroom or asparagus soup
4 potatoes, cut up
4 carrots, cut up
1 onion, cut up (opt.)

Place large enough piece of foil in baking pan to cover all food. Place beef in center of foil; pour soup over beef. Cover with foil. Bake at 350 degrees for 30 minutes. Unfold foil; add vegetables and reseal. Cook for 30 minutes longer or until vegetables are tender. Yield: 4 servings.

Alene Andriseski, Winnacunnet H.S.
Hampton, New Hampshire

SECOND-DAY DELUXE

1 c. frozen peas and sliced carrots
2 strips bacon, quartered
1 onion, chopped
2 c. cubed leftover beef roast
1/2 tbsp. Worcestershire sauce
1 bouillon cube, crumbled
1 can cream of mushroom soup

Cook peas and carrots in 1 cup simmering salted water until almost done. Fry bacon in large skillet until browned. Add onion and beef; brown. Scoop vegetables with slotted spoon into skillet; reserve liquid. Add Worcestershire sauce and bouillon cube to reserved liquid. Add mushroom soup to beef mixture; rinse soup can with hot bouillon mixture. Add 1 soup can liquid to beef mixture; stir until gravy is smooth. Simmer for 30 minutes. Serve over buttered noodles if desired. Yield: 4 servings.

Mrs. Jeanette Rontala, Ellsworth Sr. H.S.
Ellsworth, Wisconsin

VIENNA HASH

4 c. boiled, diced potatoes
1 med. onion, chopped
2 c. diced cooked roast beef
1 tsp. salt
1/4 tsp. pepper

Mix potatoes, onion, beef and seasonings together lightly; add 2 cups cold water. Cook for about 20 minutes at 225 degrees in an electric skillet. Serve piping hot. Yield: 6-8 servings.

Margaret Lieb, Atchison Co. Comm. H.S.
Effingham, Kansas

BEEF CANTONESE

1 lb. beef chuck steak
Flour
2 tbsp. Wesson oil
1   8-oz. can tomato sauce
1 tbsp. soy sauce
1/2 tsp. garlic powder

1 c. celery, cut into 1/2-in. strips
1 green pepper, sliced vertically

Cut steak into thin strips. Dredge with flour. Panfry in hot oil. Mix tomato sauce, soy sauce and garlic powder; pour over steak strips. Simmer for several minutes. Add celery and pepper to heated ingredients; cook only until crisp tender. Serve over rice. Yield: 4 servings.

Mrs. Sue Purcell, New Deal H.S.
New Deal, Texas

CHINESE BEEF WITH BROCCOLI

1 lb. flank steak
2 tbsp. soy sauce
1 tbsp. Sherry or dry vermouth
1 tbsp. cornstarch
1 tsp. sugar
1/2 bunch broccoli
4 tbsp. peanut oil
1 tsp. salt
1/4 c. chopped onion

Cut steak across grain into thin bite-sized pieces. Pour soy sauce and Sherry over steak. Sprinkle with cornstarch and sugar; mix well. Cut broccoli into thin slices. Peel stem; slice into 2-inch pieces. Pour half the oil into skillet or Dutch oven. Add salt and broccoli. Cook over high heat, stirring constantly, for 2 minutes. Remove from skillet. Add remaining oil and onion; stir. Add steak; cook for 2 minutes. Add broccoli; mix thoroughly and serve. Yield: 4 servings.

Mrs. Barbara S. Brannen
Lincoln-Sudbury Reg. H.S.
Sudbury, Massachusetts

MEAL-IN-ONE

1 beef round steak
Flour
4 med. potatoes, shredded
2 carrots, shredded
1 onion, chopped
1 1/2 tsp. salt
1/4 tsp. pepper

Cut steak into large pieces. Dredge with flour. Brown lightly on both sides. Place potatoes, carrots, onion, salt and pepper on steak. Simmer in small amount of water for about 15 minutes or until done. Add more water, if needed. Yield: 4 servings.

Mrs. John Krupala, Ballinger H.S.
Ballinger, Texas

Meats

FLANK STEAK SUPREME

1 flank steak
Onion salt to taste
1 can mushroom steak sauce

Place steak on 12 x 24-inch piece aluminum foil. Season with onion salt. Spread mushroom sauce over steak; roll steak. Wrap with foil and seal. Bake in preheated 350-degree oven for 1 hour and 30 minutes or place in pressure cooker for 45 minutes. Yield: 4 servings.

Mrs. Joyce Ferrce, McLean-Waynesville H.S.
McLean, Illinois

BAKED ROUND STEAK

1/2 c. butter
1   2-lb. round steak 1 in. thick
1 can mushrooms
1 env. dry onion soup mix

Spread butter on steak. Sprinkle mushrooms over steak; cover with soup mix. Wrap in 2 thicknesses of foil; place in roaster with rack. Bake, covered, for 2 hours at 325 degrees. Yield: 6-8 servings.

Arlene Lenort, Pine Island H.S.
Pine Island, Minnesota

BLANQUETTE OF BEEF

Salt and pepper to taste
Flour
1 lb. tenderized round steak
1 can cream of mushroom or onion soup

Salt and pepper steak; dredge with flour. Brown quickly in skillet in small amount of fat. Drain on paper towel. Place steak in casserole. Pour soup over steak; add 1 soup can water. Bake, covered, at 350 degrees for 15 minutes. Yield: 4-6 servings.

Lillian S. Aplin, Harrisonburg H.S.
Harrisonburg, Louisiana

HERBED PEPPER STEAK

1   2-lb. beef round steak 1 1/2 in. thick
2 tbsp. shortening
3 tomatoes, sliced
2 bell peppers, sliced thick
2 chili peppers, minced
1 sm. onion, sliced
1 tsp. salt

1 tsp. meat tenderizer
1 tsp. fine herbs
1/2 tsp. cumin seeds
1 clove of garlic
3 tbsp. chopped fresh parsley

Pound steak on both sides. Brown well in shortening. Add enough water to partially cover. Simmer, covered, for 1 hour and 10 minutes. Add remaining ingredients. Cook, uncovered, for 15 to 20 minutes longer to allow juice to evaporate. Yield: 6 servings.

Ruth H. Methvin, Fall River H.S.
McArthur, California

BROWN FRICASSEE OF VEAL

1 1/2 lb. veal steak
2 tbsp. flour
1/2 tsp. salt
Pepper to taste
1/2 c. chili sauce

Cut veal into serving pieces; brown in small amount of fat. Add enough water to almost cover. Simmer for 30 minutes. Combine flour, salt, pepper, chili sauce and 1/2 cup cold water; pour over veal. Stir until boiling. Simmer 30 minutes. Yield: 6 servings.

Mrs. Mary McKinney
Thornton Fractional H.S.
Calumet City, Illinois

VEAL SCALLOPINI

8 thin veal cutlets
1/4 c. unsifted all-purpose flour
1/2 tsp. salt
1/4 tsp. pepper
1/4 c. salad oil
1/4 c. diced green pepper
3   8-oz. cans tomato sauce
2 tbsp. dry onion flakes
1 tsp. garlic powder
1   3-oz. can mushrooms and juice

Cut veal into 2 1/2-inch pieces. Sprinkle with flour, salt and pepper. Toss until each piece is well coated. Heat oil in skillet. Brown veal on both sides over medium heat. Drain on paper toweling. Combine veal, pepper, tomato sauce, onion flakes, garlic powder and mushrooms in large skillet. Simmer over low heat for 10 minutes or until veal is tender, turning occasionally. Serve hot. Yield: 4 servings.

Eunice Wood, Glendo Public School
Glendo, Wyoming

FAST CHILI

1 lb. ground beef
2 tbsp. chopped celery
2 tbsp. chopped onion
1 can tomato soup
1 can kidney beans
Salt and pepper to taste
Chili powder to taste

Brown ground beef, celery and onion. Add tomato soup and beans; mix well. Add salt, pepper and chili powder. Simmer for 5 minutes and serve. Yield: 4 servings.

Gail K. Peterson, Gaylord Comm. School
Gaylord, Minnesota

JALAPENO CHILI

1 lb. ground beef or chuck
1 tbsp. shortening
2 c. tomato juice
1 pkg. instant chili mix
1 c. cooked pinto beans or kidney beans
1 lg. jalapeno pepper, diced

Brown beef in shortening. Add tomato juice. Boil slowly for 5 minutes. Add instant chili mix; mix thoroughly. Add beans and pepper. Simmer over low heat for about 10 minutes. Yield: 5-6 servings.

Mrs. Brenda Appleton, Maypearl H.S.
Maypearl, Texas

MOUNTAIN PASS CHILI

1/2 lb. ground beef
4 green onions, chopped
1 tbsp. salad oil
1 No. 2 can pinto beans
1 8-oz. can tomatoes
1 4-oz. can chopped green chili peppers
1 tsp. salt
1 tsp. pepper
1 tbsp. chili powder

Cook meat and onions in fat, in heavy skillet, stirring with fork. Add remaining ingredients with 1 cup water. Bring to a boil. Serve immediately or simmer until serving time. Yield: 4 servings.

Mrs. Virginia Patterson, Page H.S.
Page, Arizona

QUICK CHILI CON CARNE

2 tbsp. oil
1/2 lb. ground beef
1/2 c. chopped onion
2 cloves of garlic, finely minced
1 8-oz. can tomato sauce
1 can tomato soup
4 c. undrained cooked kidney beans
1 tbsp. chili powder
1/2 tsp. salt

Heat cooking oil in skillet. Add ground beef, onion and garlic. Cook until meat is crumbly and onion golden in color. Add tomato sauce, tomato soup, beans, chili powder and salt. Cook about 5 minutes. Serve with crisp crackers. Yield: 6 servings.

Mrs. Avis Crawford, Hutchinson H.S.
Hutchinson, Kansas

SPEEDY CHILI

2 tbsp. oil
1/2 c. chopped onion
1/4 c. chopped green pepper
1 lb. ground beef
2 8-oz. cans tomato sauce
1 1-lb. can kidney beans
1 tsp. salt
Chili powder

Melt oil in pan. Add onion, green pepper and beef; cook until meat is lightly browned. Pour off fat. Add tomato sauce; cook on low heat for 5 minutes. Add kidney beans and salt. Heat. Stir in at least 1 teaspoon chili powder. Yield: 5-6 servings.

Mrs. Lola McClure
Toluca Comm. Unit Schools
Toluca, Illinois

BEEF-VEGETABLE CHOWDER

1 lb. ground beef
1 c. chopped onions
1 tbsp. butter
2 c. tomatoes
2 bouillon cubes
1 tbsp. salt
1/8 tsp. pepper
1/2 bay leaf
1 c. sliced celery
1/2 tsp. Worcestershire sauce
1 pkg. frozen mixed vegetables
1/2 tsp. thyme (opt.)

Saute ground beef and onions in butter until well browned. Add tomatoes, 4 cups hot water, bouillon cubes, salt, pepper, bay leaf, celery and Worcestershire sauce. Bring to a boil; cover. Simmer for 30 minutes. Add mixed vegetables and thyme. Bring to a boil again. Simmer for 15 minutes longer. Yield: 6-8 servings.

Helen Buettner, Bishop Ludden School
Syracuse, New York

SESAME PASTRY-TOPPED STEW

1 tbsp. minced onion
1/2 tsp. dry oregano leaves
1/2 10-oz. package pie crust mix
1 1-lb 14-oz. can Chef Boy-Ar-Dee
    Meatball Stew
1 egg white
1 tbsp. sesame seed

Add onion and oregano to dry pastry mix. Prepare pastry according to package directions. Roll out dough on lightly floured board. Cut into 8 ovals, 2 inches in length. Place meatball stew in 6 x 10-inch baking dish. Bake in preheated 400-degree oven for 10 minutes. Beat egg white until frothy. Spread each pastry oval with egg white. Sprinkle sesame seed over top of pastry. Remove stew from oven. Place pastry ovals on top of stew. Return to oven. Bake for 15 minutes longer. Yield: 3-4 servings.

Photograph for this recipe on page 2.

MEATBALL STEW

1 1/2 lb. ground beef
1 egg, slightly beaten
1 c. small bread cubes
1/4 c. finely chopped onion
1 tsp. salt
1 10 1/2-oz. can condensed beef broth
1 10 3/4-oz. can condensed tomato soup
1/4 tsp. thyme leaves, crushed
1 16-oz. can sliced carrots, drained
1 16-oz. can whole white potatoes, drained
1 8-oz. can sm. whole onions, drained

Combine beef, egg, bread cubes, onion and salt; mix well. Shape into 50 meatballs. Brown meatballs in a large heavy pan; pour off fat. Add remaining ingredients. Heat thoroughly; stir occasionally. Yield: 6-8 servings.

Photograph for this recipe on page 33.

JIFFY HAMBURGER STEW

1 lb. lean hamburger
1 pkg. frozen mixed vegetables
1 can tomato juice
1 can stewed tomatoes

Brown hamburger; pour off fat. Cook vegetables according to package directions. Add hamburger, tomato juice and tomatoes. Simmer for 15 to 20 minutes until bubbling. Yield: 6 servings.

Linda Wilson, South Side H.S.
Memphis, Tennessee

MEXICALI SOUP

1/4 lb. ground beef
3/4 tsp. chili powder
1/4 tsp. salt
Dash of pepper
2 tbsp. minced onion
1 tbsp. margarine or butter
1 can tomato soup

Combine beef, 1/2 teaspoon chili powder, salt and pepper; shape into 12 meatballs. Brown meatballs and onion in margarine. Add soup, remaining chili powder and 1 soup can water. Simmer about 5 minutes. Yield: 2-3 servings.

Mrs. Luella John, Amery H.S.
Amery, Wisconsin

MULLIGAN STEW

1 lb. ground beef
2 beef bouillon cubes
1 tsp. salt
1/4 tsp. pepper
2 c. cooked mixed vegetables

Brown beef. Drain off excess fat. Add bouillon cubes, 2 cups water, salt and pepper. Simmer for 15 minutes. Add vegetables; cook until warmed. Serve with hot corn bread. Yield: 4 servings.

Mrs. Ruth Stephens, Southside H.S.
San Antonio, Texas

QUICK GOULASH

1 lb. ground meat
1/2 c. chopped onion
1 tsp. seasoned salt
1/2 tsp. seasoned pepper
2 tbsp. oil
1 c. Fluffy Dumplets
1 15-oz. can tomato sauce

Saute meat, onion and seasonings in oil. Cook on medium heat about 10 minutes or until all pink color is gone from meat. Cook Fluffy Dumplets in 3 cups boiling salted water about 10 minutes or until soft; drain. Add Dumplets and tomato sauce to meat mixture. Serve hot. Yield: 4-6 servings.

Mrs. Violet Leissner, Furr Jr.-Sr. H.S.
Houston, Texas

QUICK POT OF STEW

1 onion, chopped
1 or 2 c. celery pieces

3 carrots, cut into lg. pieces
2 med. potatoes, quartered
1 lb. (or more) ground beef
2 tbsp. bacon drippings
1 sm. can whole kernel corn
1 No. 2 can tomato juice

Cook onion, celery and carrots in boiling, salted water for 10 minutes. Add potatoes. Cook until vegetables are tender. Cook ground beef in bacon drippings until pink color disappears. Leave meat in small chunks. Add corn, tomato juice and meat to vegetables. Season to taste. Simmer 5 minutes more. Yield: 6 servings.

Mrs. Edith Conner, Hooks H.S.
Hooks, Texas

SALMAGUNDI

1 lb. ground beef
2 tbsp. flour
Salt and pepper to taste
1 can vegetable soup
1 can mushroom soup
1/2 soup can milk

Brown meat. Sprinkle with flour, salt and pepper. Add soups and milk. Cook on top of stove at medium temperature. Serve over Chinese noodles, toast or mashed potatoes. Yield: 4 servings.

Mrs. Carole Smith, Fowler H.S.
Fowler, Michigan

KOREAN MEATBALLS

2 tbsp. sesame seed
1 green onion, minced
1 clove of garlic, minced
2 tsp. soy sauce
1/2 tsp. Accent
1 tbsp. salad oil
1 lb. ground beef

Toast sesame seed in frypan. Add all ingredients except oil to ground beef; mix well. Form into balls the size of walnuts. Fry until brown in oil. Yield: 4 servings.

Mrs. George Schwartz, Fort Lee H.S.
Fort Lee, New Jersey

MEATBALLS IN CHICKEN SOUP

1 lb. hamburger
1 c. prepared dry dressing mix

1 tsp. ground sage
Salt and pepper to taste
2 eggs
Milk
1 can cream of chicken soup

Mix hamburger, dressing mix, sage, salt, pepper, eggs and 3/4 cup milk. Shape into small meatballs, using an ice cream scoop. Brown in small amount of fat. Pour soup diluted with 1 soup can milk over meatballs. Simmer about 30 minutes. Yield: 5-6 servings.

Mrs. Erleen Johnson, Clay H.S.
Oregon, Ohio

PORCUPINE MEATBALLS

1 can tomato soup
1/2 c. uncooked rice
1 lb. hamburger
1 onion, finely chopped
1 1/2 tsp. salt
1/4 tsp. pepper

Mix soup with 1 soup can water. Combine rice, hamburger, onion, seasonings and 4 tablespoons soup; mix well. Form into balls. Place in casserole; cover with remaining soup. Bake, covered, at 350 degrees about 1 hour and 30 minutes. Remove the cover for the last 15 minutes of baking. Yield: 5 servings.

Mrs. Mary A. Nelson, Traverse City Jr. H.S.
Traverse City, Michigan

SWEDISH MEATBALLS

1/3 c. skim milk powder
1 egg
1 tsp. salt
1/4 tsp. pepper
1/4 tsp. allspice
1/8 tsp. cloves
1/2 c. fine dry bread crumbs
1/3 c. finely minced onion
1 lb. ground beef

Combine 1/4 cup water and skim milk powder in a bowl. Beat in egg and seasonings. Stir in bread crumbs. Add onion and ground beef; mix thoroughly. Form into balls. Melt a small amount of fat in a frypan. Add meatballs. Brown over medium heat; turn. Reduce heat and cook thoroughly. Remove from pan. Drain on absorbent paper; keep warm. Yield: 4 servings.

Mrs. Jean Bauer, Hilda H.S.
Hilda, Alberta, Canada

Meats

DELICIOUS MEAT LOAF

1 1/2 lb. ground meat
3/4 c. quick-cooking oats
1/2 c. dill relish
1/2 c. grated cheese
Salt and pepper to taste
1 sm. onion, diced
1 egg
1/2 c. evaporated milk
1 sm. can tomato sauce
1 sm. can tomato sauce with hot sauce

Combine all ingredients except hot tomato sauce. Place in slightly greased casserole. Bake at 350 degrees for 30 minutes. Top with hot tomato sauce. Cook 30 minutes longer. Yield: 4-6 servings.

Virginia Swanzey, Silsbee H.S.
Silsbee, Texas

BUSY DAY MEAT LOAF

1 lb. ground beef
2/3 c. evaporated or skim milk
1 env. dry onion soup mix

Mix beef, milk and onion soup mix in a 1 1/2-quart mixing bowl. Place mixture in an ungreased shallow baking pan; shape into a loaf. Bake in a preheated 350-degree oven for 50 to 60 minutes. This recipe may be doubled. Yield: 4 servings.

Jean Cook, Clarksdale H.S.
Clarksdale, Mississippi

SURPRISE MEAT LOAF

1 1/2 lb. ground beef
1/2 c. chopped onion
1/4 c. dry bread crumbs
2 eggs
1/4 c. chili sauce
1 tsp. salt
1 tsp. parsley flakes
1 tsp. Worcestershire sauce
1/4 tsp. dry mustard
1/8 tsp. pepper
1/4 c. chopped bell pepper
1/4 tsp. monosodium glutamate
Potato Filling

Combine first 12 ingredients. Turn half the mixture into greased 9 x 5-inch loaf pan. Spread with Potato Filling. Top with remaining meat mixture. Bake at 350 degrees for 50 to 60 minutes. Let stand for 5 to 10 minutes; invert onto serving plate. Spread with additional chili sauce. Sprinkle chopped parsley on top for garnish.

Potato Filling

2 tbsp. butter
1/2 tsp. salt
1/3 c. milk
1 1/2 c. mashed potato flakes
1 egg, slightly beaten
1/4 c. grated Cheddar cheese

Heat 3/4 cup water, butter and salt to boiling point in saucepan. Remove from heat. Add milk. Stir in mashed potato flakes. Let stand until flakes are soft and moist, about 30 seconds. Whip lightly with fork. Stir in egg and grated Cheddar cheese. Yield: 8 servings.

Mrs. J. E. Little, Pearland H.S.
Pearland, Texas

TWENTY-MINUTE MEAT LOAVES

1 1/2 lb. ground beef
1/2 tsp. salt
1/8 to 1/4 tsp. pepper
1 to 2 tbsp. dehydrated onion flakes
1 lg. egg
1 c. soft bread crumbs
1   8-oz. can tomato sauce

Combine all ingredients for meat loaf. Shape into 8 oval loaves. Bake at 450 degrees for 15 minutes. Spoon off excess grease.

Sauce

1   8-oz. can tomato sauce
1 to 2 tbsp. brown sugar
1 to 2 tbsp. parsley flakes
1 tsp. Worcestershire sauce

Combine all ingredients. Pour over meat loaves. Bake 5 minutes longer. Yield: 4 servings.

Mrs. Rogene Moss, Page H.S.
Page, North Dakota

JUICY BROWN MEAT LOAF

3/4 lb. ground beef and veal
1/4 c. Ralston cereal
1 tsp. salt
1 1/2 tbsp. finely chopped onions
Dash of pepper
1 egg, slightly beaten
1/4 c. skim milk

Mix all ingredients thoroughly. Shape into 4 x 4 1/2 x 3-inch loaf. Place in lightly buttered 8-inch pie plate. Bake in preheated 350-degree oven 45 minutes or until brown. Yield: 1 loaf.

Lenora Hudson, Oklahoma School for Deaf
Sulphur, Oklahoma

CORNY CASSEROLE

1/4 c. green pepper, chopped
2 tbsp. chopped onion
1 lb. lean ground beef
2 tbsp. vegetable shortening, melted
1 12-oz. can yellow whole kernel corn,
   undrained
1 16-oz. can tomatoes
1 1/2 tsp. salt
1/8 tsp. pepper
1 tbsp. soy sauce
1 c. elbow macaroni, uncooked

Brown green pepper, onion and ground beef in melted shortening in heavy frypan. Stir in corn, tomatoes and seasonings; cover. Simmer over low heat about 20 minutes, stirring occasionally. Uncover; stir in macaroni. Simmer an additional 10 minutes or until macaroni is tender, stirring occasionally. Yield: 4-6 servings.

Miss Judy A. Rogers, Stuart H.S.
Stuart, Virginia

HURRY-UP SKILLET MEAL

1 8-oz. box beef-flavored Rice-A-Roni
1/2 lb. ground beef
1/3 c. chopped celery
1/3 c. chopped green pepper
1/2 tsp. salt
1/4 tsp. pepper
Grated cheese

Prepare Rice-A-Roni according to package directions. Brown ground beef, celery and pepper. Add salt and pepper. Add to Rice-A-Roni and continue cooking. Top with grated cheese. Heat in 350-degree oven until cheese is melted. Yield: 6 servings.

Mrs. Marian G. Craddock, Colorado H.S.
Colorado City, Texas

HAMBURGER-MACARONI-CHEESE DINNER

2 tbsp. butter
3 tbsp. chopped onion
1 lb. ground beef
1 tsp. salt

2 c. tomato juice
1 pkg. macaroni-cheese dinner

Heat butter in skillet. Add onion and brown. Add meat and salt. Stir until browned. Add tomato juice and macaroni-cheese dinner; cover. Simmer 30 minutes or until as much of liquid as desired has evaporated. Yield: 6 servings.

Eupha Watson, Liberty-Eylan Jr. H.S.
Texarkana, Texas

FAMILY SKILLET MEAL

1/2 lb. ground beef
2 tbsp. fat
2 1/2 c. canned tomatoes
1 tsp. Worcestershire sauce
1 1/2 c. chopped cabbage
1 sm. onion, chopped
2 tbsp. chopped parsley
1 tsp. salt
1 c. uncooked elbow macaroni
1/2 c. grated cheese (opt.)

Brown ground beef in fat. Add tomatoes and Worcestershire sauce. Bring to a boil. Add cabbage, onion, parsley, salt and macaroni. Cover and reduce heat. Cook 15 to 30 minutes. Sprinkle cheese on top if desired. Yield: 4 servings.

Alberta A. Zink, Sterling Twp. H.S.
Sterling, Illinois

GROUND BEEF IN SOUR CREAM

1 lb. ground beef
1 c. chopped onion
3 c. medium noodles
3 c. tomato juice
1 tsp. salt
1 1/2 tsp. celery salt
Dash of pepper
2 tsp. Worcestershire sauce
1/4 c. chopped green pepper
1 c. sour cream
1 3-oz. can sliced mushrooms

Lightly brown ground beef in large skillet. Add chopped onion; cook until tender, but not brown. Place noodles in layer over meat. Combine tomato juice, salt, celery salt, pepper and Worcestershire sauce; pour over noodles. Bring to a boil; cover. Simmer over low heat 20 minutes. Add green pepper; cover. Cook 10 minutes or until noodles are tender. Stir in sour cream and mushrooms. Heat just to boiling point. Season to taste. Yield: 6 servings.

Andrea Fletcher, Mountain Pine H.S.
Mountain Pine, Arkansas

Meats

EASY GROUND BEEF-CARROT CASSEROLE

1 lb. ground beef
1 pkg. dry onion soup mix
2 bouillon cubes
1/4 c. parsley flakes
1 c. sliced carrots
1 8-oz. package curly noodles

Brown ground beef in an electric skillet; drain. Add onion soup mix, 4 1/2 cups boiling water, bouillon cubes, parsley and sliced carrots. Simmer for 15 minutes. Add noodles; cover. Simmer until tender. Yield: 4 servings.

Mrs. Joanne Healea, Lewiston H.S.
Lewiston, Idaho

FAVORITE LASAGNA CASSEROLE

1 lb. ground beef
2 tsp. salt
2 cloves of garlic, crushed
1/2 tsp. pepper
1 1-lb. 8-oz. can tomatoes
1 8-oz. can tomato sauce
1 pkg. spaghetti sauce mix
1/2 lb. lasagna noodles
1/2 lb. mozzarella cheese, sliced
1/2 c. Parmesan cheese

Brown meat in Dutch oven or deep kettle. Add salt, crushed garlic and pepper. Simmer about 10 minutes. Add canned tomatoes, tomato sauce, and spaghetti sauce mix. Stir thoroughly; cover. Simmer for 30 minutes. Boil noodles in salted water until almost tender; drain and rinse. Pour 1/4 of the meat sauce into 12 x 8 x 2-inch baking dish. Cover with 1/3 of the cooked noodles. Arrange 1/3 of the mozzarella cheese over noodles. Repeat layers 2 more times, ending with meat sauce. Top with Parmesan cheese. Bake at 350 degrees for 20 minutes. Yield: 6-8 servings.

Nancy Holdridge, Knoxville H.S.
Knoxville, Illinois

LEFTOVER GOULASH

1/2 lb. hamburger
2 tbsp. chopped onion
Chopped green pepper (opt.)
1/2 tsp. salt
1/2 No. 202 can whole kernel corn
Leftover vegetables
1 10 1/2-oz. can tomato soup

1 c. noodles
1 tbsp. chili powder (opt.)
1/2 c. cheese, sliced

Saute hamburger, onion and green pepper in Teflon pan or iron skillet. Season with salt. Add vegetables, soup and water if necessary to cook noodles. Bring to a boil. Add noodles; cover. Reduce heat; cook until noodles are tender, about 10 minutes. Stir in chili powder. Place cheese slices on top. Cover and continue heating until cheese melts. May be baked in 350-degree oven until cheese melts and browns slightly. Yield: 4 servings.

Mrs. Eleanor R. Haner, Moses Lake H.S.
Moses Lake, Washington

HAMBURGER HEAVEN

1 lb. ground beef
Onion salt to taste
Salt and pepper to taste
1/2 lb. American cheese, sliced
1 c. chopped celery
1 sm. can sliced ripe olives
2 c. fine, dry noodles
1 No. 2 can tomatoes

Brown beef slightly in skillet. Season with onion salt, salt and pepper. Add remaining ingredients in layers in order given. Rinse out tomato can with 1/4 cup water and pour over all. Sprinkle with additional salt and pepper; cover. Cook on high temperature until steaming; reduce to low or simmer and cook for 30 minutes. Yield: 6 servings.

Mrs. Hazel Abbey, Nogales H.S.
Nogales, Arizona

EASY ITALIAN SPAGHETTI SAUCE

1 lb. ground beef
Seasonings to taste
1 sm. onion, chopped
3 tbsp. chopped green pepper
Bacon drippings or oil
1 can tomato soup
1 can cream of mushroom soup
1 tbsp. chili powder

Brown ground beef, seasonings to taste, onion and green pepper in a small amount of bacon drippings. Add soups and 1/2 cup water; mix well. Add chili powder. Simmer 10 to 15 minutes. Serve hot over spaghetti. Yield: 4-5 servings.

Mrs. Karen Rackow, Southern Door H.S.
Brussels, Wisconsin

ITALIAN-STYLE SPAGHETTI

1 lb. ground beef
2 tbsp. minced onion
1 pkg. Italian-style instant spaghetti
    sauce mix
2 cans tomato sauce
10 to 12 oz. spaghetti, cooked

Brown hamburger and onion in a large skillet. Drain off all but 1 tablespoon fat. Add spaghetti sauce mix, tomato sauce and 3 sauce cans water; cover. Simmer 10 to 20 minutes. Cook spaghetti in boiling salted water until tender. Serve with meat sauce. Yield: 4-6 servings.

Roma Talbott, Palisade H.S.
Palisade, Colorado

MEXICAN SPAGHETTI

1 lb. ground beef
1/2 bell pepper, chopped
1 onion, chopped
1 can tomato sauce
Salt and pepper to taste
2 tsp. cumin or chili powder
1 pkg. long spaghetti
1 c. grated cheese

Brown meat, pepper and onion in skillet. Add tomato sauce and 1 sauce can water. Add seasonings; simmer for 15 minutes. Cook spaghetti in salted water until tender; drain. Place in casserole. Pour meat sauce over spaghetti. Sprinkle grated cheese over meat sauce. Bake at 350 degrees only until cheese melts. Yield: 4-6 servings.

Allene McDougall, Luling H.S.
Luling, Texas

SKILLET SPAGHETTI

1 lb. ground beef
1 c. chopped onion
2 med. cloves of garlic, minced
1 8-oz. can tomato sauce
1 to 2 6-oz. cans tomato paste
1 16-oz. can tomato juice
1 tbsp. chili powder
2 tsp. salt
Dash of pepper
1 tsp. sugar
1 tsp. oregano
1 8-oz. package spaghetti
Onion rings (opt.)
Green pepper rings (opt.)
Parmesan cheese

Combine first 11 ingredients and 1 1/2 cups water in large skillet; mix well. Cover. Bring to a boil. Reduce heat and simmer 30 minutes. stirring occasionally. Add spaghetti; stir to separate strands. Simmer, covered, 30 minutes longer or until spaghetti is tender, stirring frequently. Add onion and green pepper rings the last 5 minutes of cooking time. Sprinkle with grated Parmesan cheese. Serve with slices of crisp French bread. Yield: 4-6 servings.

Mrs. Nina D. Sonnier, Leesville H.S.
Leesville, Louisiana

SPEEDY SPAGHETTI AND MEATBALLS

1 lb. ground beef
1/2 c. fine dry bread crumbs
1 1/2 tsp. onion salt
1/8 tsp. pepper
2/3 c. undiluted evaporated milk
2 tbsp. flour
2 tbsp. shortening
2 10-oz. cans prepared spaghetti sauce
4 c. cooked spaghetti
Parmesan cheese

Mix beef, bread crumbs, seasonings and milk until well blended. Shape into about 20 small balls. Roll in flour. Melt shortening in frypan or electric skillet. Brown balls on all sides. Pour spaghetti sauce over meatballs. Cook over low heat 15 minutes. Serve with cooked spaghetti and Parmesan cheese. Yield: 6 servings.

Judith A. Sims, Callisburg H.S.
Gainesville, Texas

TWENTY-FIVE MINUTE SPAGHETTI

1 sm. onion, chopped
1/4 c. chopped green pepper
1/2 c. diced celery
1 lb. ground beef
1 sm. can tomato sauce
4 c. tomato juice
1/2 tsp. garlic salt
1 tsp. Tabasco sauce
Salt and pepper to taste
1 bay leaf
1/4 lb. uncooked spaghetti

Brown onion, pepper and celery in a skillet with ground beef over medium heat. Add tomato sauce, tomato juice and seasonings. Bring to a boil. Add uncooked spaghetti broken in small pieces; cover. Cook over low heat for 25 minutes. Yield: 6-8 servings.

Julia P. Burroughs, Wadley H.S.
Wadley, Alabama

Meats

DELUXE ITALIAN SPAGHETTI SAUCE

1 c. sliced onions
1 lb. ground beef
1 clove of garlic, minced
1 c. diced celery
3 tbsp. salad oil
3/4 c. chopped green pepper
1/2 c. stuffed olives, sliced
1 5-oz. can mushrooms, sliced
1 13-oz. can tomato sauce
1 6-oz. can tomato paste
2 tsp. salt
1/2 tsp. pepper

Combine onions, beef, garlic, celery and oil. Bring to a simmer in pressure saucepan. Stir in remaining ingredients. Cook at 15 pounds pressure for 20 minutes. Reduce pressure under cold water. Serve over long cooked spaghetti on a large platter. Yield: 8-10 servings.

Mrs. Thordis K. Danielson
New Rockford H.S.
New Rockford, North Dakota

SPAGHETTI WITH TOMATO SAUCE

1/2 lb. hamburger
Salt to taste
1 c. catsup
1 tsp. Worcestershire sauce
1/2 tsp. Tabasco sauce
1 med. onion, diced
1 c. tomato sauce
1 c. uncooked spaghetti
1/2 c. grated cheese

Heat hamburger in very small amount of fat. Season with salt. Mix remaining ingredients, except spaghetti and cheese, with 1/2 cup water. Mix tomato sauce mixture with meat. Simmer about 20 minutes. Cook spaghetti according to package directions; drain. Serve meat sauce over spaghetti. Top with grated cheese. Yield: 8 servings.

Louise Paxton, Greenfield H.S.
Greenfield, Oklahoma

HAMBURGER CHOW MEIN

1 lb. hamburger
1/2 c. butter
2 tsp. salt
Dash of pepper
2 c. diced celery
1 med. onion, chopped
2 16-oz. cans bean sprouts, drained
    and rinsed

2 tbsp. cornstarch
1 tbsp. soy sauce
1 tsp. sugar
1 sm. can mushrooms, drained and sliced

Fry hamburger in butter until light brown. Add salt, pepper, celery, onion and 1 1/2 cups water. Bring to a boil; cover. Let simmer for 20 minutes. Add rinsed bean sprouts; heat. Combine 2 tablespoons water, cornstarch, soy sauce and sugar. Add to hot vegetable mixture; stir until thickened. Add mushrooms; heat to serving temperature. Serve hot over chow mein noodles or over steamed rice. Yield: 6 servings.

Mrs. Illene Stuckey, Wauzeka H.S.
Wauzeka, Wisconsin

BEEF-TOMATO PAISANO

1 lb. ground beef
3/4 c. chopped onions
1 clove of garlic, finely chopped
1/2 tsp. salt
1/8 tsp. oregano leaves
Dash of pepper
2 cans tomato sauce with mushrooms
1 1/2 c. milk
1 1/3 c. Minute rice
4 cheese slices

Brown beef in skillet over high heat. Add onions and garlic. Cook over medium heat until onions are tender. Stir in remaining ingredients. Bring to a boil. Simmer 5 minutes, stirring occasionally. Garnish with cheese slices. Yield: 6-8 servings.

Mrs. Evangelena L. Barber, Saluda H.S.
Saluda, North Carolina

CHILI A LA CREOLE

1 1/2 c. chopped onions
1 c. chopped bell peppers
2 tbsp. margarine
2 1/2 lb. ground beef
3 15-oz. cans of chili beans
1 8-oz. can Spanish-style tomato sauce
4 c. cooked rice
Salt and pepper to taste
Tabasco sauce to taste

Cook onions and bell peppers in margarine. Add ground beef; cook until brown. Heat chili beans and tomato sauce; add to meat mixture. Add rice. Season to taste. Serve on toast while hot. Yield: 10-12 servings.

Sister Mary George, S.B.S.
Saint Paul H.S.
Marty, South Dakota

SKILLET SPANISH RICE

1 tbsp. vegetable oil
1 med. onion, chopped
1/2 med. green pepper, chopped
1/2 lb. ground beef
1 c. regular rice, uncooked
2 8-oz. cans tomato sauce
1 tsp. prepared mustard
1 tsp. salt
Dash of pepper

Heat oil in skillet. Add onion and green pepper to beef and rice in the skillet. Stir over medium-high heat until lightly browned. Add tomato sauce, 1 1/3 cups hot water, mustard, salt and pepper; mix well. Bring quickly to a boil; cover tightly. Simmer 25 minutes. Yield: 4 servings.

Mrs. Patricia Edwards, Rock Ridge School
Wilson, North Carolina

QUICKIE STEAKS

1/2 lb. ground beef
1 tbsp. chopped onion
2 tsp. flour
1/4 c. evaporated milk
1/4 tsp. salt
1/8 tsp. savory (opt.)
4 slices bread
2 tbsp. softened butter
1 tbsp. mustard
2 tbsp. shortening

Mix beef, onion, flour, milk and seasonings together. Toast bread slices on one side. Spread untoasted side with butter and mustard. Spread beef mixture on toast to edges. Heat shortening in frying pan. Place bread with meat side down in frypan. Cook 5 minutes or until beef is golden brown. Yield: 4 servings.

Mary B. Lewis, Gilbert H.S.
Gilbert, South Carolina

BISCUIT CHEESEBURGERS

1/2 lb. hamburger
2 tbsp. minced onion or 1/4 tsp. onion salt
1/2 tsp. salt
1/8 tsp. pepper
2 c. Bisquick
12 3/4 x 3-in. thin slices cheese

Mix hamburger and seasonings. Form into 6 thin patties, 2 1/2 inches in diameter. Mix Bisquick according to package directions. Roll out 1/8 inch thick. Cut into 12 circles 3 inches in diameter. Place a meat patty between 2 circles and seal edges by moistening edge of lower circle and pressing edges together. Prick top. Bake at 400 degrees for 15 minutes. One minute before removing from the oven, crisscross 2 slices of cheese across each biscuit. Yield: 2 or 3 servings.

Magde Landis Capel, Woden H.S.
Woden, Texas

FIESTA PATTIES

1 lb. ground beef
1 c. crushed corn flakes
1 c. cooked or canned tomatoes
1 egg
1 sm. onion, minced
1 tsp. salt
1/4 tsp. pepper
8 slices bacon

Combine beef, corn flakes, tomatoes, egg and seasonings. Shape into 3/4 to 1-inch thick patties. Wrap slice of bacon around each patty; fasten with a wooden pick. Place patties on broiler rack about 2 to 3 inches from heat. Broil 10 to 12 minutes; turn and continue broiling until other side is brown, about 8 minutes. Yield: 6-8 servings.

Mrs. Jewell Spivey, Harmony School
Gilmer, Texas

A MEAL IN FOIL

4 hamburger patties
1 lg. onion, sliced
4 potatoes, quartered
4 carrots, sliced thin
4 tbsp. butter
Salt and pepper to taste

Tear 4 pieces of foil large enough to enclose hamburger patty and vegetables. Place 1 hamburger patty on each piece of foil; add a slice of onion. Place quartered potato on onion slice; add sliced carrots. Top with 1 tablespoon butter. Season with salt and pepper. Pull foil together; fold at top. Bake at 375 degrees for 1 hour and 30 minutes. Serve immediately. Yield: 4 servings.

Janet H. Lee, Gunston Jr. H.S.
Arlington, Virginia

MOCK FILET MIGNON

1 lb. ground chuck
1 tsp. salt
1/4 tsp. pepper
4 slices bacon

Combine ground chuck with salt and pepper. Shape into 4 patties. Wrap each patty in bacon; secure with toothpicks. Broil on one side; turn and broil on the other side. Serve hot. Yield: 4 servings.

Emmy Curlee, Woodrow Wilson H.S.
Portsmouth, Virginia

Meats

BEANBURGERS

1/2 lb. ground beef
1 tbsp. salad oil
1/2 tsp. salt
1/8 tsp. pepper
1/3 c. sliced green onion
1   1-lb. can pork and beans, drained
1/2 c. catsup
8 round buns

Brown ground beef in oil in large skillet. Add salt, pepper and onion. Cook slowly until well done. Add pork and beans and catsup. Heat through. Spoon into buns and serve. Yield: 8 servings.

Mrs. John Fullmer, Waupaca H.S.
Waupaca, Wisconsin

SOUPER HAMBURGER MIX

1 lb. ground beef
1 can onion soup

Cook beef in a small amount of fat until it loses red color. Add undiluted soup; cook until thick. Serve in hamburger buns. Yield: 8-10 servings.

Mrs. Mary Davis Faison, Weldon H.S.
Weldon, North Carolina

LEFTOVER MEAT LOAF SANDWICHES

1/4 c. chopped green peppers
4 slices buttered bread or English muffins
4 slices leftover meat loaf
4 slices American cheese

Fry green peppers in large buttered skillet until tender. Place buttered bread in pan until bread is toasted on one side. Remove to dishes. Add meat loaf to skillet and cook on hot heat until meat is hot. Place one slice cheese on each slice meat loaf; heat until cheese is melted. Place on bread. Garnish with peppers. Yield: 4 servings.

Mrs. Linda K. Hogan, Jay H.S.
Jay, Maine

ONION BOATS

1 lb. hamburger
2 tbsp. flour
2 cans onion soup
4 French bread rolls
Butter

Brown hamburger in 10-inch skillet. Pour off grease, if necessary, leaving 2 tablespoons in skillet. Stir

flour into hamburger. Add onion soup and 1 soup can water to hamburger. Cook on low heat for 10 minutes. Cut rolls in half. Butter and toast rolls. Spoon onion-hamburger mixture over toasted rolls. Yield: 4 servings.

Marlene K. Wilson, San Lorenzo H.S.
San Lorenzo, California

OVEN-EASY DILLBURGERS

1 lb. ground chuck
1/2 c. evaporated milk
1/4 c. chopped onion
1/4 c. chopped green pepper
1/2 tsp. dillweed
1/2 tsp. salt
1/8 tsp. pepper
3 to 4 individual French rolls
3 to 4 slices American cheese

Mix ground chuck, milk, onion, green pepper, dillweed, salt and pepper in mixing bowl. Divide meat mixture into 8 parts. Split rolls in half lengthwise. Spread meat mixture evenly over tops of rolls to the edges. Place on baking sheet. Bake at 350 degrees for 25 to 30 minutes. Remove from oven. Cut cheese slices in half at an angle. Place 1/2 slice cheese on top of each roll. Return to oven for 2 to 3 minutes longer. Serve at once. Yield: 6-8 servings.

Mrs. Gary L. Petersen, Seward Sr. H.S.
Seward, Nebraska

SATURDAY NIGHT JOES

1 lb. ground beef
2 tsp. oil
1/2 c. chopped onion
1   10 1/2 or 11-oz. can chicken gumbo soup
2 tsp. catsup
2 tsp. prepared mustard
Pepper to taste
1/2 tsp. salt
Grated cheese

Brown ground beef in hot oil. Add onion; cook until golden. Add remaining ingredients except cheese. Simmer over low heat about 30 minutes. Serve on hamburger buns. Cover with grated cheese just before serving. Let melt. Yield: 6-8 servings.

Susie McDonald, Monterey H.S.
Lubbock, Texas

PIZZABURGER

1/4 c. chopped onion
2 tbsp. shortening

1 lb. ground beef
1 10 1/2-oz. can condensed tomato soup
1/2 c. shredded sharp cheese
1/8 tsp. oregano
Dash of pepper
12 buns, split and toasted
Mozzarella cheese

Brown onion in shortening. Add beef; cook until browned. Stir often to separate meat particles. Add soup, cheese, oregano and pepper. Simmer 10 minutes. Spread mixture on buns; place strips of cheese on top. Broil until cheese melts.

Mrs. Judith Anderson, Stillwater Sr. H.S.
Stillwater, Minnesota

PIZZA BREAD

1/2 loaf French bread
1 lb. ground beef
1/2 c. chopped onions
1 tsp. garlic salt
1/2 tsp. pepper
2 1/2 c. tomato sauce
1 1/2 tsp. each oregano, basil, thyme
1/2 c. sliced black olives
2 c. shredded Cheddar or mozarella cheese

Slice bread horizontally into 2 layers. Place in pan with cut side up. Brown ground beef, onions, garlic salt and pepper in a frypan; pour off excess fat. Add tomato sauce, oregano, basil and thyme. Simmer for 10 minutes. Stir in black olives. Spoon over bread. Top with shredded cheese. Heat in a 400-degree oven for about 15 to 20 minutes or until cheese melts. Yield: 4 servings.

Mrs. M. L. Evans, Fremont H.S.
Sunnyvale, California

PIZZA SPECIAL

1 c. biscuit mix
1/4 lb. sausage
1/2 lb. ground beef
3 oz. pepperoni
1 8-oz. can tomato sauce
1 tbsp. sugar
1 tbsp. mustard
1/4 tsp. oregano
1/4 tsp. anise
1/4 tsp. fennel seed
1/2 tsp. salt
Dash of pepper
1 tbsp. dried onion
1/4 c. Cheddar cheese
3 tbsp. Parmesan cheese

Mix biscuit mix and 1/3 cup water to form dough. Spread dough thinly in 12-inch round pizza pan. Prick with fork. Bake in preheated 425-degree oven for 5 to 7 minutes. Remove from oven. Reduce heat to 375 degrees. Brown sausage and ground beef; drain. Combine meats with tomato sauce, sugar, mustard, seasonings and onion. Bring to a boil; simmer for 10 minutes. Spread meat mixture and Cheddar cheese on dough. Top with Parmesan cheese. Bake 10 minutes. Yield: 6 servings.

Dixie B. Williams, Pinedale H.S.
Pinedale, Wyoming

INDIVIDUAL PIZZAS

1/4 lb. hamburger
3/4 c. tomato sauce
1/2 tsp. oregano
1/4 tsp. salt
Pinch of garlic salt
1 can refrigerator biscuits
3/4 c. grated cheese

Brown hamburger. Add tomato sauce, oregano, salt and garlic salt. Roll out biscuits to 5 inches in diameter. Place on cookie sheet. Spread with hamburger mixture. Sprinkle with grated cheese. Garnish with additional oregano. Bake at 450 degrees for 10 minutes. Yield: 10 servings.

Dolores Beebe, Washington Union H.S.
Fresno, California

MEATZA PIE

1 lb. ground beef
2/3 c. evaporated milk
1/2 c. fine dry bread crumbs
1 tsp. garlic salt
1/3 c. tomato paste or catsup
1 2-oz. can sliced mushrooms
1 c. shredded sharp Cheddar cheese
1/4 tsp. oregano, crumbled finely
2 tbsp. grated Parmesan cheese

Place beef, milk, bread crumbs and garlic salt in 9-inch pie plate. Mix together thoroughly with fork. Pat mixture firmly and evenly onto bottom and side of pie plate. Spread tomato paste over meat mixture. Drain mushrooms; arrange at random on top of tomato paste. Top with Cheddar cheese and over this sprinkle oregano. Top with grated Parmesan cheese. Bake in a 375-degree preheated oven for 25 minutes or until meat is baked to taste and cheese is lightly browned. Yield: 5-6 servings.

Mrs. Mildred Beck, Fairhope H.S.
Fairhope, Alabama

Meats

CHEESEBURGER PIE

1 lb. ground beef
1 tbsp. minced onion
1 tsp. salt
1/4 tsp. pepper
3/4 tsp. Italian seasoning
2 6-oz. cans tomato paste
1 can refrigerated quick crescent
    dinner rolls
4 mozzarella cheese slices
1/4 c. butter

Brown ground beef in skillet. Drain off fat. Add onion, salt, pepper, 1/2 teaspoon Italian seasoning and 1 can tomato paste; blend well. Unroll and separate dough into 8 triangles. Place in ungreased 9-inch pie pan, pressing pieces together to form a crust. Turn meat mixture into unbaked crust. Top with cheese slices. Bake at 375 degrees for 25 to 30 minutes. Serve with a sauce made from combining remaining ingredients with 3/4 cup water. Yield: 4-6 servings.

Mrs. Mary M. Thomas, Healy Jr. H.S.
Pierz, Minnesota

HAMBURGER AND TATER TOTS

2 lb. ground beef
1 med. onion, diced
Salt to taste
1 can mushroom soup
1 1/2 to 2 lb. frozen Tater Tots

Brown ground beef and onion lightly. Season with salt. Add mushroom soup diluted with 1/2 soup can water. Place in greased 2-quart casserole. Place Tater Tots on top of ground beef mixture. Bake for 30 to 45 minutes in 375-degree oven. Yield: 8 servings.

Mrs. Bonnie Shaw, Clarkfield Pub. School
Clarkfield, Minnesota

SHANNON TORTE

4 servings instant mashed potatoes
2 eggs, slightly beaten
1/3 c. finely cut green onion
2/3 c. sifted flour
1 tsp. baking powder
1/2 tsp. salt
1/4 c. shredded sharp Cheddar cheese

Prepare mashed potatoes according to package directions. Stir in eggs and onion. Sift together flour, baking powder and salt; combine with potatoes. Turn into 2 lightly greased and floured 8-inch round cake pans. Sprinkle with cheese. Bake at 375 degrees for 30 to 35 minutes. Turn out of pans.

Filling

1/2 lb. ground beef
1/4 c. chopped onion
2 tbsp. green pepper
1 3/4-oz. package brown gravy mix
1 tsp. salt
1/2 tsp. Worcestershire sauce
1/8 tsp. pepper

Brown ground beef, chopped onion and green pepper in skillet. Stir in gravy mix. Add 3/4 cup water, salt, Worcestershire sauce and pepper. Bring to a boil. Simmer for 1 minute. Spread filling on one baked layer; cover with remaining layer. Yield: 4 servings.

Mrs. Patsy Smith, Ninnekah H.S.
Ninnekah, Oklahoma

RICE-STUFFED PEPPERS

3 lg. green peppers, halved
1 chopped onion
1 lb. ground beef
1/4 c. rice, cooked or 1 cup leftover rice
1 egg
1 tsp. salt
3 tsp. dried parsley
2 c. tomato juice

Remove seeds from peppers. Cook in boiling water for 10 minutes; drain. Place in baking dish. Cook chopped onion in fat until yellow; remove from heat. Add ground beef, cooked rice, egg, salt, parsley and enough tomato juice to moisten. Fill peppers. Pour remaining tomato juice over peppers. Bake at 375 degrees for 30 minutes. Yield: 6 servings.

Nancy W. Quinn, Jefferson Davis H.S.
Hampton, Virginia

CHEESEY STUFFED PEPPERS

4 bell peppers
1 1/2 lb. ground beef
1 med. onion, chopped
1/2 tsp. salt
1/2 lb. cheese, cubed
3 tomatoes, cubed

Cut tops from peppers; remove seeds. Cover with water; boil 8 minutes. Place ground beef, chopped onion and salt in pan; cook until meat is brown. Turn off heat. Add cheese and tomatoes. Stuff mixture into peppers. Bake for 20 minutes at 350 degrees. Yield: 4 servings.

Mrs. Kathryn Williams, Ruidoso H.S.
Ruidoso, New Mexico

STUFFED WHOLE PEPPERS

8 Ry-Krisp crackers or 2 slices cubed
   diet bread
4 med. green peppers
1/2 lb. ground beef
1/2 tbsp. fat
1/4 c. finely cut onion
1/4 c. finely cut celery
1/3 c. broken and drained canned tomatoes
3/4 to 1 tsp. salt
1/8 tsp. pepper (opt.)
1 tsp. Worcestershire sauce (opt.)

Roll crackers into coarse crumbs. Wash green peppers; slice off tops. Remove seeds. Cover with boiling
water; boil gently for 5 minutes. Drain. Brown beef
in hot fat. Add Ry-Krisp crumbs, onion, celery,
tomatoes, salt and pepper; mix well. Fill peppers
with beef mixture. Stand peppers upright in baking
dish. Add 1 inch of hot water; cover. Bake at 350
degrees on rack slightly below center of oven for 1
hour. Yield: 4 servings.

Grace L. Hollen, Turner Ashby H.S.
Dayton, Virginia

QUICK TAMALE PIE

1 onion, diced
1 bell pepper, diced
2 tbsp. butter
1 lb. ground chuck
1 can tamale sauce
1 med. can cream-style corn
1 can sliced black olives
1/2 c. cornmeal
1 to 2 tbsp. chili powder
Salt and pepper to taste

Saute onion and bell pepper in butter. Add chuck;
cook until crumbly. Add remaining ingredients and 1
sauce can water; mix well. Cover. Simmer 25 to 30
minutes, stirring occasionally. Yield: 6-8 servings.

Mrs. Lynn Ackerman, Ventura H.S.
Ventura, California

ORANGE-GLAZED LAMB CHOPS
WITH ONIONS

8 lamb chops
Salt and seasoned salt to taste
2 tbsp. corn oil margarine
2 doz. canned sm. white onions
1 6-oz. can concentrated orange
   juice, thawed

Sprinkle lamb chops with salt and seasoned salt.
Brown chops on both sides in hot margarine. Arrange chops and onions in roasting pan. Stir concentrated orange juice into drippings in skillet. Pour
over meat; cover. Bake at 350 degrees for 30 minutes. Uncover; continue to bake, basting frequently
until meat is tender. Yield: 8 servings.

Virginia S. Sharbutt, Vincent H.S.
Vincent, Alabama

LIVER BUNDLES WITH GREEN
BEANS

1/4 c. flour
1/2 tsp. salt
1/8 tsp. pepper
1/2 tsp. celery salt
1 1/2 lb. beef liver, sliced into 6 slices
   1/4 to 1/2 in. thick
6 tbsp. sweet pickle relish, drained
1 16-oz. can whole green beans
3 tbsp. oil or drippings
1/4 c. finely chopped onion
1 c. cooked or canned tomatoes
1 tsp. Worcestershire sauce

Combine flour, salt, pepper and celery salt. Dredge
liver slices in flour mixture. Place 1 tablespoon relish, additional salt, pepper and celery salt on each
slice. Drain beans, reserving 1/4 cup liquid. Top relish with 7 or 8 whole green beans. Roll as for jelly
roll; fasten with toothpicks or string. Brown in oil.
Pour off excess fat. Combine reserved bean liquid,
onion, tomatoes and Worcestershire sauce. Add to
liver; cover. Cook 25 to 30 minutes. Thicken cooking liquid with flour for gravy, if desired. Yield: 6
servings.

Laverne C. Frederick, Ovid Cen. School
Ovid, New York

TENDER LIVER AND ONION

1 med. onion, thinly sliced
1/2 c. quick meat broth
1/2 tsp. Worcestershire sauce
1/4 tsp. caraway seed
4 slices veal or calf liver, cut
   about 1/2 in. thick

Place onion in skillet with broth, sauce and caraway
seed; cover. Cook until onion is transparent and
almost tender. Remove onion with a slotted spoon.
Add liver to skillet. Simmer in broth about 2 minutes; turn pieces. Place onion slices on top. Continue
cooking about 2 minutes longer or just until liver is
tender; serve. Yield: 4 servings.

Sister Mary Philothea, C.S.S.F.
Good Counsel H.S.
Chicago, Illinois

Meats

CRANBERRY-GLAZED CANADIAN BACON

10 1/4-in. thick slices Canadian bacon
1 tbsp. grated orange peel
1/2 tsp. sugar
1/8 tsp. cloves
Dash of nutmeg
1 c. whole cranberry sauce

Arrange Canadian bacon in an 11 3/4 x 7 1/2 x 1 3/4-inch baking dish. Sprinkle slices with mixture of grated orange peel, sugar, cloves and nutmeg. Spread cranberry sauce over bacon slices. Bake, uncovered, at 350 degrees for about 25 minutes. Serve with sauce spooned over bacon slices. Yield: 5 servings.

Sandra M. Cuchna, Webb H.S.
Reedsburg, Wisconsin

BROILED HAM MEAL

1 can string or lima beans
1 can sweet potatoes
1 1/2-in. center cut ham slice
Brown sugar to taste
Cinnamon to taste
1 sm. can pineapple slices
4 marshmallows

Place beans in bottom of broiler pan. Heat beans in oven. Heat sweet potatoes in small pan on top of stove. Clip edges of ham; place on beans on broiler rack. Brown ham. Mash sweet potatoes with mixer. Season with brown sugar and cinnamon. Turn ham. Place pineapple slices topped with mound of sweet potatoes around ham on broiler. Heat thoroughly. Just before removing, push marshmallow into each sweet potato mound. Yield: 4 servings.

Mrs. Louis Ivanish, Malta H.S.
Malta, Montana

CHEESE-TOPPED HAM SANDWICH

6 slices ham
6 slices pineapple, drained
1 10-oz. can Cheddar cheese soup or
   cheese sauce
3 English muffins, split

Brown slices of ham and pineapple in butter in skillet. Heat cheese soup. Toast muffin halves. Top each muffin with ham, pineapple and hot cheese sauce. Yield: 6 servings.

Marilyn Oelschlager, Flanagan H.S.
Flanagan, Illinois

CREAMED HAM

6 tbsp. margarine
1 med. onion, cut fine
1/2 green pepper, chopped
6 tbsp. flour
2 c. diced ham
1 can cream of chicken soup
2 c. milk
Juice of 1 lemon
1/2 c. grated Cheddar cheese
Biscuits

Heat margarine; add onion and green pepper. Saute until tender. Add flour, ham and soup. Stir in milk gradually. Cook until thickened. Stir in lemon juice and Cheddar cheese. Serve over biscuits. Yield: 6 servings.

Mrs. Thomas Mitchell, Kingsland H.S.
Kingsland, Arkansas

HAM GUMBO

4 slices bacon
1/4 c. chopped onion
1 c. diced cooked ham
1/2 lb. fresh okra
1/4 tsp. salt

Lightly brown bacon and tear into pieces. Lightly brown onions. Add all ingredients. Simmer about 10 minutes. Cook mixture until okra is done, about 15 minutes. Yield: 4 servings.

Ruth Gill, Tuloso-Midway H.S.
Corpus Christi, Texas

VEGETABLE HAM HASH

1 tbsp. oil
2 c. diced ham
2 tbsp. minced onion
1 sm. package frozen mixed vegetables
1 c. diced frozen hash browned potatoes

Heat oil; brown ham and onion in heavy skillet. Add 1/2 cup boiling water and vegetables; cover. Bring to a boil. Reduce heat. Simmer until vegetables are just tender, about 6 to 10 minutes. Do not overcook vegetables. Yield: 4 servings.

Mrs. M. E. Friels, Empire H.S.
Duncan, Oklahoma

Recipe on page 20.

HAM WITH POTATOES AND EGGS

1/3 c. chopped onion
1/2 c. cooked ham or bacon
5 to 6 sliced boiled potatoes
3 eggs, beaten slightly
1/4 c. milk
Salt and pepper to taste

Melt 2 tablespoons fat in skillet; partially fry onion. Add ham and potatoes. Fry until mixture is hot; reduce heat. Beat eggs; add milk, salt and pepper. Pour eggs over potatoes; cover skillet. Cook until eggs are done, turning potatoes and eggs occasionally. Serve immediately. Yield: 6 servings.
This is an old German dish that my grandmother used to prepare.

Mrs. Cathrene Lynch
Wessington Springs H.S.
Wessington Springs, South Dakota

EXOTIC PORK CHOPS

6 pork chops, cut 3/4 inch thick
2 tbsp. drippings
1 tsp. salt
1/4 c. finely chopped onion
1/4 med. green pepper, cut in strips
1 clove of garlic, minced
1 1/2 tbsp. cornstarch
1 tbsp. brown sugar
1   13 1/2-oz. can pineapple tidbits
3 tbsp. tomato sauce
2 tbsp. vinegar
1 tbsp. soy sauce
1 tsp. grated lemon rind
1/2 tsp. curry powder
1/8 tsp. pepper
1/4 c. pecan halves (opt.)

Brown pork chops in drippings. Transfer to a 13 x 9-inch baking dish. Sprinkle with 1/2 teaspoon salt. Pour drippings from frypan, reserving 2 tablespoons drippings. Add onion, green pepper and garlic to reserved drippings. Stir in cornstarch and brown sugar. Add pineapple tidbits including syrup, 1/3 cup water, tomato sauce, vinegar, soy sauce, lemon rind, 1/2 teaspoon salt, curry powder and pepper. Mix well. Cook slowly for 5 minutes, stirring constantly. Pour sauce over pork chops. Cover slowly for 5 minutes, stirring constantly. Pour sauce over pork chops. Cover tightly. Bake in 350-degree oven for 45 minutes. Remove cover. Bake for 15 minutes longer. Sprinkle with pecan halves. Yield: 6 servings.

Photograph for this recipe on page 12.

Recipe on page 42.

PORK CHOPS AND RICE

6 to 8 pork chops
6 to 8 tbsp. rice
6 to 8 slices onion
6 to 8 slices tomato
6 to 8 slices bell pepper
1 can chicken broth

Brown pork chops on both sides. Grease casserole well. Place 1 tablespoon rice for each pork chop in bottom. Place chops on rice. Place slice of onion, tomato and pepper on each chop. Cover with chicken broth. Bake for 1 hour at 350 degrees. Yield: 6-8 servings.

Mrs. C. D. Huston, Greenwood Jr. H.S.
Greenwood, Mississippi

PORK CHOPS SUPREME

4 pork chops, about 1 inch thick
Salt and pepper to taste
4 slices onion
4 slices tomato

Wash chops; place in shallow pan. Sprinkle lightly with salt and pepper. Place onion slice on top of each chop. Sprinkle with salt and pepper. Place tomato slice on top of onion. Season. Add enough water to cover bottom of pan. Bake at 350 degrees for 1 hour. Add more water if needed. Yield: 4 servings.

Eunice F. Lewis, Indian River H.S.
Chesapeake, Virginia

BAKED STUFFED PORK CHOPS

6 double-cut pork chops
2 tbsp. butter or margarine
1/4 c. diced onion
1/4 c. diced celery
3 slices bread, diced
1/2 tsp. salt
1/2 tsp. pepper
1 tsp. poultry seasoning
1 can cream of mushroom soup, undiluted

Have butcher cut chops about 1/2 inch thick. Cut a pocket in chops with a sharp boning knife. Melt butter in frypan; add onion and celery. Cook until onion turns clear. Add diced bread, salt, pepper and poultry seasoning. Stuff dressing into pocket of chops; secure with a toothpick. Arrange chops in baking dish. Cover with mushroom soup. Bake at 325 degrees for 2 hours. Serve in baking dish. Yield: 6 servings.

Arline Kelly, West Babylon Jr. H.S.
West Babylon, New York

Meats

SKILLET CHOPS AND BEANS

4 pork chops
4 slices onion
Salt and pepper to taste
1   1-lb. can pork and beans with
       tomato sauce
2 tbsp. finely chopped dill pickle
2 tsp. prepared mustard

Brown chops in skillet. Top each with onion slice. Season with salt and pepper. Cover. Cook over low heat 45 minutes or until tender. Push chops to one side; add remaining ingredients. Cover. Cook 5 minutes, stirring. Yield: 5 servings.

Mrs. J. W. Williams, Independence H.S.
Independence, Mississippi

CHINESE PORK AND RICE

2/3 c. uncooked rice
2 tbsp. salad oil
1 tsp. salt
1 bouillon cube
2 tsp. soy sauce
1 med. onion, chopped
2 stalks celery, chopped
1 green pepper, chopped
1 1/2 c. diced cooked pork

Cook rice in hot oil until golden brown. Add salt, 1 1/2 cups water, bouillon cube and soy sauce; cover. Cook 20 minutes. Add remaining ingredients and 1/4 cup more water if necessary. Cover tightly. Cook 10 minutes more. Yield: 4-6 servings.

Mrs. LaVera Kraig, Monroe Jr H.S.
Aberdeen, South Dakota

PORK BARBECUE

1/2 c. diced celery
1/2 c. diced onions
2 c. leftover pork, cut up in sm. pieces
1/2 c. catsup
1 tsp. chili powder
Salt to taste
8 sandwich buns

Cook celery and onions in 1/2 cup water until tender. Remove from heat and mash. Combine pork, catsup and chili powder. Simmer for 10 minutes. Season with salt. Serve on sandwich buns. Garnish with an olive on a toothpick. Yield: 8 servings.

Phoebe Stout, Stephen Decatur School
Berlin, Maryland

PORK IN MILK GRAVY

2 lb. pork tenerloin, cut 3/4 in. thick
Flour for dredging
Salt and pepper to taste
2 tbsp. butter
2 c. milk

Trim excess fat from tenderloin. Dredge tenderloin with flour. Season with salt and pepper. Brown in butter at 350 degrees in electric skillet. Reduce temperature to 225 degrees; cover skillet. Cook for 30 minutes to 1 hour or until pork is tender. Add milk. Heat, uncovered, until bubbling hot. Serve immediately. Yield: 6-8 servings.

Mrs. A. F. Burnett
Eminence Consolidated School
Eminence, Indiana

SAUSAGE GOULASH

1 lb. pork sausage
4 diced med. potatoes
1 No. 303 can pork and beans
1 tsp. chili powder
Salt and pepper to taste

Fry sausage in pan, breaking into small pieces. Add diced potatoes; fry until almost done. Add remaining ingredients. Heat and serve.

Joyce Real, Judson School
Converse, Texas

PIGS IN A BLANKET

1 can crescent or butterhorn
     refrigerator rolls
10 sausage links

Wrap each roll around a sausage link. Follow baking instructions on can to brown. Yield: 10 servings.

Mrs. Sandra Moore, Roseville H.S.
Roseville, Illinois

PORK SAUSAGE DINNER

1 sm. onion, diced
1 green pepper, chopped
1 lb. pork sausage
1   12-oz. package frozen corn

Brown onion, green pepper and sausage in skillet. Add corn; cover. Cook 5 minutes; serve. Yield: 4 servings.

Mrs. Lew Renard, Blair H.S.
Blair, Nebraska

SPICY SPAM

1 can Spam or canned ham
Whole cloves
1/4 c. (firmly packed) brown sugar
2 tbsp. prepared mustard

Place Spam in baking dish. Score and insert cloves as desired. Blend sugar and mustard; smooth over top of meat. Bake in preheated 325-degree oven for about 20 minutes. Baste with juices while cooking. Yield: 4-6 servings.

Peggy Baker, Monterey H.S.
Monterey, Tennessee

LUNCHEON MEAT CUPS

2 tbsp. butter or margarine
2 tbsp. flour
1 c. milk
Salt and pepper to taste
1 10-oz. package frozen peas, cooked
1 tbsp. cooking oil
8 thin slices luncheon meat

Melt butter; blend in flour and milk slowly. Cook until thickened, stirring constantly. Add salt and pepper. Add peas to sauce; heat. Heat fat; brown lunch meat, allowing edges to curl and form cups. Fill cups with creamed peas. Yield: 4 servings.

Carolyn Houts, Marsing H.S.
Marsing, Idaho

QUICK PEPPERONI PIZZAS

1 sm. can pizza sauce
6 hamburger buns, split
1 pkg. pepperoni, sliced thin
1 6-oz. package sliced mozarella cheese

Spread pizza sauce on cut sides of buns. Place 5 or 6 slices pepperoni on each bun. Cover with cheese; place on broiler pan. Broil at middle position for 10 minutes or until cheese melts. Serve hot. Yield: 6 servings.

Mrs. Nola Rolston, Forsyth H.S.
Forsyth, Montana

JIFFY-BROILED PIZZAS

1 can luncheon meat, cut into 8 slices
3 tbsp. mustard
8 slices bread
8 slices cheese
1 8-oz. can tomato sauce

1/2 tsp. garlic powder
1 tsp. salt
1/2 tsp. pepper
1/2 tsp. oregano

Spread each slice of meat with mustard. Place bread on broiler pan and brown one side; remove from pan. Place slice of meat on each untoasted side of bread; top with slice of cheese. Combine remaining ingredients. Bring to a boil. Place pizzas back under broiler until cheese is melted. Spoon hot sauce over top and serve. Yield: 8 servings.

Mrs. Hazel L. Seaton, Twiggs Co. H.S.
Danville, Georgia

SUDDENLY SUPPER

1 12-oz. can luncheon meat, cut into strips
1 med. onion, thinly sliced
2 tbsp. butter or margarine
1 10 1/2-oz. can cream of mushroom soup
1/2 c. milk
2 c. cubed cooked potatoes
2 tbsp. chopped parsley
Dash of pepper

Lightly brown meat. Add onion and butter Cook until onion is tender. Blend in soup and milk. Add remaining ingredients. Cook over low heat about 10 minutes or until flavors are blended, stirring occasionally. Yield: 4 servings.

Madge Arlene Humphrey, Weston H.S.
Cazenovia, Wisconsin

PRIZE BISCUIT LOAF

1 c. cooked diced meat
1 c. drained cooked English peas or
    lima beans
2 tbsp. chopped pimento
1 1/2 c. grated cheese
2 tbsp. grated onion
2 c. biscuit dough, prepared
Melted butter

Combine first 5 ingredients; toss lightly to blend. Roll dough into a thin 10 x 14-inch rectangle. Place on ungreased baking sheet. Spread meat mixture down center of dough, covering a space about 3 inches wide. Along each side, make 8 or 9 cuts about 3 inches long and about 1 inch wide. Starting at top, bring first 2 opposite strips over filling. Continue to cross opposite strips over filling. Brush lightly with melted butter. Bake in preheated 425-degree oven for 20 to 25 minutes or until nicely browned. Serve immediately with favorite sauce. Yield: 10-12 servings.

Mrs. Roy Cousins, Hogansville H.S.
Hogansville, Georgia

Meats

MIGHTY LUCY LINKS

1/2 c. catsup
2 tsp. chili powder
2 lg. cans Vienna sausage
1 c. crushed Fritos

Mix catsup and chili powder. Stick a toothpick in end of each sausage. Roll in catsup mixture, then crushed Fritos. Broil until of desired doneness; serve hot. Yield: 8 servings.

Faye L. Greenway, Stephenville H.S.
Stephenville, Texas

BAKED BEANS AND FRANKFURTERS

1 No. 2 can pork and beans
4 tbsp. catsup
2 tbsp. molasses
2 tbsp. brown sugar
2 tbsp. bacon drippings
3 drops of Tabasco sauce
Minced onion
Salt to taste
Frankfurters

Combine all ingredients except frankfurters; mix well. Place in a greased shallow ovenproof dish. Cover top with sliced frankfurters. Bake at 375 degrees for 30 minutes. Yield: 7-8 servings.

Mrs. Stanley W. James, Fairfield Jr. H.S.
Richmond, Virginia

CREOLE FRANKS

1 lb. wieners, cut in thin slices
1 lg. onion, chopped
1/2 green pepper, chopped
4 tbsp. margarine
1 can tomatoes, drained
1 can tomato soup, undiluted
1 tsp. chili powder
1 tsp. salt
1 tsp. sugar
Dash of pepper

Brown wieners, onion and green pepper in skillet with margarine on medium-high heat. Add tomatoes, soup and seasoning; cover. Bring to steaming over high heat; turn to low for 15 minutes. Serve over steamed rice. Yield: 8 servings.

Mrs. Louise Simpson, New Site School
Alexander City, Alabama

GOURMET FRANKFURTERS

3 slices bacon
1 lb. skinless frankfurters, sliced
1/2 c. sliced mushrooms
1 1-lb. can tomatoes
1 10-oz. package frozen lima beans
1 tsp. Worcestershire sauce

Cook bacon until crisp; remove from pan. Saute frankfurters and mushrooms in bacon fat. Add tomatoes, beans and seasonings; mix well. Simmer on top of stove for 15 minutes. Or bake in 375-degree oven for 35 minutes or until hot. Crumble bacon and sprinkle over mixture just before serving. Yield: 8 servings.

Mrs. Evelyn Rosenbaum, East Bernard H.S.
East Bernard, Texas

HAWAIIAN FRANKS

2/3 c. drained crushed pineapple
4 tbsp. mustard
1 lb. franks
8 slices white bread

Mix drained pineapple and mustard. Split franks in half lengthwise, almost through center. Heat franks in ungreased skillet. Remove and place diagonally across bread slices. Spoon pineapple mixture into frank slits. Wrap bread around each frank, overlapping corners. Secure with toothpicks. Fry in skillet in butter; brown all sides. Yield: 8 servings.

Betty Scheffler, Sauk Rapids Sr. H.S.
Sauk Rapids, Minnesota

POTATO-STUFFED FRANKS

12 frankfurters
3 c. seasoned mashed potatoes
1 c. grated Cheddar cheese
Paprika

Split frankfurters lengthwise; lay cut side up in shallow baking pan. Spoon potatoes over frankfurters in light, fluffy peaks. Sprinkle on cheese and paprika. Bake in 425-degree oven for 15 to 20 minutes. Serve immeidately with sauerkraut. Yield: 6 servings.

Mrs. Marlo Brackelsberg, Mohall H.S.
Mohall, North Dakota

SAUCY FRANKS

1/2 c. chopped onion
1 tbsp. oil
1 14-oz. bottle catsup

1 tbsp. vinegar
1 tbsp. sugar
1/4 c. pickle relish
1/4 tsp. salt
Dash of pepper
8 to 10 frankfurters
8 to 10 buns

Heat skillet to 250 degrees. Cook onion in oil. Add remaining ingredients except buns with 1/4 cup water; cover. Simmer 15 minutes at 220 degrees. Place mixture in buns. Yield: 8 servings.

Dorothy Pruitt, J. F. Webb H.S.
Oxford, North Carolina

FRANKS IN BARBECUE SAUCE

1 sm. onion, chopped
2 tbsp. chopped green pepper
2 tbsp. oil
3/4 c. canned pineapple juice
1/2 c. catsup
1/8 tsp. chili powder
8 frankfurters
1 c. pineapple chunks

Saute onion and green pepper in hot fat in large heavy frypan over low heat 10 minutes or just until onion is tender. Stir in pineapple juice, catsup and chili powder. Bring to a boil. Reduce heat; simmer 10 minutes. Cut frankfurters into bite-sized pieces; add to sauce. Add pineapple chunks. Simmer 5 minutes or until frankfurters and pineapple are heated through. Yield: 4 servings.

Thelma Leigh, Quincy Jr.-Sr. H.S.
Quincy, California

TATER DOGS

1/2 c. plus 3 tbsp. butter or margarine
1 tsp. instant minced onion
1 tsp. parsley flakes
1/2 tsp. salt
3 c. mashed potato flakes
1/2 c. sour cream
1 egg, slightly beaten
3 to 4 tsp. prepared mustard
10 to 12 frankfurters

Place 3 tablespoons butter, onion, parsley flakes, salt and 1 cup water into 1 1/2-quart saucepan. Bring to a boil. Remove from heat. Stir in 2 cups potato flakes with fork just until moistened. Let stand about 30 seconds. Add sour cream, egg and mustard. Stir lightly with a fork until combined. Mold potato mixture around frankfurters. Roll in remaining potato flakes. Melt remaining butter in 13 x 9 x 2-inch pan; add frankfurters. Bake at 400 degrees for 25 to 30 minutes, turning occasionally. Yield: 4-6 servings.

Mrs. Mavis G. Dear, Stringer H.S.
Stringer, Mississippi

VENISON CHILI

1 lb. ground venison
Salt to taste
1 pkg. chili mix
1 can tomatoes or tomato sauce

Brown venison in small amount of fat. Add salt, chili mix and tomatoes. Simmer about 15 to 20 minutes. Yield: 4 servings.

Mrs. Dorothy Griffin, Snook H.S.
Snook, Texas

BEEF STEW AND DUMPLINGS

1   1 1/2-lb. can beef stew
1 pkg. prepared biscuits

Place stew in 3-quart saucepan. Rinse with 1/4 cup water; blend. Bring to a boil over medium heat. Place biscuits on simmering stew; cover tightly. Turn heat to low; simmer 10 to 12 minutes. Serve immediately. Yield: 4 servings.

Marie B. King, Ligonier Valley Sr. H.S.
Ligonier, Pennsylvania

FAST-FIX BRUNSWICK STEW

1 med. onion, coarsely chopped
1 green pepper, coarsely chopped
1 c. coarsely chopped celery
1/4 c. butter or margarine
1   1-lb. can mixed vegetables
1   8-oz. can cut okra
1   1-lb. can cream-style corn
1   6-oz. can tomato paste
1 tbsp. Worcestershire sauce
1/4 tbsp. Tabasco sauce
1 1/2 tsp. salt
1/2 tsp. pepper
1   12-oz. can roast beef
1 c. fine bread crumbs (opt.)

Saute onion, green pepper and celery in butter over low heat until just tender. Mix in remaining ingredients except bread crumbs; cover. Cook over low heat 30 minutes. If stew is not thick enough, stir in crumbs just before serving. Yield: 6-8 servings.

Mrs. Sue C. Hope, Northeast H.S.
Pasadena, Maryland

QUICK TAMALE PIE

1 c. quick grits
1 tsp. salt
2 15-oz. cans chili without beans
1 c. Cheddar cheese (opt.)

Boil grits in 4 cups water with salt according to package directors. Spread half the cooked grits in 9-inch square baking pan. Top with chili. Add another layer of cooked grits. Cook, uncovered, in 350-degree oven for 20 minutes. Spread sliced or grated cheese over top during last 10 minutes of cooking. Yield: 4 servings.

Marion Gillespie, Sanford Jr. H.S.
Sanford, Florida

TASTY TAMALE CASSEROLE

2 cans hot tamales
1 onion, chopped
1/2 lb. American cheese, grated
1 can chili without beans

Place 1 can unwrapped hot tamales in bottom of greased casserole. Add half the onion, 1/4 pound grated cheese and half the chili on top. Repeat for second layer. Bake at 350 degrees about 20 minutes. Yield: 8 servings.

Mrs. Ann R. Duco, Coushatta H.S.
Coushatta, Louisiana

CAN-CAN CHICKEN

1 10 1/2-oz. can cream of chicken soup
1 10 1/2-oz. can cream of celery soup
1 1/3 c. Minute rice
1 12-oz. can boned chicken or 1 1/2 c.
   diced cooked chicken
1 3-oz. can chow mein noodles or 1 can
   French-fried onion rings

Combine all ingredients except noodles with 1 soup can water in large skillet. Stir to mix and bring quickly to a boil. Cover; reduce heat. Simmer 7 minutes. Remove from heat; stir. Serve with noodles. Yield: 6 servings.

Mrs. Annie Clark Millikin
Deep River School
Sanford, North Carolina

CHICKEN WITH DUMPLINGS

1 can chicken with rice soup
1 egg

1/2 c. milk
1 c. flour
1/2 tsp. salt
1 tsp. baking powder

Heat soup in 1 1/2-quart saucepan; add 1 soup can water. Slightly beat egg; add milk. Mix dry ingredients together. Add to egg mixture; stir until well mixed. Drop by tablespoonfuls into hot soup mixture. Let cook until completely done, about 8 to 10 minutes. Serve immediately. Yield: 2-4 servings.

Marlene K. Lien, Minneota Public School
Minneota, Minnesota

CHICKEN AND YELLOW RICE

1 canned whole chicken
1 pkg. yellow rice

Remove chicken from bone, retaining broth. Prepare rice according to package directions, using broth as part of required liquid. Place chicken in skillet or electric frypan with rice and broth. Simmer for 30 minutes. Yield: 4 servings.

June Dixon, Lake Wales H.S.
Lake Wales, Florida

CHINESE CHICKEN WITH RICE

1 4-oz. can sliced mushrooms
1 10 1/2-oz. can cream of celery soup
1 5-oz. can boned chicken or 3/4 c.
   leftover chicken
1 5 1/4-oz. can water chestnuts, drained
   and sliced
1 tbsp. soy sauce
3 c. cooked rice
Chow mein noodles

Drain mushrooms; reserve 1/4 cup liquid. Combine soup, chicken, chestnuts, soy sauce, mushrooms and reserved liquid in saucepan; heat. Serve over rice; top with noodles. Yield: 4 servings.

Mrs. Una Ray Barnett, Century H.S.
Century, Florida

BISCUIT-TOPPED CHICKEN PIE

1 sm. can peas and carrots
1 canned chicken
Milk
1/2 c. diced celery
4 tbsp. butter
4 tbsp. flour
Salt and pepper to taste
2 cans refrigerator biscuits

Drain peas and carrots, reserving liquid. Combine liquid and stock from chicken with enough milk to measure 2 cups; set aside. Saute celery in butter until tender; add flour and liquid. Cook until thick. Add chicken, peas and carrots and seasoning. Pour into 1 1/2-quart casserole. Top with biscuits. Bake at 400 degrees until biscuits are brown. Yield: 6 servings.

Helen White, Wilmot Public School
Wilmot, Arkansas

CHICKEN A LA KING

1/4 c. melted butter or margarine
3 tbsp. flour
1 can chicken broth
1 c. milk
1 tsp. salt
2 c. diced cooked chicken
1   3-oz. can broiled sliced mushrooms, drained
1/4 c. chopped pimentos

Blend butter with flour. Blend in broth and milk. Cook, stirring constantly, over low heat until sauce is thick. Add salt, chicken, mushrooms and pimentos; heat through. Serve over hot toast points.

Mrs. Mary Helen Kirby, Conroe H.S.
Conroe, Texas

CHICKEN POOR BOYS

2 c. diced cooked chicken
1 1/2 c. diced celery
1/4 c. toasted slivered almonds
1 tbsp. grated onion
1 tbsp. lemon juice
1/2 c. cut green grapes
1/8 tsp. sesame seed
1 tsp. salt
1/2 c. mayonnaise
1 lg. loaf French bread
1/4 lb. Cheddar cheese, grated

Combine all ingredients except bread and cheese. Cut off top of French bread; scoop out center. Fill with chicken mixture. Place in baking pan; sprinkle with cheese. Bake at 350 degrees until cheese begins to bubble. Yield: 6 servings.

Joan D. Hawkos, Union H.S.
Middleton, Wisconsin

CHICKEN SPAGHETTI

1 1/2 c. cooked chicken
2 c. consomme or broth
1/2 c. tomato soup

3/4 clove of garlic, chopped
3 tbsp. chopped onion
2 whole cloves
3 tbsp. mushroom pieces
3/4 tsp. salt
3/4 c. broken spaghetti

Cut chicken into 1-inch pieces. Combine chicken, consomme, soup, garlic, onion and cloves in saucepan. Add mushrooms. Cook over moderate heat 10 minutes. Season with salt. Add spaghetti. Boil gently for 10 minutes or until spaghetti is tender. Serve hot. Yield: 6 servings.

Mary Jo Baty, Shelbyville Sr. H.S.
Shelbyville, Texas

CHICKEN SUPREME

2 c. noodles
1 c. diced chicken
1/2 c. sour cream
1 can cream of chicken soup
1/2 tsp. sage
1 tsp. salt
1/2 tsp. pepper

Cook noodles until almost tender. Combine all ingredients in casserole. Sprinkle with paprika if desired. Bake 30 to 40 minutes at 350 degrees. Serve hot. Yield: 6 servings.

Mrs. Doreene Snowdon, Barker Cen. School
Barker, New York

CORONATION DISH

3 c. chicken broth
2 c. cooked diced chicken
1 green pepper, chopped
1 onion, chopped
1 sm. can whole kernel corn
2 tbsp. pimento, chopped
1/8 tsp. pepper
1 tsp. salt
1 sm. can mushrooms
1/2 lb. American cheese, cubed
3 c. uncooked noodles

Pour chicken broth into 4-quart saucepan. Add chicken, green pepper, onion, corn, pimento, seasonings and mushrooms. Add cheese. Do not stir. Spread noodles over all; press into broth to moisten, using back of spoon. Cover pan. Cook on high heat until steam pours from cover of pan. Reduce to lowest heat; cook for 30 minutes. Stir to distribute ingredients throughout the dish and serve. Yield: 8 servings.

Mrs. Mabel Brill, Moorefield H.S.
Moorefield, West Virginia

Poultry

QUICK CREAMED CHICKEN

1   10 1/2-oz. can cream of mushroom soup
1/4 c. milk
2 c. diced cooked chicken
1 pimento, diced
1/4 c. chopped celery

Combine soup and milk; heat, stirring constantly. Add chicken, pimento and celery. Cook for several minutes to blend flavors. Serve on toast, in a rice or noodle ring, or on split corn bread squares. Yield: 4-6 servings.

Mrs. Esther M. Hight, Weare H.S.
Weare, New Hampshire

SCALLOPED CHICKEN

2 1/2 c. cooked chicken, cut up
2 1/2 c. rich chicken gravy
1 c. fine dry bread crumbs or cracker crumbs
Butter

Place alternate layers of first 3 ingredients in greased 1 1/2-quart casserole. Dot with butter. Bake at 350 degrees for 20 to 30 minutes. Yield: 6 servings.

Hilda G. Rohlf, Tallmadge H.S.
Tallmadge, Ohio

SEALED CHICKEN SANDWICHES

1 c. chopped chicken
1/3 c. diced celery
1/2 c. grated sharp cheese
1 tbsp. chopped onion
1/4 c. mayonnaise
1/4 tsp. salt
Hot dog buns or rolls

Mix all ingredients except buns together in bowl. Spread on hot dog buns or rolls. Wrap individual sandwiches in aluminum foil; twist ends securely. Place on cookie sheet. Bake for 20 minutes at 250 degrees. Serve immediately. Foil will keep sandwich warm until ready to eat. Yield: 4 servings.

Carol Reed, Greater Latrobe Sr. H.S.
Latrobe, Pennsylvania

CHICKEN SUPREME

2 c. dry herb dressing
1   3-lb. chicken, cut up
1 c. buttermilk
Paprika

Line 9 x 13-inch baking pan with foil. Roll dressing so it will be fine crumbs; put into plastic bag. Dip chicken in buttermilk. Shake in bag with crumbs until covered. Place in pan; sprinkle with paprika. Bake in 350-degree oven 1 hour and 15 minutes or until chicken is tender. Serve hot but is also delicious when served cold. Yield: 4 servings.

Alice M. Ford, Central H.S.
Cheyenne, Wyoming

CORN FLAKE CHICKEN

1 frying chicken, cut up
1/4 lb. margarine, melted
1 box corn flake crumbs or 1 1/2 c. crushed
    corn flakes
Salt and pepper to taste
Onion salt to taste

Dip chicken pieces in melted margarine. Coat with corn flake crumbs. Sprinkle with seasonings. Place in uncovered baking dish. Bake at 350 degrees for 1 hour and 30 minutes or until done. Yield: 4 servings.

Mrs. Rita Anne Miller, Sheffield H.S.
Sheffield, Pennsylvania

CURRIED ORANGE CHICKEN

1 c. English-style orange marmalade
1 tbsp. curry powder
1 tsp. salt
1 broiler-fryer, quartered

Combine marmalade, curry powder, salt and 1/2 cup water. Place chicken pieces, cut side down, in buttered 9 x 13-inch baking pan. Spoon marmalade sauce over chicken. Bake, uncovered, in a 350-degree oven for 45 minutes. Spoon sauce over chicken several times during baking. Add an additional 1/4 cup water if sauce begins to stick to bottom of pan. Remove chicken. Serve sauce hot with chicken. Serve buttered noodles with this dish. Garnish both noodles and chicken with parsley; encourage the eating of parsley as it is rich in vitamins. Yield: 4 servings.

Photograph for this recipe on page 34.

LEMON BUTTER CHICKEN

Salt to taste
1 med. fryer, cut up
Pepper to taste
1 c. butter
Juice of 3 lemons
2 tbsp. paprika

Salt chicken generously on all sides. Season with pepper. Place chicken in shallow baking dishes with bony sides up. Melt butter; add lemon juice and paprika. Pour over chicken. Bake for 30 minutes at

425 degrees. Turn and baste. Bake for 30 minutes longer. Serve with rice, using lemon sauce over rice. Yield: 6 servings.

Verlee Heard, Sherman H.S.
Sherman, Texas

PHILIPPINE CHICKEN

1 fryer, cut up
Garlic salt to taste
Salt to taste
1 1/2 tbsp. light corn syrup
1/4 c. soy sauce
1/4 c. vinegar

Lay chicken flat in casserole or banking dish. Add salts. Mix corn syrup, soy sauce and vinegar. Pour over chicken; cover. Bake at 350 degrees for 1 hour. Yield: 4-6 servings.

Marcia F. Swanson, Henry Co. H.S.
McDonough, Georgia

STEWED CHICKEN IN BARBECUE SAUCE

1 2 to 2 1/2-lb. cut-up fryer
1 16-oz. bottle prepared barbecue sauce

Arrange layer of chicken in buttered baking dish or iron skillet. Add half bottle sauce. Arrange remaining pieces; pour remaining sauce over chicken. Bake at 350 degrees for 1 hour and 30 minutes. May also be cooked on top of stove. Yield: 4 to 5 servings.

Mrs. Jean Coldewey, Patton Springs H.S.
Afton, Texas

TURKEY CROQUETTES

1 c. very thick white sauce
1/2 tsp. salt
1/4 tsp. pepper
2 c. chopped or ground cooked dark turkey
     meat
1 tsp. poultry seasoning
Spices to taste (opt.)
Sifted crumbs
1 egg, beaten

Combine all ingredients except crumbs and egg. Season well. Spread on a plate and chill. Shape 1 rounded tablespoon mixture for each croquette. Roll in crumbs, then egg and again in crumbs. Fry in 375 to 385-degree fat. May brush with fat and bake at 400 degrees. Yield: 6-7 servings.

Alice E. Grealy, Victor Cen. School
Victor, New York

EASY AND DELICIOUS TURKEY

1 c. milk
1 egg
1 tbsp. cooking oil
1 c. pancake mix
1/8 tsp. thyme
1 sm. onion, grated
1/2 c. diced cooked turkey
Hot cranberry sauce

Place milk, egg and oil in shaker or glass jar. Add pancake mix, thyme and onion. Shake vigorously 10 to 15 minutes or until batter is fairly smooth. Pour about 1/4 cup batter for each pancake onto hot, lightly greased griddle. Sprinkle with diced turkey before turning. Bake to a golden brown, turning only once. Stack two pancakes together, spooning cranberry sauce between and over the pancakes. Yield: 4 servings.

Mrs. L. O. Freeman, Chickasaw Co. H.S.
Houston, Mississippi

TURKEY DIVAN

1 pkg. frozen broccoli spears
1 pkg. sliced turkey
1 c. cheese sauce
1/2 c. grated cheese

Prepare broccoli according to package directions. Line bottom of casserole with broccoli. Lay turkey slices on top; cover with cheese sauce. Sprinkle grated cheese on top. Bake 15 to 20 minutes at 350 degrees. Yield: 4 servings.

Margaret Gomez, Eureka H.S.
Eureka, Kansas

TURKEY WITH GOURMET FLAIR

2 tbsp. margarine
3/4 c. white rice
1 env. dry onion soup mix
2 c. cut-up cooked turkey or chicken

Melt margarine; saute rice, stirring until golden brown. Add soup mix and 2 cups water; stir. Simmer, covered, 20 to 25 minutes or until water is absorbed and rice is tender. Add turkey; cover. Heat through. Serve with coconut, chopped peanuts, raisins or chutney if desired. Yield: 6 servings.

Willie Mae Cornwell, Midway H.S.
Waco, Texas

Quick Seafood Dishes

Seafood, an elegant and delectable taste treat no matter how you serve it, is probably the fastest of the fast when it comes to preparing meals in a hurry. The tender meat of seafood and fish needs only a small amount of cooking time to highlight its delicate flavor. And even better, seafood is versatile! The unmistakably fine flavor of most fish and seafood makes it perfectly suited to the use of herbs and seasonings — especially basil, chives, oregano, paprika, and curry. Fish and seafood are also excellently complemented by garnishes of almonds, mushrooms, onion rings, pimentos, and by a spoonful or two of lemon-butter, tartar, or cocktail sauce.

Fish and seafood can be ready in a hurry, almost whenever you want. Fresh shrimp and lobster, for example, can be cleaned, then thrown into a pot of boiling, seasoned water, and be ready almost before you know it. Simple adorned with only lemon slices, pats of butter, and a sprinkling of herbs, flavorful fish such as trout, flounder, haddock, and snapper can be baked and served in about 30 minutes. And, for those last minute meals, you can also turn to traditional favorites like canned salmon and tuna for quick casseroles, loaves, and croquettes. Shrimp, crab, and lobster, and other favorite delicacies from the sea are also available canned and frozen. So, an elegant crab meat souffle, a shrimp casserole, or sumptuous lobster dish is a possibility any time of the year, even if you live hundreds of miles from the seashore.

Seafood and fish offer yet another advantage: most any variety is extremely high in nutrition and wonderfully low in calories. In fact, many cooks would say that seafood does it all — it helps you watch your weight, it keeps your meal nutritious, it saves you time, yet it's elegant enough for even the most discriminating guests and taste-appealing enough for every member of the family. As Home Economics Teachers already know, you can count on seafood, and the best in seafood recipes, to assure you a great meal anytime, and in a jiffy, too.

Seafood

FISH KABOBS

2 lb. fish
3/4 c. cooking oil
1/2 c. lemon juice
1/4 tsp. powdered bay leaf
Soy sauce to taste
2 cucumbers, sliced
1 lg. green pepper, sliced

Cut fish into 1-inch cubes; place in glass or stainless steel pan. Marinate for 30 minutes in mixture of oil, lemon juice, bay leaf and soy sauce. Stir once or twice to coat fish. Thread fish cubes on skewers alternating with thick slices of cucumber and green pepper. Broil or grill for 10 minutes, turning frequently and basting with marinade. Yield: 6 servings.

Mrs. Jancie Arnold, Harper Creek, Sr. H.S.
Battle Creek, Michigan

OLD-FASHIONED FISH CHOWDER

1 lb. fish fillets
2 tbsp. chopped salt pork
1/2 c. chopped onions
1 c. mixed vegetables
2 c. milk
3/4 tsp. salt
Dash of pepper

Cut fillets into 1-inch cubes. Brown salt pork; add onions. Brown lightly; add 2 cups hot water and vegetables. Cook for 10 minutes or until vegetables are partially tender. Add fish; cook until it flakes easily with a fork. Add milk and seasoning; heat. Serve immediately with chopped parsley sprinkled over top.

Carol Snoke, McCool Junction Schools
McCool Junction, Nebraska

FISH CHOWDER FOR TWO

1/4 or 1/2 c. fish
1 tsp. oil
1/2 sm. onion, chopped
1 sm. potato, sliced
1 c. milk
Salt and pepper to taste

Cook fish in salted water. Heat oil in saucepan; brown onion. Add cooked fish, sliced potato and 1/2 cup water in which fish was cooked. Cover; cook for 15 minutes or until potato slices are tender. Add milk and seasonings. Yield: 2 servings.

Mrs. Rolina C. Jackson
Cook Co. Training School
Adel, Georgia

CRUSTY BAKED HADDOCK

1 egg
1 pkg. frozen haddock, thawed
1 c. crushed corn flakes
2 tbsp. butter
1 tsp. Tabasco sauce

Beat egg; add 1 tablespoon water. Cut fish in serving pieces. Dip each piece in egg, then in corn flakes. Place on cookie sheet. Melt butter; drizzle over fish. Sprinkle with Tabasco sauce. Bake at 350 degrees for 30 minutes. Yield: 5 servings.

Betty E. Cuneo, Williamson Jr.-Sr. H.S.
Tioga, Pennsylvania

ZESTY HADDOCK

1 lb. haddock fillets
Salt to taste
1/2 c. sour cream
1/8 tsp. dry mustard
1/8 tsp. ground ginger
Paprika
Parsley

Lightly grease a 10 x 6 x 2-inch baking dish. Divide fillets into 3 serving pieces; sprinkle with salt. Place in single layer in baking dish. Mix sour cream, mustard and ginger together; spread on top of fillets. Bake in preheated 400-degree oven for 20 to 25 minutes. Sprinkle with paprika and parsley.

Judy Stoltz, Belle Fourche School
Belle Fourche, South Dakota

OVEN-FRIED PERCH

2 lb. frozen or fresh perch fillets
1/2 c. milk
2 tsp. salt
1/2 c. cornmeal
1/2 c. flour
2 tbsp. chopped parsley
2 tbsp. melted butter
2 tbsp. lemon juice

Thaw frozen fillets; remove skin. Combine milk and salt. Combine cornmeal, flour and parsley. Dip fillets in milk. Put 2 fillets together, sandwich fashion; roll in cornmeal mixture. Place in a well-greased 12 x 15-inch casserole. Sprinkle remaining mixture over fish. Combine butter and lemon juice; drizzle over fish. Bake in 500-degree oven for 12 minutes or until fish flakes. Serve with lemon wedges and parsley. Yield: 6 servings.

Mrs. Ward McDuffee, Bellefontaine Sr. H.S.
Bellefontaine, Ohio

BAKED SOLE

1 lg. onion, sliced
4 fillets of sole
Salt and pepper to taste
1 tbsp. dried parsley
1 No. 303 can tomatoes

Place half the onion slices in a lightly greased casserole. Place sole on top. Sprinkle with salt, pepper and parsley. Place remaining onion over fish; pour canned tomatoes over all. Bake in a 350-degree oven for 35 minutes or until fish is tender. Yield: 4 servings.

Mrs. Forrest Schaad, Del Campo H.S.
Fair Oaks, California

BROILED SALMON STEAK

4 4 to 5-oz. salmon steaks
1/4 c. lemon juice
1 tsp. grated lemon peel
1 clove of garlic, crushed
2 tsp. chopped chives
1/2 tsp. paprika

Place salmon steaks in shallow baking dish. Combine lemon juice, lemon peel, garlic, chives and paprika in a small jar with airtight lid. Shake to blend thoroughly. Pour over salmon steaks. Refrigerate 1 hour; turn steaks once. Remove from marinade. Broil on lightly greased rack 6 inches from heat for 5 minutes. Turn; brush with marinade. Broil 5 to 8 minutes longer or until fish flakes easily when tested with a fork. Yield: 4 servings.

C. Anne Hollingsworth, Smithsburg Sr. H.S.
Smithsburg, Maryland

QUICK SALMON PUFFS

1 1-lb. can red salmon
1/2 c. bread crumbs
2 eggs, well beaten
1 tbsp. butter, melted
Dash of salt
1 tbsp. lemon juice

Remove skin and bones from salmon; flake. Mix with bread crumbs, eggs, butter, salt and lemon juice. Pack in greased custard cups; place in pan of hot water. Bake for 30 minutes at 375 degrees. Unmold onto serving dish; garnish. Yield: 4-6 servings.

Mrs. Zetta Robb, Napoleon Sr. H.S.
Napoleon, Michigan

SALMON CROQUETTES

1 flat can pink salmon
14 saltine crackers, crushed
1 egg
1 tbsp. grated Parmesan cheese
1 tbsp. lemon juice
2 tbsp. white cornmeal
1 tbsp. shortening, melted

Mix together salmon, crackers, egg, cheese and lemon juice. Form mixture into croquettes; roll in cornmeal. Brush with shortening. Brown in Teflon skillet at 360 degrees. Yield: 4 servings.

Judy Ferguson, Paradise H.S.
Paradise, Texas

DEEP-DISH SALMON PIE

2 10 1/2-oz. cans pea or asparagus soup
1 1-lb. or 2 7 3/4-oz. cans salmon
1/2 c. milk or cream
1 1-lb. can sm. potatoes, drained
1 1-lb. can sm. onions, drained
1/8 tsp. white pepper
1/4 tsp. oregano
1/4 tsp. sweet basil
1 pkg. refrigerator buttermilk biscuits

Combine soup, liquid from salmon and milk in saucepan. Stir in salmon, potatoes, onions and seasonings; heat until sauce begins to simmer, stirring occasionally. Place in 2-quart casserole or baking dish; top with biscuits. Bake in preheated 400-degree oven for 15 to 20 minutes or until biscuits are brown. Garnish with watercress. Yield: 4 servings.

Mrs. Alma Cross, Winnacunnet H.S.
Hampton, New Hampshire

SALMON FRITTERS

1 c. sifted flour
1 1/2 tsp. baking powder
1/2 tsp. salt
1/8 tsp. pepper
1/4 c. cornmeal
3/4 c. milk
1 egg, beaten
1 1-lb. can salmon
1 tbsp. lemon juice

Sift dry ingredients in bowl. Add milk and egg; beat until smooth. Remove skin and bone from salmon; flake with fork. Sprinkle with lemon juice; fold into batter. Fry in hot grease by dropping from a tablespoon. Yield: 6-8 servings.

Mrs. Elizabeth Potts, Lott H.S.
Lott, Texas

Seafood

WILDA'S SALMON LOAF

1 can cream of celery soup
1 1-lb. can salmon
1 tbsp. ReaLemon
1 1/2 c. cracker crumbs or 2 c. prepared
    bread crumbs

Add soup to salmon; add ReaLemon and crackers.
Shape into loaf. Bake at 350 degrees for 45 minutes.
Yield: 6 servings.

Mrs. Wilda Ash
Wenona Unit Dist. No. 1 School
Wenona, Illinois

SALMON LOAF SUPREME

1 1-lb. can salmon
1/2 tsp. salt
1/4 tsp. pepper
2 eggs
2 tbsp. lemon juice
2 tsp. instant onion
1 c. cracker crumbs
1 c. milk

Flake salmon with fork; remove skin and bones. Add
salt and pepper. Beat eggs. Add lemon juice, instant
onion, cracker crumbs and milk; mix well. Stir into
salmon. Grease a 9 x 5 x 3-inch loaf pan or line with
foil paper. Place salmon mixture in pan. Bake 1 hour
in preheated 340-degree oven. Remove from pan to
serve. Yield: 6 servings.

Katherine W. Rebbe
Wakefield Comm. School
Wakefield, Nebraska

STEAMED SALMON LOAF

1 c. milk
1 c. bread crumbs
1 lg. can salmon
Salt and pepper to taste
4 eggs, beaten

Add milk to bread crumbs; combine with salmon
and juice. Season with salt and pepper; add eggs.
Pour into well-buttered mold or pan. Steam for 1
hour. Serve with a rich white sauce to which canned
peas have been added, if desired. Yield: 4-6 servings.

Olive Smith, Victoria H.S.
Victoria, Kansas

SALMON-POTATO PUFF

2 c. flaked salmon
3 c. mashed potatoes

2 eggs, separated
1/2 tsp. salt
1/4 c. finely minced onion
1 tbsp. minced parsley

Flake salmon; mix with mashed potatoes, beaten egg
yolks, salt, minced onion and parsley. Fold in stiffly
beaten egg whites; pour into greased casserole. Bake
in 350-degree oven for 30 minutes. Yield: 6 servings.

Sister Marie Jean, Regional H.S.
St. Basile, Madawaska
New Brunswick, Canada

NAOMI'S SALMON PUFF

8-oz. slamon or tuna
1 c. skim milk
1/2 c. mushrooms, cut into slices
1/4 c. chopped green pepper or pimento
Salt and pepper to taste
2 eggs, separated

Combine salmon, skim milk, mushrooms and green
pepper in shallow baking dish. Season with salt and
pepper. Heat in 375-degree oven. Beat egg yolks.
Beat egg whites until stiff. Fold egg whites into
yolks, a little at a time. Pour over hot fish. Return to
oven for 10 minutes longer. Serve hot. Yield: 3
servings.

Naomi N. Risner, Fads Creek School
Fads Creek, Kentucky

SCALLOPED SALMON

25 (about) saltine crackers
1/3 c. butter or margarine
1 tbsp. finely chopped onion
1 tsp. minced parsley
Dash of pepper
1 7 3/4-oz. can salmon, drained
1 c. milk

Crush saltines with a rolling pin; measure 2 cups
crumbs. Melt butter over low heat. Saute onion in
butter. Combine with saltines, parsley and pepper.
Place half the mixture in bottom of lightly oiled
8-inch pie pan; spoon in salmon. Cover with remaining crumbs; add milk. Bake in preheated 400-degree
oven for 20 minutes. Yield: 4-5 servings.

Mrs. Anna Marie Rittinger, South Lake H.S.
St. Clair Shores, Michigan

SWEDISH SALMON SOUFFLE

1/2 c. flour
1/2 c. butter

1 pt. milk
4 egg yolks, beaten
2 c. salmon or tuna
4 egg whites, stiffly beaten
Salt and pepper to taste

Cook flour, butter and milk to make a white sauce. Add beaten egg yolks and salmon. Fold in beaten egg whites; season with salt and pepper. Place in 1 1/2-quart casserole. Bake at 350 degrees for 30 to 35 minutes.

Darlene Tuinstra, Mallard Comm. School
Mallard, Iowa

PINK SALMON STEW

1 med. potato, diced
1 sm. onion, diced
1 qt. milk
1/4 c. margarine
1 1-lb. can pink salmon
1 tsp. salt
1/2 tsp. pepper

Cook diced potato and onion in 2-quart saucepan with 1 cup water until tender. Drain water from potato and onion. Add milk, margarine, salmon, salt and pepper. Simmer for 15 minutes. Serve hot with crackers. Yield: 4 servings.

Mrs. Frances S. Bell, Edmunds H.S.
Sumter, South Carolina

CRUNCHY TUNA BAKE

1 med. package potato chips
2 cans tuna, drained
1 can chicken soup with rice
1 can cream of mushroom soup

Grease a 1 1/2 to 2-quart casserole. Crush potato chips; reserve 1/2 cup for top. Combine remaining potato chips with tuna and undiluted soups. Place in casserole. Cover with reserved potato chips. Bake in preheated 350-degree oven for 30 minutes. Yield: 8 servings.

Marjorie Hall, Normantown H.S.
Normantown, West Virginia

CREAMED TUNA AND EGGS

1 can cream of mushroom soup
1/3 can evaporated milk
1 lg. can tuna
4 hard-cooked eggs, cut up
Salt and pepper to taste

Tabasco sauce to taste
Italian seasoning herbs to taste

Combine soup, milk, tuna and eggs; season to taste with remaining ingredinets. Heat; serve on hot crisp toast. Yield: 4 servings.

Mrs. Margaret J. Perry, Christiana H.S.
Christiana, Tennessee

QUICK BARBECUE TUNA CASSEROLE

2 7-oz. cans tuna, drained
1 lg. package barbecue potato chips, crushed
1 can cream of mushroom soup
1/2 can milk
1/2 c. grated sharp cheese

Flake 2/3 of a can of tuna in buttered 1 1/2-quart casserole. Add 1/3 of the potato chips. Add another 2/3 can flaked tuna. Top with half the remaining potato chips and the remaining tuna. Combine soup and milk; pour over mixture. Add remaining potato chips; sprinkle with cheese. Bake in 350-degree oven for 30 minutes. Yield: 4-5 servings.

Mrs. Darlene Kelly, Los Bonos H.S.
Los Bonos, California

CREAMY TUNA CASSEROLE

2 cans cream of mushroom soup
2 7-oz. cans tuna
2 c. crushed Fritos or corn chips

Dilute soup according to can directions, using 1/2 the amount of liquid. Arrange ingredients in alternate layers in buttered 1 1/2-quart baking dish, ending with Fritos. Bake in preheated 350-degree oven for 25 minutes. Serve hot.

Mrs. Julia J. Stegall, Sallisaw H.S.
Sallisaw, Oklahoma

CRISPY TUNA CASSEROLE

1 med. can tuna
1 can mushroom soup
3 c. Rice Krispies

Mix tuna and mushroom soup; fold in Rice Krispies. Place in greased casserole. Bake 45 minutes at 350 degrees. Yield: 4 servings.

Mrs. P. W. Johnson, Hays H.S.
Hays, Kansas

Seafood

TUNA AU GRATIN

2 6 1/2 or 7-oz. cans tuna in vegetable oil
1 can cream of celery coup
1 1-lb. can peas
1 tsp. Worcestershire sauce
1 c. grated process American cheese
1 c. soft bread cubes
1 tbsp. butter

Drain oil from tuna into saucepan; add undiluted celery soup and liquid drained from peas. Stir in Worcestershire sauce. Bring to a boil, stirring occasionally. Add tuna, peas and cheese. Heat to serving temperature. Place in serving dish. Toss bread cubes with butter; place on baking sheet. Bake in 425-degree oven for 5 minutes. Sprinkle over tuna mixture. Yield: 4 servings.

Mrs. Ada Colquhoun, Pershing Co. H.S.
Lovelock, Nevada

JIFFY TUNA SKILLET

1 med. onion, chopped
1 tbsp. butter
1 c. cream of shrimp soup
1/2 c. milk
1 c. frozen peas
1 can tuna, broken into chunks
Dash of pepper

Cook onion in butter until almost tender. Add soup, milk and peas; cover. Heat just to boiling, stirring occasionally. Add tuna and pepper; heat through. Serve over crisp oven-warmed chow mein noodles or hot rice. Yield: 4 servings.

Mrs. Audrey Buhl, Milaca H.S.
Milaca, Minnesota

BUSY DAY TUNA CASSEROLE

1/2 c. crushed potato chips
1 7-oz. can tuna
1 10 1/2-oz. can cream of mushroom soup
1/2 soup can milk

Place half the crushed potato chips in bottom of baking dish. Cover with tuna. Add soup and milk mixture. Sprinkle remaining potato chips over the top. Bake at 400 degrees for 30 minutes. Leftover vegetables such as corn or peas may be added to the casserole. Shredded cheese may be added as a topping. Yield: 4 servings.

Mrs. Carol McCord, Chelsea H.S.
Chelsea, Oklahoma

TUNA-CASHEW CASSEROLE

1 sm. can tuna, drained
1 sm. bag cashew nuts
1 c. chopped celery
1 can mushroom soup
1/4 c. milk
Salt and pepper to taste

Place all ingredients in buttered casserole. Mix in dish. Bake at 325 degrees for 30 minutes or until heated through. Yield: 4 servings.

Mrs. Sharon Petry, Du Quoin High
Du Quoin, Illinois

BISCUIT-TOPPED TUNA PIE

1 can mushroom soup
1 c. peas, drained
1 7-oz. can tuna
1 can biscuits

Combine soup, peas and tuna. Place in casserole. Arrange biscuits on top of mixture. Bake in 425-degree oven for 15 minutes or until biscuits are golden brown. Yield: 4 servings.

Mrs. Naomi Hofacket, Canton H.S.
Canton, Oklahoma

TUNA-FRITO PIE

1 can tuna
2 1/2 c. Fritos
1 can mushroom soup
Several slices cheese

Place tuna and Fritos in layers in casserole. Heat mushroom soup in saucepan; pour over mixture. Place cheese slices over top. Bake in 375-degree oven for 30 minutes. Yield: 4 servings.

Mrs. Janie Vandiver, Sulphur Bluff School
Sulphur Bluff, Texas

CLAM CHOWDER

2 med. potatoes
1 med. onion
1/4 c. chopped celery tops
1 tbsp. butter
1 tsp. chopped parsley
1 can minced clams
3 c. milk

Pare and cut potatoes and onion into pieces. Add celery, butter, 1 cup water and parsley. Cook until tender; mash slightly. Add clams and milk; heat but do not boil. Serve with bread sticks or croutons. Yield: 4-6 servings.

Phyllis P. Nash, Conestoga Sr. H.S.
Berwyn, Pennsylvana

DELICIOUS CLAM APPETIZER

1 7 1/2-oz. can minced clams
1/2 lb. cottage cheese
1/2 sm. onion, grated
1 tsp. Worcestshire sauce
Dash of garlic salt
1 tsp. celery salt

Drain clams well, reserving 1 tablespoon liquid. Place clams and cottage cheese in blender container; blend. Add onion, Worcestershire sauce, garlic salt, celery salt and reserved clam juice; blend until smooth. Serve on Melba toast rounds, green pepper squares or cucumber slices. Yield: 1 1/2 cups.

Sande J. Speck, Watertown Sr. H.S.
Watertown, Minnesota

DEVILED CRAB IN SHELLS

1 1-lb can crab meat
2 tbsp. chopped onion
4 tbsp. butter, melted
2 tbsp. flour
3/4 c. milk
1/2 tsp. salt
Dash of pepper
1/2 tsp. dry mustard
1 tsp. Worcestershire sauce
1/2 tsp. sage
Dash of cayenne pepper
1 tbsp. lemon juice
1 egg, beaten
1 tbsp. chopped parsley
1/4 c. dry bread crumbs

Remove any shell or cartilage from crab meat. Cook onion in 3 tablespoons butter until tender; blend in flour. Add milk gradually; cook until thick, stirring constantly. Add seasonings and lemon juice. Stir a little of the hot sauce into egg; add to remaining sauce, stirring constantly. Add parsley and crab meat. Place in 6 well-greased individual shells or 5-ounce custard cups. Combine remaining butter and crumbs; sprinkle over top of each shell. Bake in 350-degree oven for 15 to 20 minutes or until brown. Yield: 6 servings.

Mrs. Eleanor Puckett
No. Mecklenburg School
Huntersville, North Carolina

CRAB AU GRATIN

4 pkg. Alaska King crab in wine sauce
3 pkg. Welsh Rarebit
1 box Minute rice

Combine crab and rarebit in large double boiler. Heat 35 to 40 minutes over boiling water. Place in chafing dish. Serve over prepared rice. Yield: 4 servings.

Janet Allen, Mt Lebanon H.S.
Pittsburgh, Pennsylvania

BLUE RIBBON CRAB STEW

2 c. cooked crab meat
2 tbsp. diced onion
1 can cream of celery soup
1/4 c. fat-free evaporated milk
2 tbsp. cooking sherry wine (opt.)

Combine all ingredients except sherry with 1 cup water in heavy saucepan. Simmer on low heat for 25 minutes. Add sherry; continue to simmer for 5 minutes. Serve with buttered toast. Yield: 4 servings.

Mrs. Betty R. Waller, Groves H.S.
Garden City, Georgia

CRAB MEAT BISQUE

1 can frozen potato soup
1 can milk
1 sm. can crab meat

Heat soup, milk and crab meat in small saucepan until simmering; serve. Yield: 4 servings.

Mrs. Becky Edens, Humble H.S.
Humble, Texas

BROILED CRAB SANDWICHES

1 6 1/2-oz. can crab
1/4 c. minced onion
1 c. shredded American cheese
1 c. mayonnaise
French bread slices

Mix together all ingredients except bread. Spread on French bread slices. Cut to desired thickness. Place under broiler until bubbly and brown. Yield: 6 servings.

Eleanor V. Harmon, Scobey H.S.
Scobey, Montana

Seafood

DELICIOUS DEVILED CRAB

1 tbsp. butter
1 1/2 tbsp. cracker crumbs
3/4 c. milk
2 eggs, well beaten
1/4 tsp. salt
1 1/2 tsp. prepared mustard
Few grains of cayenne pepper
1 1/2 c. crab meat

Melt butter in saucepan; add cracker crumbs and milk. Boil until mixture is thick. Remove from heat. Add eggs, salt, mustard, cayenne and crab meat; mix well. Place in crab shells. Brown and serve.

Mrs. Carrie Alice Wade, Sam Rayburn School
Ivanhoe, Texas

BAKED SHRIMP EN CASSEROLE

1 lb. frozen shrimp, thawed
2 tbsp. lemon juice
1/2 c. melted butter
1 c. fine bread crumbs
1 garlic clove, crushed
1 tsp. dried parsley
2 tbsp. Parmesan cheese
1 tsp. oregano

Place shrimp in 8 x 8-inch baking dish. Sprinkle with lemon juce. Mix butter, bread crumbs and remaining ingredients. Spread over shrimp. Bake at 350 degrees for 15 minutes. Broil for 3 minutes. Yield: 4 servings.

Mrs. Virginia Verrill, H.S.
Rangeley, Maine

CHINESE SHRIMP AND RICE

2 tbsp. oil
2 tbsp. chopped onion
1 c. diced shrimp
1 1/3 c. Minute rice
2 eggs, scrambled in sm. pieces
1 c. chicken broth
1   3-oz. can mushrooms
1 c. cooked peas
1 tsp. soy sauce

Heat oil in skillet. Saute onion, shrimp and rice until shrimp are pink. Remove from heat; stir in eggs. Bring broth, mushrooms with liquid, peas and soy sauce to a boil. Stir in rice mixture; cover. Let stand 5 minutes. Stir before serving. Yield: 4 servings.

Sharon Bell, Nome H.S.
Nome, Alaska

SHRIMP CREOLE

1/4 c. butter
1 c. coarsely chopped onions
1 c. diced celery
1 sm. clove of garlic, finely minced
2 tbsp. flour
1 tsp. salt
1 tsp. sugar
Dash of cayenne pepper
1 tsp. paprika
1/2 sm. bay leaf
4 drops of Tabasco sauce
1/2 c. diced green pepper
1   1-lb. 3-oz. can tomatoes
2 c. cooked cleaned shrimp

Melt butter in frypan. Add onions, celery and garlic. Cook slowly until tender but not brown. Add flour and seasonings; stir until blended. Stir in green pepper and tomatoes. Cook for 10 minutes over low heat, stirring occasionally. Add shrimp; heat thoroughly. Yield: 6 servings.

Cheese Rice

1 tbsp. butter
1 tsp. salt
1 1/2 c. uncooked rice
2 c. shredded American cheese
2 tbsp. finely chopped onion
1 tsp. prepared mustard

Bring 3 cups water to boiling point. Add butter, salt and rice. Bring to a boil. Reduce temperature to low. Cook, covered, until tender, about 20 to 25 minutes. Stir cheese, onion and mustard into hot rice. Line hot 2-quart casserole with Cheese Rice. Fill center with Shrimp Creole. Yield: 6 servings.

Photograph for this recipe on page 44.

HURRY-SCURRY SHRIMP CURRY

1/2 c. chopped onion
1 tbsp. butter or margarine
1 can frozen cream of shrimp soup
1 c. sour cream
1/2 tsp. curry powder
1 c. cleaned, cooked or canned shrimp
Dash of paprika

Cook onion in butter until tender, but not brown. Add shrimp soup; heat, stirring until smooth. Stir in sour cream and curry powder. Add shrimp; heat. Sprinkle with paprika. Serve over hot rice with the following condiments: salted peanuts, chopped hard-cooked eggs, chutney and kumquat preserves. Yield: 4 servings.

Mrs. Billye P. Bronson, Travis Jr. H.S.
Temple, Texas

JIFFY SHRIMP SKILLET

1 can frozen cream of shrimp soup
2/3 c. instant rice
1 8-oz. package frozen cleaned shrimp or
    1 can shrimp, washed and drained
1/2 c. diced celery
1/2 c. diced green pepper
1/2 tsp. salt
Dash of pepper
1/2 c. sliced, pitted ripe olives (opt.)
1/4 c. toasted, slivered blanched almonds

Place shrimp soup in skillet. Add 3/4 cup boiling water; cover. Bring to a boil. Stir in rice, shrimp, celery, green pepper, salt and pepper; cover. Bring to a boil. Cook for 10 minutes or until rice and shrimp are done. Just before serving, add olives. Sprinkle with toasted almonds. Yield: 6-8 servings.

Mrs. Beryl Lenington, Nashua H.S.
Nashua, Montana

GWEN'S SHRIMP CURRY

1/4 c. chopped green pepper
1/2 c. chopped celery
1/4 c. chopped onion
1/3 c. margarine
3 tbsp. flour
2 c. milk
1/2 c. chopped apple
2 tsp. lemon juice
1/2 lb. frozen cleaned shrimp
2 tsp. curry powder
3/4 tsp. salt
1/2 tsp. ginger
1 c. sour cream
Yellow rice

Cook green pepper, celery and onion in margarine until tender, but not brown. Add flour; stir into margarine. Stir in milk; continue stirring until thickened. Add apple, lemon juice, shrimp and seasonings. Cook over low heat about 15 minutes or until shrimp are tender and thoroughly cooked. Add sour cream just before serving. Serve over hot yellow rice with the following condiments: coconut, peanuts, raisins, chopped hard-cooked eggs and chutney. Yield: 4-6 servings.

Gwen Holland, Stryker Local School
Stryker, Ohio

SHRIMP AND RICE MEDLEY

1 c. diced celery
1 med. green or red pepper, diced
1 med. onion, diced
2 tbsp. light salad oil

1 10-oz. can mushrooms, drained
1 can bean sprouts, drained
1 4 to 5-oz. can shrimp, drained
1 c. long-grain rice
2 tbsp. soy sauce

Saute celery, pepper and onion in salad oil in large heavy frypan until tender. Add mushrooms, bean sprouts and shrimp; cover. Let ingredients heat through over low heat. Add rice to 2 cups boiling salted water with 1 tablespoon soy sauce in saucepan. Cook over low heat, without removing cover, for 15 minutes. Remove from heat; let stand for 3 minutes longer. Sprinkle remaining soy sauce over shrimp mixture. Add rice and serve. Yield: 6 servings.

Mrs. Sandra Cook
Weymouth Consolidated School
Weymouth, Nova Scotia, Canada

SEAFOOD NEWBURG

1 10-oz. can cream of shrimp soup
1/2 c. milk
1 tsp. lemon juice
1 c. chopped lobster or shrimp
Cooked rice or patty shells

Combine soup and milk. Heat; stir occasionally. Do not boil. Add lemon juice and seafood; heat. Serve over rice or in patty shells. Yield: 4 servings.

Carol Wisnewski, Stratford H.S.
Stratford, Wisconsin

SHRIMP AND OKRA GUMBO

3 lb. deveined shrimp
1 lb. crab meat
1 Shrimp Boil bag
1/2 stick margarine
2 qt. fresh or frozen okra
2 med. onions, chopped
2 med. bell peppers, chopped
1 c. chopped celery
Salt and pepper to taste
1/2 tsp. paprika

Place shrimp, crab meat and Shrimp Boil in large open pot. Simmer in 2 quarts water. Heat margarine in small saucepan to light browning stage; add cut okra. Cook okra slowly until tender and reduced to half its bulk. Add remaining ingredients. Continue cooking very slowly until onions, celery and bell peppers are wilted and clear. Add okra mixture to shrimp mixture; remove Shrimp Boil bag. Continue cooking 30 minutes. Serve with steamed rice. Do not use file with okra. Yield: 8-10 servings.

Mrs. M. Scroggins, Readhimer H.S.
Chestnut, Louisiana

Quick Vegetable Dishes

There is no other food quite like vegetables, because no other variety of food seems to offer so much in both color diversity, taste appeal, and vitamin content. The many shades of green, yellow, and red that are particular to vegetables is a gift from nature to let us know just how important these foods are in our everyday diets. Most important of all, most vegetables have only to be cooked for a few minutes before they are at their best in flavor, texture, color, and nutrition. For all these reasons, vegetables are the quick and easy cook's everyday delight. Moreover, they are available fresh, frozen, canned, and pickled; and, from asparagus to zucchini, there are virtually no duplicates in taste and appearance in the choice of vegetables available to the menu planner.

Vegetables are so adaptable! Brought fresh from the garden or market, there is almost no end to the imaginative ways in which vegetables can be presented at the table. There is hardly anything more palate-pleasing than an array of crisp, colorful vegetables accompanied by a tangy dip, arranged together on an appetizer tray. And, a dish like this requires no cooking and very little clean up. In the summer, these same vegetables, cooked just to the peak of tender-crispness, make the perfect meatless dinner entree. Or, they can be stored in the freezer to appear on the menu in the dead of winter, and still display nature's best in flavor and freshness. Vegetables can be baked, boiled, steamed, or fried, and be featured in the most memorable of casseroles, soups, and salads. Herbs, seasonings, and sauces add endless dimensions to the zesty and exciting things a cook can do with single and combination vegetable dishes.

The cook who finds herself in a rush at mealtime never has to sacrifice nutrition or eye appeal in a quick and easy dinner when she depends on vegetables. These recipes for superb vegetable dishes-in-a-snap from Home Economics Teachers prove that without question.

Vegetables

BASIC HERBED LEMON BUTTER

1/4 c. butter
1 tsp. fresh grated lemon rind
1 tbsp. fresh lemon juice
1/2 tsp. each parsley, marjoram, oregano,
    minced onion, tarragon, paprika

Melt butter; add lemon rind and lemon juice, blending well. Add seasonings. Keep warm while preparing vegetables. Substitute 1 teaspoon dillweed or basil for seasoning combinations, if desired.

Lemon Butter Patties

Use Basic Herbed Lemon Butter ingredients. Cream butter, adding lemon rind and lemon juice. Stir in parsley and desired seasonings. Shape into 1 x 5-inch roll. Refrigerate to harden. Slice roll into 8 butter pats. Serve on vegetables.

Lemon-Broiled Tomatoes

Basic Herbed Lemon Butter
1/4 c. soft bread crumbs
3 lg. tomatoes, cut in half

Use Basic Herbed Lemon Butter ingredients. Cream butter, adding lemon rind and lemon juice. Stir in desired seasoning and bread crumbs. Spread mixture on tomato halves. Broil until lightly browned.

Lemon-Stuffed Mushrooms

Basic Herbed Lemon Butter
1/2 c. soft bread crumbs
20 lg. mushroom caps, rinsed, drained

Use Basic Herbed Lemon Butter ingredients. Cream butter, adding lemon rind and lemon juice. Stir in desired seasoning and bread crumbs. Spoon mixture into mushroom caps. Place in shallow baking pan, filling-side up. Pour in 1/4 cup hot water. Bake for 15 minutes at 375 degrees.

Herbed Orange Butter: Substitute same amounts orange peel and juice for lemon rind and juice. Add desired seasonings. Excellent on carrots. Follow directions for Lemon Butter Patties to make Orange Butter Patties.

Photograph for this recipe on page 67.

DILL BUTTER WITH VEGETABLES

1/3 c. butter
1 tsp. lemon juice
1/2 tsp. dillweed
2 c. sliced carrots, cooked and drained
1 c. sliced celery, cooked and drained

Melt butter. Add lemon juice and dillweed. Add 1/2 of the dill butter to each of the hot vegetables; mix well.

Photograph for this recipe on page 54.

MUSTARD CREAM SAUCE WITH CABBAGE

1 sm. head cabbage, cut in wedges
3 tbsp. butter
3 tbsp. flour
1/2 tsp. salt
1/8 tsp. pepper
1 1/2 c. milk
2 tsp. prepared mustard
1/2 tsp. Worcestershire sauce

Cook cabbage just until tender-crisp; drain. Melt butter in saucepan. Blend in flour, salt and pepper. Add milk slowly. Cook over low heat, stirring constantly until sauce is smooth and thickened. Add mustard and Worcestershire sauce; mix well. Serve over hot cabbage wedges.

Photograph for this recipe on page 54.

ASPARAGUS CASSEROLE

2 c. bread crumbs or cracker crumbs
1 can asparagus
1 can cream of chicken soup
Butter or margarine

Place a layer of bread crumbs, asparagus and cream of chicken soup in casserole. Top with layer of bread crumbs. Dot with butter. Bake at 350 degrees for 15 to 20 minutes. Yield: 8 servings.

Mrs. Rebecca D. Harmon, Lexington H.S.
Lexington, South Carolina

ASPARAGUS WITH QUICK HOLLANDAISE

1   10 1/2-oz. can cream of celery, chicken
    or mushroom soup
2 tbsp. lemon juice
1/4 c. mayonnaise
1   10-oz. package frozen asparagus spears,
    cooked and drained

Blend soup, lemon juice and mayonnaise. Stir over low heat until just bubbling and hot. Do not allow to boil. Arrange asparagus in a serving dish. Cover with sauce. Serve. Yield: 2-3 servings.

Mrs. Dorothy M. Hardin, Lebanon Comm. H.S.
Lebanon, Illinois

ASPARAGUS SUPREME

1 No. 2 can asparagus tips, drained
1 8-oz. can cream of mushroom soup
1 8-oz. can fried onion rings

Pour asparagus tips into a 1-quart baking dish. Cover with mushroom soup. Top with fried onion rings. Bake in 350-degree oven until hot and bubbly, about 15 minutes. Yield: 6 servings.

Mrs. Melba Wood, Hooks H.S.
Hooks, Texas

ASPARAGUS AU GRATIN FOR ONE

1/2 c. evaporated milk
1 1-in. cube yellow cheese, cut up
6 or 7 cooked asparagus stalks

Heat evaporated milk in top of double boiler to prevent burning. Place cheese in hot milk. Heat until the cheese melts. Serve the hot cooked asparagus on toast. Pour the cheese sauce over all. Garnish with a strip of pimento or parsley.

Anna M. Young, Boonton H.S.
Boonton, New Jersey

BAKED PORK AND BEAN CASSEROLE

2 No. 303 cans pork and beans
1/3 c. (packed) brown sugar
1 sm. onion, finely chopped
1/4 c. catsup
4 to 6 slices bacon

Pour pork and beans into 1 1/2-quart casserole. Add brown sugar and onion. Add catsup. Top with slices of bacon. Bake in 350-degree oven for 2 hours. Yield: 6 servings.

Mrs. Ann Nichols Pope, Newton Co. School
Covington, Georgia

BACON-TOPPED BEANS

1 16-oz. can pork and beans
1 tbsp. brown sugar
1/4 tsp. dry mustard
1/4 c. catsup
2 strips bacon, cut in small pieces

Combine all ingredients except bacon. Bake in casserole at 350 degrees for 20 minutes. Top with strips of bacon and bake 20 minutes longer. Yield: 4 servings.

Dudley Hambright, Roby H.S.
Roby, Texas

BAKED BEANS WITH CHEESE

1 1-lb. 2-oz. jar B & M Baked beans
3/4 c. Cheddar cheese, grated
1 sm. onion, diced
2 tbsp. light corn syrup
2 tbsp. catsup
1/4 c. sour cream

Combine all ingredients in 1-quart casserole; mix. Bake at 400 degrees for 1 hour. Yield: 5-6 servings.

Mrs. David Murrish, Sentinel H.S.
Missoula, Montana

BOSTON-STYLE BEANS

2 1-lb. cans pork and beans with tomato sauce
1/4 c. catsup
2 tbsp. brown sugar
1 tbsp. minced onion
1 1/2 tsp. prepared mustard

Combine all ingredients in a 1 1/2-quart casserole. Bake at 350 degrees for 1 hour. Yield: 6 servings.

Mrs. Marjorie West, Northeast H.S.
Lauderdale, Mississippi

PORK AND BEAN LUAU

1 med. green pepper, cut in 1-in. squares
1/4 c. diagonally sliced green onions
1 med. clove of garlic, minced
2 tbsp. butter or margarine
1 1-lb. can pork and beans with tomato sauce
1/2 c. pineapple tidbits
1/4 c. sliced water chestnuts
1 tsp. soy sauce

Cook green pepper, onions and garlic in butter until tender. Add remaining ingredients. Heat, stir occasionally. Yield: 2-3 servings.

Mrs. Wanda Montgomery
Jefferson Davis Jr. H.S.
Jacksonville, Florida

CREAMY GREEN BEANS

2 cans green beans
1 can cream of celery soup

Drain liquid from beans reserving 1/2 cup. Mix liquid with soup. Arrange beans in casserole. Pour soup over beans; cover. Bake in 425-degree oven about 45 minutes. Yield: 6-8 servings.

Lucille Cook, Wilmer-Hutchins H.S.
Hutchins, Texas

Vegetables

CALICO BEAN CASSEROLE

1 No. 303 can green beans, drained
8 sm. cooked potatoes, sliced
Celery salt to taste
1 can cream of mushroom soup
1 sm. onion, grated
1/2 c. milk
1 c. grated, sharp Cheddar cheese

Alternate layers of green beans and potatoes in a banking dish. Sprinkle each layer with celery salt. Mix soup, onion and milk; pour over vegetables. Arrange a border of cheese around outside of casserole. Bake at 350 degrees about 30 minutes or until heated through. Yield: 6-8 servings.

Grace Montgomery, Kiona Benton School
Benton City, Washington

FAMILY FAVORITE GREEN BEANS

1 to 2 cans French-style or cut green beans
1 can cream of mushroom soup
1 sm. can fried onion rings, crushed

Mix beans, soup, part of crushed onion rings in a casserole. Sprinkle crushed onion rings on top of casserole. Bake in 350 to 375-degree oven for 20 to 30 minutes. Yield: 6 servings.

Mrs. Helen Garrett, Federal-Hocking H.S.
Stewart, Ohio

GREEN BEAN-ALMOND CASSEROLE

1 No. 3 can mushroom soup
2 cans green beans
1/2 tsp. salt
1/4 tsp. pepper
1 c. crushed potato chips
1/2 c. slivered almonds, Brazil nuts or
   broken pecans
Butter

Dilute soup with 1/2 soup can water. Alternate layers of green beans and mushroom soup in casserole. Sprinkle with salt and pepper. Sprinkle with crushed potato chips and almonds. Dot with butter. Bake in 325-degree oven until the top is brown. Yield: 8-10 servings.

Bettie Riggs, Antwerp Local School
Antwerp, Ohio

VIRGINIA'S GREEN BEANS

1 pkg. frozen beans
1 beef bouillon cube

1/2 tsp. Lawry's seasoned salt
1/4 tsp. dried basil

Cook beans in water seasoned with a bouillon cube. Drain. Season with Lawry's salt and basil. Serve hot. Yield: 4 servings.

Mrs. Virginia H. Brown
Soddy-Daisy Jr. H.S.
Daisy, Tennessee

GREEN BEANS IN HERB SAUCE

1 lg. onion, thinly sliced
1 lg. stalk green celery, thinly sliced
1 tbsp. dried parsley flakes
1 tbsp. margarine
1/4 tps. garlic salt (opt.)
3/4 tsp. salt
Generous dash of black pepper
1 tbsp. cornstarch
1 9-oz. package frozen cut green beans

Saute onion, celery and parsley flakes in margarine in medium saucepan until onion is golden. Mix garlic salt, salt, pepper and cornstarch; slowly stir in 1 cup water to form a smooth paste. Add mixture and green beans to onion; cover. Gently cook for 10 minutes or until beans are tender-crisp and sauce has thickened slightly. Yield: 4 servings.

Mrs. Betty West Reinhardt, Southeast H.S.
Bradenton, Florida

GREEN BEANS ORIENTAL

1 No. 303 can green beans
2 tbsp. almonds, sliced
1 tbsp. cooking oil
1/2 c. coarsely sliced celery
2 tsp. dry chicken stock
1 tsp. soy sauce
1 tsp. sugar
1 tsp. white vinegar
2 tsp. cornstarch mixed with 1 tbsp. water

Drain beans, reserving 1/2 cup liquid. Brown almonds in oil. Add celery; saute 2 minutes. Add bean liquid, chicken stock, soy sauce, sugar and vinegar. Cover; simmer 3 minutes. Stir in beans. Heat. Add cornstarch mixed with water; heat until thickens. Yield: 4 servings.

Margaret Schlotz, Waldport H.S.
Waldport, Oregon

OVENIZED GREEN BEANS

1 No. 2 can French-cut green beans
1 can cream of chicken soup

1/2 c. grated longhorn cheese
1/4 c. toasted bread crumbs

Alternate layers of beans, soup and cheese in greased 1 1/2-quart casserole. Sprinkle with bread crumbs. Bake at 325 degrees for 1 hour. Yield: 8-10 servings.

Mrs. Linda McAnelly, Estacado Jr. H.S.
Plainview, Texas

NEHME'S GREEN BEANS

1 No. 2 can cut green beans, drained
1 1-lb. can tomatoes
1/2 tsp. to 1 tsp. grated garlic
2 tbsp. butter
Salt and pepper to taste

Combine all ingredients in saucepan. Heat until warm and flavors blend. Yield: 6 servings.

Mrs. William D. Bowen, Parsons Jr. H.S.
Parsons, Kansas

GREEN BEANS AND WATER CHESTNUTS

1 1-lb. can green beans
1 can mushroom soup
1/4 c. soy sauce
1 sm. can water chestnuts, sliced
1 can onion rings

Mix beans, soup, soy sauce and water chestnuts in a casserole. Bake in a 350-degree oven for 20 minutes. Remove from oven. Sprinkle onion rings on top. Place in oven for 5 to 10 minutes longer. Yield: 6 servings.

Frances L. Fischer, Burlington-Edison H.S.
Burlington, Washington

STRING BEANS WITH SMOKED SALT

1 lb. string beans
1 can bouillon
1 tsp. smoked salt
1/2 tsp. monosodium glutamate

Remove the tips and strings from young beans. French the beans by cutting lengthwise. Place in saucepan. Cover two-thirds full with mixture of equal parts bouillon and water. Add smoked salt and monosodium glutamate. Simmer, covered, until tender. Yield: 4 servings.

Mrs. Winnie C. Perry, Lockport East H.S.
Lockport, Illinois

BAKED LIMA BEANS AND TOMATOES

1 tbsp. margarine
1 med. onion, chopped
1 med. bell pepper, chopped
1 1/2 c. canned tomatons
2 c. cooked lima beans
Salt and pepper to taste
3 strips bacon, cooked crisp

Heat margarine in small frying pan. Brown the onion and bell pepper. Add tomatoes. Cook slowly for a few minutes. Add cooked beans and season to taste. Place in a casserole. Bake at 450 degrees until slightly brown. Garnish with crisp bacon. Yield: 4 servings.

Mary Louise Myers, Belzoni H.S.
Belzoni, Mississippi

BARBECUED LIMA BEANS

1 med. onion, chopped
1 c. chopped green pepper
1/2 c. chopped celery
3 tbsp. margarine
3 15-oz. cans dried lima beans
1 c. catsup
3/4 c. (packed) brown sugar

Saute onion, green pepper and celery in margarine over low heat. Combine with remaining ingredients in a large baking dish. Bake at 350 degrees for 30 minutes. Yield: 10 servings.

Mrs. Ouida Williamson, Graham H.S.
Graham, Texas

SAVORY BEETS IN ORANGE SAUCE

6 tbsp. sugar
3 tbsp. flour
1 tsp. salt
3 c. beet liquid
1 1/2 c. orange juice
1 tbsp. grated orange rind
3 c. sliced cooked beets
3 tbsp. margarine

Blend together dry ingredients. Stir in beet liquid, orange juice and rind. Add beets and margarine. Cook over low heat until sauce thickens and is clear. Yield: 6 servings.

Mrs. Hilda Calderan
Waymart Pre-Voc. School
Waymart, Pennsylvania

BEETS AND PINEAPPLE

1 can whole small beets
1 can pineapple tidbits
1 1/2 tbsp. vinegar
2 tbsp. cornstarch

Drain juice from beets and pineapple, reserving half of each. Heat reserved beet juice and vinegar in saucepan. Mix cornstarch with cold pineapple juice. Add cornstarch mixture to saucepan containing hot liquids. Stir and heat until mixture thickens. Add pineapple tidbits and beets. Simmer until heated through. Yield: 4-5 servings.

Mrs. Edith Hawks, St. Joseph Sr. H.S.
St. Joseph, Michigan

BEETS CARAWAY

1 tbsp. sour cream
1/4 c. buttermilk
1 tbsp. butter or margarine
1 tbsp. lemon juice
Pepper to taste
1/2 lb. sliced beets, cooked
1/2 tsp. caraway seed

Mix sour cream and buttermilk; set aside. Melt butter in warm skillet. Add remaining ingredients. Toss and warm thoroughly. Add sour cream mixture. Toss and warm until mixed well. Do not boil. Yield: 6 servings.

Mrs. Fay Foster
Brownsboro Indep. Sch. Dist.
Brownsboro, Texas

BEETS IN SOUR CREAM

1 No. 303 can beets
1 beef bouillon cube
4 tbsp. butter
1 tsp. flour
1 c. sour cream
3/4 tsp. allspice
1 1/2 tbsp. red wine
Pinch of salt and pepper

Drain beets, reserving juice. Crush bouillon cube in beet juice; boil for a few seconds. Add beets; heat. Drain. Melt butter; blend in flour. Add sour cream, allspice, wine, salt and pepper gradually. Add beets. Cook over low heat until hot and well mixed. Serve. Yield: 4 servings.

Rosalie Osowski, Buffalo H.S.
Buffalo, Minnesota

ORANGE-BEETS SUPREME

1 tbsp. cornstarch
1/2 c. sugar
1/4 c. vinegar
1/4 c. orange juice concentrate
2 tbsp. butter
1/4 c. thinly sliced onion
2 1-lb. cans baby beets

Mix cornstarch and sugar. Stir in vinegar and orange juice. Stir until mixture is well mixed. Add butter, onion and beets. Place into covered casserole. Bake in preheated 325-degree oven for 35 to 40 minutes. Yield: 6-8 servings.

Grace Smith, North Whitfield H.S.
Dalton, Georgia

BROCCOLI WITH CHEESE

1 10-oz. package frozen broccoli
1 c. coarsely cut Velveeta or Chef's
   Delight cheese

Cook broccoli according to package directions until tender. Do not drain. Add cheese. Replace cover. Cook over low heat until cheese melts, about 5 minutes. Serve hot. Yield: 4 servings.

Althea LeSage, Edgewood H.S.
San Antonio, Texas

BROCCOLI WITH LEMON BUTTER

2 10-oz. packages frozen broccoli spears
3 tbsp. butter or margarine
Juice of 1 lemon
Salt to taste

Cook broccoli according to package directions. Place broccoli in a warmed serving bowl. Melt butter in saucepan. Add lemon juice. Season to taste. Shake pan to blend flavors. Pour over the broccoli. Yield: 8 servings.

Mrs. G. T. Lilly, Murray H.S.
Murray, Kentucky

BROCCOLI SUPREME

2 pkg. frozen broccoli
1/2 c. mayonnaise
1/2 tsp. onion salt
1 tbsp. lemon juice
1/8 tsp. powdered thyme
4 hard-cooked egg yolks, sieved

Cook broccoli according to package directions. Combine mayonnaise, onion salt, lemon juice and thyme. Spoon sauce over hot broccoli in serving dish. Top with sieved egg yolks. Yield: 4 servings.

Mrs. Oleta M. Smith, O'Donnell H.S.
O'Donnell, Texas

CREAMED BROCCOLI

1   10-oz. package frozen broccoli
1/2 c. cubed cheese
1 can cream of mushroom soup

Grease 1-quart casserole. Place frozen broccoli in casserole. Add cheese cubes; spoon on soup. Cover. Bake in 350-degree oven for 1 hour or until broccoli is tender. Yield: 4-6 servings.

Laura Howell, Ashley Township H.S.
Ashley, Illinois

STEAMED CABBAGE

2 beef or chicken bouillon cubes
1 med. cabbage, quartered
Salt to taste

Dissolve bouillon cubes in 1/2 cup water. Bring to a boil. Add cabbage. Bring to a boil again. Cook for 5 minutes. Season to taste. Yield: 8 servings.

Annette Braswell, Monroe Area H.S.
Monroe, Georgia

APPLE-GLAZED CARROTS

2 c. sliced hot cooked carrots
1 1/2 tbsp. melted butter
3 tbsp. brown sugar
1/4 c. applesauce

Combine carrots, butter, brown sugar and applesauce. Heat and serve. Season cold cooked carrots as suggested above, and place in baking dish. Cover. Bake in oven at 350 degrees for 15 minutes. Yield: 6 servings.

Mary Ann Page, Bountiful H.S.
Bountiful, Utah

CANDIED CARROTS

5 to 6 med. carrots, sliced crosswise
    1/2 inch thick
1/2 tsp. salt

1/4 c. butter or margarine
1/4 c. jellied cranberry sauce
2 tbsp. brown sugar

Place carrots in small amount of boiling salted water. Boil until tender, about 6 to 10 minutes. Combine butter, cranberry sauce and brown sugar in skillet. Heat slowly, stirring until cranberry sauce melts. Add drained carrots. Heat, stirring occasionally, until glazed on all sides, about 5 minutes. Yield: 4 servings.

Katharine Rigby, Starr Washington H.S.
Union Furnace, Ohio

CHEESE-TOPPED CARROTS

1 can diced carrots or 5 or 6 med. carrots
1/4 c. grated Cheddar cheese
Salt and pepper to taste
1/2 tsp. minced parsley

Simmer carrots for 5 minutes or until tender in medium saucepan. Strain; return to heat. Sprinkle with grated cheese; cover. Let stand until cheese melts. Sprinkle with salt and pepper to taste; stir to mix. Top with minced parsley. Yield: 5-6 servings.

Mrs. John Reuben Floyd, Newberry H.S.
Newberry, South Carolina

SCALLOPED CARROTS

12 carrots, sliced
1 sm. onion, chopped
1/4 c. butter
1/4 c. flour
1 tsp. salt
1/4 tsp. dry mustard
2 c. milk
1/8 tsp. pepper
1/4 tsp. celery salt
1/2 lb. cheese, sliced
3 c. buttered crumbs

Cook carrots; drain. Gently cook onion in butter in saucepan for 2 or 3 minutes. Stir in flour, salt and mustard. Add milk. Cook, stirring until smooth. Add pepper and celery salt. Arrange layers of carrots and cheese in 2-quart casserole. Repeat until all ingredients are used, ending with carrots. Pour on sauce; top with crumbs. Freeze until ready for use. Remove from freezer; thaw. Bake at 350 degrees for 1 hour. Yield: 12 servings.

Mrs. Mark Thomas, East Limestone H.S.
Athens, Alabama

Vegetables

GOLDEN-GLAZED CARROTS

1 lb. carrots, cut into 2-in. strips
2 tbsp. Wesson oil
2 tbsp. brown sugar
1/4 tsp. salt

Cook carrots in Wesson oil over medium heat until lightly browned. Combine 1/4 cup water with brown sugar and salt. Pour over carrots; cover. Cook over low heat until tender, about 15 minutes. Yield: 4 servings.

Mrs. Lewis Vance
Jefferson-Morgan Jr.-Sr. H.S.
Jefferson, Pennsylvania

ORANGE-GLAZED CARROTS

3 c. thinly sliced peeled carrots
1/3 c. orange juice
2 to 3 tbsp. sugar
1/4 tsp. cloves (opt.)
1/4 tsp. salt
1/2 5-oz. jar pineapple cheese spread

Cook carrots in a medium saucepan until tender, from 6 to 20 minutes. Drain. Mix orange juice, sugar, cloves, salt and cheese spread. Pour over carrots. Cook over low heat, stirring constantly until the cheese melts and the mixture thickens. Do not boil. Yield: 6 servings.

Mrs. Lillian Cockram, Floyd Co. H.S.
Floyd, Virginia

PIQUANT CARROTS

2 c. sliced carrots, canned
1 tbsp. cornstarch
1 tbsp. Tang
1 tbsp. butter
1/4 tsp. salt
2 dashes of ground nutmeg
Chopped parsley (opt.)

Drain carrots, measuring liquid. Add water to liquid to make 3/4 cup liquid. Blend cornstarch and liquid in a saucepan. Add Tang, butter, salt and nutmeg. Bring to a boil, stirring constantly. Reduce heat. Cook and stir until thickened. Add carrots; heat thoroughly. Sprinkle with parsley. Yield: 4 servings.

Mrs. Marvin Henning, Glasco H.S.
Glasco, Kansas

GOLDEN CARROTS AND PINEAPPLE

3/4 tsp. salt
2 c. sliced carrots

2 1/2 c. pineapple chunks
3 tbsp. butter or margarine
2 tbsp. cornstarch

Add 1/2 teaspoon salt to 1 1/2 cups water. Add carrots; cook until tender. Drain, reserving 1 cup liquid. Drain pineapple chunks, reserving pineapple juice. Melt butter; stir in cornstarch. Slowly add carrot and pineapple juices, stirring constantly. Bring to a boil. Add remaining salt. Fold in drained carrots and pineapple. Heat to serve. Yield: 6 servings.

Mrs. Janice Larson, Iron River H.S.
Iron River, Michigan

SLICED CARROTS WITH PARSLEY

10 med. carrots, pared and thinly sliced
    diagonally
1/2 tsp. salt
1 tbsp. chopped parsley

Cook carrots, covered in boiling salted water in a medium saucepan for 10 minutes or until tender; drain. Sprinkle with parsley; toss to mix. Yield: 6 servings.

Dorothy Newman, Union Free School Dist. 3
Hawthorne, New York

SAVORY CARROT STICKS

6 med. carrots, scraped and cut into 2-in.
    sticks
6 tbsp. chopped onion
3 tbsp. nonfat margarine
1/4 tsp. thyme, rosemary or marjoram
Salt and pepper to taste
Parsley

Place carrot sticks into top of double boiler; add onion, margarine and thyme. Cover. Cook over boiling water for 30 minutes or until crunchy. Do not overcook. Season with salt and pepper. Sprinkle with minced parsley. Yield: 4 servings.

Opal Carpenter, Mentone H.S.
Mentone, Indiana

FRIED CAULIFLOWER

1 pkg. frozen cauliflower
Dash of salt
1/2 c. butter or margarine
1/4 c. bread crumbs
1/4 c. Parmesan cheese

Boil cauliflower in salted water for 4 minutes. Melt butter in skillet. Add cooked cauliflower; sprinkle with bread crumbs and Parmesan cheese. Toss lightly; saute until a light golden brown. Yield: 3-4 servings.

Mrs. Margaret McAuliffe, Spaulding H.S.
Barre, Vermont

BRAISED CELERY

4 c. 2-in. pieces celery
1 chicken bouillon cube
1 tbsp. cooking oil
1 onion, peeled and minced
1/4 c. minced green pepper
1/4 lb. fresh mushrooms, sliced
Salt and pepper to taste

Cook celery in lightly salted water for 25 minutes. Drain and reserve 1/4 cup liquid. Dissolve bouillon cube in reserved liquid. Heat oil in a heavy skillet. Saute onion, green pepper and mushrooms for 10 minutes. Add cooked celery and celery liquid. Season with salt and pepper; cover. Cook over low heat 30 minutes. Yield: 4 servings.

Frieda O. Furman, Wellsboro Sr. H.S.
Wellsboro, Pennsylvania

CREOLE-SCALLOPED CELERY

3 c. 1-in. pieces celery
1 c. strained tomatoes
1 tsp. salt
3 tbsp. butter
2 tbsp. minced green pepper
2 tbsp. minced onion

Place celery, tomatoes and salt in saucepan; cover. Cook slowly until celery is tender. Melt butter in pan. Add green pepper and onion; brown. Add celery and tomatoes to pepper and onion; stir well. Serve hot. Yield: 6 servings.

Mrs. Henry Duncan, West Smith Co. H.S.
Kensington, Kansas

PEPPER CORN

2 to 3 slices bacon
1/2 onion, chopped
1 pkg. frozen whole kernel corn
1 8-oz. can whole tomatoes
1/2 green pepper, chopped
Salt to taste

Fry bacon and onion. Drain off half the fat. Add corn, tomatoes, green pepper and salt. Cook for 15 to 20 minutes. Yield: 4 servings.

Mrs. Carolyn Gregory, Western H.S.
Latham, Ohio

SCALLOPED CORN

2 c. cut cooked corn, drained
2 eggs, well beaten
1/2 tsp. salt
3/4 c. cracker crumbs
2 tbsp. butter
1 c. milk

Combine corn, eggs and salt. Place alternate layers of corn mixture and crumbs in greased baking dish. Dot each layer with butter. Pour in milk. Bake in a 325-degree oven about 30 minutes. Yield: 6-8 servings.

Ethel Spradling, Bixby H.S.
Bixby, Oklahoma

SPANISH CORN

1/2 green pepper, finely chopped
1 tbsp. butter
2 c. canned or frozen corn
2 tbsp. milk
1 tsp. salt
1/4 tsp. paprika
Dash of pepper
1 pimento, cut up

Saute green pepper in butter until just tender. Add corn and remaining ingredients. Cook slowly, covered, stirring occasionally to prevent sticking. Yield: 4-5 servings.

Mrs. Gladys G. Halfhill
Bethel-Tate Sr. H.S.
Bethel, Ohio

EGGPLANT CASSEROLE

1 med. eggplant, peeled and cubed
2 tbsp. margarine
1/2 c. bread or cracker crumbs
1 tsp. salt
1/4 tsp. pepper
1/4 c. milk
1 egg, beaten
1/2 c. American cheese, grated

Cook eggplant in small amount of boiling, salted water until tender. Drain and mash. Add margarine, bread crumbs, salt, pepper, milk, beaten egg and 1/4 cup grated cheese; mix well. Pour into buttered casserole. Top with remaining cheese. Bake at 350 degrees for about 20 minutes.

Janelle F. Stage, Ridgewood Jr. H.S.
Shreveport, Louisiana

Vegetables

EGGPLANT SPECIAL

1 lg. eggplant
2 tbsp. butter
1/2 c. chopped onion
1 minced clove of garlic
1 1/4 c. fine dry bread crumbs
3/4 lb. ground beef
1 egg, slightly beaten
1/4 tsp. salt
Pepper to taste
1 tbsp. salad oil
2 tbsp. Parmesan cheese

Cut eggplant lengthwise; scoop out inside leaving a 3/4-inch shell. Place shells on slightly oiled shallow pan. Chop eggplant pulp. Cook in butter until clear. Add onion and garlic. Cool. Add bread crumbs, ground beef and egg. Season with salt and pepper. Mound eggplant shells with mixture. Brush lightly with oil. Sprinkle with additional bread crumbs and Parmesan cheese. Bake at 325 degrees for 45 minutes. Serve with chili sauce or hot catsup. Yield: 4 servings.

Orla J. Ells, Willits Jr.-Sr. H.S.
Willits, California

STUFFED EGGPLANT

1 med. eggplant
1 1/2 c. cooked rice
1/4 clove of garlic, minced
2 tbsp. chopped green pepper
1/2 lb. cooked cleaned shrimp
1 tsp. grated onion
1/4 c. skim milk
Salt to taste
Paprika to taste
1/4 c. bread crumbs
Sapsago cheese

Cut the top from eggplant; scoop out pulp. Drop pulp into a small quantity of boiling, salted water; cook until tender. Drain well and mash. Combine with remaining ingredients except bread crumbs and cheese. Fill the eggplant shell. Cover the top with bread crumbs. Sprinkle with sapsago cheese. Place the eggplant in oven. Bake at 350 degrees until heated through.

Betty Berk, Othello H.S.
Othello, Washington

EGGPLANT PROVENCAL

2 eggplant, peeled and chopped
3 lg. tomatoes, chopped
Juice of 1 lemon
Pinch of dried tarragon

2 green olives, chopped
Salt and pepper to taste

Place eggplant and tomatoes in small saucepan. Add lemon, tarragon and olives, reserving some for garnish. Simmer for 30 minutes, covered, over low heat. Sprinkle with olives for garnish. Yield: 2 servings.

Sarah C. Riggio, Thayer H.S.
Thayer, Kansas

HOMINY-CHILI CASSEROLE

1   1-lb. 13-oz. can hominy, drained
2 tbsp. bacon drippings
Salt and pepper to taste
1   2-oz. jar pimentos, chopped
1 can chili
4 oz. cheese, grated
1 c. coarsely chopped onions
Sliced olives

Fry hominy in bacon drippings for a few minutes. Add salt, pepper and pimentos. Heat chili in skillet, stirring to blend. Place hominy in greased casserole. Sprinkle a layer of cheese and onions over hominy. Top with chili. Add remaining cheese and onions on top of chili. Garnish with sliced olives. Bake in 350-degree oven for 20 minutes or until heated through. Do not overbake; onions should be crisp and crunchy. Yield: 4-6 servings.

Margaret Feild, Marshall Sr. H.S.
Marshall, Texas

HOT CUCUMBER STICKS

3 cucumbers
1 1/2 tsp. salt
1/8 tsp. mace

Wash cucumbers; dry thoroughly. Do not remove skins. Cut in half lengthwise. Cut each half into long strips. Place in saucepan with salt and mace; cover. Cook gently over low heat, allowing cucumbers to cook in own juice, about 15 minutes; drain. Serve hot as a vegetable or as a garnish. Yield: 3-4 servings.

Barbara MacRitchie, Northville Cen. School
Northville, New York

EASY LENTILS

2 c. dried lentils
1 tbsp. salt
2 tbsp. corn oil or olive oil
1   8-oz. can tomato sauce
1 sm. clove of garlic, chopped

Place lentils and salt in 2 1/2 quarts water in pan; bring to a boil. Boil for 45 minutes to 1 hour, stirring occasionally. Place oil, tomato sauce and garlic in small frying pan; heat thoroughly. Simmer for about 20 minutes; set aside. Add tomato sauce to cooked lentils. Simmer for about 10 minutes. Serve hot with French bread and green salad. Yield: 4 servings.

Mrs. Norma Macri, Kellogg Jr. H.S.
Kellogg, Idaho

MUSHROOM SOUP

2 1/2 c. skim milk
1 med. onion, chopped
1 c. chopped mushrooms
1/4 tsp. each salt, pepper, celery salt and
　paprika

Scald milk with onion in top of a double boiler. Add mushrooms and seasonings. Cook for 20 minutes. Yield: 4 servings.

Mrs. Barbara Manns
Edmund Partridge Jr. H.S.
Winnipeg, Manitoba, Canada

TOMATO-STUFFED MUSHROOMS

12 lg. mushrooms
2 green onions, chopped
1/2 c. mashed garlic
1/4 c. butter
2 med. peeled tomatoes
1/2 tsp. salt
1/2 c. soft bread crumbs

Remove and chop mushroom stems. Saute stems with onions and garlic in butter. Cook tomatoes; add salt. Remove from heat. Add bread crumbs; stir. Fill mushrooms with tomato mixture. Place in pan with 1/2 inch water. Bake at 350 degrees for 25 minutes. Yield: 12 servings.

Kathryn Davison, Hot Springs Co. H.S.
Thermopolis, Wyoming

BAKED ONIONS

2 tbsp. melted butter or margarine
2 tbsp. flour
1 c. milk
1 c. shredded Cheddar cheese
2　1-lb. cans sm. white onions, drained
　　or 18 to 20 sm. onions, cooked
Toasted slivered almonds

Blend butter and flour; gradually stir in milk. Cook slowly until thick, stirring constantly. Add cheese;

stir until melted. Add onions; place in casserole. Bake at 350 degrees until bubbly, about 30 minutes. Sprinkle with toasted slivered almonds, if desired. Yield: 6-8 servings.

Mrs. George Richards, Belmond Comm H.S.
Belmond, Iowa

ONION PIE

1/4 c. butter or margarine
2 c. sliced onions
2 tbsp. flour
1 tsp. salt
1/2 tsp. pepper
1 c. milk
3 eggs, well beaten

Melt butter. Add onions; stir over medium heat until lightly brown. Sprinkle with flour and seasonings; blend well. Add milk gradually while stirring over low heat. Stir mixture gradually into beaten eggs. Bake in 400-degree oven about 20 minutes until set. Yield: 4-6 servings.

Mary Lee Hartley, Crisp Co. H.S.
Cordele, Georgia

PARTY PEAS

1 No. 2 can peas, drained
Salt and pepper to taste
2 tbsp. milk or cream
1/2 c. grated mild cheese
Paprika

Pour peas into buttered baking dish. Sprinkle with salt and pepper; add milk. Cover with cheese. Broil under moderate heat until very lightly browned. Garnish with paprika. Serve hot. Yield: 8 servings.

Mrs. Wilma H. Horton, Harrold H.S.
Harrold, Texas

POTATO WAFERS

Potatoes
Butter
Salt and pepper to taste
Minced parsley

Scrub potatoes well; rub with butter. Cut, without peeling, in rounds 1/4 inch thick. Place in generously buttered skillet, flat-side down. Sprinkle with salt and pepper; cover. Bake in 375-degree oven for 20 minutes or until tender. Turn slices when brown. Serve garnished with minced parsley.

Marilyn Opfer, Central Comm. H.S.
Elkader, Iowa

Vegetables

BAKED SLICED POTATOES

4 med. baking potatoes, peeled and sliced
1/4 c. chopped green pepper
1/4 c. chopped onion
Parsley flakes
Salt and pepper to taste
Margarine

Place evenly divided potatoes, green pepper and onion on 4 pieces of foil. Sprinkle with parsley, salt and pepper. Dot with margarine. Seal each packet in foil. Bake at 400 degrees about 30 minutes. Yield: 4 servings.

Mrs. Pat Bowdell, Southern Wells Jr. H.S.
Poneto, Indiana

BAKED STUFFED IDAHO POTATOES

6 med. Idaho potatoes
3/4 c. hot skim milk
1 tsp. grated onion
1 tsp. salt
1/8 tsp. pepper
1 egg, separated
2 tbsp. grated American cheese

Scrub the potatoes under running water. Pierce with a fork. Bake at 350 degrees until tender. Shave a slice from the flat side of each potato and carefully scoop out pulp. Add the milk, onion, salt, pepper and egg yolk to pulp. Mix with an electric mixer until creamy. Season to taste. Beat the egg white until stiff and fold into the mixture. Fill the potato shells and sprinkle with grated cheese. Place in 350-degree oven for 20 minutes or until heated through. The mixture thickens as it heats. Yield: 6 servings.

Mrs. Aletha Mittelstaedt
Kaukauna Voc. School
Kaukauna, Wisconsin

OVEN-CHIPPED IDAHO POTATOES

4 unpared Idaho potatoes, thinly sliced
1/4 c. butter or margarine
1 tbsp. grated onion
1 tsp. salt
1/8 tsp. pepper
1 tbsp. chopped parsley
1/2 tsp. dried leaf thyme
1 1/2 c. shredded Cheddar cheese

Layer potato slices in a greased 13 x 9 x 2-inch baking dish. Melt butter in a small saucepan. Stir in grated onion, salt and pepper. Brush potato slices with butter mixture. Bake in a 425-degree oven for 45 minutes or until potatoes are tender. Sprinkle with parsley, thyme and shredded cheese. Bake 15 minutes longer or until cheese is melted. Yield: 4-6 servings.

Photograph for this recipe on page 68.

EASY-SCALLOPED POTATOES

3 to 4 c. thinly sliced or coarsely grated
    potatoes
1 tbsp. minced onion
Salt and pepper to taste
Butter
1 1/4 c. hot milk

Arrange potatoes in layers in 1 1/2-quart baking dish. Sprinkle each layer with minced onion, salt and pepper; dot with butter. Add hot milk. Bake in pre-heated 350-degree oven about 1 hour and 15 minutes. Yield: 4 servings.

Mrs. Catherine R. Trotter
Independence H.S.
Independence, Louisiana

MOCK BAKED POTATOES

3/4 c. instant potato flakes
3 tbsp. sour cream
1 tsp. frozen chopped chives
4 tbsp. grated cheese

Prepare mashed potatoes according to package directions. Fold in sour cream and chives. Divide into equal parts. Place in potato foil boats with sides at least 1 1/2 inches high. Top with cheese. Place in hot oven until cheese melts. Yield: 2-4 servings.

Daisymae Eckman, Pawnee H.S.
Pawnee City, Nebraska

GOLDEN OVEN FRENCH FRIES

1 tbsp. salad oil
3 med. potatoes, cut into strips
Salt to taste

Mix oil and 1 tablespoon water in a bowl. Add potato strips; mix until coated with mixture. Place in a shallow pan. Bake for 30 minutes at 475 degrees. If further browning is desired, place under broiler. Salt lightly and serve hot. Yield: 4 1/2 cups.

Alice McMeekin, Rapelje H.S.
Rapelje, Montana

Recipes on page 56.

EASY OVEN FRENCH FRIES

4 med. potatoes, cut into 1/4 to 1/2-in.
  strips
1 tbsp. corn oil
Salt to taste

Pour oil into baking pan; add layer of potatoes, stirring to coat potatoes with oil. Bake in preheated 425-degree oven for 40 minutes. Turn once after 30 minutes. Season with salt and serve. Yield: 4 servings.

Jane Senese, Wissahickon Sr. H. S.
Ambler, Pennsylvania

FRIED MASHED POTATO PATTIES

1 1/2 c. leftover mashed potatoes
2 tbsp. milk
1 egg
1/2 tsp. salt
Dash of pepper
1/4 c. flour
1/4 c. cooking oil

Mash cold potatoes with fork until soft. Add milk; mix well. Add egg, salt, pepper and flour; mix until well blended. Shape into patties. Fry in oil until golden brown on both sides. Yield: 4 servings.

Mrs. Jo Nell Baker, Scurry-Rosser H.S.
Scurry, Texas

PAN-FRIED POTATO PATTIES

2 c. seasoned mashed potatoes
1 egg, slightly beaten
1/2 c. grated American cheese
1 tbsp. grated onion
2 tbsp. Bisquick

Combine the seasoned mashed potatoes egg, cheese, onion and Bisquick. Mix until well blended. Chill in refrigerator until cold. Shape into patties using 2 tablespoons mixture. Coat each patty well with flour. Panfry over medium heat until golden brown. Serve hot. Yield: 4 servings.

Mrs. Henriette Harris, West H.S.
West, Texas

EASY POTATO PANCAKES

1 12-oz. package potato patties, thawed
1/4 c. milk
2 eggs, slightly beaten
2 tbsp. all-purpose flour

Recipe on page 66.

1/4 tsp. salt
Dash of pepper
Shortening

Place potato patties in bowl; break into small pieces with a fork. Stir in milk, eggs, flour, salt and pepper. Heat shallow amount of shortening in a skillet. Drop potato mixture by tablespoonfuls into hot shortening. Cook until brown on both sides, turning only once. Yield: 6 servings.

Gail Speron, Dye Jr. H.S.
Flint, Michigan

POTATO PANCAKE SURPRISE

2 c. instant mashed potatoes
4 eggs
1 pkg. dry onion soup mix

Combine all ingredients, adding enough water to hold mixture together. Shape into desired size patties. Fry in hot fat until lightly browned on both sides. Yield: 8 pancakes.

Mrs. Marilyn L. Anderson, Wheaton H.S.
Wheaton, Minnesota

QUICK POTATO PANCAKES

1 sm. onion, grated
2 med. potatoes, grated
1 egg, beaten
1 tsp. salt
1/4 tsp. pepper

Add grated onion and potatoes to egg. Add seasonings; mix lightly. Drop in small amount of hot fat; flatten with fork. Fry until tender and golden brown. Yield: 3 servings.

Mrs. Kenneth Harter, Pella Comm. H.S.
Pella, Iowa

GOLDEN POTATO PUFFS

1 c. mashed potatoes
1 egg
2 tsp. baking powder
2 tbsp. flour
Shortening

Mix first 4 ingredients together. Drop by teaspoonfuls into hot shortening. Cook until golden brown. Drain. Potato puffs are an excellent addition to most meals. Yield: 4 servings.

Lillian Thompson, Salina H.S.
Salina, Oklahoma

Vegetables

CORNY POTATO PUFFS

1 c. leftover mashed potatoes
2 eggs
3 tbsp. milk
1 tsp. baking powder
1 c. fresh or canned corn
1/2 c. flour
1 tsp. chopped parsley
1 tsp. salt

Mix all ingredients together thoroughly. Drop by tea-spoonfuls into hot deep fat. Cook until brown. Drain on paper. Yield: 8 puffs.

Mrs. Alice V. McKelvie
Sandy Creek School No. 1
Fairfield, Nebraska

GOLDEN POTATO CASSEROLE

6 med. white potatoes, peeled and sliced
2 med. white onions, peeled and sliced
1 can golden mushroom soup
1 soup can milk
1/2 stick butter
Salt and pepper to taste

Arrange potatoes and onions in layers in 1 1/2-quart casserole. Add soup and milk to casserole. Chip butter over top. Add salt and pepper. Bake in 350-degree oven for 1 hour and 30 minutes or until potatoes are fork tender. Yield: 8-10 servings.

Mrs. Mildred R. Bowles, Mooreville H.S.
Mooreville, Mississippi

POTATO FLUFF CASSEROLE

2 c. whipped potatoes
1 egg, beaten
1/4 c. canned evaporated milk
1/4 tsp. salt
Dash of pepper
1 tbsp. margarine or butter

Beat together potatoes, egg, milk, salt and pepper. Pour into small buttered casserole. Dot with margarine. Bake in 350-degree oven for 30 minutes or until lightly browned. Sprinkle with shredded cheese before serving, if desired. Yield: 4 servings.

Beatrice P. Grace, Dardanelle H.S.
Dardanelle, Arkansas

POTATOES MARGARET

1 c. sour cream
1/2 c. milk
1 tbsp. instant dried onion
5 c. diced cooked potatoes

Salt and pepper to taste
2 tbsp. dry fine crumbs
1 tbsp. butter

Combine sour cream, milk and onion. Pour half the mixture over half the potatoes in 10 x 6 x 1 1/2-inch pan or in large casserole. Sprinkle with salt and pepper; repeat. Add crumbs and butter mixed together. Bake at 350 degrees for 20 to 25 minutes. Convenient to prepare ahead and heat when needed. Yield: 6-8 servings.

Mrs. Fay Jean Dean, Valley Heights H.S.
Blue Rapids, Kansas

QUICK CHEESY POTATOES

8 servings instant mashed potatoes
1/4 tsp. garlic salt
1 tbsp. onion flakes
1 c. grated cheese

Prepare instant mashed potatoes according to package directions, adding garlic salt and onion flakes with thn potato flakes. Spread in greased shallow casserole. Sprinkle with grated cheese. Bake at 400 degrees for 10 minutes or until cheese is melted. Yield: 8 servings.

Mrs. Barbara Wiemer, Mason City H.S.
Mason City, Illinois

EASY SPINACH CASSEROLE

2 pkg. frozen chopped spinach
1 pkg. dry onion soup mix
1 sm. carton sour cream
1/2 c. Ritz cracker crumbs

Cook spinach according to package directions. Drain. Add onion soup mix and sour cream; mix gently. Place in greased casserole. Sprinkle cracker crumbs over top. Bake in 350-degree oven for 25 minutes. Yield: 6 servings.

Mrs. M. Judelle Jones, Turlock H.S.
Turlock, California

FLORENTINE RICE

1 c. rice
1 10-oz. package frozen chopped spinach
3 tbsp. chopped onion
1 tsp. salt
1/4 c. butter or margarine
1/4 tsp. pepper
1 8-oz. package Cheddar cheese, cubed

Add rice, spinach and onion to 2 1/2 cups boiling salted water; cover. Reduce heat and simmer for 25 minutes. Add remaining ingredients; mix well. Yield: 6-8 servings.

Mrs. Sue Kidd, Crockett Jr. H.S.
Odessa, Texas

GOURMET SPINACH

1 pkg. frozen chopped spinach
1 3-oz. package cream cheese
Dash of nutmeg

Cook spinach according to package directions. Remove from heat. Drain off excess liquid. Stir in cream cheese. Serve sprinkled with nutmeg. Yield: 2-3 servings.

Dora R. Wray, Brookland Jr. H.S.
Richmond, Virginia

CHINESE-STYLE SPINACH

2 lb. fresh spinach
2 tbsp. oil
3/4 tsp. salt
1 tsp. sugar
1/4 tsp. Accent
Bits of crisp bacon, ham or hard-cooked eggs

Wash and drain spinach, removing any wilted leaves. Heat oil over high heat. Add spinach; stir until oil is thoroughly mixed with spinach. Add seasonings; cover. Cook for 2 minutes. Garnish with bits of bacon, ham or eggs. Yield: 4-6 servings.

Mrs. Carolyn Eberle, Moon Union Jr. H.S.
Coraopolis, Pennsylvania

CROOKNECK SQUASH WITH TOMATOES

1 tbsp. minced onion
1 tbsp. butter
1 1-lb. can tomatoes, drained
1/4 tsp. basil
1 1/2 lb. crookneck squash, thinly sliced

Brown onion in the butter in a 2-quart saucepan. Add remaining ingredients; cover. Bring to a boil. Cook over medium heat, stirring occasionally until squash begins to soften, about 10 to 15 minutes. Remove cover and continue to cook until squash is tender, about 15 to 20 minutes longer. Yield: 4 servings.

Dana Ray Owens, Schleicher Co. Indep. H.S.
Eldorado, Texas

SQUASH IN A SKILLET

2 c. chopped squash
1/2 c. chopped green pepper
1/2 c. chopped celery
1 med. onion, chopped
1 tbsp. Wesson oil
1 lg. tomato, peeled and chopped
1/2 tsp. salt
1/8 tsp. pepper
1/4 tsp. chili powder
Dash of each comino and oregano

Saute squash, green pepper, celery and onion in oil for approximately 10 minutes or until tender. Add tomato and seasonings; cover. Simmer for 10 minutes longer, stirring occasionally. Yield: 4 servings.

Wanda Frix, Mojave H.S.
Mojave, California

BAKED ZUCCHINI SUPREME

1 12-in. long and 3-in. round zucchini
2 slices crisp fried bacon, chopped
1/2 c. chopped onion
4 fresh tomatoes or whole canned
Salt and pepper to taste

Slice zucchini in half lengthwise and remove seeds. Place chopped bacon, onion and tomatoes in hollows. Season to taste. Place in 9-inch cake pan. Bake for 45 minutes in 350-degree oven. To serve cut each half zucchini in half and serve. Yield: 4 servings.

Mrs. Eileen H. MacDonald, Jenifer Jr. H.S.
Lewiston, Idaho

NO-CAL ZUCCHINI

4 med. zucchini, sliced
2 ripe tomatoes, cut into wedges
1/2 c. frozen chopped onion
1 tsp. salt
1/4 tsp. garlic powder
Pinch of oregano
1 tbsp. tomato juice

Place all ingredients in medium covered saucepan. Cook for 5 minutes, stirring occasionally. Uncover and cook for 10 minutes longer. Watch carefully to be sure liquid has not evaporated. Add liquid if necessary, 1 tablespoon at a time. Yield: 4-6 servings.

Mrs. Beverly Sachs, Westlake H.S.
Thornwood, New York

Vegetables

QUICK SWEET POTATOES

2 tbsp. butter or margarine
3/4 c. (packed) brown sugar
1/8 tsp. salt
1/8 tsp. cinnamon
1 1-lb. 2-oz. can sweet potatoes

Simmer butter, brown sugar, 1/2 cup water, salt and cinnamon in large skillet. Reduce heat to low; add sweet potatoes. Cook, uncovered, turning frequently every 15 minutes until flavors blend and sweet potatoes are heated through. Yield: 4 servings.

Mrs. Sandra Rachel, Bradford Township H.S.
Bradford, Illinois

SWEET POTATO CASSEROLE

2 lb. sweet potatoes
2 tbsp. butter or margarine
1/2 c. milk
1/4 tsp. nutmeg
Pinch of salt
1/4 tsp. cinnamon
8 marshmallows

Cook potatoes; peel and mash. Add butter, milk, nutmeg and salt. Place in a buttered casserole. Sprinkle with cinnamon. Push marshmallows down into mixture. Bake in a 350-degree oven until marshmallows are brown, about 15 minutes. Yield: 6 servings.

Mrs. Lou R. Gaston, Hurricane H.S.
Pontotoc, Mississippi

BAKED TOMATO HALVES

2 lg. fresh tomatoes
1/4 tsp. salt
1/2 tsp. prepared mustard
1/2 tbsp. chopped onion
1 tbsp. chopped parsley
1 tbsp. chopped celery leaves
1/2 tsp. butter or margarine

Prepare tomatoes by removing stem ends, washing and cutting in half crosswise. Sprinkle tomato halves with salt; spread sparingly with mustard. Combine onion, parsley and celery leaves; spread over mustard. Dot tomatoes with small bits of butter. Bake in a 350-degree oven for 30 minutes or until tender. Yield: 4 servings.

Mrs. Evelyn Suomi, Sr. H.S.
New London, Wisconsin

CHAK-CHOUKA-TUNSIA

5 or 6 lg. onions, sliced thinly
Oil
5 or 6 lg. tomatoes, sliced
3 green peppers, finely chopped
Sweet red pimentos, chopped
1 clove of garlic, chopped (opt.)
Pinch of paprika (opt.)
6 eggs

Brown onions in oil. Add tomatoes, green peppers and red pimentos. Cook vegetables slowly in the frying pan until soft. Add garlic and paprika. Place mixture in 6 separate earthenware dishes. Break an egg on top of each. Bake in 325-degree oven until the egg is set, about 10 minutes. Yield: 6 servings.

Valerie Hillcox, Hope Secondary School
Hope, British Columbia, Canada

BROILED TOMATO AND ONION CUP

4 med. ripe tomatoes, halved
2 sweet onions, sliced
Salt and pepper to taste
4 tbsp. butter

Prepare 4 bowl-shaped containers using foil. Place tomatoes in foil cups. Add generous slice of onion. Season with salt and pepper. Top with 1 tablespoon butter. Place on broiler rack. Broil for 15 minutes. May be served from individual foil containers. Yield: 4 servings.

Idella I. Alfson, Woonsocket H.S.
Woonsocket, South Dakota

CHEESE-TOMATO GRILL

4 ripe tomatoes
1 lb. creamed cottage cheese
1 c. grated Cheddar cheese
Salt and pepper to taste

Cut each tomato into 3 thick slices. Broil on one side and turn. Mix cheeses; add salt and pepper. Spread generously on tomato slices. Broil until golden brown and bubbly. Yield: 6 servings.

Wilma Brereton Gross, Catalina H.S.
Tucson, Arizona

TURNIPS SUPREME

1 tbsp. shortening
1 tsp. chopped onion
2 c. mashed turnips
1/4 tsp. salt

2 tsp. sugar
1/8 tsp. pepper
Pinch of paprika
1 egg, separated

Melt shortening. Add onion; fry until delicate brown. Add turnips and seasonings; combine well. Add beaten egg yolk. Fold in stiffly beaten egg white. Place in a greased casserole. Bake, covered, at 375 degrees for 20 to 25 minutes. Yield: 5 servings.

Barbara Body, Nutrition & Food Specialist
Ext. Branch, Dept of Agriculture
Winnipeg, Manitoba, Canada

SAUCY VEGETABLES

1 pkg. frozen vegetables
2 tbsp. butter
2 tbsp. finely chopped onion
1/2 c. sour cream
Pinch of pepper

Cook vegetables according to package directions, using water and salt, only until tender. Pour off water. Add butter, onion, sour cream and pepper to vegetables. Stir and heat just to serving temperature.

Mrs. Kathy Hufstedler, Pampa H.S.
Pampa, Texas

BEAN CHOWDER

4 slices bacon, cut in sm. pieces
2 lg. onions, chopped
1 lg. or 2 sm. cans baked beans
1 No. 2 can tomatoes
1 med. potato, peeled and sliced paper thin
1/2 tsp. salt
1/4 tsp. freshly ground pepper

Saute bacon and onion until golden brown. Add to beans, tomatoes, 2 cups water, potato and seasonings in a deep saucepan. Simmer 20 to 30 minutes. Yield: 6 servings.

Mrs. Mary P. Sprague, Parksley H.S.
Parksley, Virginia

CREAMY VEGETABLE SOUP

1 lg. potato, diced
1 med. carrot, diced
1 med. onion, diced
2 pieces celery, diced
1 tsp. salt

1 tbsp. butter or margarine
1 tsp. Accent
Pepper to taste
1/8 tsp. garlic salt
1 1/2 c. milk

Place 2 cups water with all ingredients except milk in large saucepan. Cook, covered, over medium heat for 20 minutes. Mash vegetables with a potato masher or a rotary beater. Do not force vegetables through a food mill. Add milk. Bring to a boil. Serve at once. For richer soup use cream; for less calories use non-fat milk. Yield: 4-6 servings.

Mrs. Winifred McCoy, Follansbee H.S.
Follansbee, West Virginia

GARDEN SOUP

2 qt. clarified beef stock
2 tsp. salt
1/2 tsp. oregano
1/2 tsp. marjoram
1/2 tsp. celery seed
1/8 tsp. cumin seed
6 peppercorns
1 clove of garlic, crushed
1 lg. onion, chopped
1/4 c. chopped parsley
4 carrots, scraped and sliced
1 lg. green pepper, scalded, skinned and cut
    into strips
1 c. green beans
3 ears sweet corn, cut into 3-in. lengths
2 lg. tomatoes, skinned and quartered

Simmer stock with salt, spices and garlic for 30 minutes. Add onion, parsley, carrots, green pepper and beans. Simmer for 20 minutes. Add corn; simmer 15 minutes. Add tomatoes; simmer 15 minutes. Yield: 8 servings.

Angeline Strom, Canton H.S.
Canton, South Dakota

HEARTY VEGETABLE SOUP

3 or 4 med. carrots, diced
1/2 cabbage, chopped
1/2 med. onion, chopped fine
1/2 c. chopped celery
2 cans tomato soup
Salt and pepper to taste

Boil vegetables together in water to cover. Add soup and season to taste. Stir well. Yield: 6 servings.

Mrs. M. H. McPherson, Branton School
Calgary, Alberta, Canada

Easy Casseroles

What could be a faster way to serve a meal than to cook and serve it all in one dish? Well, that is why casseroles are such a favorite among homemakers in a hurry. The "one-pot" method of cooking dates back several hundred years, even though casserole cookery seems to be at its most popular peak today. Modern homemakers value highly any cooking method that presents her a choice of foods at their very best, and with very little fuss and bother on her part. That's the beauty of cooking in a casserole — almost any favorite food can be the featured ingredients in a bubbling, aromatic casserole.

Most meals seem incomplete without a meat entree, and when combined with other flavorful ingredients in a casserole, meat creates a delightful, taste-tempting, and nutritious meal that is complete with just a salad and bread. A casserole is also a natural feature dish for poultry because its flavor combines so easily with such a variety of other foods. And, it is no mistake that famous restaurants everywhere feature seafood in a casserole. There is no better way to catch every bit of the delicate flavor of shrimp, oysters, crab, salmon, tuna, and all the other fish and seafood favorites. There is probably a side dish casserole recipe that is right for any day of the year, because it could highlight vegetables, pasta, cereal, cheese, or eggs. A dessert casserole is welcome in quick and easy cookery, too, because it can taste scrumptious and look elegant, and still be simple to prepare. Best of all, casseroles are a natural for the freezer. The cook who puts a premium on the time she spends in the kitchen always makes two of the same casserole recipe. She cooks one and freezes the other, so that it is there whenever she needs it.

Casseroles are economical with the efficient cook's time and money. Once in the oven to bake, they cook with little or no stirring, watching, or attention from the cook. This is an unequaled advantage for the hostess who prefers to spend her time visiting with her guests rather than basting, whipping, mixing and timing the foods in the kitchen. And, when more people than expected arrive for a casual supper, a small amount of food can go a long way in flavor when featured in a casserole.

No collection of quick and easy recipes would be complete without recipes for casseroles and skillet dishes. This section contains favorites from Home Economics Teachers everywhere, and these casseroles will become your favorite "fast foods" from now on.

Casseroles

INDIVIDUAL STEAK DINNER

1 minute steak or 1 ground round patty
1 slice potato, 1 in. thick
1 carrot, sliced lengthwise
1 slice onion, 1/2 in. thick
1 green pepper ring (opt.)
Salt and pepper to taste

Wrap all ingredients in 1 square aluminum foil. Place on cookie sheet. Bake in 350-degree oven for 1 hour.

Mrs. Jacquelyn Sanders, Taft H.S.
Taft, Texas

LEFTOVER SPECIAL

1/4 to 1/2 lb. leftover roast or chicken
1 1-lb. can mixed vegetables or leftover
    vegetables
Thickened vegetable liquid or 1/2 can
    mushroom soup
1 can refrigerator biscuits

Mix roast, vegetables and liquid in casserole. Top with biscuits. Bake at 350 degrees until biscuits are golden brown.

Wanda Sparks, T. A. Dugger Jr. H.S.
Elizabethton, Tennessee

SWISS STEAK CASSEROLE

1 1/2 lb. steak, cut thick
2 tbsp. flour
1 tsp. salt
2 tbsp. cooking oil
2 c. pared quartered potatoes
1 lg. whole onion
2 c. pared sliced carrots

Rub steak with flour and salt; brown in oil. Place steak in roaster or covered pan. Place potatoes, onion and carrots in pan with steak. Pour in 1 cup hot water. Season vegetables. Bake in 300 to 325-degree oven 1 hour or longer.

Wilma Durbin Wood, Amanda Jr. H.S.
Middletown, Ohio

DELICIOUS BEEF AND VEGETABLES

3 tbsp. finely chopped onion
Dash of leaf thyme
1 tbsp. butter
1 10 3/4-oz. can beef or mushroom gravy
1 1/2 c. cubed cooked beef
1 c. cooked peas and carrots
4 servings prepared instant mashed potatoes

Cook onion with thyme in butter until tender. Combine with gravy, beef, peas and carrots in 1 1/2-quart casserole. Press potatoes through cookie press around top of casserole or spoon around edge of casserole. Bake at 450 degrees for 20 minutes or until hot.

Vivian Delene, Baraga H.S.
Baraga, Michigan

BEEF AND BEAN CASSEROLE

1 lb. hamburger
1 sm. onion, diced
1 can green beans
1 can tomato soup

Brown hamburger and onion in skillet. Add green beans with part of liquid and soup. Bake for 45 minutes to 1 hour in 350-degree oven. Top with buttered bread or cracker crumbs or grated cheese. Yield: 6 servings.

Mrs. Gladys Hetherton, Cascade H.S.
Cascade, Montana

GREEN CHILI AND TORTILLA CASSEROLE

3 tbsp. vegetable oil
12 corn tortillas
1 lb. lean ground beef
1 1/2 tbsp. chili powder
1 tsp. salt
1/4 tsp. pepper
1 can cream of mushroom soup
1 c. chopped onions
1 8-oz. can roasted green chilies
1 sm. can chopped ripe olives
1 1/2 c. grated longhorn cheese

Heat vegetable oil over medium-high heat. Place one tortilla at a time in oil for 15 seconds on each side to soften; set aside. Repeat. Pour off oil. Brown ground beef with seasonings over medium heat. Tear 4 tortillas into 6 pieces; layer in casserole. Cover with 1/4 of the meat, soup, chopped onions, chilies, olives and cheese. Repeat layers, ending with cheese on top. Bake at 325 degrees until bubbling hot.

Mollie S. Olson, McClintock H.S.
Tempe, Arizona

CHEESEBURGER CASSEROLE

1 lb. ground beef
1/4 c. chopped onion

1/4 c. chopped green pepper
1 8-oz. can tomato sauce
1/4 c. catsup
1/8 tsp. pepper
6 slices American cheese
1 can refrigerator biscuits

Brown ground beef with onion and green pepper in skillet. Drain off fat. Add tomato sauce, catsup and pepper; heat. Alternate meat mixture and cheese slices in ungreased 1 1/2-quart casserole. Arrange biscuits around edge of casserole. Bake at 400 degrees for 20 to 25 minutes until golden brown. Yield: 4-6 servings.

Mrs. Diane Bagley, Todd Co. H.S.
Mission, South Dakota

CHOW MEIN-CASHEW BAKE

1 lb. ground beef
1 med. onion, chopped
2 stalks celery, chopped
1 can chicken with rice soup
1 can cream of mushroom soup
1 8-oz. package chow mein noodles
1 c. salted cashews

Brown ground beef, onion and celery. Add soups and noodles. Place in buttered 2-quart casserole. Bake 30 minutes at 350 degrees. Sprinkle with cashews. Bake 10 to 15 minutes longer. Yield: 6-8 servings.

Mrs. Shirley Glenn, Centennial Jr. H.S.
Circle Pines, Minnesota

SPEEDY GROUND BEEF CASSEROLE

1 med. onion, chopped
1 lb. ground beef
1 10-oz. can chili soup
1 10-oz. can tomato soup
1/4 tsp. salt
1 6 or 7-oz. package Fritos
1 c. grated cheese

Brown onion and ground beef in frying pan. Add chili and tomato soups. Bring to a simmer. Add salt. Line casserole with half the Fritos. Pour in beef mixture; place remaining Fritos on top. Sprinkle with grated cheese. Bake at 400 degrees until cheese is melted, about 20 minutes.

Mrs. Kathryn Whitten, Hanford H.S.
Hanford, California

EASY ENCHILADAS

24 soft tortillas
1/2 lb. longhorn cheese, grated
1 med. onion, chopped
1 can prepared enchilada sauce, mixed with
    1/2 c. water
1 can chopped green banana peppers
1/2 to 1 lb. cooked hamburger

Place 6 tortillas flat on a cookie sheet with sides. Top with small amount of cheese, onion and sauce. Repeat layers until all is used, creating 6 stacks of 4 tortillas each. Pour any remaining sauce over top. Sprinkle green peppers and cooked hamburger over the top. Cover with foil. Bake at 350 degrees for 35 to 45 minutes, or until onions are soft. Yield: 6 servings.

Mrs. Sandra P. Beck, Crawford H.S.
Crawford, Texas

CORN CHOWDER CASSEROLE

1 lb. hamburger
1/3 c. finely diced onion
3 c. cooked macaroni
1/2 c. shredded American cheese
2 c. cream-style corn or 1 No. 303 can corn
1 tsp. salt
1/2 tsp. pepper

Brown hamburger and onion; drain. Add to remaining ingredients in large bowl; stir well. Place in a well-greased casserole. Bake at 350 degrees until bubbly, about 20 to 30 minutes. Yield: 6-8 servings.

Mrs. Jim Eckhout, Ansley H.S.
Ansley, Nebraska

EASY SUPPER CASSEROLE

1/2 c. chopped onion
1 lb. ground beef
1 c. cooked macaroni
1 c. chopped celery
1 8-oz. can tomato sauce
1/2 c. grated cheese
Salt and pepper to taste

Cook onion until golden in skillet. Crumble and brown ground beef. Combine macaroni, celery, tomato sauce, cheese, salt, pepper, onion and hamburger in casserole. Bake, uncovered, at 350 degrees 25 minutes or until heated through. Yield: 6 servings.

Mrs. Bobbie Sharpe, Irving College H.S.
McMinnville, Tennessee

Casseroles

COTTAGE BEEF BAKE

1 7-oz. package elbow macaroni
2 c. cream-style cottage cheese
1 med. onion, chopped
2 tbsp. butter
1 lb. lean ground beef
1 tsp. salt
1 tbsp. flour
2 tsp. Italian seasoning
1 8-oz. can tomato sauce
2 c. process American cheese, shredded
Buttered bread crumbs

Cook macaroni according to package directions; drain well. Combine with cottage cheese; set aside. Saute onion in butter until transparent. Add ground beef. Cook until lightly brown. Stir in salt, flour, Italian seasoning and tomato sauce. Cook for 1 minute. Pour 1/3 of the meat mixture into buttered 2-quart casserole. Top with 1/2 of the macaroni mixture, then 1/2 of the shredded cheese. Repeat layers using last 1/3 of the sauce on top. Sprinkle buttered bread crumbs over top. Bake, uncovered, in a 325-degree oven for 45 minutes. Let stand 10 minutes before serving. Yield: 6-8 servings.

Photograph for this recipe on page 74.

BAKED HAMBURGER AND MACARONI

1 lb. lean hamburger
1 box macaroni dinner
1 can cream of mushroom soup
5 soda crackers, crushed

Brown hamburger; pour off fat. Cook macaroni in boiling salted water for 8 minutes; stir occasionally. Add cheese mix from macaroni dinner to drained macaroni. Add mushroom soup and hamburger; stir well. Sprinkle crackers on top. Bake 20 to 30 minutes at 350 degrees. Yield: 4-6 servings.

Mrs. Kay Darmer, R.C.S. Jr.-Sr. H.S.
Ravena, New York

SOUTHERN-STYLE MACARONI

1 lb. ground beef
1/2 lb. bacon, diced
1 med. onion, finely cut
1/2 green pepper, finely cut
1 tsp. salt
Pepper to taste
1 1-lb. can red beans, drained
1 1-lb. can peas, drained
1 1-lb. can tomatoes
1 12-oz. package shell macaroni, cooked
1/4 lb. American cheese, cubed

Brown ground beef and bacon; drain off excess fat. Add onion and green pepper; cook until tender. Season with salt and pepper. Add beans, peas, tomatoes and macaroni. Pour into large casserole or baking dish. Sprinkle cheese over top. Bake at 350 degrees for approximately 45 minutes or until entire surface is bubbly and cheese is melted. Yield: 15-20 servings.

Mrs. Margaret G. McIntosh, Lostant H.S.
Lostant, Illinois

BEEF PATTIES IN GRAVY

1 1/4 lb. ground beef
1 c. bread crumbs
3/4 c. grated sharp Cheddar cheese
2 tsp. onion flakes
1/4 c. chopped parsley
Salt and pepper to taste
Dash of garlic powder
1 egg, beaten in 1/4 c. cold water
1 can cream of mushroom soup
1 2-oz. can sliced mushrooms

Combine all ingredients in order given except soup and mushrooms. Form into small patties about 2 1/2 inches in diameter and 1 inch thick. Brown on both sides in Teflon skillet or in small amount of margarine in plain skillet. Arrange in single layer in 7 x 11 x 2-inch casserole. Top with undiluted soup and mushrooms with liquid; cover. Bake in 350-degree oven until gravy bubbles and turns slightly brown, about 25 minutes. Patties may be browned and frozen for future baking with soup and mushrooms. Yield: 6-7 servings.

Rose Hagopian, Arcata H.S.
Arcata, California

BEEF-NOODLE BAKE

1 8-oz. package noodles
1 lb. ground chuck
1 2/3 c. tomato sauce
1/2 c. chopped onion
1/4 c. chopped green pepper
1 tsp. seasoned salt
1/8 tsp. pepper
2 c. cottage cheese
1 3-oz. package cream cheese, softened

Cook noodles according to package directions; drain well. Brown chuck in skillet; remove from heat. Pour off excess fat. Stir in tomato sauce, onion, green pepper, salt and pepper. Blend cottage cheese with cream cheese until smooth and creamy. Spoon half the noodles into buttered 2-quart casserole; cover with cheese mixture. Add remaining noodles; pour meat sauce over noodles. Place in refrigerator until

30 minutes before serving. Bake, uncovered, in 350-degree oven for 30 to 35 minutes or until bubbly. Yield: 8 servings.

Carolyn Willis Robinson, Highland H.S.
Highland, Indiana

HAMBURGER ROMANOFF

1 box Noodles Romanoff
1 lb. hamburger
1 can mushroom soup
1 can mushroom stems and pieces
Grated cheese

Cook noodles according to package directions. Brown hamburger. Combine noodles, hamburger, soup, mushrooms and sauce from package with milk as directed. Place in casserole. Bake at 350 degrees for 15 minutes. Garnish with grated cheese. Yield: 5 servings.

Mrs. Lorn Pracht, New Richmond Sr. H.S.
New Richmond, Wisconsin

MORE

1 lb. ground beef
1/2 c. chopped onions
1/2 c. chopped green pepper
1 c. chopped celery
1   5-oz. package egg noodles
1   8-oz. can tomato sauce
1   12-oz. can niblet corn
2 tbsp. chili powder
Salt and pepper to taste
1 c. grated cheese

Brown ground beef in small amount of oil. Add onions, green pepper and celery. Cook slowly for several minutes. Cook noodles in salted water until tender. Add with tomato sauce, corn, chili powder, salt and pepper to ground beef; mix well. Pour into baking dish. Cover with grated cheese. Bake in 350-degree oven for 20 minutes. Yield: 6-8 servings.

Mrs. Clifford E. Wheeler,
Woodville Attendance Center
Woodville, Mississippi

JACKPOT CASSEROLE

2 tbsp. shortening
1/2 c. chopped onion
1 lb. ground beef
1 can tomato soup
2 oz. noodles
1 no. 2 can cream-style corn

1 c. grated cheese
Salt and pepper to taste

Melt shortening in saucepan. Add onion and ground beef; cook until done. Add tomato soup, 1 1/2 cups water and noodles; mix well. Add corn and 1/2 cup cheese; mix. Season with salt and pepper. Pour into greased casserole. Sprinkle remaining cheese on top. Bake 45 minutes at 350 degrees. Yield: 6 servings.

Ada Goff, Hinton H.S.
Hinton, West Virginia

EASY CHILI RICE BAKE

1/2 lb. ground beef
1 sm. onion, chopped
2 c. cooked rice
1 can cream of tomato soup
2 tsp. chili powder
1 c. English peas
1/2 c. crushed cheese crackers

Cook ground beef and onion until tender and slightly browned. Combine with 1/2 cup water and remaining ingredients except crackers. Place in buttered 1 1/2-quart casserole. Sprinkle cracker crumbs over top. Bake at 375 degrees for 20 to 25 minutes. Yield: 4-6 servings.

Mrs. Grace Callaway, Green Co. H.S.
Greensboro, Georgia

POOR BOY SUPPER

1 1/2 lb. ground beef
1 sm. potato, peeled and grated
1 sm. onion, peeled and grated
1/2 carrot, grated
1/2 c. dry bread crumbs
1 egg
1 1/2 tsp. salt
1/8 tsp. pepper
2 tbsp. shortening
1   10 1/2-oz. can cream of mushroom soup
1 soup can milk
1/2 c. precooked rice

Combine ground beef, grated vegetables and bread crumbs. Add egg, salt and pepper; mix until well blended. Shape into meatballs. Brown in shortening over medium heat. Combine soup, milk and rice in a casserole. Add meatballs; cover. Bake at 350 degrees for 30 minutes. Yield; 6-8 servings.

Mrs. Jane Asche, Blue Earth H.S.
Blue Earth, Minnesota

Casseroles

TEXAS HASH

1 c. chopped onions
2 tbsp. shortening
1 lb. ground beef
1 c. chopped green pepper
2 tsp. salt
1/4 tsp. pepper
1 1/2 tsp. chili powder
1/2 c. rice
1 No. 2 1/2 can tomatoes

Saute onions in shortening in 10-inch skillet until brown. Stir in ground beef, green pepper, salt, pepper, chili powder and rice. Place in casserole. Pour tomatoes over mixture; cover. Bake at 350 degrees about 30 minutes. Yield: 6 servings.

Mrs. James R. Risinger, McKinney H.S.
McKinney, Texas

BISCUIT-TOPPED SKILLET DINNER

1 lb. hamburger
1 can vegetable soup
Salt and pepper to taste
1 can refrigerator biscuits

Brown hamburger in ovenproof skillet; drain excess fat. Add vegetable soup and 1/4 soup can water; season. Cover mixture with canned biscuits. Bake in 400-degree oven until biscuits are golden brown. Yield: 6 servings.

Mrs. Juanita Cochran, Holly Ridge H.S.
Holly Ridge, Louisiana

SPAGHETTI-GROUND BEEF CASSEROLE

1 tsp. salt
1/4 lb. spaghetti
1 1/2 tsp. oil
1 med. onion, chopped
1 med. green pepper, chopped
1 lb. ground beef
1 can tomato soup
1 can tomato paste
1/4 tsp. pepper
1/2 tbsp. melted butter or margarine
1/2 c. soft bread crumbs

Place 6 cups water and salt in a kettle; bring to a boil. Add spaghetti; cook for 15 minutes. Drain in a sieve and rinse under cool water; drain again. Heat oil in frying pan; brown onion and green pepper. Add ground beef; brown. Add tomato soup, tomato paste and pepper; mix well. Add spaghetti; mix gently. Pour into greased baking dish. Combine

melted butter with bread crumbs. Top casserole with prepared bread crumbs. Bake at 375 degrees for 30 minutes. Serve hot. Yield: 4 servings.

Mrs. Kathleen K. Horne, Powell Valley H.S.
Big Stone Gap, Virginia

QUICKIE SUPPER CASSEROLE

1 1/2 lb. hamburger
1 tsp. salt
1/2 c. chopped onion
3 tbsp. shortening
1   10-oz. can vegetarian vegetable soup
1 can Franco-American spaghetti
Chow mein noodles

Brown hamburger, salt and onion in shortening. Mix with soup and spaghetti. Place in casserole. Bake about 35 minutes at 350 degrees. Serve with chow mein noodles. Yield: 6 servings.

Mrs. Arlene Block, Sauk Prairie H.S.
Prairie du Sac, Wisconsin

FAMILY BEEF-VEGETABLE CASSEROLE

2 c. sliced potatoes
1/2 c. sliced carrots
3/4 lb. hamburger, cooked
1 can vegetable-beef soup
1 can mushroom soup

Place a layer of potatoes and carrots alternately in a greased 1 1/2 to 2-quart casserole. Place crumbled hamburger on top. Pour in vegetable and mushroom soups. Stir gently with spoon. Bake 1 hour and 30 minutes at 325 degrees. Yield: 5-6 servings.

Mrs. Eleanore M. Dahl, Belgrade H.S.
Belgrade, Minnesota

GROUND BEEF SURPRISE

2 lb. ground beef
Salt and pepper to taste
1 med. onion, chopped
2 boxes frozen French fries
1 can cream of chicken soup
1 can mushroom soup

Press ground beef evenly over bottom of buttered 9 x 13-inch pan. Season with salt and pepper. Sprinkle onion over meat. Sprinkle frozen French fries evenly over onion. Mix chicken and mushroom soups together; add 3/4 cup water. Stir; pour carefully over meat and potato mixture. Bake at 325 degrees for 1 hour and 30 minutes. Yield: 8 servings.

Mrs. Peg Latimer, Encina H.S.
Sacramento, California

BUSY DAY BEEF DISH

1 lb. hamburger
2 tbsp. chopped onion
1 can tomato soup
1 No. 303 can mixed vegetables, drained

Brown hamburger and onion; pour off fat. Add tomato soup and mixed vegetables. Place in 2-quart casserole. Bake in 400-degree oven for 15 minutes. Serve plain or over biscuits. Yield: 4 servings.

Mrs. Janet Mayer, Reinbeck Comm. School
Reinbeck, Iowa

GROUND BEEF PIE WITH BISCUITS

1 lb. ground beef
1 sm. onion, chopped
1 tbsp. shortening
2 med. potatoes, sliced
2 carrots, sliced
Salt and pepper to taste
1 1/2 c. medium brown gravy
1 can refrigerator biscuits

Brown ground beef and onion in shortening. Cook potatoes and carrots in small amount of water until tender; drain. Add to ground beef mixture. Season with salt and pepper. Pour brown gravy over mixture. Place into casserole. Top with canned biscuits. Bake in 450-degree oven until biscuits are brown.

Mrs. Bobbie Clay, Timpson H.S.
Timpson, Texas

HAMBURGER HOT DISH

1 8-oz. can tomato soup
1 No. 303 can corn
1 c. chopped cheese
2 c. chopped potatoes
1 lb. hamburger, cooked
Salt and pepper to taste

Mix tomato soup, corn and cheese together. Place a layer of potatoes in a greased baking dish, then a layer of hamburger. Place the tomato mixture on top; season. Repeat layers. Bake in 350-degree oven for 1 hour. Yield: 8 servings.

Ilene Bastian, Tyler Public School
Tyler, Minnesota

HOBO DINNER

1 lb. ground beef
1/4 c. canned milk
Salt and pepper to taste
6 lg. potatoes
2 lg. onions
1/4 lb. sharp cheese
1 can cream of mushroom soup

Press ground beef in bottom of 2 1/2-quart casserole. Sprinkle with canned milk, salt and pepper. Slice potatoes over milk; slice onions over potatoes. Cube cheese onto potatoes and onions; cover with mushroom soup. Bake, covered, at 350 degrees for 1 hour or until potatoes are done. Yield: 6 servings.

Mrs. Marjorie M. Gorton, Flagler H.S.
Flagler, Colorado

MEAL-IN-ONE

1 lb. hamburger
2 med. potatoes, sliced thin
1 onion, sliced thin
1 No. 303 can green beans, drained
Dash of salt
1/2 tsp. pepper
1 can tomato soup

Brown hamburger in a 9-inch skillet with lid. Drain off grease, except for 2 tablespoons. Add potatoes and onions to hamburger. Add green beans to meat mixture. Add salt and pepper with tomato soup. Mix; cover. Bake at 350 degrees for 1 hour. Yield: 4-6 servings.

Opal M. House, Orland Union H.S.
Orland, California

ONE-DISH MEAL

3 lg. potatoes
1/2 c. milk
1/2 c. butter
Salt and pepper to taste
1 lb. ground beef
1 sm. onion, chopped
1 No. 3 can cut green beans
1 can cream of chicken soup

Cook potatoes; mash with milk and butter. Form into balls. Add salt and pepper to ground beef. Mix with chopped onion. Place green beans in 9-inch casserole; cover with meat and onion mixture. Pour soup over meat and beans. Top with mashed potato balls. Bake at 350 degrees for 10 to 15 minutes or until meat is done. Yield: 6-8 servings.

Mrs. William B. Raley, Leakesville H. S.
Leakesville, Mississippi

Casseroles

LAMB AND RICE MIX-UP

2 c. diced cooked lamb
1 onion, grated
1 c. canned tomatoes
2 c. beef stock
1 tsp. salt
1/4 tsp. freshly ground pepper
1 tbsp. butter or margarine
1/2 c. rice
2 tbsp. Worcestershire sauce

Place lamb, onion, tomatoes, stock, salt and pepper in casserole. Bake in 350-degree oven for 10 minutes. Melt butter in skillet. Add rice; saute, stirring constantly, until light brown. Stir rice and Worcestershire sauce into casserole. Continue to bake for 35 minutes or until rice is tender. Serve in casserole. Yield: 6 servings.

Sister M. Roseleen, O.S.F.
Mount Assisi Academy
Pittsburgh, Pennsylvania

BAKED LIVER AND RICE

1 lb. sliced liver, cut into 1-in. squares
1/4 c. chopped green pepper
1/2 c. chopped celery
1 med. onion, diced
2 tbsp. bacon drippings
1 8-oz. can tomato sauce
1 16-oz. can tomatoes
1 1/2 tsp. salt
1/2 tsp. pepper
1/8 tsp. thyme
2 c. hot cooked rice
1/2 c. grated sharp Cheddar cheese

Cook liver, green pepper, celery and onion in drippings until liver is very lightly browned and vegetables are tender. Pour off drippings. Add tomato sauce, tomatoes, salt, pepper, thyme and rice. Pour into greased 1 1/2-quart casserole. Sprinkle cheese over top. Bake at 350 degrees for 20 to 30 minutes. Yield: 4-5 servings.

Sandra Eschbach Carnes, Sinton H.S.
Sinton, Texas

HAM-CHEESE SURPRISE

12 slices white bread
3/4 lb. sliced sharp process cheese
1 10-oz. package frozen chopped broccoli,
    cooked and drained
2 c. diced ham
6 eggs, slightly beaten
3 1/2 c. milk
1/4 tsp. salt

1 tsp. instant onion
1/4 tsp. dry mustard

Arrange half the bread slices in a 13 x 9 x 2-inch pan. Cover with cheese, cooked broccoli, and ham. Top with remaining bread. Mix eggs, milk, salt, onion and mustard. Pour over ingredients in pan. Bake, uncovered, at 325 degrees for 55 minutes. This dish may be refrigerated overnight and baked the following day. Yield: 6 servings.

Mrs. Lois Brown, Riverdale Schools
Blue River, Wisconsin

EASY HAM AND VEGETABLE DISH

1 No. 303 can green peas, drained
1 No. 303 can green lima beans, drained
1 No. 303 can vegetables in layers, drained
1 No. 303 can yellow cream-style corn
Diced ham
1 tbsp. Worcestershire sauce
1 tsp. garlic salt
Salt to taste
1 can refrigerator biscuits

Combine peas, beans, layered vegetables with corn, ham, Worcestershire sauce, garlic salt and salt; mix well. Pour in round 8-inch greased casserole. Arrange biscuits to cover most of the top. Bake in 350-degree oven for 15 to 20 minutes or until biscuits are brown. Yield: 6-8 servings.

Mrs. Sondra Allen, Hughes Springs Jr. H.S.
Hughes Springs, Texas

HAM AND ASPARAGUS BAKE

1 12-oz. can chopped ham
1 10 1/2-oz. can cream of mushroom soup
1/2 c. milk
1 1-lb. 3-oz. can white asparagus spears
1 3 1/2-oz. can French-fried onion rings

Slice chopped ham into 4 equal parts. Blend together mushroom soup and milk. Place chopped ham slices in a 2-quart casserole. Arrange asparagus spears on top of the ham. Pour soup mixture over the asparagus. Sprinkle onions over top of the casserole; cover. Bake in a 375-degree oven for about 20 minutes. Serve hot. Yield: 4 servings.

Amy H. Redfearn, Cheraw H.S.
Cheraw, South Carolina

CREAMY HAM-CHEESE CASSEROLE

1 env. creamy mushroom sauce mix
1 env. cheese sauce mix

1 c. cubed cooked ham
4 hard-cooked eggs, sliced
1 10-oz. package frozen asparagus spears
2 tbsp. margarine or butter, melted
1 c. bread crumbs

Prepare mushroom and cheese sauce mixes according to package directions. Combine ham, sauces and eggs. Place in buttered casserole, reserving 1/4 cup. Arrange asparagus over top. Mound remaining ham mixture in center. Combine melted margarine with bread crumbs. Sprinkle over top of casserole. Bake, uncovered, in 365-degree oven for 30 minutes. Yield: 4 servings.

Mrs. Raye L. Evers, McGregor H.S.
McGregor, Texas

HAM AND NOODLES

2 c. cooked noodles
1 c. cubed cooked ham
1/2 c. cubed Cheddar or American cheese
1 c. cream of mushroom soup
1/2 soup can milk

Combine all ingredients in 1 1/2-quart casserole. Bake at 375 degrees for 25 to 30 minutes. Leftover cooked peas or other vegetable may be added. Yield: 4 servings.

Myrna Neff, Upper Scioto Valley H.S.
McGuffey, Ohio

HAM DIVINE

1 pkg. frozen broccoli
4 slices white bread, toasted
4 slices precooked ham
1 c. sour cream
1 tsp. prepared mustard
1/2 c. grated Cheddar cheese

Cook broccoli according to package directions. Drain well. Place toast slices in a single layer in casserole. Cover with ham slices. Top with hot broccoli. Blend sour cream with mustard. Spoon over broccoli. Sprinkle with grated cheese. Bake at 400 degrees for 10 minutes. Yield: 4 servings.

Mrs. Oleta Lovell, Crosbyton H.S.
Crosbyton, Texas

MEAL-IN-ONE CASSEROLE

1 c. rice
1 can asparagus
1 can mushroom soup
4 pork chops

1 tsp. salt
1 tsp. pepper

Place rice in bottom of 1-quart casserole. Drain asparagus, reserving liquid. Arrange layer of asparagus spears on rice. Combine soup and asparagus liquid; pour over asparagus. Place pork chops on top. Season with salt and pepper. Bake at 350 degrees for 1 hour. Yield: 4 servings.

Mrs. Edward Felknor, White Pine School
White Pine, Tennessee

PORK CHOPS WITH WILD RICE

1 6-oz. box long grain and wild rice
1 10 1/2-oz. can cream of mushroom soup
1 16-oz. can Chinese vegetables, drained
6 lean pork chops
Pepper to taste

Mix rice, soup and 1 1/4 cups water in a 2-quart casserole. Add Chinese vegetables. Arrange pork chops on top. Sprinkle with pepper. Bake for 1 hour and 20 minutes at 350 degrees. Serve with Chinese noodles and soy sauce. Veal chops or chicken may be substituted. Yield: 5-6 servings.

Mrs. Michael Buero, Alcoa H.S.
Alcoa, Tennessee

GOLDEN PORK CHOP CASSEROLE

4 pork chops
Salt and pepper to taste
1 can golden mushroom soup
1 box long grain and wild rice

Brown pork chops in small amount of fat; season. Heat mushroom soup, 3/4 soup can water, rice mix and mix seasonings. Pour over pork chops. Bake in 300-degree oven about 1 hour or until tender. Yield: 4 servings.

Mrs. Michael Ginsburg, Hector Comm. School
Hector, Minnesota

SO-EASY PORK CHOP CASSEROLE

2 med. potatoes, cut into pieces
1 can green beans
6 pork chops

Place potatoes in bottom of casserole. Pour green beans and liquid over potatoes. Place pork chops on top. Bake for 45 mintues in a 350-degree oven.

Helen Long, Laverne Public School
Laverne, Oklahoma

Casseroles

BEANS AND SAUSAGE BAKE

1 pkg. frozen lima beans
3 No. 303 cans baked beans
2 No. 2 cans kidney beans, drained
1 lb. pork link sausage or Italian link
    sausage
1/2 lb. smoked ham, cubed
1 tbsp. salt
1/2 tsp. pepper
1/2 tsp. dry mustard
1 8-oz. can tomato sauce
1/2 c. catsup
1/4 c. (packed) brown sugar
1 med. onion, chopped

Prepare lima beans according to package directions, cooking only 10 minutes; drain. Mix with baked beans and kidney beans. Place sausage in skillet. Add small amount of water; cover. Simmer for 5 minutes; drain. Panfry until brown. Cut each sausage link into 2 or 3 pieces. Add sausage and ham to beans. Combine seasonings, tomato sauce, catsup, brown sugar and onion; add to beans. Pour bean mixture into 3-quart baking dish. Bake in preheated 400-degree oven, uncovered, for 1 hour. Yield: 10-12 servings.

Marion Francone, Crauthus H.S.
Crauthus, California

ASPARAGUS-CHICKEN DELIGHT

2 c. cooked chicken, diced
1 1/2 c. cooked asparagus, cuts and tips
1/2 c. sliced water chestnuts
1 1/2 c. chicken consomme
1 1/2 tbsp. flour
1/2 tsp. salt
1/2 tsp. pepper

Combine chicken, asparagus and water chestnuts in greased casserole. Heat consomme; blend in flour and seasonings. Pour over chicken mixture. Bake in preheated 325-degree oven for 20 minutes. Yield: 4-6 servings.

Mrs. Mary Pinkson Whaley, Tuscaloosa Co. H.S.
Northport, Alabama

BAKED CHICKEN AND BEANS

4 chicken legs or breasts
1 10 1/2-oz. can cream of mushroom or
    chicken soup
1 12-oz. can cut green beans, drained
1 pkg. frozen onion rings

Place chicken and soup in casserole. Bake in preheated 375-degree oven for 30 minutes. Pour beans in casserole with chicken. Place onion rings on top.

Return to oven for about 15 minutes or until chicken is tender and onion rings are heated through. Yield: 4 servings.

Jann Campbell, Elgin H.S.
Marion, Ohio

BAKED CHICKEN WITH ZUCCHINI

1 frying chicken, disjointed
1 med. onion, sliced
2 med. tomatoes, peeled and sliced
1 lb. zucchini, sliced
1/4 tsp. oregano
1/2 tsp. salt
1/8 tsp. pepper

Broil chicken pieces for 12 to 15 minutes or until light brown, turning once. Remove to a 3 1/2-quart casserole or baking dish. Add sliced onion, tomatoes and zucchini. Sprinkle with oregano, salt and pepper; cover. Bake in 350-degree oven until chicken is tender, about 45 to 50 minutes. Cover may be removed the last 10 minutes of baking. Yield: 4 servings.

Mrs. Elvi Salmela, Hudson H.S.
Hudson, Massachusetts

CHICKEN AND BROCCOLI CASSEROLE

1 pkg. frozen broccoli, cooked
2 tbsp. canned pimento
2 c. cubed cooked chicken
1/4 c. light cream
2 c. chicken gravy
1/4 tsp. salt
Dash of pepper
1/2 c. slivered toasted almonds

Place broccoli in a shallow buttered casserole. Cut pimento into strips 1/2 inch long and 1/4 inch wide. Combine chicken, pimento, cream, gravy, salt and pepper; pour over broccoli. Top with almonds. Bake in a preheated 350-degree oven for 25 minutes. Yield: 4 servings.

Lela Carlile, Bray H.S.
Bray, Oklahoma

CHICKEN STUFFING CASSEROLE

2 c. favorite stuffing mix
2 c. cooked chicken, diced
1 can cream of chicken soup

Place stuffing in bottom of a buttered casserole. Layer chicken on top of stuffing. Cover with soup and 2 tablespoons water; cover. Bake at 350 degrees for 45 to 60 minutes. Yield: 4-6 servings.

Judith Radcliff, Springdale Sr. H.S.
Springdale, Pennsylvania

CHICKEN AND TORTILLAS

1/4 c. chopped onions
1 can cream of chicken soup
1 sm. can green chilies, chopped
1 sm. can boned chicken or 1 c. cooked
   cut-up chicken
6 to 8 corn tortillas
Grated cheese to taste

Fry onions in a small amount of fat until brown. Add soup, green chilies, chicken and 1 soup can water. Cook, stirring often, until mixture bubbles. Remove from heat; set aside. Line a casserole with corn tortillas. Spoon chicken mixture over tortillas until covered. Add a layer of cheese, tortillas and chicken mixture, ending with cheese on top. Bake in 350-degree oven for 20 to 30 minutes. Yield: 6 servings.

Mrs. Doris Ann Brownfield, Dell City H.S.
Dell City, Texas

QUICK CHICKEN TETRAZZINI

1 sm. onion, chopped
2 tbsp. chopped green pepper
2 tbsp. chopped celery
1 tbsp. margarine
1   8-oz. can boned chicken
1 can cream of mushroom soup
1 box chicken and noodles dinner, cooked

Saute onion, green pepper and celery in margarine. Add chicken, soup, and chicken and noodles dinner. Turn into casserole. Bake at 325 degrees for 25 minutes. Yield: 6 servings.

Freda Richey, Marshall Co. H.S.
Guntersville, Alabama

CHICKEN-STRING BEAN CASSEROLE

1 can cream of chicken soup
1 can cream of mushroom soup
1/3 c. milk
1 c. cooked string beans
1 c. cooked noodles
1 tsp. minced onion
2 tbsp. minced pimento
1   5-oz. can chicken
1/2 c. buttered crumbs

Thin soups with milk. Add string beans, noodles, onion and pimento; mix with chicken. Place in greased casserole. Cover with buttered crumbs. Bake in 400-degree oven for 25 minutes. Yield: 6 servings.

Genevieve Overvaag, Mt. Lake Pub. School
Mt. Lake, Minnesota

PLYMOUTH CHICKEN SPECIAL

2 c. medium egg noodles
2 tbsp. all-purpose flour
1/2 tsp. salt
1/2 tsp. Accent
1/2 tsp. celery salt
1 tbsp. salad oil
1 1/2 c. skim milk
2 c. cubed cooked chicken
2 slices day-old bread, cubed

Cook noodles according to package directions; drain thoroughly. Stir flour, salt, Accent and celery salt in salad oil in a large saucepan. Slowly add milk; cook, stirring constantly, until thickened and smooth. Stir in chicken cubes; bring to a boil. Mix together drained noodles and chicken mixture in a 2-quart casserole. Top with bread cubes. Bake in preheated 375-degree oven for 15 minutes or until cubes are golden brown. Serve immediately. Add 1/2 pound browned mushrooms to cream sauce, if desired. Yield: 6 servings.

Mrs. Barbara Knowlton, Wellman H.S.
Wellman, Texas

EASY CHICKEN DINNER

1   14-oz. package Minute rice
1 lg. frying chicken, cut up
1 1/2 c. milk
1 can mushroom soup
1 can cream of celery soup
1 pkg. dry onion soup mix

Place Minute rice in bottom of greased 9 x 13-inch baking dish. Arrange chicken, skin side up, on top of rice. Combine milk and soups in saucepan; pour mixture over rice and chicken. Sprinkle onion soup mix over the soup mixture. Bake, uncovered, at 350 degrees about 45 minutes or until chicken is done. Serve immediately. Canned chicken may be substituted, if desired, but reduce baking time to 30 minutes. Yield: 4-6 servings.

Mrs. Mary Lou Siewert, McIntosh H.S.
McIntosh, South Dakota

Casseroles

CHEESE-TOPPED CHICKEN AND RICE

1 fryer, disjointed
Salt and pepper to taste
1 c. rice
1 can cream of mushroom soup
Celery salt to taste
Oregano to taste
2 cheese slices

Season chicken with salt and pepper. Place rice in bottom of a casserole. Arrange chicken over the top of rice. Pour mushroom soup diluted as directed over rice. Sprinkle with celery salt and oregano. Cut cheese slices into pieces over the top. Bake at 325 degrees for 1 hour. Yield: 4 servings.

Mrs. Bill Reynolds, Knobel School
Knobel, Arkansas

QUICK CHICKEN AND RICE CASSEROLE

1 c. rice
2 cans mushrooms
2 cans consomme
1 3-lb. fryer, disjointed

Place rice, mushrooms and consomme into large casserole. Lay chicken pieces on top, skin side up. Bake in preheated 350-degree oven for 2 hours. Serve hot. Yield: 6 servings.

Mrs. H. W. Sebern, Cummings School
Brownsville, Texas

SCALLOPED TURKEY AU GRATIN

2 c. chopped leftover turkey
1/2 c. slivered almonds
2 c. leftover giblet gravy or plain gravy
1 c. crushed potato chips
1 c. grated cheese

Mix chopped turkey with slivered almonds. Layer turkey, gravy, potato chips and 1/2 cup cheese in greased 2-quart casserole. Bake at 350 degrees for 20 minutes. Add remaining cheese and bake for 10 more minutes. Yield: 4-6 servings.

Mrs. Dorothy M. Grace, Sumter Co. H.S.
York, Alabama

GOOD-BYE TURKEY CASSEROLE

5 tbsp. sifted flour
1 tsp. salt
1/4 tsp. onion salt

1/4 c. melted butter
2 1/2 c. milk
1 1/3 c. Minute rice
1 1/2 c. turkey or chicken broth
1/2 c. grated cheese
1 1/2 c. cooked asparagus
2 c. sliced turkey
2 tbsp. toasted slivered almonds

Sift flour, 1/2 teaspoon salt and onion salt into butter. Stir in milk. Cook over hot water, stirring occasionally until thickened. Pour rice into 2-quart shallow baking dish. Combine broth and remaining salt; pour over rice. Sprinkle half the cheese over rice. Top with asparagus, then turkey. Pour on sauce. Sprinkle with remaining cheese. Bake at 375 degrees for about 20 minutes. Top with almonds. Yield: 6 servings.

Ivadine G. Blevins, Ider School
Ider, Alabama

BAKED CRAB MEAT AND NOODLES

1 8-oz. package pimento cheese
1/4 lb. butter
1/2 pt. cream
1 lb. mushrooms
1 lg. onion, chopped
1 12-oz. box fine noodles, cooked
1 1-lb. can crab meat
Salt and pepper to taste

Melt cheese and half the butter together; add cream slowly. Saute mushrooms and onion in remaining butter. Add noodles, crab meat, mushrooms and onion to cheese mixture. Season with salt and pepper. Place in buttered casserole. Bake in 325-degree oven about 25 minutes. Buttered crumbs may be placed on top before baking, if desired. Yield: 5-6 servings.

Esther P. Leed, Wiscasset H.S.
Wiscasset, Maine

SAUCY CRAB WITH MACARONI

2 1/2 to 3 c. macaroni
2 c. medium white sauce
1 c. grated cheese
1 6 1/2-oz. can crab meat
1 sm. can mushroom pieces
1/2 c. sliced ripe olives
Buttered bread crumbs
Paprika (opt.)

Cook macaroni; drain. Prepare white sauce. Add grated cheese, stirring until cheese melts. Combine macaroni, sauce, crab, mushroom pieces and olives. Place in greased baking dish. Top with buttered bread crumbs. Additional grated cheese and paprika may be added, if desired. Bake at 350 degrees until bubbly. Yield: 6 servings.

Mrs. Bonnie Greene, Bellevue Christian H.S.
Bellevue, Washington

EASY CRAB CASSEROLE

1 can mushroom soup
1/3 c. salad dressing
1/3 c. milk
6 oz. crab meat
1 can water chestnuts, drained
1 c. diced celery
Pinch of coarsely ground pepper
Small amount of onion
2 c. cooked macaroni
2 tbsp. paprika

Blend all ingredients in baking dish. Sprinkle top with paprika. Bake at 350 degrees 30 to 40 minutes. Yield: 6 servings.

Mrs. Joan Murphy, Chinook H.S.
Chinook, Montana

CAPRICIOUS CRAB CASSEROLE

1 6-oz. package seasoned white and wild rice mix
1 lg. peeled onion, finely chopped
1 lg. stalk green celery with leaves, chopped
2 tbsp. salad oil
1 apple, pared and chopped
1 to 2 tsp. curry powder
1/2 tsp. monosodium glutamate
3 6-oz. packages frozen King crab meat, thawed and drained
2 tbsp. raisins

Cook rice mix according to package directions, omitting butter and decreasing cooking time to 20 minutes. Saute onion and celery in salad oil in large skillet until onion is golden. Stir in apple, curry, monosodium glutamate, crab, raisins and rice. Turn into a 2-quart casserole; cover. Bake in preheated 375-degree oven for 20 minutes. Yield: 6 servings.

Kathy M. Lazun, Bethlehem Cath. H.S.
Bethlehem, Pennsylvania

FLOUNDER FILLETS EN CASSEROLE

1/2 lb. frozen flounder fillets
3 tbsp. butter
1 can mushroom soup
1 1/4 c. milk
1/4 c. finely chopped onion
1/4 tsp. salt
Dash of pepper
1 1/3 c. precooked rice
1 10-oz. package thawed frozen peas
1/2 c. grated Cheddar cheese
Dash of paprika

Saute fillets in butter; cut in cubes. Combine soup, milk, onion, salt and pepper in saucepan. Bring to a boil, stirring occasionally. Add rice, flounder and peas. Place in casserole. Top with cheese; sprinkle with paprika. Bake, covered, 20 minutes at 375 degrees. Yield: 4 servings.

Mrs. Nannie C. Edwards, Oxford Area H.S.
Oxford, Pennsylvania

QUICK FISH AND NOODLE CASSEROLE

1 can cream of vegetable, celery, chicken or mushroom soup
1/2 c. milk
1 to 1 1/2 c. cooked or canned fish
2 c. cooked noodles
1/2 c. cooked peas or green beans
2 tbsp. buttered bread crumbs, slightly crushed corn flakes or herb-seasoned stuffing mix

Blend soup and milk in 1 1/2-quart casserole. Stir in fish, noodles and vegetables. Top with crumbs. Bake at 350 degrees for 30 minutes or until hot. Yield: 3-4 servings.

Annette O'Rourke, Goodrich H.S.
Fond du Lac, Wisconsin

FISH FILLETS WITH RICE

1/4 c. chopped onion
5 tbsp. butter
2 c. cooked rice
2 tbsp. lemon juice
1 egg, slightly beaten
Salt and pepper to taste
1 lb. frozen fish fillets, partially thawed

Cook onion in 2 tablespoons butter until slightly tender; stir into rice. Mix in lemon juice, egg, and a dash of salt. Place half the fillets in a buttered 10 x 6 x 1 1/2-inch baking dish. Season with salt and pepper. Top with rice mixture, then remaining fillets. Brush with remaining melted butter. Sprinkle with salt, pepper and paprika. Bake at 375 degrees about 35 minutes, brushing occasionally with additional melted butter. Yield: 4 servings.

Velva Johnson, Adams H.S.
Adams, Minnesota

Casseroles

CAN OPENER CASSEROLE

1 1-lb. can green beans, drained
1 1-lb. can salmon, drained
1 1/2 c. shredded Cheddar cheese
1/4 c. all-purpose flour
2 tbsp. instant minced onion
1 10 1/2-oz. can tomato soup
1/2 c. milk
1 tsp. parsley flakes
1 recipe baking powder biscuit dough

Place beans, salmon and 1 cup cheese in 2 1/2-quart casserole. Sprinkle with flour and 1 tablespoon onion. Add soup and milk; stir gently. Add remaining cheese, onion and parsley to biscuit dough. Drop by spoonfuls around edge of casserole. Bake in 450-degree oven for 25 to 30 minutes. Yield: 6 servings.

Karen Tinseth, Sauk Rapids Jr. H.S.
Sauk Rapids, Minnesota

SALMON-NOODLE BAKE

1 8-oz. package med. noodles
2 10 1/2-oz. cans cream of mushroom soup
1 c. grated Cheddar cheese
1/2 tsp. Worcestershire sauce
1 16-oz. can salmon
1/2 c. fine cracker crumbs
2 tbsp. butter
3 hard-cooked eggs, sliced

Cook noodles according to package directions. Heat soup and 1 cup water over medium heat. Add cheese and Worcestershire sauce. Stir until smooth; remove from heat. Add flaked salmon and noodles; blend well. Pour into greased 1 1/2-quart casserole. Sprinkle cracker crumbs over top; dot with butter. Garnish with egg slices. Bake in a preheated 350-degree oven for 40 to 50 minutes. Yield: 8 servings.

Mrs. Anna Brandon, Brewer Jr. H.S.
Fort Worth, Texas

DIFFERENT TUNA CASSEROLE

2 cans tuna
2 1/2 c. bread stuffing mix
2 tbsp. melted butter
1 c. tomato juice
3 beaten egg yolks
3 stiffly beaten egg whites

Combine ingredients in order listed. Place in a greased baking dish. Bake at 350 degrees for about 25 minutes. Yield: 4-6 servings.

Virginia T. Harbour, Wakefield H.S.
Arlington, Virginia

TUNA WITH MACARONI AND CHEESE

2 cans macaroni and cheese
2 cans chunk tuna
Grated cheese

Alternate layers of macaroni and tuna in greased casserole until all ingredients are used. Sprinkle cheese on top. Bake, uncovered, at 300 degrees for 30 minutes. Yield: 4-5 servings.

Mrs. Aleen Hartman, Hyattville H.S.
Manderson, Wyoming

TUNA TEASER

1 can cream of mushroom soup
1/2 c. milk
1 7-oz. can flaked tuna, drained
1 1/2 c. cooked macaroni
1 8-oz. can green peas, drained
1 c. crushed potato chips

Combine soup and milk in 1 1/2-quart casserole. Fold in tuna, macaroni and peas. Sprinkle crushed potato chips on top. Bake 25 minutes at 350 degrees. Yield: 4 servings.

Mrs. Carol Short, Greenbelt Jr. H.S.
Greenbelt, Maryland

HURRY-UP TUNA DISH

1 6 1/2-oz. can tuna
1 can cream of mushroom soup
1 lg. can chow mein noodles
1 soup can milk

Mix all ingredients well. Place in greased casserole. Bake at 350 degrees for 25 to 30 minutes. Yield: 6 servings.

Jo Ann Thompson, Moscow H.S.
Moscow, Idaho

TUNA-NOODLE CRISP

4 oz. noodles
1/4 c. Crisco
1/3 c. chopped onion
2 tbsp. chopped green pepper
1 10 1/2-oz. can cheese soup
1/2 c. milk
1 tbsp chopped pimento
1 tsp. salt
1/8 tsp. pepper
1 6 1/2 or 7-oz. can tuna
1/2 c. bread crumbs

Cook noodles in boiling salted water according to package directions; drain. Melt Crisco in large skillet; add onion and green pepper. Cook until tender. Stir in soup, milk, pimento, salt and pepper. Bring to a boil. Add cooked noodles and tuna. Place mixture in a 1 1/2 or 2-quart casserole. Sprinkle bread crumbs on top. Bake in preheated 350-degree oven for 25 to 30 minutes. Yield: 4-6 servings.

Mrs. Betty Porter, Oilton H.S.
Oilton, Oklahoma

FIVE-CAN CASSEROLE

1   11 1/2-oz. can cream of chicken soup
1   6 1/2-oz. can tuna
1   11 1/2-oz. can cream of mushroom soup
1 can chow mein noodles
1   5-oz. can evaporated milk or 1/4 c.
     plus 1 tbsp. whole milk
Bread crumbs or crushed potato chips

Combine all ingredients except bread crumbs in 1-quart casserole. Sprinkle bread crumbs on top. Bake for 1 hour at 350 degrees. Yield: 4 servings.

Janet White Stafford, Hanover Comm. School
Hanover, Illinois

TUNA-CASHEW CASSEROLE

1   3-oz. can chow mein noodles
1 can cream of mushroom soup
1 can chunk-style tuna
1/4 lb. cashews
1 c. finely diced celery
1/4 c. minced onions
Dash of pepper
Salt to taste

Set aside 1/2 cup chow mein noodles. Combine remaining noodles and next 6 ingredients with 1/4 to 1/2 cup water in 1 1/2-quart casserole. Season with salt. Sprinkle reserved noodles over top. Bake at 350 degrees for 40 minutes. Up to 1 1/2 cups liquid may be used. Yield: 5 servings.

Joan McCready, Missour Valley Comm. School
Missouri Valley, Iowa

NUTTY TUNA CASSEROLE

2 cans cream of mushroom soup
2 c. noodles, cooked and drained
2 cans tuna
1/2 c. grated Cheddar cheese
1 sm. jar olives, sliced
1/4 lb. cashews, chopped

1/2 c. milk
Potato chips, crushed
Paprika

Pour 1 can mushroom soup into a buttered casserole. Add noodles, tuna, cheese, olives and cashews. Top with remaining soup and milk; stir gently. Top with potato chips and paprika. Bake at 350 degrees until bubbly and golden brown on top. Yield: 6-8 servings.

Mrs. Nancy W. Grammer, Ripley H.S.
Ripley, Tennessee

TUNA-OLIVE CASSEROLE

2   6 1/2-oz. cans tuna
1 can cream of mushroom soup
10 chopped stuffed olives
6 oz. egg noodles, cooked and drained
1/2 c. grated Cheddar cheese

Combine tuna, soup and olives. Place half the noodles in a casserole. Cover with half the tuna mixture. Repeat the process with remaining noodles and tuna. Sprinkle on grated cheese; cover. Bake at 400 degrees for 20 minutes. Uncover and cook for 10 minutes longer or until top is lightly browned. Yield: 6 servings.

Anita Dugger, West Phoenix H.S.
Phoenix, Arizona

TUNA CREOLE

1/2 c. chopped celery
1/2 c. chopped green pepper
1/2 c. minced onion
2 tbsp. Wesson oil
1 sm. can pimentos, mashed
1 c. rice
1 1/2 tsp. salt
1 can chunk-style tuna or 1 can cleaned
     shrimp, cooked
1 can cream of tomato soup
1 tbsp. Worcestershire sauce
1/4 stick margarine

Saute celery, green pepper and onion in oil; add pimentos. Add rice, salt and sauteed mixture to greased casserole. Add tuna. Top with soup blended with 2 cups water and Worcestershire sauce. Dot with margarine. Bake, covered, at 400 degrees for 20 minutes. Remove cover; stir. Cover and bake for 10 to 15 minutes more. Use mushroom soup with tuna and tomato with shrimp. Yield: 6 servings.

Carla Sue Park, Dayton H.S.
Dayton, Texas

Casseroles

TUNA-BROCCOLI BAKE

1 box frozen broccoli
1 sm. can tuna
1/2 can mushroom soup
1/3 c. crushed potato chips

Paritally cook frozen broccoli according to package directions. Layer broccoli, tuna and mushroom soup in small baking dish. Cover with crushed potato chips. Bake, uncovered, at 350 degrees for 45 to 60 minutes. Yield: 3 servings.

Sharon Schlafmann, Worthington Sr. H.S.
Worthington, Minnesota

FISHERMAN'S CASSEROLE

1 pkg. frozen mashed potatoes or 2 c. cooked
   potatoes, mashed
1 3-oz. can mushrooms, chopped
1 10 1/2-oz. can cream of mushroom soup
1 c. grated American cheese
1 med. onion, chopped
1/2 green pepper, chopped
1/2 tsp. salt
1/4 tsp. pepper
3 hard-cooked eggs, sliced
2 6 1/2-oz. cans tuna

Grease a 2-quart casserole. Prepare frozen mashed potatoes according to package directions. Toss mushrooms with cream of mushroom soup and 1/2 cup grated cheese. Cook over a low heat until cheese melts. Add onion, green pepper and seasonings. Arrange a layer of egg slices over bottom of casserole. Cover with a layer of drained tuna and a layer of sauce. Repeat the layers ending with sauce. Spread mashed potatoes over surface. Sprinkle with remaining cheese. Bake in preheated 350-degree oven for 30 to 35 minutes. Yield: 6 servings.

Mrs. Effie G. Hoyle, Warwick H.S.
Newport News, Virginia

BISCUIT-TOPPED TUNA

2 tbsp. butter
1/2 c. diced onion
2 tbsp. flour
1 c. milk
1 c. drained peas
1 family-sized can tuna, drained
1/2 tsp. salt
1/8 tsp. pepper
1 can refrigerator biscuits or 1/2 biscuit
   recipe

Melt butter in 1 1/2-quart Corning Ware casserole on top of stove. Saute onion in butter at low tempera-

ture until onion turns yellow. Add flour and milk to make a white sauce. Cook until sauce thickens. Add peas, tuna, salt and pepper; stir lightly. Top with biscuits. Bake at 425 degrees for 15 minutes or until biscuits are baked. Yield: 4 servings.

Mrs. Yvonne Wilson, Clarkston H.S.
Clarkston, Michigan

HOMINY-TUNA CASSEROLE

1 No. 2 can hominy
1 family-sized can tuna
1 can mushroom soup
1/4 c. finely chopped onion
1/2 c. fine crumbs
1/2 c. (or more) grated cheese
1/2 stick margarine

Place alternate layers of hominy, tuna and soup combined with onion in greased baking dish. Cover with crumbs. Sprinkle with cheese. Dot with margarine. Bake in a 350-degree oven until cheese melts and casserole is thoroughly heated. Yield: 6 servings.

Mrs. H. M. Thomas, Breckenridge H.S.
Breckenridge, Texas

QUICK CHINESE SUPPER

1 3-oz. can crisp chow mein noodles
1 15-oz. can peas, drained
1 10 1/2-oz. can mushroom soup
2 7-oz. cans tuna
1/2 soup can milk
2 tbsp. chopped celery
1 tsp. chopped onion
1/2 c. cashew nuts
1/2 c. canned mandarin oranges, drained

Reserve 1/2 cup noodles. Combine all ingredients except mandarin orange segments. Pour into buttered 1 1/2-quart casserole. Top with reserved noodles. Bake at 350 degrees for 25 to 30 minutes. Garnish top with mandarin orange segments. Yield: 4 servings.

Mrs. Norma Booshey, Sumner H.S.
Sumner, Washington

BETTY'S TUNA-BROCCOLI CASSEROLE

1 pkg. frozen broccoli
1 7-oz. can tuna, flaked
1 10 1/2-oz. can cream of mushroom soup
1/2 soup can milk
1/2 c. crushed potato chips

Split broccoli stalks. Cook in small amount of water for 3 minutes; drain. Place in 1 1/2-quart baking dish. Cover with tuna. Mix soup and milk; pour over tuna. Sprinkle potato chips over top. Bake in pre-heated 450-degree oven for 15 minutes. Yield: 4 servings.

Mrs. Betty Addison, Lipan H.S.
Lipan, Texas

CREAMY TUNA CASSEROLE

1 c. cream of mushroom soup
1/2 c. milk
1 c. tuna, drained
1 c. cooked green peas, drained
1 c. crushed potato chips

Place mushroom soup in a small casserole. Add milk; stir until well blended. Add tuna, green peas and about 3/4 of the potato chips to soup; mix well. Sprinkle remaining potato chips over top. Bake in preheated 350-degree oven for 25 minutes. Serve hot in casserole. Yield: 6 servings.

Mrs. Mildred W. Jordan, Riverview H.S.
Waynesboro, Mississippi

TUNA DELIGHT

2 7-oz. cans tuna, drained
1 can cream of chicken soup
1 pkg. frozen French-style green beans
1 sm. package Tater Tots

Combine tuna with undiluted soup and precooked green beans. Brown Tater Tots in oven. Place on top of casserole. Bake in 300-degree oven until mixture is bubbly, about 20 minutes. Yield: 4 servings.

Mrs. Irene Patton, Merryville H.S.
Merryville, Louisiana

TASTY TUNA-GREEN BEAN CASSEROLE

1 can tuna
1 can French-style green beans
1 can cream of celery or mushroom soup
Chopped onion and green pepper to taste
Buttered bread crumbs

Place all ingredients except crumbs in alternating layers in greased casserole. Cover with buttered bread crumbs. Bake for 30 minutes at 375 degrees. Yield: 4-6 servings.

Jean C. Vandergrift, Patrick Henry H.S.
Roanoke, Virginia

SO-GOOD SHRIMP

1 13-oz. can shrimp or crab meat
1/3 c. chopped green pepper
1/3 c. chopped pimento
1 1/2 c. chopped celery
1/3 c. almonds
Mushrooms to taste
1 10-oz. can cream of mushroom or
    shrimp soup
1/2 c. small macaroni
1 c. bread crumbs, corn flakes or Wheaties
1 tbsp. butter

Combine all ingredinets except bread crumbs and butter. Place in a casserole. Saute bread crumbs in butter; place on top of shrimp mixture. Bake in a 350-degree oven for 35 minutes. Yield: 6 servings.

Kathleen A. Popp, Owatonna H.S.
Owatonna, Minnesota

SEAFOOD CASSEROLE SUPREME

1 can white crab meat
2 cans shrimp
1/2 c. chopped green pepper
3/4 c. chopped celery
1 c. grated cheese
2 tsp. Worcestershire sauce
1/2 tsp. salt
Cracker crumbs

Toss all ingredients lightly except crumbs. Place in buttered casserole. Sprinkle crumbs on top. Bake 30 minutes at 350 degrees. This casserole freezes well. Yield: 6 servings.

Mrs. Rachel Nicholson, Union H.S.
Union, Mississippi

SPAGHETTI-BEAN CASSEROLE

1 can spaghetti and tomato sauce
1 c. grated cheese
1 med. onion, chopped
1 sm. package corn chips
1 can pork and beans

Cover bottom of 2-quart casserole with spaghetti. Alternate layers of cheese, onion and corn chips on spaghetti. Pour pork and beans over mixture and level in casserole. Alternate layers of remaining cheese, onion and corn chips. Place in preheated 350-degree oven about 20 minutes. Yield: 6 servings.

Billie F. Franke, Buda H.S.
Buda, Texas

Casseroles

CORNED BEEF AND NOODLE CASSEROLE

1 8-oz. package noodles
1 can corned beef
1 can mushroom soup
1 sm. can peas
1 sm. onion, chopped

Cook noodles; drain. Layer with remaining ingredients in casserole. Top with crumbs, if desired. Bake 45 minutes in 350-degree oven. Yield: 6 servings.

Elenor Rollins, Fort Myers Jr. H. S.
Fort Myers, Florida

RUTH'S CORNED BEEF DINNER

1 med. onion, chopped
1 green pepper, diced
2 tbsp. bacon drippings
1 can corned beef
1 can mushroom soup
Cooked wide noodles
1/2 c. bread crumbs
2 tbsp. butter or margarine

Saute onion and green pepper in bacon drippings. Add corned beef, breaking apart with fork. Add soup. Place small amount of beef mixture in casserole; add layer of noodles. Spread remaining corned beef over noodles. Brown crumbs in melted butter; sprinkle over casserole. Bake at 350 degrees for 45 minutes. Yield: 6 servings.

Ruth A. Fanelli, East Bay H. S.
Riverview, Florida

CHIPPED BEEF-NOODLE CASSEROLE

1/4 lb. sliced dried beef
1 pkg. frozen peas
1/2 c. diced celery
1 can cream of chicken soup
1/2 c. milk
1/4 tsp. garlic salt
1/4 tsp. pepper
1 5-oz. can chow mein noodles

Shred beef into pieces. Cover with boiling water; drain. Separate frozen peas by running water over them. Combine all ingredients except noodles. Arrange alternate layers of noodles and beef mixture in 1 1/2-quart casserole, beginning and ending with noodles. Bake in 375-degree oven for 30 minutes. Yield: 4 servings.

Lucille Johnston, Litchfield Sr. H. S.
Litchfield, Illinois

DRIED BEEF AND MACARONI

1/4 c. chopped onion
1/4 c. chopped celery
1/4 lb. dried beef, shredded
1/4 c. oil
1/4 c. flour
2 c. milk
2 c. cooked macaroni
1/2 tsp. salt
1/2 tsp. pepper
1 tbsp. minced parsley
1/3 c. grated American cheese

Cook onion, celery and dried beef in hot oil until onion is golden. Stir in flour. Add milk gradually; stir until slightly thickened. Add macaroni, seasonings and parsley. Pour into greased 1 1/2-quart casserole. Sprinkle with grated cheese. Bake in preheated 350-degree oven for 15 minutes. Yield: 6 servings.

Mrs. Garry C. Pittman, Darien H. S.
Darien, Georgia

FRANKFURTER-VEGETABLE PIE

1 10-oz. package frozen mixed vegetables
1/2 lb. frankfurters
2 tbsp. melted butter
1 8-oz. package corn bread mix

Place vegetables in 1-quart saucepan; add 2 tablespoons water. Bring to a slow boil. Reduce heat to low and cook 10 minutes. Cut frankfurters into 8 crosswise slices, about 1/2 inch thick. Spread in casserole. Drain cooked vegetables. Add butter; pour over frankfurters. Prepare corn bread mix according to package directions. Spread over casserole mixture. Bake at 375 degrees about 20 minutes. Yield: 6-8 servings.

Karen A. Boytz, Bellevue H. S.
Bellevue, Washington

WIENER-BEAN CASSEROLE

2 1-lb. cans pork and beans
1 env. dry onion soup mix
1/3 c. catsup
2 tbsp. brown sugar
1 tbsp. prepared mustard
1 lb. frankfurters, sliced

Combine all ingredients with 1/4 cup water in a 2-quart casserole. Bake, uncovered, at 350 degrees for about 1 hour. Yield: 6-8 servings.

Mrs. Mary Westman, Alameda Sr. H. S.
Denver, Colorado

GLAZED FRANKFURTER CASSEROLE

2 1-lb. cans pork and beans with tomato
   sauce
6 frankfurters
2 tbsp. brown sugar
1 tsp. prepared mustard
1 tsp. Worcestershire sauce

Pour beans into shallow baking dish. Slash skin of frankfurters; arrange on beans, cut side up. Combine brown sugar, mustard and Worcestershire sauce. Spread over frankfurters. Bake at 450 degrees for 20 minutes or until beans are hot and frankfurthers are browned. Yield: 4 servings.

Mildred Wood, Gaffney H.S.
Gaffney, South Carolina

WIENER-MACARONI CASSEROLE

1 c. shell macaroni
1 lb. wieners, chopped
1 1/2 c. mixed vegetables
1 can cream of chicken soup
1/2 tsp. salt
1/2 tsp. pepper
1/2 tsp. sugar
1 tsp. oregano
1 can onion rings

Cook macaroni in 2 cups salted water for 8 minutes; drain. Arrange layers of macaroni, wieners, vegetables and soup in casserole. Sprinkle with salt, pepper, sugar and oregano. Place onion rings on top. Bake, covered, at 325 degrees for 40 minutes. Yield: 4 servings.

Mrs. Jency Ree Henderson, Summer Hill H.S.
Clinton, Mississippi

DINNER-IN-A-DISH

1 No. 2 can sliced apples
1 1-lb. 7-oz. can syrup-packed
   sweet potatoes
1 can luncheon meat, sliced
1/4 c. (packed) brown sugar
1/2 tsp. cinnamon
1/2 tsp. thyme

Arrange alternate layers of sliced apples and sweet potatoes in 2-quart baking dish. Place slices of luncheon meat on top. Sprinkle with brown sugar, cinnamon and thyme. Bake at 400 degrees for 25 minutes. Yield: 4 servings.

Sister M. Aloysius, PBVM, O'Gorman H.S.
Sioux Falls, South Dakota

PANTRY-SHELF SPECIAL

1 sm. can sweet potatoes or 4 cooked med.
   sweet potatoes, halved
1 12-oz. can luncheon meat
4 pineapple slices
Pineapple syrup
1/4 c. (packed) brown sugar
1 tbsp. cornstarch
1/4 tsp. salt
1/4 c. cooking Sherry or 2 tbsp. lemon juice
2 tbsp. butter

Arrange potatoes in 10 x 6 x 2-inch baking dish. Cut luncheon meat into 4 lengthwise slices; place on top of potatoes. Place pineapple slices on top of meat. Heat pineapple syrup, sugar and cornstarch; cook 2 to 3 minutes until thickened and clear. Add salt, Sherry and butter. Pour over foods in baking dish. Bake, uncovered, in 375-degree oven 40 minutes. Yield: 4 servings.

Mrs. Yvonne Haug, Lincoln H.S.
Alma Center, Wisconsin

MEXI-CHILI CASSEROLE

1 6-oz. package corn chips
2 c. shredded sharp process American cheese
1 15-oz. can chili with beans
1 15-oz. can enchilada sauce
1 8-oz. can seasoned tomato sauce
1 tbsp. instant minced onion
1 c. sour cream

Reserve 1 cup corn chips and 1/2 cup cheese. Combine remaining chips and cheese with chili, sauces and onion. Pour into casserole. Bake at 375 degrees for 20 minutes. Remove from oven; spread top with sour cream. Sprinkle with reserved cheese. Arrange remaining corn chips around edge. Bake 5 minutes longer. Yield: 6 servings.

Betty Herbel, Turtle Mt. Comm. School
Belcourt, North Dakota

BELL PEPPER CASSEROLE

2 bell peppers, chopped
1 pkg. crackers, crumbled
1 8-oz. package Cheddar cheese, grated
Butter
Milk

Boil bell peppers for 10 minutes; drain. Place bell peppers, crackers and cheese in casserole. Dot with butter. Add enough milk to cover ingredients. Bake at 400 degrees for 30 minutes or until brown, stirring occasionally. Yield: 6 servings.

Marjorie B. Turner, Mississippi School for Blind
Jackson, Mississippi

Casseroles

SCALLOPED LOGS

1 box frozen asparagus, cooked
Milk
2 tbsp. butter
2 tbsp. flour
1/2 tsp. salt
1 c. grated Cheddar cheese
3 hard-cooked eggs, sliced
1/3 c. chopped nuts
1 c. coarsely crushed potato chips
Paprika

Drain liquid from asparagus; add enough milk to equal 1 cup. Melt butter; blend in flour and salt to make a smooth paste. Add liquid; cook until thickened, stirring frequently. Remove from heat. Add cheese; stir until cheese is melted. Alternate layers of asparagus, hard-cooked eggs, cheese sauce and nuts in greased 2-quart casserole. Top with coarsely crushed potato chips; sprinkle with paprika. Bake at 350 degrees for 30 minutes. Yield: 10-12 servings.

Laura Ann Good, Inola H.S.
Inola, Oklahoma

SCALLOPED BROCCOLI CASSEROLE

1 tsp. salt
1 pkg. frozen broccoli
3 tbsp. butter or margarine
2 tbsp. chopped onions
3 tbsp. flour
1 1/2 c. milk
1/2 c. grated cheese
1/2 c. bread crumbs

Add 1/2 teaspoon salt to 1/2 cup boiling water; add broccoli. Return to a boil. Cook 5 minutes; drain. Melt 2 tablespoons butter in a 1-quart saucepan. Add chopped onions. Cook until golden. Add remaining salt and flour; mix well. Add milk. Cook, stirring constantly, until thickened. Remove from heat; stir in grated cheese. Place cooked drained broccoli in a 1-quart casserole; pour cheese sauce over top. Mix remaining melted butter and bread crumbs. Sprinkle over top of casserole. Bake 20 to 25 minutes in 350-degree oven. Yield: 4 servings.

Mrs. Floy Rossetter, Rains Indep. School
Emory, Texas

CONFETTI CORN PUDDING

1 No. 2 can cream-style corn
2 eggs, beaten
2 tbsp. butter
1 tbsp. sugar
1/2 tsp. monosodium glutamate
1 tbsp. pimento, chopped

1/2 c. cooked brown rice
1/2 c. milk
1/2 c. cracker crumbs
4 sprigs parsley

Mix first 8 ingredients together. Pour into casserole. Sprinkle cracker crumbs over top. Bake at 350 degrees for 15 minutes. Remove from oven. Garnish with parsley. Yield: 8 servings.

Mrs. G. W. Sorrells, Stuttgart Sr. H.S.
Stuttgart, Arkansas

EASY PARTY CARROTS AND ONIONS

1 lb. carrots
1 lb. small whole white onions
1 can mushroom soup
1 tbsp. chopped parsley
1/4 tsp. paprika

Cut carrots lengthwise about 3 inches long. Cook carrots and onions in water for 30 minutes or until tender in covered saucepan; drain. Stir in soup, 1/2 cup water, parsley and paprika. Pour into casserole. Bake in 350-degree oven for 15 to 20 minutes. Yield: 6-8 servings.

Delores Vondrak, Elk Point H.S.
Elk Point, South Dakota

EGG-MUSHROOM CASSEROLE

1 lg. onion, chopped fine
1 green pepper, chopped
1/2 c. chopped celery
1/4 c. butter
6 hard-cooked eggs, chopped
1 c. cooked mushrooms
2 c. thin cream sauce
1/2 tsp. salt
1 can refrigerator biscuits, unbaked

Fry onion, green pepper and celery in butter until golden brown. Mix with hard-cooked eggs and mushrooms. Stir in cream sauce and salt. Pour into greased baking dish. Cover with unbaked biscuits. Bake in 400 to 450-degree oven until biscuits are brown, about 10 to 12 minutes. Casserole may be frozen. Canned celery or mushroom soup may be substituted for thin cream sauce. Yield: 4-6 servings.

Mrs. Dorothy A. Foster, Mathews H.S.
Mathews, Virginia

ASPARAGUS-CARROT CASSEROLE

1 can asparagus
1 can carrots
1 can Cheddar cheese soup

1/2 c. slivered almonds
1 can onion rings or Chinese noodles

Drain asparagus and carrots. Mix with soup and slivered almonds in a casserole. Bake in 350-degree oven about 10 minutes or until warm. Top with canned onion rings. Yield: 3-4 servings.

Rosalyn M. Lester, Greenville H.S.
Greenville, Florida

BAKED TOMATO-ZUCCHINI CASSEROLE

4 med. zucchini squash
6 med. tomatoes
1 sm. onion, minced
1 tsp. salt
1/2 c. bread crumbs
1/4 c. grated cheese

Cut ends off zucchini; do not peel. Slice in 1/4-inch slices. Peel tomatoes; cut up. Combine with zucchini, onion and salt. Place in casserole. Sprinkle with bread crumbs and grated cheese. Bake 45 minutes at 350 degrees.

Maxine J. Rader, Boone Grove School
Boone Grove, Indiana

PEAS AND ASPARAGUS CASSEROLE

1 No. 2 can asparagus
1 No. 2 can English peas
1/2 can cream of mushroom soup
1/2 c. milk
1 1/2 c. grated cheese
1/2 c. bread crumbs

Place asparagus and peas in a buttered baking dish. Heat soup, milk and cheese over low heat until cheese is melted. Pour mixture over asparagus and peas. Cover with bread crumbs. Bake at 350 degrees for 25 minutes. Yield: 8 servings.

Mrs. Grady Nunnery, Jr., Lewisville H.S.
Richburg, South Carolina

MIXED VEGETABLE BAKE

1 can cream of mushroom soup
1/3 c. milk
1 tsp. soy sauce
Dash of pepper
2 10-oz. packages frozen vegetables
1 3 1/2-oz. can French-fried onions

Stir soup, milk, soy sauce and pepper into 1-quart casserole until smooth. Mix in vegetables and 1/2 can onions. Bake at 350 degrees for 25 minutes or until hot. Top with remaining onions. Bake 5 minutes more. Yield: 6 servings.

Barbara Monroe, Adrian H.S.
Adrian, Minnesota

SEVEN-CAN CASSEROLE

2 No. 2 cans French-style green beans
1 No. 2 can bean sprouts, drained
2 cans cream of mushroom soup
2 cans French-fried onions

Heat green beans in bean juice until boiling; drain. Place in casserole. Add bean sprouts, soup and most of the onions. Sprinkle remaining onions over top. Bake at 350 degrees 30 to 40 minutes. Yield: 6 servings.

Jean Passino, Keewatin-Nashwauk Jr. H.S.
Keewatin, Minnesota

FROZEN VEGETABLE MEDLEY

1 pkg. frozen French green beans
1 pkg. frozen corn
1 pkg. frozen peas
1 can cream of mushroom soup
1/2 c. milk
1 tsp. salt

Place 1 layer French green beans, corn and peas in casserole. Dilute mushroom soup with milk; stir in salt. Pour over vegetables in casserole; cover. Bake at 350 degrees for 1 hour. Yield: 10 servings.

Linda J. Kautzmann, Montour H.S.
McKees Rocks, Pennsylvania

LIMA BEANS WITH CHEESE SAUCE

1 pkg. frozen lima beans
1 tall can sm. onions, drained
1 sm. can mushrooms, drained
1 tbsp. butter
1 tbsp. flour
1/2 tsp. salt
1/4 tsp. pepper
1 c. milk
1/2 lb. Velveeta cheese

Cook beans in 3/4 cup salted water for 12 minutes; drain. Add onions and mushrooms. Melt butter; add flour, salt, pepper and milk; mixing well. Add cheese; stir until melted. Place beans, onions and mushrooms in casserole. Cover with cheese sauce. Bake in 350-degree oven until hot. Yield: 8 servings.

Maude Haynes, Lawhon Jr. H.S.
Tupelo, Mississippi

Easy Fruit Dishes

How can fruit help out when a meal needs to be ready in a hurry? Fruits, just like vegetables, can be purchased in so many quick-to-use ways! They are readily available to the homemaker all year through — fresh in the market from the vines and trees, frozen at the peak of their tenderness and flavor, or canned in a delicious juice. Some health food stores now feature an unusual selection of dried fruits, such as orange wedges and banana slices — in addition to the more familiar dried apricots, peaches and apples. So, flavorful fruits are always right at hand, ready to be turned into a surprising side dish, appealing appetizers, a healthy snack, or a super dessert.

As a side dish, there is hardly a better complement to a hearty meat entree than a light and sweet fruit accompaniment — they are often unexpected (but always welcome!), as well as being full of vitamins, minerals, and lots of flavor. Moreover, fruits can always be counted on to save the day for a quick meal. In the morning, a dish of fresh fruit, drizzled with a little cream and honey becomes a real eye opener for breakfast. At lunch, a fruit dish adds a refreshing balance to any soup and sandwich duo. Sparkling fruit is also nature's best dessert, as sweet and luscious as any cook could ever want. Traditionally, a plate of various fruits and pungent cheeses is considered dessert in European countries. But, there's more to fruit than just fresh, frozen and canned when it comes to dessert. Fruits can be served bubbling-hot or chilly-cold, they can be baked, made into a cold soup, caramel or chocolate coated, garnished with nuts and, of course, served alone or in combination with other sweet and delectable fruits.

As you can see in this selection of quick and easy fruit recipes from Home Economics Teachers, no one should neglect fruits in their menu plan, especially when they want a dish that can be ready quick as a wink.

Fruits

ALMOND-STUFFED APPLES

1/2 c. blanched almonds
Sugar
1/4 tsp. almond extract
8 med. baking apples
Melted butter
Sifted dry fine bread crumbs
Whipped cream

Blend almonds in electric blender until finely ground. Add 2 tablespoons water, 1/4 cup sugar and almond extract; blend until smooth. Peel and core apples; fill with almond paste. Roll apples in melted butter, then in bread crumbs and finally in sugar. Arrange fruit in buttered baking pan. Bake in a 425-degree oven for 25 minutes or until tender. Serve from baking dish with whipped cream. Yield: 8 servings.

Clare D. Ferguson, Tecumseh H.S.
Lynville, Indiana

APPLES ROSE

4 red Delicious apples
Juice of 1 lemon

Wash and polish apples; remove core. Cut apples into thin wedges. Place each apple in an individual glass dessert or sherbet dish in the shape of the whole fruit. Pour freshly squeezed lemon juice over apples and serve. Yield: 4 servings.

Opal Teaford Standiford, English-Sterling School
English, Indiana

BAKED APPLE SURPRISE

2 med. bananas
1 tbsp. lemon juice
1/4 c. sugar
Dash of salt
1/4 tsp. ground nutmeg
6 med. baking apples
1 c. orange juice

Mash peeled bananas with fork in a medium bowl. Mix with lemon juice, sugar, salt and nutmeg. Wash and core apples; place in large baking dish. Fill apples with banana mixture. Pour orange juice over apples. Bake in preheated 375-degree oven for 1 hour or until tender, basting occasionally with orange juice. Chill and serve cold. Top with orange sauce, if desired.

Mrs. J. D. Chizen, Radway School
Radway, Alberta, Canada

APPLE TAPIOCA

1/2 tsp. salt
1/3 c. quick-cooking tapioca
1 1/2 lb. cooking apples
1/2 c. sugar
2 tbsp. butter

Add 2 1/2 cups boiling water and salt to tapioca. Cook in double boiler until clear. Core and pare apples. Arrange whole apples in buttered baking dish. Fill with sugar; add tapioca mixture. Dot with butter. Bake at 350 degrees until apples are soft. Serve with sugar and cream. Yield: 6 servings.

C. Lohrer, Ridgefield Park H.S.
Ridgefield Park, New Jersey

HOLIDAY APPLES

1 c. sugar
3 tbsp. lemon juice
2 tsp. vanilla extract
Red food coloring
6 lg. Winesap apples
1 c. whipping cream
1 tbsp. powdered sugar

Combine sugar, 1 cup water, lemon juice and 1 1/2 teaspoons vanilla and food coloring in saucepan. Heat on low heat until sugar is dissolved. Simmer for 5 minutes. Wash, peel and core apples. Place in syrup; cook on low heat, uncovered, until tender. Turn once in syrup. Chill well. Combine remaining ingredients. Serve over apples. Yield: 6 servings.

Mrs. Sue Rogers, Krum H.S.
Krum, Texas

MAPLE-BAKED APPLES

4 lg. cooking apples
1/3 c. sugar
1/2 tsp. maple flavoring
1 tsp. margarine
1/8 tsp. cinnamon

Wash and core apples. Place in greased baking dish. Heat 1/2 cup water and remaining ingredients in saucepan. Pour over apples. Bake in a 400-degree oven until soft. Add more water if needed. Yield: 4 servings.

Mrs. Helen M. Godwin, Northwest H.S.
Greensboro, North Carolina

BAKED BANANA AMBROSIA

3 lg. peeled green tipped or yellow bananas
1 1/2 tbsp. melted butter or margarine
2 tbsp. lemon or lime juice
1/3 c. shredded coconut

Halve bananas crosswise, then lengthwise. Arrange in greased 10 x 6 x 2-inch baking dish. Brush well with butter, then with lemon juice. Sprinkle with coconut. Bake in preheated 375-degree oven for 15 to 20 minutes, or until fork tender. Serve warm. Yield: 6 servings.

Mrs. Jean Downes, Canton South H.S.
Canton, Ohio

BANANA TREAT

4 med. bananas
1/2 c. lemon juice
1/4 c. mayonnaise
1/2 c. chopped peanuts
4 lettuce leaves

Dip peeled bananas in lemon juice. Spread thin coat of mayonnaise over bananas; roll lightly in chopped peanuts. Refrigerate. Serve on lettuce leaf. Yield: 4 servings.

Mary Malone, Cottage Grove H.S.
Cottage Grove, Tennessee

BERRY BRAGGLE

1 pt. blackberries, raspberries, blueberries
    or strawberries
Sugar to taste
1 1/2 tsp. flour
1/2 c. cream
3/4 c. croutons

Place berries in saucepan with enough sugar to sweeten. Add flour to about 1/2 cup cream; add berries. Heat for about 5 minutes. Serve with croutons. Yield: 4 servings.

Laura Clark, Wyoming H.S.
Wyoming, Illinois

BROILED GRAPEFRUIT

1 grapefruit, cut in half
2 tsp. maple syrup

Section grapefruit halves as for breakfast fruit. Pour 1 teaspoon maple syrup over top of each segment. Place under broiler until heated through. Serve immediately. Yield: 2 servings.

Luverna Thales
Immaculate Conception Indian Mission School
Stephan, South Dakota

GREEN GRAPES WITH CREAM

1 lb. seedless green grapes, washed
    and stemmed
1/2 c. sour cream
1 c. brown sugar or to taste

Mix ingredients together and refrigerate for several hours. Pile in sherbet glasses and serve. Blueberries may be substituted for grapes. Yield: 4-6 servings.

Fae M. Briggs, Gary H.S.
Gary, South Dakota

BROILED PEACH HALVES

Butter or margarine
Canned peach halves
Coconut

Place a dot of butter on each peach half. Sprinkle shredded coconut over the tops. Broil for several minutes or until coconut begins to brown. This makes a good light dessert or snack and takes little time and energy.

Mrs. Pat Bandy, Lingleville H.S.
Lingleville, Texas

FRESH PEACHES AND SOUR CREAM

2 fresh peaches
Sour cream
Brown sugar

Place layer of peaches in bottom of sherbet dish. Top with mound of sour cream. Sprinkle top with brown sugar. Repeat, using about 3 layers of fruit. Serve chilled. Yield: 4 servings.

Mrs. Lois R. Bell, Coon Rapids Sr. H.S.
Anoka, Minnesota

Fruits

PEACHES SUPREME

8 fresh or canned peach halves
2 tbsp. melted butter
1/2 c. prepared mincemeat
Sour cream

Arrange peach halves in buttered baking dish. Brush with melted butter. Place 1 spoonful mincemeat into each half. Spoon remaining mincemeat around peach halves. Bake at 350 degrees for 15 to 20 minutes or until peaches are lightly browned. Serve topped with sour cream. Yield: 8 servings.

Photograph for this recipe on page 96.

PERSIAN PEACHES

4 c. sliced peaches
1 c. orange juice
6 tbsp. honey
1 tbsp. finely chopped candied ginger
Dash of salt

Combine all ingredients, mixing gently. Cover; chill thoroughly. Spoon into chilled sherbet glasses to serve. Yield: 5 servings.

Anna Marie Rittinger, South Lake Sr. H.S.
St. Clair Shores, Michigan

BAKED MACAROON PEARS

2 1-lb. 14-oz. cans pear halves
2 tbsp. apricot preserves
1/2 c. dry macaroon crumbs
Butter

Cut pear halves into 1/2-inch slices; drain, reserving 1/4 cup syrup. Heat syrup with apricot preserves. Pour over pears. Sprinkle pears with macaroon crumbs; dot with butter. Bake at 350 degrees for about 20 minutes or until crumbs are browned. Serve warm and plain or with ice cream. Yield: 4 servings.

Mrs. Deborah Longbothum, Mifflinburg H.S.
Mifflinburg, Pennsylvania

CARAMEL PEARS

1 1-lb. can pear halves, drained
2 tbsp. butter
1/2 c. (packed) brown sugar
2 tbsp. light corn syrup
1/4 c. pear syrup

Combine all ingredients except pears in saucepan. Simmer until smooth and blended. Place pear halves in caramel syrup. Heat, basting with syrup. Serve warm or chilled with sour or ice cream. Yield: 4 servings.

Mrs. Meeks, Willows H.S.
Willows, California

HONEY-BAKED PEARS

4 fresh pears
Juice of 1/2 lemon
1/2 c. honey
1 c. fresh cream, sour cream or
    whipped cream

Wash, halve and core pears. Combine lemon juice with enough water to cover bottom of baking pan. Place pears, cut side down, in dish. Bake, covered, at 375 degrees for 20 minutes. Remove cover and turn pears. Drizzle pears with honey and return to oven to glaze pears, about 10 to 15 minutes. May be topped with fresh, sour or whipped cream.

Mrs. Charla Mae Filla, Sterling H.S.
Sterling, Colorado

THELMA'S AMBROSIA

2 lg. oranges, peeled and sectioned
3 bananas, thinly sliced
1/4 c. confectioners' sugar
1 1/2 c. shredded coconut

Arrange alternate layers of oranges and bananas in serving bowl, sprinkling each layer with sugar and coconut. Top with coconut. Chill in freezer 10 minutes before servings. Yield: 4 servings.

Mrs. Thelma M. Ash, George Wythe Jr. H.S.
Hampton, Virginia

AMBROSIA SUPREME

1 c. seedless grapes
1 c. mandarin oranges
1 c. pineapple chunks
2 c. sour cream
1 c. flaked coconut

Combine first 3 ingredients; add sour cream. Toss lightly with coconut. Refrigerate until thoroughly chilled; serve. Yield: 8 servings.

Mrs. Joel Ferrell, Brinkley H.S.
Brinkley, Arkansas

Recipe on page 108.

AMBROSIA TROPICALE

2 lg. seedless oranges
3 lg. bananas
3 tbsp. flaked coconut
1/2 pt. orange sherbet

Peel and section oranges; press juice from remaining orange pieces. Add to sections. Peel and slice bananas; add to orange sections. Toss. Divide among 6 dessert dishes. Sprinkle each serving with 1/2 tablespoon flaked coconut and top with a dollop of sherbet. Yield: 6 servings.

Mrs. Hal Puett, North Cobb H.S.
Acworth, Georgia

GOOD AND EASY FRUIT DESSERT

1 can peach pie filling
1 can apricot halves, drained
1 can mandarin oranges, drained
1 can pineapple chunks, drained
1 can sliced peaches, drained
1 sm. package frozen strawberries,
    thawed and drained

Mix all ingredients; chill thoroughly. Yield: 15-18 servings.

Mrs. Kathryn Leischner, DeLand-Weldon H.S.
DeLand, Illinois

FIVE-STAR DELIGHT

1 8-oz. can mandarin oranges, drained
1 No. 2 can chunk pineapple, drained
1 8-oz. can shredded coconut
1 1/2 c. miniature marshmallows
1 8-oz. carton sour cream

Combine oranges, pineapple, coconut and marshmallows together thoroughly. Add sour cream and mix. Prepare a few hours before serving and refrigerate until serving time. Yield: 6-8 servings.

Berma F. Doty, Towns Co. H.S.
Hiawassee, Georgia

CHERRY-PINEAPPLE DELIGHT

1 No. 2 can pie cherries
1 No. 300 can pineapple tidbits, drained
1 banana, sliced

Recipe on page 123.

Combine all ingredients; refrigerate. Serve in individual fruit cups. Yield: 6 servings.

Mrs. Gretchen Ryan, Armour Public School
Armour, South Dakota

COMPANY COMPOTE

2 pkg. frozen whole strawberries
1 No. 303 can pineapple, crushed
1 can mandarin oranges
1 No. 303 can fruit cocktail
1 c. sugar
Dash of nutmeg

Combine all ingredients; mix well. Chill about 30 minutes. Serve with sugar cookies or spoon over ice cream. Yield: 12 servings.

Dorothy Dowell, Ripley H.S.
Ripley, Oklahoma

CREAMY FRUIT PARFAIT

1 box frozen strawberries
1 pt. sour cream or yogurt
1 8-oz. can chunk pineapple
1 banana, sliced
Dietetic sweetener

Arrange strawberries in 4 parfait glasses. Cover with 2 tablespoons sour cream in each glass. Layer pineapple and sour cream. Add bananas and a final layer of sour cream. Top off with a large strawberry rolled in dietetic sweetener. Yield: 4 servings.

Eillen Loken, Wolsey H.S.
Wolsey, South Dakota

GOURMET FRUITS

1 can chunk pineapple, drained
1 can pears, drained
4 c. watermelon chunks
2 c. cantaloupe chunks
3 lg. tart apples, cut in lg. pieces
Sprigs of fresh mint

Combine all fruits in large bowl. Cover and refrigerate for 3 to 4 hours. Garnish with mint sprigs before serving. Yield: 8-10 servings.

Mrs. Maxine Gibson, Bradford Co. H.S.
Starke, Florida

Fruits

FRUIT POTPOURRI

1 No. 2 1/2 can peach halves
1 No. 2 1/2 can pear halves
1 No. 2 1/2 can pineapple chunks
1 No. 2 1/2 can apricot halves
1 jar sliced apples
1 jar cherries
3/4 stick margarine
1 c. (packed) brown sugar
1 1/2 tsp. curry powder

Drain all fruits well. Arrange in a 3-quart casserole. Mix together margarine, brown sugar and curry powder. Pour over fruit. Bake 1 hour to 1 hour and 30 minutes in a 350-degree oven. Serve hot or cold. May be preheated. Yield: 12 servings.

Evelyn K. Kearse, Bamberg-Ehrhardt H.S.
Bamberg, South Carolina

HOT-COLD SPICED FRUIT

1   1-lb. can cling peach slices, chilled
1   1-lb. can pear slices, chilled
1 c. canned pineapple juice
1/4 tsp. ground cinnamon

Drain syrup from peaches and pears thoroughly. Bring pineapple juice and cinnamon just to a boil in a medium saucepan. Place chilled, drained fruit in serving bowl; pour pineapple juice over all. Serve immediately. Yield: 6 servings.

Mrs. Elvera M. Raff, Longford H.S.
Longford, Kansas

PINEAPPLE FRUIT BOAT

2 fresh pineapples
3 apples
2 bananas
3 lg. oranges
1 lg. bunch seedless grapes
2 pears
1 pkg. frozen melon balls
1/2 pt. blueberries

Cut pineapples in half from top to bottom. Scoop out pulp and cut into chunks. Core apples and cut into chunks; do not peel. Peel bananas and slice. Peel oranges and section. Clean grapes and separate. Core pears and slice. Defrost melon balls. Combine fruits in bowl. Drain melon balls; add to mixture. Lay pineapples on side; fill with fruit mixture. Serve on large platter. Yield: 4-6 servings.

Sabina A. Leiby, Susquenita H.S.
Duncannon, Pennsylvania

MIXED FRUIT DESSERT

2 bananas, cut up
2 pineapple rings, cut up
1 can mixed fruit, drained
1 c. miniature marshmallows
1/2 to 1 c. chopped nuts
1 pkg. Dream Whip

Mix first 5 ingredients. Prepare Dream Whip according to package directions. Fold in fruit mixture. Chill thoroughly. Yield: 6 servings.

Ida Hennigh, Hanna-Elk Mtn. H.S.
Hanna, Wyoming

MELON BOATS

Pineapple chunks
1/4 tsp. sugar or substitute
Mint to taste
Honeydew melon wedges
Cantaloupe balls
Watermelon balls
Banana slices
Green grapes
Strawberries
Shredded coconut

Drain pineapple, reserving juice. Add sugar and mint to juice. Combine all fruits together; mix well. Add juice, tossing gently to coat well. Top with shredded coconut. Yield: 4 servings.

Doris Herlick, Bigfork H.S.
Bigfork, Montana

MELON BALL DELIGHT

1 pkg. strawberry gelatin
1 c. honeydew melon balls
1 c. watermelon balls
1 c. cantaloupe balls

Prepare gelatin according to package directions. Chill until partially set. Add melon balls. Chill until firm. May be served with cottage cheese or low-calorie dressing.

Mildred Mason, Cherokee Vocational H.S.
Cherokee, Alabama

REFRESHING FRUIT CUP

1 apple, cored and sliced
2 oranges, sectioned
1 banana, sliced
1 can sliced peaches

Mix fruit lightly in bowl; chill. Serve in fruit dishes. Yield: 6 servings.

Mrs. Eldine Budden, Palmetto H.S.
Palmetto, Louisiana

SOUR CREAM FRUIT MEDLEY

1 9-oz. can crushed pineapple, drained
1 11-oz. can peaches, drained
1 11-oz. can mandarin oranges, drained
1/2 10-oz. can Angel flake coconut
1/2 pt. sour cream
12 chopped marshmallows

Mix all ingredients well; chill. Serve in individual fruit dishes. Yield: 6 servings.

Elizabeth Curry, Marianna H.S.
Marianna, Florida

TROPICAL COMPOTE WITH WINE SAUCE

1 pkg. frozen pineapple cubes
2 bananas, sliced
1 lg. grapefruit, sectioned
1 c. seeded malaga grapes
1/2 c. sugar
1/3 c. Sherry
2 tbsp. Madeira

Combine sugar and wines. Combine fruits in fruit compote. Pour wine mixture over fruits. Chill; serve. Yield: 6 servings.

Mrs. Caroline Kengen, Holyoke H.S.
Holyoke, Colorado

SPICY FRUIT

1/3 c. butter
3/4 c. (packed) brown sugar
4 tsp. curry powder
1 1-lb. can pear halves
1 1-lb. can apricot halves
1 1-lb. can peach halves
1 1-lb. can pineapple chunks
1 8-oz. jar maraschino cherries

Melt butter. Add brown sugar and curry powder. Drain fruits well. Place in 1 1/2-quart casserole. Spoon sugar mixture over fruits. Bake at 350 degrees for 30 minutes, stirring occasionally. Yield: 1 1/2 quart.

Mrs. Alease E. Raney, Hopewell H.S.
Hopewell, Virginia

SWEDISH FRUIT SOUP

1/2 lb. prunes
1 c. seeded raisins
1/4 lb. dried apricots
1/4 c. tapioca
1 c. sugar
1 stick cinnamon
1 lg. orange, sliced
1 lemon, sliced
3 apples, diced or sliced
1 pt. grape juice
1 can cherries

Soak dried fruits, tapioca, sugar, cinnamon, orange and lemon overnight in enough water to cover. Add diced apples and 1 cup water. Cook slowly until fruit is tender. Add grape juice and cherries. Serve either hot or cold. Soup may be thinned with more grape juice if served cold. Yield: 12 servings.

Mrs. Nora Estrem, Battle Lake H.S.
Battle Lake, Minnesota

DREAMY FRUIT

1 No. 2 1/2 can fruit cocktail, drained
1 11-oz. can mandarin oranges, drained
1 c. miniature marshmallows
1 c. flaked coconut
1 c. sour cream

Combine fruit cocktail, mandarin oranges, marshmallows and coconut. Fold in sour cream. Chill. Yield: 8 servings.

Mrs. Peggy Schomburg, Aldine Jr. H.S.
Houston, Texas

COLORFUL PINEAPPLE CHEESE

1 No. 303 can crushed pineapple
1 6-oz. package lemon gelatin
1 2-oz. jar chopped pimento
1 6-oz. package cream cheese, creamed
1/2 pt. whipping cream
1/4 c. chopped nuts

Drain juice from pineapple; add enough water to juice to measure 1 scant pint. Bring to a boil; pour over gelatin. Stir until gelatin is dissolved. Chill until thickened. Add pineapple and pimento; blend into cream cheese. Refrigerate until partially congealed. Fold in whipped cream; pour in an 11 x 7 1/2 x 1 3/8-inch pan. Sprinkle nuts over top; refrigerate until firm. Yield: 6-8 servings.

Mrs. Nancy Anderson, Frankfort Sr. H.S.
Frankfort, Indiana

Easy Salads

Salads meet almost every requirement set by homemakers for the best in quick and easy cookery. There is hardly a salad that is not overflowing with appetite-arousing color, taste and nutrition — everything needed to please the eye as well as the palate. Because salad means "mixture," it can encompass almost any exciting array of ingredients — vegetables, meats, poultry, fruits, seafood, pasta, eggs, and cheese. Any of these can be highlighted as the star ingredient. Or the highlight can be a superb combination of several ingredients and flavors. All in all, there is an endless list of salad ideas for jiffy meals. This is why salads are so ideally suited to quick and easy cookery.

A creative homemaker knows she can place a salad anywhere on the menu and never fail to delight the diners. A salad can become a hearty meal in itself, a delicate appetizer, a marvelously easy-to-prepare accompaniment dish, a light and refreshing snack, or the perfect lunch entree. Featuring meat in a salad is an excellent way to use leftover beef, ham, luncheon meat, poultry, and pork — and viola, you have a main dish in minutes! For elegance, even in a hurry, there is nothing that equals a seafood salad, or a molded salad, either frozen or congealed. Even though salads including either vegetables or fruits are the most typical they never have to become tiresome. It takes no time at all to vary seasonings and dressings, and to try a new combination of ingredients. For a salad that is both filling, delicious and packed with extra nutrition, choose pasta, eggs, cheese and cereals for unbeatable additions to salads. One quick idea for mealtime is to come up with your own "salad bar" selection. The salad bar includes anything — fresh garden vegetables, pickles, congealed fruit mixtures, exciting garnishes, various cheeses, a selection of salad dressings. Best of all, everyone fixes their very own! This not only insures that everyone will eat just exactly what they want, it also saves the cook lots of time and effort — and the results are always unique and memorable.

In this section, you will find a Home Economics Teacher's salute to the wonderful world of quick and easy salads. You are sure to find several that suit your fancy — plus they can be ready in the twinkling of an eye.

Salads

FAMILY SUPPER SALAD PLATE

2 peeled nectarines, peaches or plums, sliced
2 c. cantaloupe, honeydew or watermelon balls
1 avocado, pared and sliced
1 medium cucumer, cut in spears
1 tomato, cut in wedges or 1 c.
    cherry tomatoes
12 whole radishes or seedless green grapes
1 sm. red onion, thinly sliced or 8
    scallions, trimed
1 green pepper, seeded and cut in strips
1/2 lb. cooked chicken, turkey, ham or
    luncheon meat, thinly sliced
1/2 lb. sliced Swiss, American or
    Muenster cheese
Creamy Curry Dressing

Arrange fruits, vegetables, sliced meats and cheese on a large platter. Serve with Creamy Curry Dressing and slices of whole grain bread. Yield: 4 servings.

Creamy Curry Dressing

1/2 c. sour cream
1/2 c. mayonnaise
1 tbsp. honey
1/4 to 1/2 tsp. curry powder
1/8 tsp. salt

Stir all ingredients until smooth in a small bowl.

Photograph for this recipe on page 101.

RED APPLE SALAD

1 1/2 c. sugar
1/4 c. salt
1/2 c. cinnamon candies
4 firm tart apples, pared and cored
1/2 c. cottage cheese or 3-oz. package
    cream cheese
1/4 c. chopped green pepper

Combine sugar, salt, candies and 3 cups water in saucepan. Heat, stirring until candies are dissolved. Add apples; cover. Cook slowly until just tender, turning occasionally to color evenly. Drain and chill. Mix cheese with green pepper; stuff apples. Serve on watercress or lettuce. Yield: 4 servings.

Sister Mary Ignatius, O.S.F., Madonna H.S.
Chicago, Illinois

CRANBERRY-PINEAPPLE SALAD

Lettuce
1 can jellied cranberry sauce
1 can sliced pineapple

Place lettuce leaf on salad plate. Open cranberry sauce at both ends; push out whole. Cut into round slices. Place cranberry slice on lettuce leaf; place ring of pineapple on top. Garnish with salad dressing, if desired. Yield: 6 servings.

Mrs. Joan Storley, Roslyn H.S.
Roslyn, South Dakota

CREAMY CRANBERRY SALAD

3 c. whole or frozen cranberries
3/4 c. sugar
2 1/3 c. miniature marshmallows
1   8 1/2-oz. can crushed pineapple, drained
1/2 c. chopped nuts
1 c. heavy cream

Chop cranberries; add sugar. Chill for 2 hours. Add marshmallows, pineapple and nuts. Whip cream; fold into cranberry mixture. Refrigerate or freeze. Yield: 6-8 servings.

Mrs. Robert Colter, Harrison Twp. School
Gaston, Indiana

FESTIVE COCKTAIL SALAD

1 pkg. Dream Whip
1 No. 2 can fruit cocktail, drained
1 lg. lettuce leaf
Chopped nuts
4 maraschino cherries

Prepare Dream Whip according to package directions. Combine with fruit cocktail; mix well. Tear lettuce leaf into 4 sections; place on 4 plates as a lettuce nest. Fill with fruit cocktail mixture. Garnish with chopped nuts and a cherry. Chill for about 2 hours before serving. Yield: 4 servings.

Mrs. Diane Dilges, Jefferson H.S.
Jefferson, South Dakota

FRESH FRUIT SALAD

1 med. pear, diced
1 med. apple, diced
1 lg. banana, sliced crosswise
1 1/2 oz. seedless raisins
3 tbsp. mayonnaise
1/3 c. pecans, chopped (opt.)
4 candied cherries

Combine first 4 ingredients. Add mayonnaise and mix thoroughly. Add pecans. Serve on lettuce leaf; top with candied cherry. Yield: 4 servings.

Mrs. Carmen T. Moreno
Still Intermediate School
Brownsville, Texas

ANYTIME FRUIT SALAD

1 1-lb. 4-oz. can pineapple chunks, drained
2 11-oz. cans mandarin oranges, drained
1/3 c. chopped pecans
1 c. miniature marshmallows
1/3 c. mayonnaise

Combine all ingredients in order listed; toss lightly. Refrigerate. Serve in salad bowl with lettuce leaves. Yield: 6-8 servings.

Mrs. Kathryn Bebow, North Branch H.S.
North Branch, Michigan

FRUIT SALAD BOWL

1 No. 2 can fruit cocktail, drained
1 can mandarin oranges
1 c. fresh green grapes
1 banana, cubed
1/2 c. miniature marshmallows
Mayonnaise

Place fruit cocktail in serving bowl. Drain oranges; reserve liquid. Add oranges to fruit in bowl. Add grapes, banana and marshmallows. Toss together; chill well. Serve with mayonnaise thinned with a small amount of reserved orange juice. Salad may be varied by using 1/2 to 1 cup of melon balls, diced apples, raisins, fresh peaches or pears. Yield: 8-12 servings.

Jean C. Johnson, Riverside H.S.
Milan, Washington

FRUIT WITH A FLAIR

1 No. 2 can fruit cocktail, drained
1 pt. sour cream

Combine fruit cocktail and sour cream; mix thoroughly. Refrigerate for at least 30 minutes. Serve on lettuce cups. Yield: 6 servings.

Mrs. Ellen G. Powell, Sam Houston H.S.
Huntsville, Texas

MILLIONAIRE SALAD

1 11-oz. can mandarin oranges, drained
1 c. flaked coconut
1/2 c. small marshmallows
1 c. drained diced pineapple
2 tbsp. sour cream

Combine oranges, coconut, marshmallows and pineapple; mix in sour cream. Chill thoroughly. Yield: 6-8 servings.

Mrs. Madie Oliver, Centerville H.S.
Groveton, Texas

PEACH HALVES DELIGHT

1 3-oz. package cream cheese, softened
2 to 3 tbsp. salad dressing
1/4 c. chopped pecans
4 lg. peach halves

Blend cream cheese and salad dressing until smooth and creamy. Add pecans. Fill each peach half with cheese mixture. Serve on lettuce leaves. Yield: 4 servings.

Mrs. Quincy Rollins, McKinney H.S.
McKinney, Texas

CREAMY SIX-CUP SALAD

1 c. drained pineapple
1 c. drained fruit cocktail
1 c. coconut
1 c. miniature marshmallows
1 c. cottage cheese
1 c. sour cream

Combine all ingredients except sour cream. Chill for several hours but do not freeze. Add sour cream about 1 hour before serving. Yield: 10 servings.

Elizabeth Carson, Sulphur Springs H.S.
Jonesboro, Tennessee

FRUITED CUCUMBER WITH DRESSING

1 cucumber, peeled and thinly sliced
3 c. thinly sliced fresh melon or pears
Black Pepper-Lemon Dressing
Crisp lettuce
Finely chopped fresh parsley

Toss cucumber and fruit gently with small amount of dressing. Cover; chill for 2 hours or longer. Arrange on chilled lettuce-lined serving platter or individual plates. Spoon additional dressing over salad; sprinkle with chopped parsley.

Black Pepper-Lemon Dressing

1/2 c. salad oil
3 tbsp. fresh lemon juice
3/4 tsp. prepared or dry mustard
1/2 tsp. salt
1/2 tsp. freshly ground pepper
1/2 tsp. crushed dried rosemary or 3/4 tsp. finely minced fresh rosemary

Combine ingredients; beat or shake until well blended. Yield: 6 servings.

Mrs. Bertha Keller Benthien
Clermont Northeastern H.S.
Batavia, Ohio

Salads

APPLE BLUSH SALAD

2 3-oz. packages cherry gelatin
2 c. applesauce

Dissolve gelatin in 2 cups boiling water; add 1 cup cold water. Chill until slightly thickened. Stir in applesauce. Turn into 1 1/2-quart mold. Chill until firm. Yield: 6-8 servings.

Gaynelle C. James, Gardner H.S.
Gardner, Illinois

AUTUMN APPLE SALAD MOLD

1 3-oz. package lime gelatin
Dash of salt
1 7-oz. bottle ginger ale or Seven-Up
1 1/2 c. diced red apples
1 c. seedless grapes
1/2 c. flaked coconut

Dissolve gelatin and salt in 1 cup boiling water; cool thoroughly. Stir in ginger ale; chill until thickened. Fold in apples, grapes and coconut. Chill until set. Grapes may be left whole or cut in halves. Yield: 5-6 servings.

Ilene Rippe, Central Jr. H.S.
Valparaiso, Nebraska

MANHATTAN APPLE SALAD

1 3-oz. package lemon gelatin
1 tbsp. vinegar
1/2 tsp. salt
1 c. tart apples, diced
1/2 c. celery, diced

Dissolve gelatin in 2 cups hot water. Add vinegar and salt. Pour thin layer in mold. Chill until firm. Combine apples and celery; place in mold. Add remaining gelatin. Chill until firm. Unmold on crisp lettuce. Yield: 8 servings.

Mrs. Thelma Maxey, Lorenzo H.S.
Lorenzo, Texas

CRUNCHY WALDORF SALAD

1 env. unflavored gelatin
1/4 c. sugar
1/2 tsp. salt
1 1/2 c. apple juice, cider or water
1/4 c. lemon juice
2 c. diced unpeeled apples
1/2 c. diced celery

Combine gelatin, sugar and salt in a saucepan; stir in 1/2 cup juice. Stir over low heat until gelatin is dis-

solved. Add remaining juice. Chill until slightly thickened. Fold in remaining ingredients. Turn into 4-cup mold; chill until firm. Unmold on greens; serve with French dressing, if desired. Yield: 4-6 servings.

Mrs. Ray E. Alexander, Beaver Area Jr. H.S.
Beaver, Pennsylvania

RED APPLESAUCE SALAD

1 No. 303 can applesauce
1 3-oz. package cherry gelatin
1 6-oz. bottle 7-Up

Place applesauce in small saucepan; heat until bubbly hot. Add gelatin; stir until gelatin is dissolved. Cool. Stir in 7-Up; mix well. Pour into mold. Chill until set. May be served on lettuce leaves, if desired. Yield: 8-10 servings.

Mrs. Jewell Spivey, Harmony School
Gilmer, Texas

EASY APRICOT-PINEAPPLE SALAD

2 12-oz. cans apricot nectar
2 tbsp. lemon juice
2 3-oz. packages lemon gelatin
1 8-oz. can crushed pineapple

Heat apricot nectar and lemon juice in a saucepan; add gelatin. Stir until gelatin is dissolved. Stir in pineapple; pour into 9-inch square pan. Chill until firm. Yield: 6 servings.

Mrs. Madelon Matile, Burnham Jr. H.S.
Sylvania, Ohio

MIXED FRUIT SALAD

1 pkg. orange gelatin
1 baby food jar apricots and tapioca
1 tall can crushed pineapple
1 can mandarin oranges

Dissolve gelatin in 1 cup hot water; add remaining ingredients. Pour into mold. Chill until firm. Yield: 4 servings.

Mrs. Nancy Putney, Sunapee Cen. School
Sunapee, New Hampshire

CANTALOUPE FRUIT SALAD

1 3-oz. package lime gelatin
1 1/2 c. ginger ale
1 c. cantaloupe balls
1/2 c. white grapes, cut in half

2 fresh peaches, sliced
1/2 c. diced pineapple

Dissolve gelatin in 1/2 cup boiling water; cool. Add ginger ale and fruits. Pour into ring mold; chill until firm. Turn out on shredded lettuce. Yield: 8 servings.

Marion Clark, St. Edward H.S.
St. Edward, Nebraska

BING CHERRY SALAD

1 No. 303 can Bing cherries
1 6-oz. package orange gelatin
1/2 c. chopped walnuts
1 c. whipped cream
2 tbsp. mayonnaise

Drain cherries; reserve juice. Dissolve gelatin according to package directions, using reserved juice as part of liquid. Add cherries and walnuts. Pour into mold. Chill until firm. Combine whipped cream and mayonnaise for topping. Yield: 6 servings.

Mrs. Gilberta Percival, Waterville Sr. H.S.
Waterville, Maine

CRANBERRY-SOUR CREAM SALAD

1 pkg. cherry gelatin
1 can whole cranberry sauce
1/2 c. diced celery
1/4 c. chopped walnuts
1 c. sour cream

Dissolve gelatin in 1 cup hot water; add 1/2 cup cold water. Chill until slightly thickened. Break up cranberry sauce; add to gelatin. Add celery and walnuts. Fold in sour cream; chill until firm. Yield: 6 servings.

Myrna Neff, Upper Scioto Valley School
McGuffey, Ohio

MOLDED CRANBERRY RELISH SALAD

1 3-oz. package strawberry gelatin
1 9-oz. can pineapple tidbits
1 10-oz. package frozen cranberry
   relish, thawed
1/3 c. diced celery

Dissolve gelatin in 1 cup hot water. Drain pineapple, reserving syrup. Add enough water to syrup to make 3/4 cup liquid; add to gelatin. Stir in relish. Chill until partially set. Stir in pineapple and celery. Turn into 1-quart mold; chill until firm. Yield: 6 servings.

Mrs. Robert C. Powell, Atkinson Comm. H.S.
Atkinson, Illinois

FESTIVE FRUIT MOLD

1 3-oz. package lemon gelatin
1 c. pineapple syrup and water
2 oranges, diced
1 c. drained pineapple chunks
1 banana sliced
1 apple, diced
1/2 c. broken English walnuts or pecans

Dissolve gelatin in 1 cup hot water. Add pineapple syrup; chill until partially set. Add fruits and walnuts; chill until firm. Serve on crisp lettuce. Yield: 6 servings.

Mrs. G. Sue Lacy, Kermit H.S.
Kermit, West Virginia

GRAPEFRUIT SALAD MOLD

2 No. 2 cans grapefruit sections
Canned grapefruit juice
2 env. unflavored gelatin
1/2 c. sugar
1/4 tsp. salt
Strawberries
Salad greens

Drain grapefruit sections; measure syrup and add enough grapefruit juice to make 3 1/2 cups. Soften gelatin in 1 cup liquid. Heat remaining liquid. Add softened gelatin, sugar and salt; stir until dissolved. Chill until slightly thickened. Fold in 2 cups grapefruit sections. Turn into 1 1/4-quart mold or individual molds; chill until firm. Unmold and garnish with remaining grapefruit sections, strawberries and salad greens. Yield: 8-10 servings.

Betty Horn, Robert Lee H.S.
Midland, Texas

HEAVENLY HALO

1 3-oz. package lime gelatin
3/4 c. pineapple juice
1/2 c. dry milk powder
2 tbsp. lemon juice
1 c. drained pineapple

Dissolve gelatin in 1 cup boiling water; add pineapple juice. Cool until slightly thickened. Chill beaters and small mixing bowl. Whip dry milk and 1/2 cup ice water for about 3 to 4 minutes, or until soft peaks form. Add lemon juice; continue beating until stiff peaks form. Fold whipped milk and pineapple into gelatin mixture; spoon into mold. Chill until set. Serve on lettuce and garnish with parsley and pimento. Yield: 6-8 servings.

Mrs. Louisa M. Krebs, Rapid City Sr. H.S.
Rapid City, South Dakota

Salads

LEMON FRUIT SALAD WITH TOPPING

2 pkg. lemon gelatin
1/2 c. miniature marshmallows
1 lg. can crushed pineapple, drained
2 bananas, sliced

Dissolve gelatin in 2 cups boiling water. Add marshmallows; stir until marshmallows are dissolved. Add pineapple and 1 cup cold water. Chill until thickened. Slice bananas to cover bottom of 9 x 13-inch pan. Pour gelatin mixture over bananas. Chill until set.

Topping

2 tbsp. flour
1/2 c. sugar
1 c. pineapple juice
1 egg, beaten
1/2 c. prepared Dream Whip
Grated Cheddar cheese

Combine flour and sugar in small saucepan; stir in juice and egg. Place over low heat; cook, stirring constantly, until thickened. Cool. Stir in Dream Whip. Place topping on mold. Sprinkle cheese over top. Yield: 12 servings.

Diane M. Berner, South Charleston H.S.
So. Charleston, West Virginia

CRUNCHY LIME-PINEAPPLE SALAD

2 3-oz. boxes lime gelatin
1 13 1/2-oz. can pineapple tidbits, drained
1/2 lb. finely sliced celery
1/4 lb. shredded American cheese

Dissolve gelatin in 2 cups boiling water. Add 2 cups cold water. Chill until slightly thickened. Fold in pineapple, celery and cheese. Pour into a 9 x 13-inch pan. Chill until firm. Cut into squares; serve on salad plates. May use juice drained from pineapple as part of cold water, if desired. Yield: 12-15 servings.

Bertha Shaw, Holstein H.S.
Holstein, Iowa

SPECIAL MANDARIN ORANGE SALAD

1 3-oz. package orange gelatin
1 pt. orange sherbet
1 8-oz. can mandarin oranges, drained
1 c. whipped cream

Dissolve gelatin in 1 cup boiling water; add sherbet. Let stand for about 20 minutes or until thickened.

Fold in oranges and whipped cream. Chill for several hours before serving. Yield: 6 servings.

Becky Davis Kelly, Clarksdale Jr. H.S.
Clarksdale, Mississippi

GOLDEN ORANGE MOLD

1 3-oz. package orange gelatin
2 c. Hi-C orange drink
1 can mandarin oranges, drained
1 c. drained crushed pineapple

Dissolve gelatin in hot orange drink. Chill until thickened. Add fruits. Chill until firm. Unmold on crisp greens. Yield: 6 servings.

Evelyn Mangold, Warrensburg-Lathem H.S.
Warrensburg, Illinois

MOLDED ORANGE SUPREME

2 env. unflavored gelatin
1/2 c. sugar
1 6-oz. can frozen orange juice concentrate
1 tbsp. lemon juice
1/2 c. nonfat dry milk powder
3 lg. fresh oranges, peeled and sectioned
1/2 c. drained pineapple chunks

Combine gelatin, sugar and 1 cup water in top of double boiler. Cook, stirring, until gelatin dissolves. Stir in orange juice. Chill until consistency of unbeaten egg whites. Combine 1/2 cup cold water, lemon juice and dry milk. Beat until stiff. Stir fruits into gelatin mixture; fold in whipped mixture. Pour into 1-quart mold. Chill until firm. Yield: 8 servings.

Mrs. Shirley Hofacker, Holcombe H.S.
Holcombe, Wisconsin

TEA GARDEN SALAD

1 3-oz. package orange gelatin
1 c. hot black tea
1 11-oz. can mandarin oranges
1 9-oz. can crushed pineapple
1 5-oz. can water chestnuts, sliced

Dissolve gelatin in hot tea. Drain and reserve juice from oranges and pineapple. Add 1 cup reserved juice to gelatin. Add orange juice to equal 1 cup if needed. Stir. Chill until gelatin begins to thicken. Add water chestnuts, pineapple and orange sections; spoon into well-oiled molds. Refrigerate until set. Yield: 8 servings.

Mrs. Marjory Fuller, Seitz Jr. H.S.
Riverview, Michigan

ORANGE-GRAPE SALAD

1 3-oz. package orange gelatin
2 tbsp. lemon juice
1/4 tsp. salt
2 seedless oranges, peeled and sectioned
1 lg. grapefruit, peeled and sectioned
1/2 c. grapes, halved

Dissolve gelatin in 1 cup boiling water; stir in 3/4 cup water, lemon juice and salt. Chill until slightly thickend. Fold in fruits. Pour into molds. Chill until firm. Serve on greens. Yield: 6 servings.

Mrs. George Schwartz, Fort Lee H.S.
Fort Lee, New Jersey

SPICED PEACH SALAD

1 env. unflavored gelatin
1 tbsp. sugar
1/4 tsp. salt
1 1-lb. can sliced peaches
6 whole cloves
1 stick cinnamon
1/4 c. vinegar

Combine gelatin, sugar and salt in a saucepan. Drain peaches, reserving liquid. Add enough water to syrup to make 1 3/4 cups liquid. Add syrup mixture to gelatin with cloves and cinnamon. Place over low heat; simmer for 10 minutes. Strain; stir in vinegar. Chill to unbeaten egg white consistency. Fold in peaches. Turn into a 2-cup mold or individual molds; chill until firm. Unmold on serving plate; garnish with parsley. Yield: 4 servings.

Marilyn Miller, Spooner Sr. H.S.
Spooner, Wisconsin

SUNSET PEAR SALAD

2 1-lb. cans pear halves
1 8 1/2-oz. can pineapple slices
Red food coloring
1 3-oz. box each orange and
    pineapple gelatin
2 oranges, peeled and diced
1 tbsp. lemon juice
Salad greens

Drain fruits, reserving syrups. Add a few drops of food coloring to a small amount of syrup. Brush on 8 pear halves to give a blush. Dice remaining pears. Add enough water to fruit syrups to make 3 1/2 cups liquid. Heat half the syrup to boiling point; pour over gelatin. Stir until dissolved. Add remaining cold syrup. Chill until partially set. Add diced pears, oranges and lemon juice; pour into 1 1/2-quart mold. Chill until firm. Turn out on serving plate; garnish

with greens. Cut pineapple slices in half; arrange around base of mold, rounded side out. Stand a pear on each piece of pineapple. Garnish tips of pears with mint sprigs. Yield: 8 servings.

Amelia Davis, Frank W. Cox H.S.
Virginia Beach, Virginia

BLUSHING PEAR SALAD

1 3-oz. package lime gelatin
6 pear halves
Red food coloring

Prepare gelatin according to package directions. Tint pear halves a soft pink with a solution of red food coloring and water. Arrange pears, cut side down, in 9 x 9 x 1 3/4-inch pan. Pour gelatin into pan; chill until firm. Serve on salad greens with fruit dressing. Yield: 6 servings.

Mrs. LeRoy Kurtenbach, Wilsey H.S.
Wilsey, Kansas

GINGER PEARS

1 3-oz. package raspberry or lemon gelatin
1 1/2 tsp. lemon juice
1 c. ginger ale
1 c. diced fresh pears

Dissolve gelatin in 1 cup boiling water. Add lemon juice and ginger ale. Chill until very thick. Add pears. Spoon into mold. Chill until firm; unmold to serve. Yield: 6 servings.

Mary Jo Udovich, Durand H.S.
Durand, Wisconsin

CANADIAN PINEAPPLE SALAD MOLD

2 env. unflavored gelatin
1/3 c. sugar
1/4 tsp. salt
1 20-oz. can pineapple chunks
1/3 c. lemon juice
1 c. grated carrots
1 1/2 c. diced oranges

Combine gelatin, sugar and salt in a saucepan. Drain pineapple, reserving syrup. Add enough water to syrup to make 2 cups liquid. Blend 1 cup syrup into gelatin mixture; cook over low heat, stirring constantly, until gelatin is dissolved. Remove from heat; stir in remaining syrup mixture and lemon juice. Turn into bowl; cover. Chill until thick. Fold in carrots, oranges and pineapple chunks. Turn into 5-cup mold; chill until set. Yield: 6-8 servings.

Mrs. Joan Corey, Petitcodiac Reg. H.S.
Petitcodiac, New Brunswick, Canada

Salads

RASPBERRY-APPLESAUCE SALAD

1 box raspberry gelatin
1 10-oz. package frozen red raspberries
1 c. applesauce
1 c. sour cream (opt.)
2 c. miniature marshmallows (opt.)

Dissolve gelatin in 1 cup boiling water. Add frozen raspberries; stir until raspberries have thawed and mixture begins to thicken. Stir in applesauce; turn into a 9-inch square pan. Chill until set. Combine sour cream with marshmallows; spread over top. Yield: 9 servings.

Mrs. Loretta Stock, Murdock Consolidated School
Murdock, Nebraska

RASPBERRY-LEMONADE SALAD

2 3-oz. boxes raspberry gelatin
1 10-oz. package frozen raspberries
1 6-oz. can frozen lemonade
1 c. cream, whipped

Dissolve gelatin in 1 cup boiling water. Stir in frozen raspberries and lemonade. Chill until partially set. Fold in whipped cream. Pour into mold. Chill until firm. Serve on salad greens. Yield: 6-8 servings.

Marilyn Kelley, Wadena Sr. H.S.
Wadena, Minnesota

RHUBARB SALAD MOLD

3 c. chopped rhubarb
3/4 c. sugar
1 3-oz. package strawberry gelatin

Cook rhubarb with sugar and 1 cup water until tender. Skim foam from rhubarb; add gelatin. Stir until dissolved. Pour into mold. Serve with cream cheese ball. Yield: 6 servings.

Dorothy Westergard, Romulus Sr. H.S.
Romulus, Michigan

STRAWBERRY-SOUR CREAM SALAD

1 3-oz. package strawberry gelatin
1 10-oz. package frozen strawberries
1 c. dairy sour cream
1 c. chopped pecans

Dissolve gelatin in 1 cup boiling water. Add frozen strawberries. Stir until strawberries separate and thaw. Pour half the mixture into mold; chill until set. Mix sour cream and pecans; spread over straw-

berry layer. Add remaining strawberry mixture; chill until firm. Yield: 6-8 servings.

Mrs. Eleanor Weatherford, Tupelo Sr. H.S.
Tupelo, Mississippi

CARROT FRUIT SALAD

1 3-oz. package orange or lemon gelatin
1 No. 2 can crushed pineapple
2 carrots, grated

Dissolve gelatin in 1 cup boiling water; cool. Add undrained pineapple and carrots. Pour into mold; refrigerate for 2 hours. Unmold; place on large dish. Garnish with lettuce leaves. Yield: 6-8 servings.

Elena Yatarola, Leavenworth Cen. School
Walcott, New York

GOLDEN SALAD SUPREME

1 env. unflavored gelatin
2 tbsp. sugar
1/4 tsp. salt
1/2 c. orange juice
2 tbsp. vinegar
1/2 c. drained crushed pineapple
1/2 c. drained orange sections
1/2 c. grated carrots

Mix gelatin, sugar and salt together. Add 1 cup hot water; stir until gelatin is thoroughly dissolved. Add orange juice and vinegar. Chill to unbeaten egg white consistency. Fold in pineapple, orange sections and carrots. Turn into a 3-cup mold or individual molds; chill until firm. Unmold on salad greens; serve with salad dressing, if desired. Yield: 6 servings.

Mrs. Ruth Hale, Cheyenne-Eagle Butte School
Eagle Butte, South Dakota

SUNSET PINEAPPLE SALAD

1 3-oz. package lemon gelatin
1/2 tsp. salt
1 8-oz. can crushed pineapple
   or pineapple tidbits
1 tbsp. lemon juice
1 c. coarsely grated carrots

Dissolve gelatin and salt in 1 1/2 cups boiling water. Add pineapple and lemon juice. Chill until thick. Fold in carrots. Pour into individual molds or a 1-quart mold. Chill until firm. Unmold. Garnish with additional pineapple, if desired. Yield: 6 servings.

Sister Anita Beaton, C.N.D.
Mabou Consolidated School
Mabou, Nova Scotia, Canada

COTTAGE CHEESE CARNIVAL

2 8 1/2-oz. cans crushed pineapple
1 env. unflavored gelatin
1 lg. stalk celery, chopped
1 tsp. finely minced onion (opt.)
1 lb. creamed cottage cheese
2 carrots, cut in sticks
8 saltine crackers

Drain part of syrup from pineapple into a medium saucepan. Stir in gelatin; let stand for 5 minutes to soften. Heat, stirring constantly, until gelatin is dissolved. Stir in pineapple with remaining syrup, celery, onion and cottage cheese. Refrigerate for at least 2 hours. Spoon mixture into lettuce cups; surround with carrot sticks and saltines just before serving. Yield: 4 servings.

Obera B. Pruitt, Belton-Honea Path H.S.
Belton, South Carolina

DELUXE CHEESE MOLD

1 3-oz. package orange gelatin
1 c. orange sherbet
1 1/2 c. cottage cheese with pineapple

Dissolve gelatin in 1 cup boiling water. Blend in sherbet. Chill until very thick. Stir in cottage cheese. Spoon into mold. Chill until firm. May be served with sour cream, if desired. May use 1 cup cottage cheese and one 8 3/4-ounce can drained crushed pineapple for cottage cheese with pineapple. Yield: 6 servings.

Mrs. Beverly A. Reed, Stamford Cen. School
Stamford, New York

DREAMY CHEESE-LIME SALAD

1 flat can pineapple
2 3-oz. packages lime gelatin
1 pt. cottage cheese
1/4 c. vinegar
1 pkg. Dream Whip
1/2 c. milk
1 tsp. vanilla extract

Drain pineapple; reserve juice. Dissolve gelatin in 2 cups boiling water; add 1 cup cold water and reserve pineapple juice. Let set until thickened. Fold in cottage cheese, pineapple and vinegar. Prepare Dream Whip according to package directions with milk and vanilla. Fold into gelatin mixture. Chill until set. Serve on a lettuce leaf. Yield: 15 servings.

Mrs. Linda Lewis, Kendrick H.S.
Kendrick, Idaho

HARLEQUIN PARTY SALAD

1 3-oz. package lemon gelatin
1 1-lb. 4 1/2-oz. can crushed pineapple
1/2 c. cottage cheese
1 c. whipped cream or prepared Dream Whip
1/4 c. chopped maraschino cherries
1/4 c. chopped blanched almonds

Dissolve gelatin in 1 cup boiling water. Drain pineapple, reserving 1/2 cup syrup. Add syrup to gelatin; chill until thick. Fold in pineapple, cottage cheese, whipped cream, cherries and almonds. Pour into individual molds or a 9 x 5 x 3-inch loaf pan. Chill until firm. Unmold and serve. Yield: 8 servings.

Mrs. Joyce S. Longest, Henrico H.S.
Richmond, Virginia

FLUFFY LIME SALAD

1 3-oz. package lime gelatin
1 10-oz. package marshmallows
1 flat can crushed pineapple
1 carton cottage cheese
1/2 c. chopped pecans
1 carton whipping cream, whipped

Dissolve gelatin and marshmallows in 2 cups boiling water, stirring until dissolved. Cool until thick; fold in pineapple, cottage cheese, pecans and whipped cream. Chill until firm. Serve squares on lettuce leaves. Yield: 10 servings.

Mrs. Tennie Isbell, Hillsboro H.S.
Hillsboro, Texas

EMERALD SALAD

1 3-oz. package lime gelatin
2 3-oz. packages cream cheese
1/2 c. fruit juice
Few drops green food coloring (opt.)
1 lg. can fruit cocktail, drained
1 c. chopped nuts
1 can pineapple chunks, drained
1 c. chopped marshmallows
1/2 pt. whipped cream

Dissolve gelatin in 1 cup hot water. Blend cream cheese, 1/2 cup cold water and juice until smooth. Stir into gelatin. Beat until foamy. Add food coloring. Chill for 1 to 2 hours or until thickened. Fold in remaining ingredients; chill until firm. Yield: 10-15 servings.

Mrs. Patricia A. Mullins, South Fulton H.S.
South Fulton, Tennessee

Salads

FROZEN CRANBERRY SALAD

1 can whole cranberry sauce
1 No. 2 can crushed pineapple
1/2 pt. sour cream
1/4 c. pecans, chopped
3 to 4 drops red food coloring

Combine all ingredients; mix thoroughly. Place in oblong or square pans. Freeze until firm. Cut in squares; serve on lettuce. Yield: 8-10 servings.

Mrs. Louise S. Barton, Herrin H.S.
Herrin, Illinois

THE EASIEST FROZEN FRUIT SALAD

1 No. 303 can fruit cocktail
4 to 5 lettuce leaves
Whipped cream or salad dressing

Freeze can of fruit cocktail. Open both ends of the can; push contents out. Slice. Serve on lettuce; garnish with whipped cream or salad dressing. Serve immediately. Yield: 4-5 servings.

Catherine Thomas, Dyer H.S.
Dyer, Tennessee

RASPBERRY SHERBET SALAD

1   6-oz. package raspberry gelatin
1 pt. raspberry sherbet
1   3-oz. package lime gelatin
1 c. cold fruit juice
1   13 1/2-oz. can pineapple tidbets, drained

Dissolve raspberry gelatin in 2 cups hot water; add sherbet. Stir until melted. Pour into 2-quart mold; freeze. Dissolve lime gelatin in 1 cup hot water; add juice and pineapple tidbits. Pour over frozen layer; refrigerate for about 30 minutes. Unmold on greens. Yield: 8-12 servings.

Mrs. Jeanette Weiss, Revere H.S.
Sedgewick, Colorado

HAM AND CHEESE LOAF

1 env. unflavored gelatin
1/4 c. vinegar
1/4 tsp. salt
1 c. diced cooked ham
1 c. grated American cheese
1/4 c. diced celery
1/4 c. diced sweet pickles or pickle relish

Sprinkle gelatin on 1/2 cup cold water to soften; add 3/4 cup hot water. Stir until gelatin is thoroughly dissolved. Add vinegar and salt. Chill until mixture mounds when dropped from spoon. Fold in ham,

cheese, celery and pickles. Turn into loaf pan; chill until firm. Unmold on salad greens. Yield: 4-6 servings.

Evia C. Arnold, Rio Vista H.S.
Rio Vista, Texas

LUNCHEON HAM SALAD

2 c. diced ham or Spam
2 hard-boiled eggs, chopped
1/2 c. chopped pickles
1/2 c. salad dressing
1/8 tsp. salt
1/8 tsp. pepper

Combine all ingredients; toss lightly. Place on lettuce leaf; garnish with cheese, olive or green pepper. Leftover chicken or roast may be used. Yield: 5-6 servings.

Doris Hartman, Neches H.S.
Neches, Texas

WINTER SALAD BOWL

1/2 sweet onion, cut fine
2 tomatoes
1 lg. carrot, diced
2 c. cooked peas (opt.)
2 to 3 Jerusalem artichokes, scraped
   and thinly sliced
1/2 sm. green pepper, thinly sliced
2/3 c. cubed ham or tongue
1 sm. head lettuce
Low-calorie salad dressing

Toss vegetables and ham together in bowl; place in refrigerator to chill. Tear lettuce apart; place on salad dishes. Add salad dressing to vegetables; toss. Place on lettuce to serve. Yield: 6 servings.

Berniece M. Cobb, Westminster H.S.
Westminster, Colorado

JELLIED MEAT SALAD

1 env. unflavored gelatin
2 bouillon cubes
1 1/2 tbsp. lemon juice
1 tsp. grated onion
1 c. finely diced cooked meat
1/2 c. diced celery
1/2 c. cooked or canned peas, well drained

Sprinkle gelatin in 1/2 cup cold water to soften. Combine bouillon cubes with 1 1/4 cup water, lemon juice and onion; heat until bouillon cubes are completely dissolved. Add softened gelatin; stir until thoroughly dissolved. Chill to unbeaten egg white consistency. Fold in meat, celery and peas. Turn into

4-cup loaf pan. Chill until firm; cut into slices and serve. Yield: 6 servings.

Maurine Pierce, Trimble School
Trimble, Tennessee

ROAST BEEF SALAD

1 c. diced cooked beef
2 hard-cooked eggs, sliced
2 tomatoes, quartered
1 sm. head lettuce
French dressing or mayonnaise

Arrange first 3 ingredients on lettuce. Serve with French dressing. Diced cooked ham, tongue or corned beef may be substituted for beef. Yield: 6 servings.

Mrs. Johnnie Mae Proctor, Dilley H.S.
Dilley, Texas

LAMB SALAD

2 c. cooked diced lamb
1 head lettuce, broken into pieces
1 c. sliced celery
2 c. diced cooked potatoes
1 c. chopped fresh dill
1/4 c. French dressing
1/4 c. mayonnaise
1/3 c. chopped stuffed olives
2 tbsp. vinegar
Salt and pepper to taste

Combine lamb, lettuce, celery, potatoes and dill; toss lightly. Chill. Combine remaining ingredients; mix well. Add to lamb mixture. Toss lightly, but thoroughly. Yield: 6 servings.

Mrs. Delia McClurg, Merino H.S.
Merino, Colorado

CHICKEN MOUSSE

1 env. unflavored gelatin
1 c. very hot chicken stock
1/4 tsp. onion salt
2/3 c. cold evaporated milk
1 tbsp. lemon juice
1 1/2 c. cooked, diced or flaked chicken

Soften gelatin in 1/2 cup cold water; add to hot stock. Add onion salt; stir until gelatin is dissolved. Cool until the consistency of unbeaten egg white. Whip evaporated milk; beat in lemon juice. Beat gelatin until fluffy. Combine whipped evaporated milk, gelatin and chicken. Turn into 4-cup mold; chill until firm. Unmold and garnish as desired. Bouillon may be used for broth. Yield: 8 servings.

Sister M. Carolita, F.S.P.A.
Hayes Catholic H.S.
Muscatine, Iowa

APPLE-CHICKEN SALAD

1   3-oz. package lemon or lime gelatin
1 c. boiling broth or hot water
1 tsp. onion juice
1 tbsp. lemon juice or vinegar
Salt and pepper to taste
1/2 c. chopped apple
2 tbsp. chopped pimento
3/4 c. finely chopped celery
1 1/2 c. diced cooked chicken

Soak gelatin in 1/4 cup cold water until softened; add hot chicken broth, onion juice, lemon juice, salt and pepper. Stir until gelatin is dissolved. Pour in mold; chill until thick. Stir in apple, pimento, celery and chicken. Chill until firm. Serve on crisp lettuce leaves. Any desired meat or fish may be substituted for chicken. Yield: 6 servings.

Mrs. Carmen Kazen Ferris, Consultant
Texas Education Agency
Austin, Texas

MAIN DISH CHICKEN SALAD

1 tsp. lemon juice
1/2 c. boiling chicken broth
1 env. unflavored gelatin
1/4 c. mayonnaise
2 egg yolks
1/4 tsp. dry mustard
2 drops of Tabasco sauce
2 sprigs of parsley
1 slice onion
Dash of pepper
1/4 green pepper, seeded
2 stalks celery, cut into 1-in. pieces
2 c. diced cooked chicken
1 c. canned cooked peas

Place first 3 ingredients in blender container; cover and run on low speed until gelatin is dissolved. Add remaining ingredients except chicken and peas; cover and run on low or medium speed just until vegetables are coarsely chopped. Add chicken to container; cover and run on speed high just until all chicken goes through blades. Pour into a 1 1/2-quart mold or a loaf pan; stir in peas. Chill until set. Yield: 6 servings.

Mrs. Louise Smith, Dexter Municipal School
Dexter, New Mexico

117

Salads

SILHOUETTE SALAD

1 env. unflavored gelatin
1 10 1/2-oz. can cream of chicken or
   mushroom soup
1 tbsp. lemon juice
Dash of pepper
1 5-oz. can boned chicken or turkey, flaked
1/2 c. chopped celery
1/4 c. chopped green pepper
2 tbsp. chopped pimento
2 tsp. grated onion

Sprinkle gelatin on 1/2 cup water to soften. Place
over low heat; stir until gelatin is dissolved. Remove
from heat; blend in soup until smooth. Add 1/2 cup
water, lemon juice and pepper. Chill to unbeaten egg
white consistency. Fold in chicken, celery, green
pepper, pimento and onion. Turn into a 3-cup mold
or individual molds. Chill until firm. Unmold on
serving plate; garnish with salad greens. Yield: 4
servings.

Mrs. Anona Moore, Alvin Jr. H.S.
Alvin, Texas

TOMATO-CHICKEN SALAD MOLD

2 env. unflavored gelatin
1 10 1/2-oz. can consomme
1 17 1/2-oz. can tomato juice
1/2 tsp. salt
2 tbsp. lemon juice
1/4 tsp. Tabasco sauce
3 c. diced cooked chicken
1 c. chopped celery
1/2 c. chopped cucumber
1/4 c. chopped stuffed olives (opt.)

Sprinkle gelatin on 1 cup consomme to soften. Place
over low heat; stir until gelatin is dissolved. Remove
from heat; stir in remaining consomme, tomato
juice, salt, lemon juice and Tabasco. Chill to consistency of unbeaten egg white. Fold in chicken, celery,
cucumber and olives. Turn into 6-cup mold; chill
until firm. Unmold on serving plate; garnish with
salad greens. Yield: 8-10 servings.

Sister Helene Michael, St. Mary H.S.
Westfield, Massachusetts

MACARONI-CHICKEN SALAD

1 tbsp. salt
2 c. macaroni
2 c. diced chicken
1 c. diced celery
2 sweet pickles, chopped
2 tbsp. grated onion
1 can pimento, chopped
1/3 c. salad dressing
Juice of 1 lemon

1/8 tsp. dry mustard
Dash of Tabasco sauce

Add salt to 3 quarts boiling water. Add macaroni
gradually so water continues to boil. Cook, uncovered, stirring occasionally, until tender. Drain in
colander. Rinse with cold water; drain again. Combine remaining ingredients; toss lightly with macaroni. Season with pepper, if desired. Chill. Garnish
with tomato wedges. Yield: 4 servings.

Mrs. Janell Samford, C.O. Wilson Jr. H.S.
Nederland, Texas

WESTERN TURKEY SALAD

6 tbsp. corn oil
3 tbsp. vinegar
1 tbsp. sugar
1 1/2 lb. cooked turkey, diced
3 tbsp. unflavored gelatin
2 c. hot turkey stock or water and
   2 chicken bouillon cubes
2 tbsp. lemon juice
1 tbsp. grated onion
1 tsp. creamed horseradish
Salt and pepper to taste
2 tbsp. chopped red pepper
1/2 c. diced celery
2 hard-boiled eggs, diced
2 oz. sliced almonds (opt.)

Combine oil, vinegar and sugar; mix well. Add turkey. Set aside to chill. Soften gelatin in 1/4 cup cold
water; dissolve in hot stock. Add lemon juice, onion
and horseradish; season with salt and pepper. Chill
until partially set. Blend in turkey mixture, red pepper, celery, eggs and almonds. Pour into mold. Chill
for several hours or overnight until firm. Turn out.
Garnish with avocado slices and watercress. Serve
with low-calorie salad dressing or mayonnaise. Yield:
6 servings.

Mrs. Irene B. Knudsen, Del Norte H.S.
Crescent City, California

INDIVIDUAL TURKEY SALAD MOLDS

2 tbsp. unflavored gelatin
2 tbsp. lemon juice
1 1/2 c. diced cooked turkey
1 tsp. sugar
1 tsp. salt
1/2 tsp. dry mustard
1/2 tsp. paprika
1/4 tsp. onion salt
1 10 1/2-oz. can cream of chicken soup
1/4 c. diced celery
1/4 c. diced cucumber

2 tbsp. chopped pimento
2 tbsp. chopped green pepper

Sprinkle gelatin on 1 1/2 cups cold water to soften. Place over low heat until gelatin is thoroughly dissolved, stirring constantly. Remove from heat. Pour lemon juice over turkey; blend well. Add to gelatin. Cool until consistency of unbeaten egg whites. Fold in remaining ingredients. Pour into individual molds. Chill until firm. Yield: 8-10 servings.

Mrs. Dolores Brown, Lexington H.S.
Lexington, Oklahoma

CALICO CLAM RINGS

1   7-oz. can minced clams
1 c. dry cottage cheese
1 tsp. garlic salt
1 tsp. Worcestershire sauce
1 med. sweet red pepper
1 med. sweet green pepper
Romaine

Drain liquid from clams into a cup. Press cottage cheese through a sieve into a medium bowl; stir in clams, 1/4 cup clam liquid, garlic salt and Worcestershire sauce. Chill for at least 1 hour. Cut each pepper into 4 rings; remove seeds. Place 1 red and 1 green ring on each of 4 romaine-lined salad plates. Spoon clam mixture into each, dividing evenly. Yield: 4 servings.

Mrs. Barbara Elledge, Grand Prairie Sr. H.S.
Grand Prairie, Texas

NORTHWEST CRAB SALAD BOWL

1 lb. crab meat
1 qt. mixed salad greens
2 tomatoes, cut into wedges
1 c. corn chips
1/2 c. sliced pitted ripe olives
1/4 c. chopped green onion
Avocado Cream Dressing
1/2 c. shredded natural Cheddar cheese
Whole pitted ripe olives

Prepare crab meat. Break crab meat into large pieces. Combine salad greens, tomatoes, corn chips, olives, onion and crab meat in a serving bowl. Add dressing; toss lightly. Sprinkle with cheese and garnish with olives. Serve immediately. Yield: 6 servings.

Avocado Cream Dressing

1/2 c. mashed avocado
1/3 c. sour cream
2 tbsp. lemon juice
1/2 tsp. sugar
1/4 tsp. chili powder

1/4 tsp salt
1/4 tsp. liquid hot pepper sauce
1 clove of garlic, crushed

Combine all ingredients; mix until smooth. Chill. Yield: 1 cup dressing.

Photograph for this recipe on page 106.

MOLDED SHRIMP SALAD

1 tbsp. unflavored gelatin
1/4 c. white wine
1 1/4 c. hot tomato juice
1 1/2 tsp. Worcestershire sauce
1/4 tsp. pepper
1 lb. shrimp, cooked and cleaned
1 green pepper, diced
2 stalks celery, sliced

Soften gelatin in wine; add tomato juice, Worcestershire sauce and pepper, stirring until dissolved. Cool for 1 hour. Beat with a rotary beater for several minutes. Add shrimp, green pepper and celery. Pour into cold water rinsed 1-quart mold. Chill for at least 4 hours. Serve with dressing, if desired. Yield: 4 servings.

Nancy R. West, Richton H.S.
Richton, Mississippi

SHRIMP ASPIC

2 c. tomato juice
1 tsp. liquid sweetener
1 tsp. salt
1/8 tsp. pepper
1 tbsp. minced onion
1 sm. bay leaf
1/2 tsp. lemon juice
1/2 tsp. Worcestershire sauce
1 tbsp. vinegar
1 tbsp. unflavored gelatin
1   5-oz. can shrimp, rinsed and cut
1 c. chopped celery
1/4 c. chopped green pepper

Combine tomato juice, liquid sweetener, salt, pepper, onion, bay leaf, lemon juice, Worcestershire sauce and vinegar. Bring to a boil; strain. Soften gelatin in 1/4 cup cold water; dissolve in hot mixture. Cool until mixture begins to thicken. Fold in remaining ingredients; pour into a 1-quart mold. Chill until firm. Serve on lettuce leaf; garnish with sliced egg. Yield: 6 servings.

Elynore J. Wilson, Calumet H.S.
Chicago, Illinois

Salads

SHRIMP-BEAN SALAD

1 c. boiled shrimp
1 No. 1 can green beans, broken
1 sm. onion, minced
1/4 c. chopped bell pepper
2 tbsp. diced mushrooms
2 tbsp. diced pimento

Combine all ingredients in order listed. Serve on crisp lettuce leaves with small amount of salad dressing. Yield: 4 servings.

Mattie Y. Miller, Newton H.S.
Newton, Texas

SHRIMP-OLIVE SALAD

3 3-oz. packages lemon gelatin
2 tbsp. lemon juice
1 1/2 c. finely chopped celery
1 sm. bottle stuffed olives, sliced
1 sm. green pepper, finely diced
2 4 1/2-oz. cans drained shrimp, cut fine

Dissolve gelatin in 3 cups hot water; add 2 3/4 cups cold water. Chill until thickened. Add remaining ingredients. Pour into individual molds; chill until firm. Serve on lettuce leaf or shredded lettuce. Yield: 20 servings.

Mrs. Clara M. Trout, Oakland Comm. School
Oakland, Iowa

TEXAS SHRIMP MOLD

1 can tomato soup
1 tbsp. vinegar
1 tbsp. Worcestershire sauce
1 3-oz. package lemon gelatin
1 sm. can shrimp, drained and rinsed
1 c. chopped celery
1/4 c. chopped green peppers
1/4 c. salad olives

Heat soup, 1 soup can water, vinegar and Worcestershire sauce. Dissolve gelatin in soup mixture. Cool. Add shrimp, celery, green peppers and olives. Place in mold; chill until firm. Yield: 6 servings.

Mrs. Nellie Hoggatt, Perryton Jr. H.S.
Perryton, Texas

SALMON-PINEAPPLE-COTTAGE CHEESE SALAD

1 1-lb. can salmon, drained
3/4 c. chopped sweet pickles
1/2 c. salad dressing
1 tsp. salt
1 to 1 1/4 c. cottage cheese
1/2 c. chopped celery
6 lettuce cups
6 slices pineapple

Bone and flake salmon. Mix lightly with sweet pickles, salad dressing, salt, cottage cheese and celery. Chill. Place in lettuce cups. Cut pineapple slices in fourths; place 4 of the cut pieces around each serving of salad. Garnish with radish roses, pickles and carrot sticks. Yield: 6 servings.

Marilyn Berousek, Maysville H.S.
Maysville, Oklahoma

INDIVIDUAL SALMON SALADS

1 3-oz. package lemon gelatin
2 tbsp. vinegar
2 7 1/2-oz. cans salmon
1/2 c. chopped celery
2 tbsp. chopped green pepper
2 tbsp. chopped pimento
1 tbsp. grated onion

Dissolve gelatin in 1 cup boiling water. Stir in 1 cup cold water and vinegar; chill until slightly thickened. Fold in remaining ingredients. Pour into 8 individual molds; chill until firm. Serve on salad greens.

Mrs. Cecile L. Herscher, Union H.S.
Dowagiac, Michigan

FESTIVE SALMON RING

1 env. unflavored gelatin
1 3/4 c. skim milk
2 egg yolks
1 can salmon or tuna, drained and flaked
1 tsp. prepared mustard
2 tbsp. lemon juice
1/2 c. chopped celery
2 tbsp. chopped pimento

Stir gelatin into 1/2 cup milk to soften. Beat egg yolks and remaining 1 1/4 cups milk together; add to gelatin mixture. Cook over low heat, stirring constantly, until gelatin is dissolved. Remove from heat; chill until slightly thickened. Combine salmon, mustard, lemon juice, celery and pimento; fold into gelatin mixture. Turn into 3-cup ring mold or individual molds. Chill until firm. Unmold; garnish with greens and tomato wedges. Fill center with English peas, if desired. Yield: 6 servings.

Mrs. Clariece Seachord, Chester H.S.
Chester, Nebraska

CAULIFLOWER RING-AROUND

1 lg. tomato
1/4 c. cottage cheese

3 tbsp. chunk tuna
Onion salt to taste
Caulifloweret, sliced

Scoop pulp from tomato. Make 8 or 10 even cuts halfway down shell. Mix cottage cheese and tuna together. Season with onion salt. Fill tomato. Insert cauliflower slices into cuts in tomato. Garnish with parsley. Serve on lettuce. Yield: 1 serving.

Mrs. Vera M. Sylvester
Weyburn Collegiate Institute
Weyburn, Saskatchewan, Canada

CRACKER CRISP SALAD

1 head lettuce, torn
2 tomatoes, diced
8 radishes, sliced
1 can tuna, drained and flaked
1 tsp. salt
1 c. mayonnaise
3 tsp. wine vinegar
1/4 tsp. Worcestershire sauce
1/2 c. cheese crackers

Place first 4 ingredients in salad bowl. Combine salt, mayonnaise, vinegar and Worcestershire sauce; mix well. Add to salad bowl; toss until well coated. Add crackers just before serving. Yield: 6 servings.

Diane M. Berner, South Charleston H.S.
South Charleston, West Virginia

TUNA CRUNCH SALAD

2 7-oz. cans tuna, flaked
1 8-oz. can water chestnuts, drained
   and sliced
1/4 c. diced celery
2 tbsp. sliced green onions
1/2 c. sour cream
1/4 c. Italian dressing
1 tbsp. lemon juice
1/2 tsp. salt
1/8 tsp. pepper
1/2 c. chopped pecans

Combine first 4 ingredients. Blend sour cream, Italian dressing, lemon juice, salt and pepper together; add to tuna mixture. Toss to blend. Chill until serving time. Stir in pecans; serve on salad greens. Yield: 6 servings.

Mrs. Margaret Bumpas, West H.S.
Wichita, Kansas

TUNA SPRING SALAD

2 c. cottage cheese
1/2 tsp. Worcestershire sauce

2 7-oz. cans dietetic tuna
1 c. shredded carrot
1 c. chopped parsley
2 tbsp. dietetic pickle relish
Salt and pepper to taste

Mix cottage cheese and Worcestershire sauce. Drain tuna; break into flakes with fork. Mix vegetables and cheese mixture. Toss lightly; season with salt and pepper. Serve on lettuce; garnish with tomato wedges. Yield: 6 servings.

Mrs. Jo Anne Tuttle, Spencer Jr. H.S.
Spencer, Iowa

TANGY TUNA SALAD

1 3-oz. package lemon gelatin
1 tsp. salt
2 tsp. vinegar
1 c. flaked tuna
2 tbsp. chopped celery
2 tbsp. chopped green pepper
2 tsp. chopped onion

Dissolve gelatin and salt in 1 cup hot water. Add 3/4 cup cold water and vinegar; chill until slightly thickened. Add tuna, celery, green pepper and onion. Pour into molds. Chill until firm. Unmold; garnish with crisp salad greens. Crab meat or shrimp may be used instead of tuna. Yield: 6 servings.

Mrs. Margaret Hambleton, Lake Weir H.S.
Summerfield, Florida

KEY ASPARAGUS SALAD

2 env. unflavored gelatin
1/2 c. sugar
1/2 c. vinegar
1/2 tsp. salt
1 c. chopped celery
1 sm. jar chopped pimento
1 15-oz. can asparagus pieces, drained
Juice of 1/2 lemon
1/2 c. chopped pecans
1 tsp. grated onion (opt.)

Soften gelatin in 1/2 cup cold water. Bring 1 cup water, sugar, vinegar and salt to a boil. Add gelatin; stir until gelatin is dissolved. Cool. Fold in celery, pimento, asparagus, lemon juice, pecans and onion. Pour into 12 individual molds; chill until firm. Serve on crisp lettuce leaf; garnish with small piece of pimento or half of a stuffed green olive.

Jane Sharon Frazier, West Rowan H.S.
Mount Ulla, North Carolina

Salads

LAST MINUTE ASPARAGUS SALAD

1 10 1/2-oz. can asparagus tips
4 lettuce leaves
2 hard-cooked eggs
1/4 tsp. salt
1/8 tsp. pepper
1 tsp. vinegar

Place equal amounts of asparagus tips on each lettuce leaf; top with slices of hard-cooked eggs. Sprinkle with salt, pepper and vinegar. Yield: 4 servings.

Mattie Y. Miller, Newton H.S.
Newton, Texas

PORK AND BEAN SALAD

1 can pork and beans with tomato sauce
1/2 c. diced celery
1 tbsp. minced green pepper
1 tbsp. minced onion
1 tsp. vinegar
1/2 tsp. salt
Dash of pepper

Combine all ingredients; mix lightly. Chill. Serve on salad greens. Yield: 4 servings.

Mary L. Lane, San Benito H.S.
San Benito, Texas

FOUR-BEAN SALAD

1 can wax beans, drained
1 can red beans, drained and rinsed
1 can French-cut beans
1 can garbanzos, drained and rinsed
1 lg. red onion, thinly sliced
1 lg. bell pepper, thinly sliced
Salt and pepper to taste
3/4 c. sugar
2/3 c. white vinegar
1/3 c. salad oil

Combine all beans. Place alternate layers of bean mixture, onion and pepper slices in salad bowl; season with salt and pepper. Mix remaining ingredients for dressing; beat until white and thick. Pour over salad; refrigerate overnight. Yield: 16 servings.

Mrs. Tharessa P. Walker, Shady Grove H.S.
Saline, Louisiana

FRENCH BEAN SALAD

1 can French-cut beans, drained
1 sm. can sweet peas, drained

4 stalks celery, diced
1 sm. green pepper, chopped
1 sm. can pimento, chopped
1/2 c. sugar
1/2 c. salad oil
1/2 c. vinegar

Combine first 5 ingredients. Combine remaining ingredients. Pour over vegetables. Marinate overnight or for at least 12 hours. Will keep for several days. Yield: 6-8 servings.

Mrs. Viola Johnson, Karnes City H.S.
Karnes City, Texas

SOUTHERN-MARINATED GREEN BEANS

3 cans green beans, drained
1/2 c. salad oil
1/2 c. vinegar
3/4 c. sugar
1/2 tsp. salt
1/2 c. chopped onion
1/2 c. chopped bell pepper
1 sm. jar pimento

Combine beans with remaining ingredients in a saucepan; cover with a tight lid. Bring to a quick simmer. Set aside to cool. Yield: 8 servings.

Mrs. Jerry Stevens, Indianola H.S.
Indianola, Mississippi

SWEET-SOUR BEANS

2 strips bacon
1 c. minced onion
1 tbsp. flour
3/4 c. vegetable liquid
1/4 c. vinegar
2 tbsp. sugar
1 tsp. salt
1/4 tsp. pepper
2 c. cooked green or waxed beans

Fry bacon until crisp. Cook onion in bacon drippings until yellow. Stir in flour. Add vegetable liquid, vinegar, sugar, salt and pepper; bring to a boil. Stir in beans. Stir gently until heated through. Sprinkle bacon over top before serving. Yield: 4 servings.

Ethelyn Richman, West Noble H.S.
Wawaka, Indiana

BEET AND ONION SALAD

6 med. cooked beets
1 1-in. onion
2 tbsp. sugar
3 tbsp. vinegar

Cut beets into small cubes. Cut onion into thin slices. Mix sugar and vinegar; pour over beets and onion. Mix gently; refrigerate until ready to serve. Yield: 6 servings.

Jessye P. MacKay, Pollock H.S.
Pollock, South Dakota

BEET AND SAUERKRAUT ASPIC

2 env. unflavored gelatin
1 tsp. salt
1/2 tsp. Sucaryl
2 c. chopped cooked beets
1 med. apple, cored peeled and chopped
1 No. 2 can sauerkraut
1 tbsp. horseradish

Soften gelatin in 1/2 cup cold water. Stir into 2 cups hot water until gelatin is dissolved. Add salt and Sucaryl. Cool. Combine with beets, apple, sauerkraut and horseradish. Mix thoroughly. Turn into a mold; chill until firm. Yield: 6 servings.

Mrs. Esther Sigmund, Christen Jr. H.S.
Laredo, Texas

LEMONY BEET SALAD RING

1 qt. canned beets
2 3-oz. packages lemon gelatin
1/3 c. vinegar
1 tsp. grated onion
2 tbsp. grated horseradish
1 c. chopped celery

Drain liquid from beets; add enough water to make 3 cups liquid. Heat; add gelatin. Stir until dissolved; add vinegar, onion and horseradish. Chill until mixture begins to thicken; add diced beets and celery. Pour into 9-inch ring mold or individual molds; refrigerate until firm. Unmold on platter; surround with salad greens. Yield: 8 servings.

Sister Mary Andrew, Flaherty H.S.
Vine Grove, Kentucky

SANDWICH IN-A-BOWL

1 head iceberg lettuce
8 slices sm. bologna
8 slices sm. salami
2 firm ripe tomatoes, quartered
2 hard-cooked eggs, sliced
Creamy Relish Dressing

Core, rinse and thoroughly drain lettuce; refrigerate. Place a slice of bologna on each salami slice; roll up. Cut lettuce lengthwise into halves. Place cut-side

down on board and slice crosswise with thin-bladed knife; place in chilled salad bowl. Arrange tomatoes, eggs and meat rolls on lettuce. Serve with Creamy Relish Dressing. Yield: 4 servings.

Creamy Relish Dressing

1 c. mayonnaise
2 tbsp. chili sauce or catsup
2 tbsp. pickle relish
1 tsp. prepared mustard

Combine mayonnaise with chili sauce, pickle relish and prepared mustard; mix well.

Photograph for this recipe on page 102.

SPECIAL CABBAGE SALAD

2 1/2 c. finely shredded cabbage
1 c. grated carrots
1/2 avocado, thinly sliced
1 tsp. salt
Salad dressing or mayonnaise

Place cabbage, carrots and avocado in a bowl; sprinkle with salt. Moisten with salad dressing; toss lightly with a fork. Serve immediately. Yield: 6 servings.

Mrs. Valentine Dyson, South Cameron H.S.
Creole, Louisiana

HOT COLESLAW WITH CHIVES

3 c. shredded cabbage
1/4 c. chopped chives
3/4 c. freshly made salad dressing

Combine all ingredients in double boiler. Cook just until heated through. Toss lightly; serve at once. Yield: 6 servings.

Lucille E. Johnston, Litchfield Sr. H.S.
Litchfield, Illinois

CABBAGE PATCH COLESLAW

2 c. shredded cabbage
1/2 c. chopped parsley
1/2 c. sliced green onions
2 to 3 tbsp. sugar
3 tbsp. vinegar
2 tbsp. salad oil
1 tsp. salt

Combine vegetables. Blend remaining ingredients, stirring to dissolve sugar. Pour over vegetables; toss. Garnish top with green pepper and onion rings. Yield: 6 servings.

Collen Lenz, Jordan Pub. School
Jordan, Minnesota

Salads

COLESLAW WITH SOUR CREAM DRESSING

3 tbsp. (heaping) sour cream
3/4 c. sugar
3/4 tsp. salt
3 tbsp. vinegar
1/2 c. milk
3 c. shredded cabbage

Combine sour cream, sugar and salt until well blended. Add vinegar; mix well. Stir in milk. Check for seasonings. Refrigerate for a few minutes to thicken. Blend in cabbage. Yield: 5-7 servings.

Mary L. Clark, Van Buren H.S.
Van Buren, Ohio

EVERLASTING SALAD

1 med. cabbage
4 to 6 carrots
6 med. onions
4 red or green sweet peppers
1/4 c. salt
1 tsp. celery seed
1 tsp. white mustard seed
2 c. sugar
2 c. white vinegar

Grind all vegetables in food chopper or blender. Add salt; let stand for 2 hours. Drain well; add celery and mustard seeds, sugar and vinegar. Place in jars; do not cook. May be kept in refrigerator for at least 6 weeks.

Mrs. Laurel Alexander Webb
Valentine Indep. School Dist.
Valentine, Texas

HOT ZIPPY COLESLAW

4 c. finely chopped cabbage
1/3 c. sliced or grated carrot
1/2 tsp. celery seed
1/2 c. salad dressing
1 tsp. dry mustard
1 tsp. horseradish
1 tsp. salt
3 tsp. vinegar
1/4 tsp. paprika
2 tbsp. chopped onions
1 tbsp. milk
1/4 tsp. pepper

Combine cabbage, carrots and celery seed. Combine remaining ingredients in skillet; heat slowly. Pour over cabbage mixture; mix lightly. Yield: 8-10 servings.

Hilda Harmon, Crowley H.S.
Crowley, Louisiana

SKILLET CABBAGE SALAD

4 slices bacon
1/4 c. vinegar
1 tbsp. brown sugar
1 tsp. salt
1 tbsp. finely chopped onion
4 c. shredded cabbage
1/2 c. chopped parsley

Cook bacon until crisp; remove from skillet and crumble. Add vinegar, sugar, salt and onion to bacon drippings in skillet. Add crumbled bacon. Heat thoroughly; remove from heat. Toss cabbage and parsley in hot dressing. Yield: 6 servings.

Mrs. Patricia Bobbitt, Kennedy H.S.
Taylor, Michigan

CRAZY KRAUT SALAD

2 1/2 c. chopped sauerkraut
1 c. chopped green pepper
1 c. chopped celery
1 c. chopped onion
1 sm. can pimento, chopped
1 c. sugar
1/2 c. vinegar

Mix all ingredients in order listed. Chill for several hours or overnight. Yield: 8-10 servings.

Frances Clark, Soper Pub. School
Soper, Oklahoma

OVERNIGHT SAUERKRAUT SALAD

1 1-lb. 4-oz. can sauerkraut
1 c. chopped green pepper
1/4 c. chopped onion
1 c. sugar
Salt and pepper to taste

Combine sauerkraut, green pepper, onion, sugar and seasonings; mix well. Refrigerate for several hours or overnight to blend flavors. Yield: 8 servings.

Ardes Hasleton, Ceres Unified H.S.
Ceres, California

CARROT-PEANUT SALAD

1 lb. fresh carrots, shredded
1 c. salted peanuts
1/2 c. salad dressing

Combine carrots, peanuts and salad dressing; mix well. Yield: 6-8 servings.

Mrs. Gary Wiltse, Power River Co. H.S.
Broadus, Montana

CARROT-RAISIN SALAD

3/4 c. grated carrots
1/4 c. chopped olives or pickles
1/2 c. chopped celery
1/2 c. raisins
Dash of salt

Combine all ingredients lightly; serve on lettuce leaves. Salad dressing may be added to salad or used as a garnish. Yield: 8 servings.

Mrs. Beth Johnson, Winston Churchill H.S.
Lethbridge, Alberta, Canada

TASTY CARROT SALAD

Juice of 1 lemon
1 tbsp. honey
1/8 tsp. salt
1/4 tsp. grated lemon rind
4 carrots, shredded

Combine lemon juice, honey, salt and lemon rind; add carrots. Mix well; chill for at least 1 hour for flavors to blend. A small amount of water may be added to lemon juice if more liquid is needed. Serve on lettuce or salad greens. Yield: 4 servings.

Mrs. Eleanor Morford, Highmore H.S.
Highmore, South Dakota

COTTAGE CHEESE AND CARROTS

1 6-oz. package lime gelatin
1 carton creamed cottage cheese
1/2 c. shredded carrots

Dissolve gelatin in 2 cups boiling water; add 2 cups cold water. Chill for 30 minutes. Add remaining ingredients. Pour into 8 x 10-inch pan. Refrigerate until firm. Cut into 8 squares; place on lettuce leaves to serve. Yield: 8 servings.

Mrs. Cheryl Ory, Covington H.S.
Covington, Louisiana

CARROT-GRAPE SALAD

1 pkg. lemon or lime gelatin
1 1/4 c. grated carrots
Halved green or red seeded grapes

Prepare gelatin according to package directions. Pour into mold. Chill until partially set. Add carrots and grapes. Chill until firm. Unmold on large salad plate. Yield: 6-8 servings.

Sister Carmela Belzile, Van Buren Dist. H.S.
Van Buren, Maine

EASY CARROT-PINEAPPLE SALAD

1 3-oz. package orange gelatin
2 lg. carrots, grated
1 sm. can crushed pineapple

Dissolve gelatin in 1 cup boiling water; add carrots. Add pineapple; mix well. Pour into molds or rectangular dish. Chill until set. Serve on lettuce. Yield: 6-8 servings.

Mrs. Edna Whitley, Laneville H.S.
Laneville, Texas

GREEN AND GOLD MOLD

1 3-oz. box lime gelatin
1 c. grated carrots
1 c. grated Velveeta cheese

Dissolve gelatin in 1 cup boiling water; add 1 cup cold water. Chill until thickened. Add carrots and cheese. Pour into a ring mold. Chill until firm. Unmold; fill center with sour cream or salad dressing. Yield: 8 servings.

Carla Sue Park, Dayton H.S.
Dayton, Texas

CUCUMBER-CABBAGE SALAD

1 sm. cabbage, shredded
1 sm. cucumber, diced
3 tbsp. minced chives or green onion
1 tsp. celery seed
Salt and pepper to taste
2 tbsp. mayonnaise

Combine crisp cabbage with cucumber. Add chives and celery seed. Season with salt and pepper; add mayonnaise to moisten. Yield: 4 servings.

Mrs. Brenda Cook, Silverton H.S.
Silverton, Texas

CUCUMBER-EGG CRISP

6 hard-cooked eggs, diced
1 c. cottage cheese
2 lg. cucumbers, peeled and diced
1 carrot, diced
2 celery sticks, chopped
1/2 tsp. salt
1/4 tsp. pepper

Combine all ingredients; toss lightly. Serve on lettuce leaf; top with favorite salad dressing. Yield: 6-8 servings.

Mrs. Dorothy Burford, Blacksburg H.S.
Blacksburg, Virginia

Salads

SWEDISH PICKLED CUCUMBERS

3 cucumbers, thinly sliced
1 red onion, thinly sliced
1 c. white vinegar
1/4 c. sugar
6 whole allspice
1 tbsp. chopped parsley
Salt and pepper to taste

Place cucumbers and onion in dish. Combine remaining ingredients; pour over cucumbers and onion. Marinate in refrigerator for 24 hours; serve as a relish. Yield: 6 servings.

Florence Hughes, Toaz Jr. H.S.
Huntington, New York

CUCUMBER-CREAM CHEESE SALAD

1 env. unflavored gelatin
2 tbsp. sugar
3/4 tsp. salt
3 to 4 tbsp. lemon juice
6 med. cucumbers, peeled and diced
1 8-oz. package cream cheese
1 c. mayonnaise or dietetic mayonnaise
1/4 c. minced onions

Soften gelatin in 2 tablespoons cold water; blend in sugar, salt and 2/3 cup hot water. Cool; add remaining ingredients. Refrigerate until firm. Yield: 8 servings.

Mrs. Claire H. Shaw, Southern H.S.
Durham, North Carolina

ENGLISH PEA SALAD

1 1/2 c. drained canned sm. English peas
2 hard-cooked eggs, chopped
2 tbsp. chopped pickle
1 pimento, chopped
1 tbsp. minced onion
1/2 c. chopped celery
1/4 tsp. salt
Low-calorie salad dressing

Combine all ingredients except dressing. Moisten with dressing; serve on lettuce. Yield: 6 servings.

Mrs. Ava Bush, Grapeland H.S.
Grapeland, Texas

MOLDED PARTY CAULIFLOWER

1 sm. cauliflower
2 pimentos, chopped
1 tbsp. grated onion
2 tbsp. green pepper, chopped
1/2 tsp. salt
1/4 c. vinegar
1 6-oz. package lemon gelatin

Break cauliflower into small flowerets; steam until tender. Combine cauliflower, pimentos, onion and green pepper; add salt and vinegar. Marinate for 15 minutes. Dissolve gelatin in 1 1/2 cups boiling water; chill until slightly thickened. Fold vegetables into gelatin; pour into mold. Chill until firm. Yield: 8 servings.

Sandra Hanson, Bell H.S.
Bell, Florida

FAVORITE POTATO SALAD

2 c. cooked or canned diced potatoes
2 hard-cooked eggs, chopped
1 sm. onion, chopped
1/3 c. chopped dill pickles
1 tsp. celery seed
1 tbsp. vinegar
1 tsp. sugar
Salt and pepper to taste
1/4 c. mayonnaise

Combine all ingredients; toss lightly to mix. Garnish as desired. Yield: 4-6 servings.

Mrs. Don McMahen, Emerson H.S.
Emerson, Arkansas

GERMAN POTATO SALAD

6 slices bacon
1/4 c. frozen minced onion
1 1/2 tsp. flour
1 tbsp. sugar
1 tsp. salt
1/4 tsp. pepper
1/4 c. vinegar
1 tsp. celery seed
2 1-lb. cans sliced white potatoes, drained
1/2 c. sliced radishes

Fry bacon until crisp; add onion to drippings. Saute until tender but not brown. Crumble bacon; add to onion. Mix flour, sugar, salt and pepper; add vinegar and 1/2 cup water, stirring until smooth. Add flour mixture to bacon mixture; simmer, stirring constantly, until thickened. Add celery seed; pour hot dressing over potatoes. Add radishes; toss. Yield: 6 servings.

Mrs. Edna Eisenhart, Bristol Jr.-Sr. H.S.
Briston, Pennsylvania

UNUSUAL TOMATO ASPIC SALAD

1 4-oz. can tomato sauce
1 3-oz. package strawberry gelatin

1/4 tsp. salt
1 tsp. grated onion
3/4 c. shredded carrots
1/2 c. diced celery
1/4 c. chopped nuts (opt.)

Combine tomato sauce and 1 1/2 sauce cans water in saucepan; heat. Add gelatin; stir until dissolved. Add salt and onion; chill until partially congealed. Add remaining ingredients; place in desired mold. Chill until set. Yield: 8 servings.

Mrs. Esther Green, Herbert Hoover Jr. H.S.
Oklahoma City, Oklahoma

BASIC TOMATO ASPIC

2 env. unflavored gelatin
2 c. tomato juice
1 tsp. salt
1 tsp. confectioners' sugar
Dash of cayenne pepper
Dash of celery salt
1 bay leaf
1 sm. onion, cut up
Celery leaves
1 tbsp. lemon juice

Soften gelatin in 1/2 cup cold water. Combine remaining ingredients except lemon juice; simmer for 15 minutes. Strain; add softened gelatin and lemon juice, stirring until dissolved. Cool; pour into 6 to 8 individual molds. Chill until firm; unmold on salad greens. Serve with mayonnaise, if desired. Yield: 6-8 servings.

Mrs. Grace Pylman, Grant-Deuel Indep. H.S.
Revillo, South Dakota

GOURMET TOSSED GREEN SALAD

1 med. head lettuce
1 sm. cauliflower
1 sm. sweet onion
1 med. green pepper, diced
1 pimento, diced
6 lg. fresh mushrooms, sliced
1/2 c. Roquefort cheese, crumbled
Low-Calorie French dressing

Tear lettuce into bite-sized pieces. Wash cauliflower; remove green stalks. Separate into small flowerets. Cut onion in paper-thin rings. Toss gently with green pepper, pimento, mushrooms and cheese. Chill for about 1 hour. Toss and serve immediately with low-calorie French dressing.

Sue Chaffin, Ithaca H.S.
Ithaca, Michigan

VEGETABLES MOLDED IN CHICKEN ASPIC

1 env. unflavored gelatin
1/2 c. cold chicken broth
1 1/2 c. hot chicken broth
1/2 tsp. salt
1/2 c. cooked peas, drained
1/2 c. cooked diced carrots, drained
1/2 c. diced celery
1/4 c. diced green pepper

Sprinkle gelatin on 1/2 cup cold broth to soften. Add hot broth and salt; stir until gelatin is thoroughly dissolved. Chill to unbeaten egg white consistency. Fold in vegetables. Turn into a 3-cup mold or individual molds. Chill until firm. Yield: 4 servings.

Mrs. Trudy Fulmer, Springfield H.S.
Springfield, South Carolina

DEVILED EGG MOLD

1 env. unflavored gelatin
1 tsp. salt
2 tbsp. lemon juice
1/4 tsp. Worcestershire sauce
1/8 tsp. cayenne pepper
3/4 c. mayonnaise
1 1/2 tsp. grated onion
1/2 c. finely diced celery
1/4 c. finely diced green pepper
1/4 c. chopped pimento
4 hard-cooked eggs, chopped

Sprinkle gelatin on 1/2 cup water to soften. Place over low heat; stir until gelatin is dissolved. Remove from heat; add salt, lemon juice, Worcestershire sauce and cayenne pepper. Cool. Stir in mayonnaise. Fold in remaining ingredients. Turn into a 3-cup mold or individual molds; chill until firm. Yield: 6 servings.

Mrs. Martha B. Wheeler, Le Roy H.S.
Le Roy, Kansas

SOUTHERN BUTTERMILK DRESSING

1 c. buttermilk
1/2 tsp. onion juice
3/4 tsp. salt
1 1/2 tbsp. lemon juice

Combine all ingredients in jar with tightfitting lid; shake vigorously to blend. Store in refrigerator; shake before using. Yield: 4-5 servings.

Mrs. Rose Evelyn H. Butler, A. L. Corbett H.S.
Wagener, South Carolina

Salads

COOKED CELERY SEED DRESSING FOR COLESLAW

2 tbsp. cornstarch
1/2 c. vinegar
1/2 tsp. dry mustard
1 tsp. paprika
1 tsp. celery seed
1/2 tsp. garlic salt
1/4 tsp. salt

Add 1 1/4 cups water slowly to cornstarch; blend until smooth. Cook over low heat until thickened, stirring constantly. Add remaining ingredients; beat well with rotary beater. Refrigerate in jar with tight-fitting cover. Shake well before using. Yield: 2 cups.

Mrs. Beverly Sampson, Redfield H.S.
Redfield, South Dakota

GARLIC-BLEU CHEESE SALAD DRESSING

1/2 tsp. dehydrated minced garlic
1 pt. cottage cheese
2 to 3 oz. bleu cheese
1/4 c. lemon juice
1 tsp. salt
1 c. mayonnaise

Soak garlic in 1 teaspoon water. Place cottage cheese, bleu cheese, lemon juice, salt and garlic in small mixing bowl; beat until smooth and creamy. Fold in mayonnaise. Refrigerate. Dressing will not keep over 2 weeks. Yield: 3 cups dressing.

Mrs. Bernice Van Woudenburg, Ferndale H.S.
Ferndale, Washington

COTTAGE CHEESE DRESSING

1 1/2 c. cottage cheese
2 tbsp. catsup
2 tbsp. chopped onion
1/4 c. chopped green pepper
1/2 tsp. salt
1/2 can tomato soup

Whip or blend cottage cheese until smooth. Add remaining ingredients; blend together. Yield: 6 servings.

Mrs. Norma M. Womble, Broadway School
Broadway, North Carolina

ROQUEFORT DRESSING

8 oz. cottage cheese
4 oz. Roquefort cheese

1 tbsp. lemon juice
3 dashes of Tabasco sauce
3 dashes of Worcestershire sauce
1 tsp. salt
Skim milk

Place all ingredients except milk in blender container. Blend on low speed until smooth. Thin to desired consistency with skim milk. Store in covered container in refrigerator.

Mrs. Doris C. Beck, Thomas Jefferson Jr. H.S.
Edison, New Jersey

PINEAPPLE JUICE DRESSING

1/2 c. pineapple juice
3 tbsp. lemon juice
1/2 c. sugar
1 1/2 tbsp. flour
2 eggs, beaten

Combine all ingredients and 1/4 cup water in top of double boiler. Cook, stirring with wooden spoon until slightly thickened. Cool and serve. Yield: 4-6 servings.

Mrs. Ialeen S. Mode, Franklinton H.S.
Franklinton, North Carolina

CHEF'S DRESSING

1/3 c. tomato sauce
1/3 c. salad oil
1/4 c. vinegar
1 tsp. salt
1/4 tsp. pepper
1/2 tsp. oregano
1/2 tsp. mustard
1/4 tsp. soy sauce

Combine all ingredients in jar with tightfitting lid. Shake well. Yield: 1 cup.

Mrs. Clyda Phillips, Star City H.S.
Star City, Arkansas

WESTERN FRENCH DRESSING

1 can tomato soup
2 tbsp. vinegar
2 tbsp. Worcestershire sauce
Juice of 1/2 lemon
Salt and pepper to taste
1 clove of garlic

Combine all ingredients. Let stand for several hours to improve flavor. Shake well before using. Yield: 8-10 servings.

Gloriann M. Katabi, Watsonville H.S.
Watsonville, California

ONION FRENCH DRESSING

1 tbsp. salt
1/2 c. sugar
1 1/2 tsp. pepper
1 tsp. dry mustard
1/2 c. vinegar
1 med. onion, chopped
1/2 c. catsup
1 c. salad oil

Combine all ingredients in blender container; blend until smooth. Dressing may also be made by combining salt, sugar, pepper and mustard. Then dissolve dry ingredients in vinegar. Chop or shred onion and add to vinegar mixture. Add catsup and salad oil. Beat by hand or shake vigorously in a bottle. Yield: 1 1/2 pints.

Renee Porter, American Fork H.S.
American Fork, Utah

PIQUANT DRESSING

1 can tomato soup
1 c. tarragon vinegar
2 tsp. salt
1/2 tsp. paprika
1 tbsp. Worcestershire sauce
1/2 c. salad oil
1/4 c. sugar
1/2 tsp. pepper
1 tsp. dry mustard
1 clove of garlic
1 sm. onion, grated
3 tbsp. horseradish

Place all ingredients in blender container; blend for 2 minutes. Refrigerate. Yield: 3 cups dressing.

Mrs. Dorothy Zimmerman, Canby Pub. H.S.
Canby, Minnesota

SMOOTH POPPY SEED DRESSING

1/2 c. sugar
1/2 tsp. salt
1 tbsp. dry mustard
1 tbsp. paprika
1 tsp. poppy seed
1/4 c. vinegar
2 tsp. grated onion
1 c. salad oil
Lettuce wedges

Combine first 7 ingredients in mixer bowl; mix well. Add salad oil in thirds, beating well after each addition. Serve on lettuce wedges, if desired. Dressing will keep for several weeks in refrigerator.

Alberta Ball Bickerdike, East Pike School
Milton, Illinois

HOMEMADE MAYONNAISE

1 egg yolk
1 tsp. (scant) vinegar or lemon juice
1/2 tsp. salt
1 tsp. dry mustard or ginger
Dash of freshly ground pepper
1/8 tsp. paprika
1/8 tsp. basil or tarragon
1 c. soy oil, olive oil or half of each

Combine all ingredients except oil in blender container; mix until well blended. Add oil slowly until just mixed. Refrigerate. Mayonnaise may also be made by the mixer method. Combine egg yolk, half the vinegar and seasonings in a mixer bowl. Add oil, drop by drop, then in increasing stream; beat as mixture thickens. Add remaining vinegar; beat slightly.

Pearl Anthony, Fallsburg Cen. School
Fallsburg, New York

SLIM JIM THOUSAND ISLAND DRESSING

1 c. sour cream
1/4 tsp. (or more) salt
1/4 c. chili sauce
1/4 c. drained pickle relish or 1 med.
    pickle, chopped
1 tbsp. minced green onion
2 hard-cooked eggs, finely chopped
1 tbsp. chopped pimento
Lemon juice to taste

Combine all ingredients lightly; chill thoroughly. Yield: 1 3/4 cups dressing.

Mrs. Irene Kathy Lee, Washington H.S.
El Dorado, Arkansas

SLIM JIM HOLLANDAISE SAUCE

1 c. (scant) cottage cheese
1/4 c. lemon juice
1/2 tsp. seasoned salt
1/2 tsp. salt
Dash of pepper and cayenne pepper
2 egg yolks

Combine cottage cheese and lemon juice in electric blender container; blend until smooth and creamy. Remove from blender to double boiler. Add seasonings; stir in egg yolks, blending thoroughly. Cook, stirring constantly with wire whisk, over hot, not boiling water, until thick. Yield: 1 1/4 cups sauce.

Mrs. Elane McCarriar, Hayti H.S.
Hayti, South Dakota

Desserts & Beverages

For special occasions or for no occasion at all, desserts are almost always a must on the menu plan. There is just no substitute for ending the perfect meal with a perfect dessert. Even when time is short, there is no reason to skip the dessert or the meal just won't seem complete. Satisfying everyone's sweet tooth doesn't have to be time-consuming, either, because there are a wealth of easy-to-prepare desserts that are right for any meal. Beverages, too, are an important part of an interesting, well-rounded meal plan. And, you don't have to feel like you are serving your family empty and needless calories when you serve them desserts and beverages, because both foods are an excellent way to include dairy products, fruit and fruit juices, nuts, eggs, and gelatin in the family's diet.

The hardest thing about serving dessert is deciding which one to serve — there is such a choice! But, when preparing a quick dessert, don't overlook all the fancy and taste-tempting things you can do with garnishes — a sprinkling of nuts here, a cherry there, chocolate curls, a dollop of whipped cream, or a dash of toasted coconut all serve to dress up what might be otherwise be a plain piece of cake or scoop of ice cream. Special beverages can be as quick as they are refreshing. Try adding a scoop of chocolate or vanilla ice cream to iced coffee, or shake iced tea and fruit juice together with slices of lemon, orange, and apple.

Home-tested, company-perfect desserts and beverages are proven favorites. Home Economics Teachers have found that these are the foods that bring out the creativity in the cook and the compliments from the diners, and you will find that the following quick and easy recipes will do the same for you, anytime.

Desserts

ANGEL FOOD DESSERT

1 angel food cake mix
1 pt. frozen strawberries, thawed
1 pt. Cool Whip

Prepare cake mix according to package directions. Bake in tube pan. Cool cake thoroughly. Cut with long sharp knife into 3 layers. Reserve 6 to 8 strawberries for garnish. Spoon 1/3 of the strawberries and juice on bottom layer. Spread 1/3 of the Cool Whip over strawberries. Repeat with middle and top layers. Decorate with reserved strawberries. Refrigerate until ready to use. Yield: 6-8 servings.

Parma Bottls, Yancey School
Yancey, Texas

APPLESAUCE CAKE WITH BROILED TOPPING

2 1/2 c. sifted all-purpose flour
1 2/3 c. sugar
1/4 tsp. baking powder
1 1/2 tsp. soda
1 tsp. cinnamon
1/2 tsp. nutmeg
1/8 tsp. ground cloves
Salt
1/2 c. soft shortening
2 eggs
1 1/2 c. applesauce
1 tsp. vanilla extract
2/3 c. (packed) brown sugar
1/4 c. melted butter
2 tbsp. milk
1 c. shredded coconut

Sift dry ingredients with 1/2 teaspoon salt into large bowl. Add shortening, eggs and about half the applesauce; beat for about 2 minutes or until smooth. Add remaining applesauce, 1/4 cup water and vanilla; beat for about 1 minute longer. Spread in a greased 13 x 9 x 2-inch pan. Bake in a preheated 375-degree oven for 40 to 45 minutes. Combine brown sugar, melted butter, 1/8 teaspoon salt, milk and shredded coconut. Spread over top of hot cake; place under broiler for several minutes until lightly browned. Yield: 18 servings.

Mrs. Marshall King, Gates H.S.
Gatesville, Texas

APRICOT DELIGHT CAKE

1 box yellow cake mix
1 c. apricot nectar
4 eggs
1/4 c. lemon juice
1/4 c. melted shortening

Combine cake mix, apricot nectar, eggs and lemon juice; beat until smooth. Blend in shortening. Pour into tube cake pan. Bake in a preheated 350-degree oven for 1 hour and 10 minutes.

Glaze

1 c. powdered sugar
Juice of 1 lemon

Combine sugar and lemon juice; mix until smooth. Pour glaze over cake while still hot.

Katherine Witty, Medina Valley H.S.
Castroville, Texas

BUTTER CAKE

1 c. butter
2 c. flour
1 c. sugar
1 egg, lightly beaten

Soften butter to room temperature. Mix in flour, sugar and egg, reserving part of egg to glaze top of cake before baking. Pat dough into a round cake pan. Brush with reserved egg. Bake in preheated 375-degree oven for 30 minutes. Serve warm. Yield: 6 servings.

Mrs. O. L. Villarreal, United H.S.
Laredo, Texas

CAKE WITH FUDGE SAUCE

1 6-oz. package chocolate chips
1 1/2 c. Bisquick
1/2 c. sugar
1/2 c. milk
1/2 c. chopped nuts
1/2 c. (packed) brown sugar

Pour 1 1/2 cups boiling water over chocolate chips; let stand until chocolate is melted. Combine Bisquick, sugar, milk and nuts; mix well. Turn into greased 8 x 8-inch pan. Sprinkle with brown sugar. Pour melted chocolate mixture over batter. Bake in preheated 350-degree oven for 40 to 45 minutes. Serve warm. Sauce will be on bottom. Ice cream or whipped cream may be used as a topping.

Mrs. Charles Corlew, Greenwood Jr. H.S.
Clarksville, Tennessee

CHOCOLATE PUDDING CAKE

1 pkg. white cake mix
1 pkg. instant chocolate pudding
2 c. milk

3 egg whites
3/4 c. chopped walnuts
3/4 c. chocolate chips

Combine cake mix, pudding mix, milk and egg whites; beat for about 4 minutes. Turn into cake pan; sprinkle walnuts and chocolate chips over batter. Bake according to cake mix directions.

Carolyn Rude, Oltman Jr. H.S.
St. Paul Park, Minnesota

CHOCOLATE SNACKING CAKE

1 1/2 c. sugar
2 1/2 c. flour
1/2 c. butter
1 1/2 c. buttermilk
2 eggs, beaten
2 sq. melted chocolate or 1/2 c. cocoa
1 tsp. vanilla extract
1 tsp. soda

Combine sugar and flour; cut in butter until crumbly. Add buttermilk gradually. Blend in eggs, melted chocolate, vanilla and soda. Pour into sheet cake pan. Bake in preheated 350-degree oven until center springs back at touch. Yield: 16 servings.

Mrs. E. G. Bryant, Cosby H.S.
Cosby, Tennessee

FREEZER FUDGE CAKE

1 box yellow cake mix
1 c. chopped nuts
1/4 c. cocoa
1 c. (packed) brown sugar

Prepare cake mix according to package directions; fold in nuts. Pour batter into 13 x 9 x 2-inch baking pan. Wrap and freeze. Combine 1 3/4 cups boiling water, cocoa and brown sugar; pour over frozen cake in pan. Bake in preheated 350-degree oven for 1 hour. Yield: 10-16 servings.

Lynda C. Carlton, Arvin Sr. H.S.
Arvin, California

HEAVENLY HASH CAKE

4 eggs
2 c. sugar
1 c. melted margarine
1 1/2 c. self-rising flour
1/4 c. cocoa
2 tsp. vanilla extract
2 c. chopped pecans
18 lg. marshmallows, halved

Beat eggs slightly; stir in sugar and margarine. Blend flour and cocoa together; stir into egg mixture. Add vanilla and pecans. Turn into greased and floured 13 x 9 x 2-inch pan. Bake in preheated 325-degree oven for 35 minutes. Remove from oven; cover with marshmallows, placing cut side down.

Cocoa Icing

1 lb. confectioners' sugar
1/4 c. melted margarine
1/2 c. canned or thin cream
1/4 c. cocoa

Combine all ingredients; mix thoroughly. Spread over marshmallows.

Mrs. Wilma Tucker, Marion H.S.
Marion, Louisiana

MINT BONBON CAKES

1 pkg. devil's food cake mix
Vanilla or chocolate ice cream
Creme de menthe

Prepare cake mix according to package directions. Bake in muffin tins. Cool; cut out centers. Fill with vanilla ice cream. Pour 1 tablespoon creme de menthe over each one. Serve immediately.

Mrs. Virginia E. McEwen, Coosa Co. H.S.
Rockford, Alabama

QUICK CHOCOLATE CAKE

1 tsp. salt
2 c. flour, sifted
1 tsp. soda
2 c. sugar
1/2 c. butter
4 sq. chocolate
2 eggs
1/2 c. sour milk
1 tsp. vanilla extract

Sift salt, flour, soda and sugar together into a bowl. Melt butter and chocolate in 1 cup boiling water; stir chocolate mixture into flour mixture. Beat in eggs. Add sour milk and vanilla; pour into 2 greased and floured 8-inch square pans. Bake in preheated 400-degree oven for 30 to 35 minutes. Yield: 9 servings.

Mrs. Olive Weidman
Conrad Weiser Area Schools
Robesonia, Pennsylvania

Desserts

QUICK LUNCHBOX CAKE

2 1/4 c. flour
2 tsp. soda
1/2 tsp. salt
1 c. (packed) brown sugar
2 eggs
1/4 c. soft butter
1 1-lb. can fruit cocktail
1/2 c. semisweet chocolate pieces
1/2 c. chopped nuts

Combine all ingredients except chocolate and nuts in large mixing bowl. Blend well on lowest mixer speed; increase to medium speed for about 2 minutes. Pour batter into greased and floured 13 x 9-inch pan. Sprinkle with chocolate pieces and nuts. Bake in preheated 350-degree oven for 30 to 35 minutes.

Mildred Gates, Claude H.S.
Claude, Texas

WHACKY CAKE

2 1/4 c. flour
1 1/2 c. sugar
4 1/2 tbsp. cocoa
1 1/2 tsp. soda
3/4 tsp. salt
1 1/2 tsp. vinegar
1 1/2 tsp. vanilla extract
1/2 c. plus 1 tsp. Wesson oil or
   melted shortening

Sift all dry ingredients into oblong 9 x 13-inch pan. Scoop out 3 holes in mixture; add vinegar to one hole, vanilla to second hole and oil in third hole. Pour 1 1/2 cups cold water over mixture. Stir with spoon until smooth. Bake in preheated 325-degree oven for 30 to 35 minutes.

Mrs. Rita Clark, Central Jr. H.S.
Olathe, Kansas

CHRISTMAS CAKE

2 c. raisins
3 tsp. cinnamon
1 tsp. cloves or 1/2 tsp. nutmeg
2 c. sugar
1 c. butter or margarine
4 c. sifted flour
1 tsp. salt
1 1/2 tsp. soda

Combine first 5 ingredients and 2 cups water in saucepan; bring to a boil. Simmer for about 15 minutes. Cool thoroughly. Add remaining ingredients. Turn into 2 small well-greased loaf or tube pans.

Bake in preheated 325-degree oven for 1 hour. Cool completely. Store in tightly covered container.

Ruth Smith, Buckley Comm. School
Buckley, Michigan

NINE-MINUTE FRUITCAKE

2 1/2 c. sifted all-purpose flour
1 tsp. soda
2 eggs, slightly beaten
2 2/3 c. mincemeat
1 15-oz. can sweetened condensed milk
1 c. coarsely chopped walnuts
2 c. mixed candied fruits and peels

Grease 9-inch tube pan. Line with waxed paper. Grease liner. Sift flour and soda together. Combine eggs, mincemeat, milk, walnuts and fruits in large mixing bowl; fold in flour mixture. Pour batter into pan. Bake in preheated 300-degree oven for about 2 hours or until cake center springs back when lightly touched with finger and top is golden. Cool cake slightly before turning out of pan and removing waxed paper. Cake top may be brushed lightly with heated corn syrup and decorated with glace cherries, candied pineapple slices and walnut halves. Yield: One 9-inch tube cake.

Elizabeth M. Turner, Algood Jr. H.S.
Algood, Tennessee

FRUIT COCKTAIL CAKE

2 1/2 c. sugar
2 c. self-rising flour
Pinch of soda
1 No. 303 can fruit cocktail
2 lg. eggs
1/2 c. (packed) light brown sugar
1 can coconut
1 c. chopped pecans
1 c. evaporated milk
1/2 c. margarine
1 tsp. vanilla extract

Sift 1 cup sugar, flour and soda into mixing bowl. Add fruit cocktail and juice. Add eggs; beat until mixed well. Pour into greased 15 1/2 x 10 1/2-inch pan. Sprinkle top with brown sugar, coconut and pecans. Bake in preheated 350-degree oven for 25 to 30 minutes. Combine remaining sugar with remaining ingredients; boil for 5 minutes. Pour over cake as soon as cake is removed from oven. Yield: 8-10 servings.

Laura Parker, Sand Rock H.S.
Leesburg, Alabama

Recipe on page 175.

DELUXE GINGERBREAD

1 pkg. gingerbread mix
1 tbsp. cornstarch
3/4 c. sugar or 2 tsp. Sucaryl solution
Grated rind and juice of 1 lemon
2 tbsp. butter
1 3-oz. package cream cheese

Prepare gingerbread mix according to package directions. Bake in rectangular pan. Prepare sauce while
gingerbread is baking. Combine cornstarch, sugar and
1 cup water; cook over medium heat, stirring constantly, until thickened. Remove from heat; blend in
lemon rind, juice and butter. Cool gingerbread for 10
minutes; spread with cream cheese. Cut into serving
pieces; top with sauce.

Mrs. Ruth Yelvington, Mildred H.S.
Corsicana, Texas

GINGERBREAD CRUNCH

2 tbsp. butter
2 tbsp. flour
2 to 4 tbsp. brown sugar
1 tsp. cinnamon
1/2 c. chopped nuts
1 pkg. of gingerbread mix

Combine first 4 ingredients by cutting together as
for pie crust; add nuts. Prepare gingerbread according to package directions. Remove from oven 5 minutes before done; sprinkle with nut mixture. Return
to oven; bake remaining 5 minutes. May be served
with whipped topping flavored with cinnamon.
Yield: 9 servings.

Mrs. E. E. Tuft, Stillwater Jr. H.S.
Stillwater, Minnesota

MOLASSES GINGERBREAD AND WHIPPED SAUCE

2 1/3 c. flour, sifted
1/2 tsp. salt
1/4 c. sugar
2 tsp. ginger
1/2 tsp. cinnamon
1 3/4 tsp. soda
3/4 c. molasses
1 c. sour milk
1/4 c. melted butter

Sift flour, salt, sugar, spices and soda together. Combine molasses, sour milk and melted butter. Stir in

Recipe on pages 14, 176, 186.

dry ingredients. Spread in 11 x 7 1/2-inch pan. Bake
in preheated 350-degree oven for 35 minutes.

Whipped Sauce

1 1/2 tbsp. lemon juice
3/4 c. milk powder
2 tbsp. sugar

Add lemon juice to 1/2 cup ice water and milk pow-
der. Beat well; chill for several minutes in freezer.
Beat again, adding sugar. Serve over gingerbread.
Yield: 24 servings.

Helen M. Campbell
Esquimalt Jr. Secondary School
Victoria, British Columbia, Canada

LEMON-ORANGE CAKE

1 box lemon supreme cake mix
1 pkg. vanilla instant pudding mix
1/2 c. salad oil
4 eggs
1/3 c. orange juice
2 tbsp. melted butter
3 c. confectioners' sugar

Combine first 4 ingredients in large mixing bowl; add
1 cup water. Blend, then beat for 4 minutes at medium speed. Turn into greased bundt pan. Bake in
preheated 350-degree oven about 40 minutes or until
cake tests done. Combine remaining ingredients for
glaze. Punch holes in top of cake with fork while
hot; pour glaze over top. Yield: 20 servings.

Mrs. Cleo Ripley, Huguenot H.S.
Richmond, Virginia

LEMON-COCONUT CAKE

1 box lemon cake mix
1 3-oz. can Angel Flake coconut
2 c. sugar
1 c. milk

Prepare cake mix according to package directions;
pour into 13 x 9 x 2-inch pan. Bake as directed.
Remove from oven; sprinkle with coconut while
warm. Bring sugar and milk to a boil, stirring constantly. Cook for 1 minute. Remove from heat;
spoon over warm cake. Yield: 12-15 servings.

Marie S. Welch, Lookout Jr. H.S.
Chattanooga, Tennessee

Desserts

LEMON SUPREME CAKE

1 pkg. lemon cake mix
1 c. apricot nectar
3/4 c. salad oil
1/2 c. sugar (opt.)
4 eggs
1 c. powdered sugar
Juice of 1 lemon

Combine cake mix, nectar, salad oil and sugar; mix well. Add eggs, one at a time, beating well after each addition. Turn into greased tube pan. Bake in preheated 325-degree oven for 1 hour. Do not open door of oven during baking time. Combine powdered sugar and lemon juice. Spread over warm cake.

Mrs. Mary Ada Parks, Anna-Jonesboro H.S.
Anna, Illinois

LEMON-APRICOT CAKE

1 angel food cake mix
1 pkg. lemon meringue pie filling mix
1/2 c. apricot marmalade
1/8 tsp. orange extract
1 pt. whipping cream, whipped

Bake angel food cake according to package directions. Cool. Cut cake into 3 equal layers. Prepare lemon pie filling according to package directions. Mix marmalade with filling; add extract while pudding is still warm. Chill. Spread between layers of cake. Ice with whipped cream. Yield: 10-12 servings.

Mrs. Anne D. Johnson, Bethel Park H.S.
Bethel Park, Pennsylvania

SOUR CREAM-LEMON CAKE

1 pkg. yellow cake mix
3/4 c. cooking oil
4 eggs
1 c. sour cream
1 pkg. instant lemon pudding mix
1/3 c. cinnamon-sugar mixture
1/3 c. chopped pecans

Combine first 5 ingredients. Beat for 2 minutes at medium speed. Pour half the batter into greased 10-inch tube pan. Sprinkle with half the cinnamon-sugar mixture and half the pecans. Add remaining batter. Sprinkle with remaining cinnamon-sugar mixture and pecans. Bake in preheated 350-degree oven for 50 to 55 minutes or until cake tests done.

Mrs. Joanie Stevenson, Oak Park Jr. H.S.
Lake Charles, Louisiana

MOCHA LAYER CAKE

1 angel food cake
1/2 lb. marshmallows
1/2 c. strong coffee
1 pt. whipping cream, whipped
Toasted slivered almonds or coconut

Split cake to make 4 layers. Melt marshmallows and coffee together; cool slightly. Fold mixture into 1 cup whipped cream. Spread between cake layers. Sweeten remaining cream; cover entire cake. Sprinkle with toasted slivered almonds or coconut. Yield: 10 servings.

Mrs. M. A. Ziegler, Lancaster H.S.
Lancaster, Minnesota

NO-FLOUR DATE CAKE

2 cans coconut
2 cans sweetened condensed milk
2 8-oz. boxes chopped dates
2 c. chopped pecans

Combine all ingredients; mix well. Batter will be thick and hard to stir. Spread in square cake pan. Bake in preheated 350-degree oven for about 1 hour.

Mrs. Mary Nell McAdams, Rosedale H.S.
Rosedale, Mississippi

EASY POPPY SEED CAKE

1 pkg. yellow cake mix
1/2 c. salad oil
1 pkg. instant banana pudding
4 eggs
1/4 c. poppy seeds
Powdered sugar

Blend cake mix, 1 cup hot water, salad oil and pudding together. Add eggs, one at a time, beating with electric mixer set at medium speed for 1 minute after each addition. Add poppy seeds; beat 1 minute longer. Pour into greased and floured bundt pan or angel food cake pan. Bake in preheated 350-degree oven for 45 to 55 minutes. Let stand in pan for 10 minutes. Turn out on cake rack; sprinkle top with powdered sugar. Yield: 12-16 servings.

Mrs. Helen Mason, Cascade H.S.
Clayton, Indiana

SOUTHERN-STYLE CRUMB CAKE

1/2 c. butter or margarine
2 c. self-rising flour
1 c. sugar

1 tsp. cinnamon
1 tsp. cloves
1 egg
1 c. milk
1 tsp. soda
1 tsp. vanilla extract

Cut butter into flour and sugar until crumbly. Remove 1/2 cup of the mixture; set aside for topping. Add remaining ingredients to remaining flour mixture; beat until smooth. Pour batter into greased 9 x 12-inch pan; sprinkle remaining topping over batter. Bake in preheated 350-degree oven for 30 to 35 minutes. Yield: 8 servings.

Verdonna Timmons, Minford H.S.
Minford, Ohio

QUICK TOMATO SPICE CAKE

1 pkg. spice cake mix
1   10 3/4-oz. can condensed tomato soup
2 eggs
1 c. chopped walnuts

Combine all ingredients except walnuts with 1/2 cup water, according to package directions. Fold in walnuts. Bake according to package directions. Frost with favorite white frosting.

Photograph for this recipe on page 130.

SPICY RHUBARB CAKE

1 pkg. spice cake mix
1 1/2 c. sugar
3 c. chopped rhubarb

Prepare cake mix according to package directions, then mix in sugar and rhubarb. Turn into greased 13 x 9 x 2 1/2-inch pan. Bake in preheated 350-degree oven for 30 to 35 minutes. Yield: 12-15 servings.

Mrs. Elaine Gutzmer, Anita H.S.
Anita, Iowa

ANGEL RASPBERRY ROLL

1 pkg. angel food cake mix
2 tbsp. confectioners' sugar
1 pkg. dessert topping mix
1 pt. raspberries

Prepare cake mix according to package directions; spread half in a 15 1/2 x 10 1/2 x 1-inch pan. Bake and cool. Remove cooled cake from pan; roll up in a towel dusted with confectioners' sugar. Prepare dessert topping mix according to package directions. Beat in 1/2 cup raspberries while whipping. Unroll

cake; spread with filling, reserving 1/2 cup for garnish. Roll as for jelly roll. Wrap well in foil; store in refrigerator for 1 hour before serving. Arrange on a serving plate; sift confectioners' sugar over top. Garnish platter with fluffs of remaining filling and remaining raspberries. Use remaining cake batter as desired. Yield: 12 servings.

Ann Watts, Adrian H.S.
Adrian, Oregan

BASIC JELLY ROLL

2 eggs
3/4 c. plus 2 tbsp. sugar
Grated rind of 1 lemon
1 c. flour
1 1/2 tsp. baking powder
1/4 tsp. salt
3 tbsp. milk
Jelly
Confectioners' sugar

Beat eggs until light; add sugar gradually, beating until thick and smooth. Add lemon rind. Sift flour with baking powder and salt; add alternately with milk to egg mixture. Pour into shallow 14 x 10-inch pan lined with waxed paper. Bake in preheated 350-degree oven for 15 to 20 minutes. Turn out onto damp cloth. Spread with jelly; roll up. Wrap in waxed paper; cool. Sprinkle with confectioners' sugar just before serving. Yield: 6-8 servings.

Mrs. Choyce K. Scott, Benton H.S.
Benton, Mississippi

STRAWBERRY SHEET CAKE

1 box white cake mix
1   10-oz. box frozen strawberries, thawed
3/4 c. Wesson oil
4 eggs
1 sm. package strawberry gelatin
1 box confectioners' sugar
1/2 c. margarine

Place cake mix in large mixing bowl. Measure 1/2 cup strawberries; add enough water to measure 1 cup. Add to cake mix. Add oil; mix well. Add eggs, one at a time, beating well after each addition. Add gelatin; beat well. Pour into greased and floured 8 x 12-inch pan. Bake in preheated 350-degree oven until top springs back when lightly touched. Mix confectioners' sugar, margarine and remaining strawberries in mixing bowl until well blended. Spread over warm cake. Yield: 20 servings.

Mrs. Joann Sanders, Spearsville H.S.
Spearsville, Louisiana

Desserts

WINE CAKE

1 pkg. yellow cake mix
1 pkg. instant vanilla pudding mix
4 eggs
3/4 c. cooking oil
3/4 c. Sherry
1 tsp. nutmeg
Powdered sugar

Combine all ingredients except powdered sugar in large mixing bowl. Beat with electric mixer for 5 minutes at medium speed. Pour batter into greased angel food cake pan. Bake in preheated 350-degree oven about 45 minutes or until cake tests done. Cool in pan for 5 minutes before turning out on rack to cool. Sprinkle with sifted powdered sugar. Yield: 8-10 servings.

Mrs. June Letcher, Mount Shasta H.S.
Mount Shasta, California

COCONUT-APRICOT UPSIDE-DOWN CAKE

1 1-lb. 6-oz. can apricot pie filling
1 · 1-layer pkg. white cake mix
1 egg
1/2 c. flaked coconut
1/2 c. chopped pecans
1/2 c. melted butter

Spread pie filling on bottom of 9 x 9 x 2-inch baking dish. Combine cake mix, 1/3 cup water and egg. Beat with electric mixer for 4 minutes on medium speed. Pour over pie filling; sprinkle with coconut and pecans. Drizzle melted butter over top. Bake in preheated 350-degree oven for 40 minutes. Serve warm. Yield: 9 servings.

Lois B. Jenkins, Franklin H.S.
Franklin, Pennsylvania

PINEAPPLE UPSIDE-DOWN CAKE

1/2 c. margarine
1 c. (packed) brown sugar
1 1-lb. 14-oz. can pineapple slices,
   drained
Maraschino cherries
Pecan halves (opt.)
1 pkg. yellow cake mix

Melt margarine over low heat in a 13 x 9 x 2-inch pan; sprinkle brown sugar over butter. Arrange pineapple slices in bottom of pan. Decorate with cherries and pecan halves. Prepare cake mix according to package directions; pour over pineapple. Bake in preheated 350-degree oven for 45 to 55 minutes. Invert pan immediately after taking cake from oven; let set

a few minutes before removing from pan. Yield: 12-15 servings.

Mrs. Jane W. Peay, Jonesville H.S.
Jonesville, South Carolina

DEEP CHOCOLATE UPSIDE-DOWN CAKE

1/2 c. butter or margarine
1 c. (packed) brown sugar
1 c. chopped nuts
1 1/3 c. flaked coconut
1 pkg. deep chocolate cake mix

Melt butter in 13 x 9 x 2-inch pan. Add 1/4 cup water; sprinkle brown sugar evenly in pan. Arrange nuts and coconut in sugar mixture. Prepare cake mix according to package directions; pour batter over mixture in pan. Bake in preheated 350-degree oven for 40 minutes or until cake tests done. Let stand for 5 minutes; invert on large platter or cookie sheet. Yield: 12 servings.

Mrs. Janis D. Thomas, Port Washington School
Port Washington, Ohio

QUICK UPSIDE-DOWN CAKE

1/4 c. margarine, melted
1/2 c. (packed) brown sugar
2 c. sliced fresh fruit
1 pkg. white cake mix

Pour melted margarine in 8 x 13 x 2-inch cake pan; sprinkle brown sugar over margarine. Add sliced fruit. Prepare cake mix according to package directions; pour over fruit. Bake as directed. Serve warm or with whipped cream. Yield: 12 servings.

Mrs. Ruth M. Bearup, Silver H.S.
Silver City, New Mexico

BROILED COCONUT FROSTING

6 tbsp. melted butter
2/3 c. (packed) brown sugar
1/4 c. cream
1 c. moist shredded coconut
1/2 tsp. vanilla extract

Combine all ingredients thoroughly; spread over warm cake. Brown lightly in broiler. Will frost one 9-inch square cake.

Maree S. Culpepper, Valley Head H.S.
Valley Head, Alabama

EASY CARAMEL FROSTING

1/2 c. butter or margarine
1 c. (packed) brown sugar
1/4 c. milk
2 c. (about) sifted confectioners' sugar
1 tsp. vanilla extract

Melt butter in saucepan; stir in brown sugar. Add milk; continue stirring until boiling. Remove from heat. Cool to lukewarm. Add sugar and vanilla while beating with mixer on low speed. Beat on high speed for about 2 minutes or until of spreading consistency. Adjust to spreading consistency with drops of hot water or additional sugar as needed. Spread on cake at once. Yield: Two 8-inch or 9-inch layers.

Mrs. Charlene Hyde, Senatobia City School
Senatobia, Mississippi

SEVEN-MINUTE FROSTING

2 egg whites
1 1/2 c. sugar

Combine egg whites, sugar and 1/4 cup water in top of a double boiler. Beat with electric mixer for 1 minute at medium speed to blend ingredients. Place over medium heat; beat for 7 minutes with electric hand mixer. Remove from heat; beat for 1 minute longer. Spread on 9 x 13-inch loaf cake or on angel food cake. Food coloring and flavoring may be added, if desired.

Lois Schommer, Twin Valley H.S.
Twin Valley, Minnesota

BEAT AND EAT CAKE TOPPING

1 egg white
1/4 tsp. cream of tartar
3/4 c. sugar or confectioners' sugar
1 tsp. vanilla extract

Mix egg white, cream of tartar, sugar and vanilla together in a small deep bowl. Add 1/4 cup boiling water; beat until stiff. Spread on cake. Yield: 2 layers.

Marguerite Holloway, Porta H.S.
Petersburg, Illinois

GOLDEN ORANGE SLICE TOPPING

1/2 c. butter or margarine
2 tbsp. grated orange rind
1/3 c. confectioners' sugar
1 pound cake, cut into 1/2-in. slices

Cream butter, orange rind and sugar together; place cake slices on an ungreased cookie sheet. Spread each slice with butter mixture. Broil 3 to 4 inches from broiler unit for 4 to 5 minutes or until golden brown. Yield: 8-10 servings.

Mrs. Jean S. McHargue, Beltsville Jr. H.S.
Beltsville, Maryland

LEMON DESSERT TOPPING

1 tbsp. lemon juice
1 tsp. vanilla extract
1/2 c. nonfat dry milk
3 tbsp. sugar

Measure 1/2 cup ice water into large bowl of electric mixer. Add lemon juice and vanilla. Sprinkle milk over water. Beat for about 7 to 10 minutes or until soft peaks form. Add sugar; continue beating for about 5 minutes or until stiff peaks form. Yield: 8-12 servings.

Mrs. Rita Thompson, Alameda H.S.
Alameda, California

PINEAPPLE SIZZLE TOPPING FOR CAKE

4 maraschino cherries with stems
Orange marmalade
Coconut
2 tbsp. melted butter
4 thick slices pound cake
4 pineapple slices

Dip each cherry in marmalade; coat with coconut. Set aside to use as garnish. Combine 1/3 cup orange marmalade, butter and 3 tablespoons coconut. Spread on cake slices. Place 1 slice pineapple on top of each cake slice. Broil slowly until bubbly. Garnish with cherry in center of pineapple. Yield: 4 servings.

Dolores Hopkins Knesel, Southwest Miami H.S.
Miami, Florida

APRICOT SAUCE

2 jars strained baby apricots
1 tbsp. lemon juice
1 tsp. grated orange rind
1 tsp. grated lemon rind

Combine all ingredients; mix well. Serve over ice cream, angel food cake or pound cake. Yield: 4 servings.

Mrs. Doris W. Larke, Peoria H.S.
Peoria, Illinois

Desserts

HOT CHOCOLATE SAUCE

1 sq. unsweetened chocolate
1/4 c. butter
1/4 tsp. salt
1 1/2 c. sugar
1 sm. can evaporated milk

Melt chocolate, butter and salt in double boiler. Add sugar, 1/2 cup at a time, stirring after each addition. Add evaporated milk, small amount at a time, stirring until well mixed. Serve hot over ice cream balls rolled in Rice Krispies. May be stored in refrigerator. Yield: 8 servings.

Mrs. Dale Fladeboe, Cosmos Public School
Cosmos, Minnesota

LAST MINUTE HOT FUDGE SAUCE

1 can sweetened condensed milk
1 can chocolate syrup

Mix ingredients together over low heat, stirring constantly until bubbly. Remove from heat immediately and serve. Yield: 12 servings.

Mrs. Martha Zimmerman, Taylorville H.S.
Taylorville, Illinois

DELUXE HOT FUDGE SAUCE

1/4 c. margarine
2 sq. unsweetened chocolate
1 1/2 c. sugar
1/8 tsp. salt
1 c. evaporated milk
1 tsp. vanilla extract

Melt margarine and chocolate in top of double boiler. Stir in sugar slowly. Blend in salt, milk and vanilla gradually. Cover. Cook, stirring occasionally, for 10 to 15 minutes. This will thicken when cooled. Yield: 6 servings.

Carol A. Nizlek, Clarkston H.S.
Clarkston, Michigan

SPECIAL HOT LEMON SAUCE

1/4 c. butter
1 egg, slightly beaten
1/2 c. sugar
Juice and grated rind of 1 lemon
Pinch of salt
Nutmeg

Melt butter in double boiler; stir in egg and sugar. Sprinkle nutmeg, juice, rind and salt over egg mixture. Cook, stirring, until mixture thickens. Delicious served over gingerbread, ice cream, pound cake or date bread. Yield: 8 servings.

Mary Virginia Wood, Bluestone H.S.
Skipwith, Virginia

EASY HOT LEMON SAUCE

1/2 c. sugar
2 tbsp. cornstarch
1/8 tsp. salt
1/4 c. lemon juice
2 tbsp. butter

Mix sugar and cornstarch with 1/4 cup water. Add 3/4 cup water. Bring to a boil; remove from heat. Stir in remaining ingredients; cool slightly. Serve over warm cake. Yield: 6 servings.

Mrs. Audrey Johnson, Kickapoo H.S.
Viola, Wisconsin

CHOCOLATE-POTATO CANDY

2 6-oz. packages chocolate chips
3 tbsp. peanut butter
1 4-oz. can shoestring potatoes
1 c. chopped pecans

Melt chocolate chips and peanut butter together in top of double boiler. Mix shoestring potatoes and chopped pecans in large bowl. Pour chocolate mixture over potatoes and pecans; stir until well coated. Drop by tablespoonfuls onto waxed paper-covered tray. Place in refrigerator until well chilled. Yield: 24 servings.

Mrs. Wilma Blair, Glenwood H.S.
Glenwood, Arkansas

FABULOUS FUDGE

2 1/4 c. sugar
3/4 c. evaporated milk
1 c. marshmallow creme or 16 lg. marshmallows
1/4 c. butter or margarine
1/4 tsp. salt
1 6-oz. package semisweet chocolate chips
1 tsp. vanilla extract
1 c. chopped nuts

Combine sugar, milk, marshmallow creme, butter and salt in heavy 2-quart saucepan. Bring to a boil, stirring constantly, over medium heat. Mixture will be bubbling all over top. Boil and stir for 5 minutes. Remove from heat. Stir in chocolate chips until completely melted; stir in vanilla and nuts. Spread in buttered 8-inch square pan. Cool. Cut into 30 pieces.

Mrs. Ruth Methuin, Fall River H.S.
McArthur, California

HEAVENLY HASH

1 12-oz. package semisweet chocolate pieces
1 can sweetened condensed milk
1 lb. miniature marshmallows
1 c. pecan halves or pieces

Melt chocolate pieces in large saucepan at 150 degrees. Stir until smooth and creamy. Remove from heat; stir in sweetened condensed milk slowly. Add marshmallows and pecans; mix until well coated. Drop by tablespoons onto greased cookie sheets. Chill until firm. Yield: 36 pieces.

Jean Foreman, Springdale Sr. H.S.
Springdale, Arkansas

PEANUT CLUSTERS

2 sm. bags chocolate chips
1 sm. bag butterscotch chips
2 14-oz. bags salted peanuts

Melt chocolate chips and butterscotch chips in a heavy pan over low heat. Pour in peanuts. Mix well. Drop by teaspoonfuls onto waxed paper. Yield: 40 servings.

Mrs. Paula Chandler, Westmer H.S.
Joy, Illinois

NUTTY CANDY

1 12-oz. package chocolate chips
3 tbsp. evaporated milk or heavy cream
6 tbsp. confectioners' sugar
1 c. chopped nuts
1 tsp. vanilla extract
Pinch of salt

Melt chocolate chips with milk over hot water. Remove from heat; add sugar, nuts, vanilla and salt. Drop from teaspoon onto waxed paper. Yield: 3 dozen.

Mrs. Carol Subera, Colby H.S.
Colby, Wisconsin

QUICK AND EASY FUDGE

3 sq. unsweetened chocolate
1/4 c. butter or margarine
3 1/2 c. sifted powdered sugar
1 egg
2 tsp. vanilla extract
1 c. chopped nuts

Melt chocolate and butter. Add about 1/2 of the powdered sugar to chocolate mixture; mix well. Beat in egg and vanilla. Blend in remaining sugar. Add nuts. Press into 8-inch square pan lined with waxed paper. Let set until firm. Turn out; cut into squares. Makes about 16 2-inch squares.

Mrs. Nancy Kores, Coronado H.S.
Scottsdale, Arizona

COCONUT CREAMS

2 3-oz. packages cream cheese, softened
2 tsp. liquid sweetener
1 tsp. grated orange rind
1/2 c. shredded coconut, toasted

Mash cream cheese; whip until creamy. Add sweetener and orange rind; mix thoroughly. Form into 24 balls about 1 inch in diameter; roll in toasted coconut. Chill. Yield: 24 servings.

Mrs. Viola Mosely, Avon Park H.S.
Avon Park, Florida

DANISH FRUIT DELIGHTS

1 box flavored gelatin
1 lb. coconut
1 can sweetened condensed milk
1/2 c. finely ground almonds

Set aside 2 or 3 teaspoons gelatin. Combine remaining gelatin with remaining ingredients; mix well. Roll and shape into desired miniature fruit. Roll in reserved gelatin. Stick green toothpicks in for stems; add green frosting leaves.

Mrs. Joanne M. Miller, Monteca Union H.S.
Monteca, California

NO-COOK PEANUT BUTTER FUDGE

1 c. creamy or chunk-style peanut butter
1 c. corn syrup
1 1/4 c. nonfat dry milk
1 1/4 c. sifted confectioners' sugar

Blend peanut butter and syrup in large mixing bowl; add dry milk and confectioners' sugar all at once. Mix with spoon, then hands, kneading on a board until smooth. Press into block 1/2 inch thick and cut in squares. Top with nuts, if desired. May blend cocoa into peanut butter mixture before adding dry ingredients, if desired. Yield: 2 pounds.

Anita Smith, Edinburg H.S.
Edinburg, Texas

Desserts

POPCORN BALLS

3/4 to 1 c. unpopped popcorn
1 10 1/2-oz. package miniature marshmallows
1/2 c. butter

Pop the corn. Remove unpopped kernels. Melt marshmallows and butter in double boiler. Add food coloring, if desired. Pour over popcorn. Shape into balls. Wrap in plastic wrap; tie with colored ribbon. Yield: 18 medium servings.

Mrs. Wayne Ditmer, Mott H.S.
Mott, North Dakota

POP SNACKS

2 1/2 qt. popped corn
1 lb. light brown sugar
1/2 c. light corn syrup
1/2 c. butter or margarine
2 tsp. salt
1 tsbp. vanilla extract
1 c. salted peanuts

Keep corn hot and crisp in 300 to 325-degree oven. Combine sugar, syrup, 1/2 cup water, butter and salt in large saucepan; cook over moderate heat, stirring occasionally, until syrup reaches hard-crack stage. Remove from heat. Stir in vanilla. Mix peanuts and popcorn in large buttered bowl or pan; pour syrup in a fine stream over mixture, mixing quickly, until completely covered and coated evenly. Spread out thin on buttered cookie sheets. Separate quickly into bite-sized clusters with 2 buttered forks. Cool. Yield: 3 to 3 1/2 quarts.

Mrs. Virginia Darnell, Apache H.S.
Apache, Oklahoma

QUICK WALNUT BUTTERSCOTCH FUDGE

1 6-oz. package butterscotch morsels
Dash of salt
1/4 c. walnuts

Melt butterscotch morsels in top of double boiler; add salt. Stir in walnuts. Drop by teaspoonfuls onto waxed paper. Yield: About 2 dozen pieces.

Judith Irvin, Richlands School
Richlands, North Carolina

SKILLET PEANUT BUTTER FUDGE

2 c. sugar
3 tbsp. butter
1 c. evaporated milk

1 c. miniature marshmallows
1 12-oz. jar chunk-style peanut butter
1 tsp. vanilla extract

Combine sugar, butter and evaporated milk in electric skillet. Set heat control at 280 degrees; bring to a boil for 5 minutes, stirring constantly. Turn off heat. Add marshmallows, peanut butter and vanilla. Stir until marshmallows and peanut butter are melted and blended. Pour into a buttered 8-inch square pan. Yield: 2 pounds.

Polly J. Hanst, Northern H.S.
Accident, Maryland

ANGELS ON HORSEBACK

4 sm. milk chocolate bars
8 lg. graham crackers
12 marshmallows

Place chocolate bars on 4 crackers. Place under hot broiler until slightly melted. Add 3 marshmallows to each cracker. Return to broiler until slightly brown. Remove; cover with remaining crackers. Yield: 4 servings.

Norma W. Keesee, Christianburg H.S.
Christianburg, Virginia

BUTTERMILK BROWNIES

1/2 c. margarine
1/4 c. cocoa
1/2 c. shortening
2 c. flour
2 c. sugar
1/4 tsp. salt
1/2 c. buttermilk
2 eggs, beaten
1 tsp. soda
1 tsp. vanilla extract

Combine margarine, 1 cup water, cocoa and shortening in saucepan; heat, stirring, until margarine and shortening is melted. Combine remaining ingredients; pour hot mixture over flour mixture. Mix well. Pour into a greased and floured 13 x 18-inch cookie sheet. Bake in preheated 350-degree oven for 20 minutes. Yield: 48 servings.

Peggy Studer, Crest Sr. H.S.
Colony, Kansas

COCOA BROWNIES

1 c. sugar
1/2 c. butter or margarine
2 eggs

1/4 c. milk
1 c. flour
1/2 c. cocoa
1 tsp. vanilla extract
1 c. chopped nuts

Combine all ingredients in bowl, adding nuts last. Spread in 10 x 14-inch pan. Bake in preheated 375-degree oven until done. Frost if desired. Cut into squares.

Mrs. Hazel Tonseth, Tri-Valley Jr. H.S.
Colton, South Dakota

COUNTRY HOUSE BUTTERSCOTCH BROWNIES

1/3 c. butter
1 c. (packed) brown sugar
1 egg
1/2 tsp. salt
3/4 c. sifted flour
1 tsp. baking powder
1/2 tsp. vanilla extract
1/2 c. coconut
1 6-oz. package chocolate chips
1/2 c. chopped nuts

Melt butter in medium saucepan. Cool. Add sugar, egg, salt, flour, baking powder and vanilla. Blend well. Add coconut, chocolate chips and nuts. Spread in greased 8 or 9-inch square pan. Bake at 350 degrees for 25 minutes. Yield: 12-16 servings.

Eleanor L. Foreman, Haslett H.S.
Haslett, Michigan

MACAROON BROWNIES

1 family-size pkg. brownie mix
1 pkg. macaroon mix

Mix each package of mix according to package directions. Spread half the brownie mix in greased 9 x 13-inch pan. Spread macaroon mix over brownie mix. Cover with remaining brownie mix. Bake at 350 degrees for 35 to 40 minutes. May be frosted with chocolate fudge frosting. Very moist and may be kept for several days.

Mrs. Karlene Mahaney, Boothbay Region H.S.
Boothbay Harbor, Maine

CHOCOLATE-BUTTERSCOTCH CRUNCH

1 c. graham cracker crumbs
1/4 lb. melted butter
1 6-oz. package chocolate chips
1 6-oz. package butterscotch chips
1 c. coconut

1 c. chopped nuts
1 c. sweetened condensed milk

Place crumbs in a 9 x 12-inch cake pan. Pour melted butter over crumbs. Combine chips, coconut and nuts. Place over crumbs. Pour milk over all. Bake at 350 degrees for 30 minutes.

Ann Marshall, Columbus H.S.
Columbus, Wisconsin

CHOCOLATE SQUARES

1/2 c. flour
1 c. sugar
1/4 c. cocoa
1/2 c. butter
2 eggs, beaten

Mix dry ingredients. Cream butter. Add flour mixture and eggs to butter mixture. Mix thoroughly; spread evenly in 9-inch square greased pan. Bake at 350 degrees for 20 minutes. Yield: 6-8 servings.

Lydia Branch, Big Sandy School
Big Sandy, Tennessee

EASY CHOCOLATE-CHERRY CHEWS

1 family-size pkg. brownie mix
1 1/2 c. shredded coconut
1 1/2 c. chopped candied cherries

Prepare brownie mix according to package directions. Add coconut and cherries. Pour into buttered 9 x 13-inch pan. Bake at 350 degrees for about 35 minutes or until toothpick inserted in center comes out clean.

Mrs. Eleanor Pritts, Mt. Auburn H.S.
Mt. Auburn, Illinois

DO-LITTLE SEVEN SQUARES

1/4 c. butter
1 c. graham cracker crumbs
1 can flaked coconut
1 6-oz. package chocolate chips
1 6-oz. package butterscotch chips
1 can sweetened condensed milk
1 c. chopped pecans

Melt butter in a 9 x 12-inch baking pan. Add ingredients in layers in order listed. Bake at 325 degrees for about 30 minutes. Press slightly with spatula while still hot. Let cool in pan; cut into squares. Yield: 24 squares.

Mary A. Campbell, Ft. Necessity H.S.
Ft. Necessity, Louisiana

Desserts

FUDGE NOUGATS

2 c. sugar
1/2 c. butter
1 c. evaporated milk
1 c. chocolate chips
3/4 c. flour
1 c. graham cracker crumbs
3/4 c. chopped walnuts
1 tsp. vanilla

Combine sugar, butter and evaporated milk in a saucepan. Bring to a boil; boil for 10 minutes, stirring constantly. Combine remaining ingredients. Pour milk mixture over chocolate mixture; mix well. Pour into greased 8 x 8-inch pan. Let cool; cut into squares.

Jeraldine Sanders, Dixie H.S.
St. George, Utah

HELLO DOLLIES

1 c. butter
1 c. graham cracker crumbs
1 c. shredded coconut
1 c. chocolate chips
1 c. chopped walnuts
1 c. sweetened condensed milk

Melt butter; pour into a 13 x 9 x 2-inch baking dish. Pour graham cracker crumbs over melted butter. Sprinkle coconut, chocolate chips and walnuts in order listed over butter and graham cracker crumb mixture. Pour milk over top. Bake at 350 degrees for about 25 minutes or until top begins to lightly brown. Allow to cool thoroughly before cutting into squares. Yield: 16 servings.

Susan Kerr, Panama Central School
Panama, New York

PEANUT-BUTTERSCOTCH SQUARES

1/2 c. butter
1/2 c. (packed) brown sugar
1 1/3 c. sifted flour
2/3 c. sugar
2/3 c. light corn syrup
1 6-oz. package butterscotch pieces
1/2 c. chunk-style peanut butter
1 1/2 c. corn flakes

Cream butter and brown sugar together; stir in flour. Press in ungreased 13 x 9 x 2-inch pan. Bake at 350 degrees for 15 minutes. Combine sugar and corn syrup in saucepan; bring to a boil. Remove from heat. Add butterscotch pieces and peanut butter. Stir until butterscotch is melted. Stir in corn flakes.

Spread over baked layer. Cool. Cut into squares. Yield: 3 dozen squares.

Ellen Jane Chase, Seymour Comm. H.S.
Seymour, Wisconsin

PRALINE COOKIE SQUARES

1 box brown sugar
4 eggs
2 c. Bisquick
1 c. chopped pecans

Mix brown sugar and eggs. Add biscuit mix and pecans. Mix well. Pour into greased 5 1/2 x 10 1/2 x 2-inch pan. Bake in preheated 350-degree oven for 30 to 40 minutes. Cool and cut into squares. Yield: 24 servings.

Mrs. Bettie Hudson, South Garland H.S.
Garland, Texas

QUICK COOKIES

2 1/2 c. graham cracker crumbs
1 can sweetened condensed milk
1 6-oz. bag chocolate chips

Combine all ingredients; mix well. Spread in a 9 x 9 x 2-inch square pan. Bake at 350 degrees for 35 minutes. Cool; cut into bars. Yield: 12 servings.

Mrs. Helen Winkelman, Triopia Jr. H.S.
Arenzville, Illinois

SOME MORE

1 lg. marshmallow
2 graham crackers
1 Hershey bar

Roast marshmallow over an open fire. Place roasted marshmallow on graham cracker. Top with a Hershey bar; cover with another graham cracker. Yield: 1 cookie.

Mrs. Geraldine G. Miracle
Jeffersonville H.S.
Jeffersonville, Indiana

COCONUT MACAROONS

2/3 c. sweetened condensed milk
3 c. moist shredded coconut
1 tsp. vanilla extract
3/4 tsp. almond extract

Blend all ingredients together in medium mixing bowl. Drop by teaspoonfuls, about 1 inch apart, onto well-greased cookie sheet. Bake in 350-degree oven for 8 to 10 minutes or until edges are lightly browned. Remove at once from cookie sheet. Yield: 1 1/2 dozen.

Mrs. Thomas L. Elliott, Three Rivers H.S.
Three Rivers, Texas

CORN FLAKE MACAROONS

1 egg white
1/4 c. white sugar or 1/3 c. (packed)
　brown sugar
1/8 tsp. salt
1/2 tsp. vanilla extract
1/3 c. corn flakes

Beat egg white until stiff, adding sugar gradually. Beat until mixture holds shape. Beat in salt and vanilla. Fold in corn flakes; drop by teaspoonfuls onto buttered cookie sheet. Bake at 300 degrees for 20 to 25 minutes. Yield: 1 dozen.

Mrs. Carl Whynacht, Lunenburg Jr.-Sr. H.S.
Lunenburg, Nova Scotia, Canada

FORGOTTEN COOKIES

2 egg whites
2/3 c. sugar
Pinch of salt
1 tsp. vanilla extract
1 c. chopped pecans
1　6-oz. package chocolate chips

Preheat oven to 400 degrees. Beat egg whites until stiff, adding sugar gradually. Beat in salt and vanilla. Fold in pecans and chocolate chips. Drop by teaspoonfuls on ungreased cookie sheet. Place in oven; turn off oven. Do not open door until oven is cool. Yield: 4-6 dozen cookies.

Mrs. Joyce Cheatham, Monterey H.S.
Lubbock, Texas

HONEY-FLAVORED MACAROONS

2 c. quick-cooking oats
1 tsp. salt
1 tsp. cinnamon
1/2 tsp. each nutmeg and allspice
1/2 tsp. vanilla extract
1/4 tsp. almond extract
1/3 c. salad oil
1/2 c. honey
1 egg, lightly beaten
1/4 c. finely chopped walnuts

Combine oats, salt, spices and extracts. Stir in oil, honey, egg and walnuts. Mix well. Chill mixture for 1 hour or longer. Press tablespoons of dough to-

gether to form cookies. Place on ungreased cookie sheet. Bake at 375 degrees for 12 minutes. Flavor of all honey-baked goods improves with age. Yield: 2 dozen.

Nancy Kay Colva, Morton H.S.
Kinnear, Wyoming

MERINGUE KISSES

1 egg white
Pinch of salt
1/3 c. sugar
1/4 tsp. vanilla extract

Beat egg white with salt until stiff but not dry. Add sugar, 1 tablespoon at a time, beating well after each addition. Beat until stiff peaks form and sugar is dissolved. Fold in vanilla. Shape with spoon or tube into spiral cones on a well-greased baking sheet. Bake in preheated 250-degree oven for 45 minutes or until dry but not browned. Yield: 24 servings.

Mrs. John Maxwell, Holton H.S.
Holton, Indiana

APRICOT JUMBLES

2 tbsp. butter
1 c. chopped dried apricots
2 eggs
1 c. sugar
1 tsp. vanilla extract
1/2 c. chopped nuts
1 c. coconut
1 c. crushed graham cracker crumbs

Melt butter in a skillet. Stir in apricots. Beat eggs well; blend in sugar. Add to apricot mixture. Cook over low heat for 15 minutes, stirring constantly. Remove from heat; stir in vanilla, nuts, coconut and crumbs. Drop by teaspoonfuls onto waxed paper. Yield: 3 1/2 dozen.

Mrs. Mary L. Burkholder, Biglerville H.S.
Biglerville, Pennsylvania

PEANUT QUICKIES

1 pkg. fluffy white frosting mix
1/2 c. flour
1/2 c. crunchy peanut butter
1/2 c. salted peanuts

Prepare frosting mix according to package directions. Fold in flour, peanut butter and peanuts. Drop dough by rounded teaspoonfuls onto greased and floured cookie sheets. Bake at 375 degrees for 10 to 12 minutes or until golden. Remove from cookie sheets immediately. Yield: 50 servings.

Mrs. Karen Williams, Perham H.S.
Perham, Minnesota

Desserts

CHOCOLATE-PEPPERMINT CREAMS

3 c. sifted flour
1 1/4 tsp. soda
1 tsp. salt
1 1/2 c. (packed) brown sugar
3/4 c. butter
2 c. chocolate bits
2 eggs, lightly beaten
Peppermint Cream

Sift flour, soda and salt together. Heat brown sugar, butter and 2 tablespoons water. Add chocolate; stir to melt. Beat in eggs; stir in flour mixture. Drop by heaping teaspoonfuls onto greased cookie sheet. Bake at 350 degrees for 8 to 10 minutes. Cool. Sandwich each pair of cookies together with 1 teaspoon Peppermint Cream.

Peppermint Cream

3 c. sifted confectioners' sugar
1/3 c. soft butter
1/8 tsp. peppermint extract
Dash of salt
1/4 c. milk

Blend 1 cup sugar with butter, peppermint extract and salt. Beat in remaining sugar alternately with ·milk. Yield: 8 dozen

Mrs. Barbara Sech, Northridge Sr. H.S.
Dayton, Ohio

COCONUT-ORANGE DROPS

1/4 c. margarine
3/4 c. (firmly packed) brown sugar
1 egg
1 c. shredded coconut
1 tbsp. grated orange rind
1 1/3 c. Bisquick

Combine margarine, brown sugar and egg thoroughly. Stir in remaining ingredients. Drop from teaspoon, 2 inches apart, onto ungreased cookie sheet. Bake in preheated 375-degree oven for about 10 minutes or until lightly browned. Do not overbake. Yield: 3 dozen cookies.

Mrs. Frances Eldridge, Central Sr. H.S.
Clifton, Illinois

EASY CHOCOLATE DROP COOKIES

2 eggs
2/3 c. shortening
1 pkg. chocolate cake mix
1/2 c. chopped nuts (opt.)

Combine eggs and shortening. Add half the dry mix. Mix thoroughly. Add remaining dry mix and nuts. Mix thoroughly. Drop by teaspoonfuls onto greased cookie sheet. Bake at 350 degrees 8 to 10 minutes or until done. Cool; frost if desired. Cherry, lemon or spice cake mix may be substituted for chocolate. Yield: 3 dozen.

Charlotte Macy, Ottawa Sr. H.S.
Ottawa, Kansas

PUDDING COOKIES

3/4 c. biscuit mix
1 egg
1/4 c. salad oil
1 3-oz. package instant vanilla pudding mix

Combine all ingredients in a mixing bowl. Mix until mixture forms a ball. Drop by teaspoonfuls onto ungreased cookie sheet. Flatten with teaspoon. Garnish top with nuts, candied cherries or raisins. Bake in 350-degree oven for 5 to 8 minutes. Yield: 20 cookies.

Mrs. Jane M. Bowles
Vinton Co. Consolidated H.S.
McArthur, Ohio

PUMPKIN NUT COOKIES

1/4 c. shortening
1/2 c. sugar
1 egg, beaten
1/2 c. pumpkin
1 c. sifted flour
2 tsp. baking powder
1/2 tsp. salt
1 1/4 tsp. cinnamon
1/4 tsp. nutmeg
1/8 tsp. ginger
1/2 c. seedless raisins
1/2 c. chopped walnuts

Cream shortening; add sugar gradually. Cream until light and fluffy. Add egg and pumpkin; mix well. Sift flour, baking powder, salt and spices together. Stir into pumpkin mixture. Add raisins and walnuts. Drop by teaspoonfuls onto greased cookie sheets. Bake at 350 degrees for 15 minutes. Yield: 2 dozen cookies.

Laoma D. Clevenger, Ohio City Liberty School
Ohio City, Ohio

SCHOOL DAY COOKIES

1 pkg. cake mix
1 c. (packed) brown sugar
2 tbsp. soft butter
2 tbsp. honey

2 eggs
1 c. chopped nuts

Combine cake mix, brown sugar, butter, honey and eggs. Stir in nuts. Drop by spoonfuls onto cookie sheet. Bake at 375 degrees for 10 to 12 minutes. One cup coconut may be substituted for nuts. Yield: 5 dozen.

Sister Ramona Ann, O.S.F., St. Mary's H.S.
Holly Springs, Mississippi

QUICK PECAN DROPS

1 pkg. yellow cake mix
1/4 c. soft butter or margarine
1 egg
1/3 c. milk
1 c. chopped pecans

Combine cake mix, butter, eggs and milk. Beat until light and fluffy. Stir in pecans. Drop by teaspoonfuls onto cookie sheet. Bake in preheated 375-degree oven until brown. Yield: 5 dozen.

Mary Finley, Baker Co. H.S.
Macclenny, Florida

STIR AND DROP COOKIES

2 eggs
2/3 c. Wesson oil
2 tsp. vanilla extract
1 tsp. grated lemon peel
3/4 c. sugar
2 c. sifted flour
2 tsp. baking powder
1/2 tsp. salt

Beat eggs with fork. Stir in Wesson oil, vanilla and lemon peel. Blend in sugar. Reserve 1 tablespoon of mixture. Sift flour, baking powder and salt together; add to egg mixture. Mix well. Drop by teaspoonfuls, about 2 inches apart, onto ungreased cookie sheets. Stamp each cookie flat with bottom of glass that has been dipped in reserved mixture and then in additional sugar. Bake in preheated 400-degree oven for 8 to 10 minutes. Remove at once from cookie sheet. If cookies are baked one cookie sheet at a time, stir dough between each batch. Yield: 60 cookies.

Mrs. Louise G. Eversole, Manley Jr. H.S.
Louisville, Kentucky

SURPRISE OATMEAL COOKIES

1 15-oz. can sweetened condensed milk
2 sq. unsweetened chocolate
1/2 c. chopped pecans
1/2 c. crunchy peanut butter
1 c. quick-cooking oats

Cook milk and chocolate in double boiler for about 6 minutes or until mixture thickens. Remove from heat. Add pecans, peanut butter and oats. Drop from teaspoon onto greased baking sheet. Bake at 350 degrees for about 10 minutes. Yield: 24 servings.

Martha Tolley, Central H.S.
Bruceton, Tennessee

CAKE MIX COOKIES

2 med eggs, well beaten
1 pkg. butter brickle cake mix

Beat eggs well; add 2 to 4 tablespoons water. Add cake mix; blend well. Shape into balls. Place on greased baking sheet. Bake at 350 degrees for 10 to 12 minutes. Yield: 3 dozen 2 1/2-inch cookies.

Mrs. Yvonne K. Knoll, North Cen. H.S.
Pioneer, Ohio

LADYFINGERS

2 c. unsifted flour
1 c. butter or margarine
1/2 c. sugar
1/2 c. chopped nuts
Powdered sugar

Place all ingredients except powdered sugar in bowl. Mix until mixture holds shape. Shape into pieces about 1/2 inch wide and 1 1/2 inches long. Place on cookie sheet. Bake at 325 degrees for 20 minutes or until golden brown. Cool for about 2 minutes. Roll in powdered sugar. Yield: 3 dozen.

Mary Ruth Reeves, Greenville H.S.
Greenville, Illinois

BOILED COOKIES

2 c. sugar
1/2 c. evaporated milk
1/2 c. margarine or butter
1/4 c. cocoa
2 1/2 c. oats
1/4 c. chopped nuts
2 tsp. vanilla extract
1/2 c. peanut butter
Powdered sugar

Combine sugar, milk, butter and cocoa in saucepan; bring to a full rolling boil. Remove from heat; add remaining ingredients except powdered sugar. Blend well. Spoon onto waxed paper or pour into a greased square pan; cut into squares. Cool. Shape into balls; roll in sifted powdered sugar. Yield: 5 dozen.

Mrs. C. P. Hooper, Elizabeth H.S.
Elizabeth, Louisiana

Desserts

CRISPY CLUSTERS

4 1/2 c. miniature marshmallows
1/2 c. margarine
5 c. rice cereal
1 c. shredded coconut
1/2 c. chopped nuts
1 6-oz. package semisweet chocolate
    pieces, melted

Melt marshmallows with margarine over low heat; stir until smooth. Add cereal, coconut and nuts; mix well. Drop by tablespoonfuls onto waxed paper. Top clusters with melted chocolate; chill. Cereal mixture may be pressed into greased pan and topped with melted chocolate, if desired. Yield: 3-4 dozen squares or clusters.

Mrs. Willie V. Hill, Neshoka Cen. H.S.
Philadelphia, Mississippi

COCONUT BALLS

1 pkg. vanilla wafers
1/2 pkg. miniature marshmallows
1 c. chopped English walnuts
1 can sweetened condensed milk
1 c. coconut

Crush vanilla wafers; add marshmallows, walnuts and milk. Mix well. Form into balls. Roll in coconut. Yield: 4 dozen.

Mrs. Florence Lester
North Mahaska Comm. School
New Sharon, Iowa

CRUNCHY CHOCOLATE CHEWIES

3 8-oz. packages chocolate chips
1 12-oz. jar crunchy peanut butter
1 7-oz. box Rice Krispies
1 15-oz. box raisins

Melt chocolate chips in top of double boiler over hot, not boiling, water. Stir in peanut butter. Toss cereal and raisins in a large bowl. Pour chocolate-peanut butter mixture over cereal; stir until well combined. Drop by spoonfuls onto waxed paper. Yield: 8-9 dozen.

Katherine McIlquham, Senior H.S.
Chippewa Falls, Wisconsin

FRYING PAN COOKIES

2 eggs
1 c. sugar
1/2 tsp. salt
1 1/2 c. chopped dates
2 tbsp. margarine
1 c. chopped nuts
2 c. Rice Krispies
1 can flaked coconut

Beat eggs; add sugar, salt and dates. Melt margarine in skillet; add date mixture. Cook over low heat for 10 minutes or until dates are very tender. Remove from heat; add nuts and Rice Krispies. Cool slightly. Form into small balls; roll in coconut.

Mrs. Doris Starkey, Spur H.S.
Spur, Texas

NO-BAKE CHOCOLATE COOKIES

2 c. sugar
1/2 c. milk
1/2 c. butter or margarine
3 tbsp. cocoa
1 tsp. salt
3 c. quick-cooking oats
1 tsp. vanilla extract
1/2 c. broken walnuts
1 c. coconut

Combine sugar, milk, butter, cocoa and salt in a large saucepan; bring to a boil. Remove from heat; stir in oats, vanilla, walnuts and coconut. Drop from teaspoon onto waxed paper. Yield: 4 dozen.

Mrs. Sara H. Barlow, Whitesburg H.S.
Whitesburg, Tennessee

POMANDER COOKIES

2 1/2 c. finely crushed vanilla wafers
1 c. finely chopped pecans or nuts
1 6-oz. package semisweet
    chocolate pieces
1/2 c. sugar
1/4 c. light corn syrup
1 tsp. orange extract
Powdered sugar

Combine crushed wafers and chopped pecans. Melt chocolate pieces in saucepan over very low heat; stir in sugar and corn syrup. Blend in 1/4 cup water. Remove from heat; pour over crumb mixture. Add extract. Mix well. Form into 1-inch balls. Roll in powdered sugar. Place in tightly covered container; let stand at least 3 days. Flavor improves with standing. Will keep 3 to 4 weeks. Yield: 4 1/4 dozen.

Mrs. L. S. Coers, Liberty Hill H.S.
Liberty Hill, Texas

NO-BAKE PEANUT BUTTER COOKIES

1/4 c. (packed) brown sugar
1/4 c. sugar
1/2 c. light corn syrup
3/4 c. peanut butter
1 tsp. vanilla extract
2 c. oven-popped rice cereal

Stir sugars and syrup together in saucepan; bring to a boil. Remove from heat. Stir in peanut butter; mix well. Add vanilla and cereal. Drop from a teaspoon onto waxed paper. Cool. Yield: 3 dozen.

Sherry Rickle, Bowsher H.S.
Toledo, Ohio

ORANGE NO-BAKE COOKIES

1   12-oz. package vanilla wafer crumbs
3/4 c. chopped nuts
1/4 c. melted butter
1   6-oz. can frozen orange juice
1 c. powdered sugar

Combine first 4 ingredients; mix well. Form into small balls. Roll in powdered sugar. Freeze. Yield: 6 servings.

Mrs. Ve Lasta Burns, Center Grove School
Lovelady, Texas

BASIC CREAM PUFFS

1/2 c. butter
1 c. flour
3 lg. or 4 med. eggs

Melt butter in 1 cup boiling water. Add flour all at once; stir vigorously. Cook until dough clings to spoon. Remove from heat. Add eggs, 1 at a time, beating well after each addition. Drop by heaping teaspoonfuls onto greased baking sheet. Bake at 450 degrees for 25 minutes. Cool; slit and fill with desired filling. Sprinkle top with powdered sugar. Yield: 18 servings.

Mrs. Nancy Simonton, Wade Hampton Sch.
Greenville, South Carolina

PINK LEMONADE CREAM PUFFS

6 tbsp. butter
3/4 c. sifted flour
Dash of salt
3 eggs
1 env. unflavored gelatin
1   6-oz. can frozen pink
    lemonade concentrate

1/2 c. nonfat dry milk powder
1 tbsp. lemon juice
2 tbsp. sugar

Bring 3/4 cup water and butter to a boil in a heavy saucepan, stirring until butter melts. Add flour and salt all at once. Reduce heat. Cook, stirring constantly, for about 1 to 2 minutes or until mixture is smooth and forms a soft ball. Remove from heat; cool slightly. Add eggs, one at a time, beating well after each addition or until batter is smooth and shiny. Drop by tablespoonfuls onto lightly greased baking sheet. Bake in preheated 400-degree oven for 25 to 30 minutes or until golden brown. Cool on wire racks. Sprinkle gelatin on 1/4 cup cold water to soften. Combine lemonade concentrate and enough water to measure 2 cups liquid; heat to boiling. Remove from heat; mix in gelatin until well blended. Chill. Chill bowl and beaters. Mix dry milk powder and 1/2 cup ice water; beat at high speed until soft peaks form. Add lemon juice; beat until stiff. Add sugar; beat until sugar is dissolved. Fold in gelatin mixture. Cut tops from cream puffs; fill. Replace tops; refrigerate until serving time. Yield: 12 servings.

Effie Lois Greene, Potts Camp H.S.
Potts Camp, Mississippi

FROZEN ANGEL FOOD DELIGHT

1 oblong angel food cake
1/2 pt. lime sherbet
1/2 pt. lemon sherbet
1/2 pt. whipping cream

Cut cake into 3 layers. Spread lime sherbet on bottom layer. Top with a cake layer. Spread second layer with lemon sherbet. Add third cake layer. Frost with whipping cream. Freeze. Remove 10 to 15 minutes before serving. Any flavor sherbets may be used, if desired. Yield: 12 servings.

Mrs. Kathleen Ochander, Mr. Pleasant Sr. H.S.
Mt. Pleasant, Michigan

APRICOT CREAM

1 lg. can peeled apricots, drained
1 c. sugar
Juice of 1 lemon
2 c. whipping cream, whipped

Sieve apricots. Add sugar; stir until dissolved. Add lemon juice; fold in whipped cream. Place in mold or freezer tray; freeze until firm. Yield: 8-10 servings.

Mrs. Louis A. Elliott
Minonk-Dana-Rutland School
Minonk, Illinois

Desserts

CREAMY CRANBERRY MOUSSE

2 1/2 c. cranberries
1 1/4 c. sugar
1 c. evaporated milk, chilled
2 tbsp. lemon juice
1/4 c. orange juice

Wash cranberries; place in saucepan. Add 1 1/4 cups water; cook until soft. Force berries through sieve; return to saucepan. Add sugar; simmer for 10 minutes. Cool. Beat milk in chilled bowl until fluffy; add lemon juice and continue beating until mixture forms peaks. Combine cranberry mixture and orange juice; fold into milk mixture. Pour into refrigerator tray; freeze until mushy. Remove to chilled bowl; beat until fluffy. Return to freezer until firm. Yield: 6-8 servings.

Cora E. Fairbanks, Rockport H.S.
Rockport, Massachusetts

FIGURE-WISE FRUIT FROST

1/4 c. jam, jelly or preserves
1/4 c. marshmallow whip
1/2 c. lemon-lime carbonated diet beverage
   or ice water
1/2 c. instant nonfat dry milk crystals
2 tbsp. lemon juice
3 drops of food coloring (opt.)

Blend jam and marshmallow whip well. Pour beverage into small mixing bowl; add milk crystals. Whip for 3 to 4 minutes or until soft peaks form; add lemon juice. Continue whipping for 2 to 4 minutes or until stiff; fold in jam mixture and food coloring. Spoon into refrigerator tray; freeze for 5 hours or until firm or spoon into sherbet glasses and serve immediately. Yield: 7-8 servings.

Sister Mary Louise, Notre Dame H.S.
Clarksburg, West Virginia

FROZEN ALMOND DELIGHT

1 c. nonfat dry milk
6 tbsp. sugar
1 tsp. almond extract
1/2 c. finely chopped nuts

Combine dry milk with 1 cup ice water in chilled bowl; beat until stiff. Beat in sugar, almond extract and nuts; spoon mixture into fluted paper baking cups. Set in muffin tins; freeze for 3 to 4 hours. Yield: 12 servings.

Mrs. Marie L. Fuller, Liberty-Eylan Sr. H.S.
Texarkana, Texas

FROZEN STRAWBERRY DESSERT

2 pkg. partially frozen strawberries
1 c. sugar
1 egg white
Juice of 1 lemon
1 pt. whipping cream, whipped
1 box vanilla wafers, crushed

Beat strawberries, sugar, egg white and lemon juice at medium speed for 30 minutes. Fold whipped cream into strawberry mixture. Place half the vanilla wafers in 9 x 13-inch pan; cover with strawberry mixture. Top with remaining vanilla wafers. Freeze for several days; cut into 15 squares to serve. Yield: 15 servings.

Mrs. Margaret Hempel, Lennox H.S.
Lennox, South Dakota

FROZEN ICE CREAM BARS

2 1/2 c. crushed Rice Chex
1 c. flaked coconut
1 c. chopped walnuts
3/4 c. melted butter or margarine
1/2 gal. slightly softened butter
   brickle ice cream

Combine Rice Chex, coconut, walnuts and butter; spread half the mixture in 9 x 13-inch cake pan. Top with softened ice cream; sprinkle with remaining Rice Chex mixture. Freeze overnight; cut into squares to serve.

Mrs. Diane M. Ryan, Aitkin H.S.
Aitkin, Minnesota

RASPBERRY FREEZE

1 env. Dream Whip
1 10-oz. package frozen raspberries or
   strawberry halves

Prepare Dream Whip according to package directions; stir in raspberries. Freeze for 6 hours or until firm. Yield: 6 servings.

Mrs. Gary Malone, Stratton H.S.
Stratton, Nebraska

CHOCOLATE ICE CREAM

1 env. unflavored gelatin
1/2 c. sugar
1/4 c. cocoa
3/4 c. white syrup
5 1/2 c. (or more) milk
1 tsp. vanilla extract

Soak gelatin in 1/4 cup cold water. Mix sugar and cocoa; stir in syrup and 1/2 cup milk. Boil for 2 minutes; cool slightly. Stir in softened gelatin. Pour into 1/2 gallon freezer container; stir in enough milk to fill container 3/4 full. Add vanilla; freeze according to freezer instructions. Yield: 12 servings.

Mrs. K. E. Sharp, Houston Jr. H.S.
Borger, Texas

PEACH ICE CREAM

3 qt. milk
9 eggs, slightly beaten
2 1/2 c. sugar
3 tbsp. cornstarch or 4 tbsp. flour
1 tbsp. vanilla extract
1 tsp. almond extract
2 c. whipping cream or 1 lg. can
   evaporated milk
1 pt. crushed fresh or frozen peaches

Scald milk over medium heat; combine eggs, sugar and cornstarch. Stir small amount of hot milk into eggs; stir back into milk. Cook over medium heat, stirring constantly, until mixture coats a spoon; remove from heat. Add vanilla and almond extracts. Cool immediately. Add cream and peaches; pour into freezer container. Place container in ice cream freezer; alternate layers of ice and ice cream salt around container. Freeze according to freezing directions; remove dasher. Pack freezer with additional ice; cover and let stand for 1 hour before serving. Yield: 12 servings.

Mrs. Minnie Lee King, Winona Jr.-Sr. H.S.
Winona, Mississippi

DREAMY ICE CREAM

6 eggs
2 c. sugar
2 tsp. vanilla extract
Dash of salt
2 pkg. Dream Whip
2 pt. half and half
1 c. milk

Whip eggs until stiff and foamy; add sugar gradually, beating until sugar is dissolved. Stir in vanilla, salt and Dream Whip; add half and half and beat well. Pour mixture into freezer container; add milk. Stir to mix. Freeze according to freezer directions. Yield: 12-16 servings.

Mrs. Barbara Amerin, Hardtner H.S.
Hardtner, Kansas

THRIFTY ICE CREAM

3 c. instant dry milk
1/4 c. flour
1 1/2 c. sugar
1/2 tsp. salt
2 eggs
1 No. 2 1/2 can crushed pineapple or
   peaches (opt.)
1/2 c. lime juice (opt.)
Food coloring (opt.)

Mix dry milk, flour, sugar and salt in saucepan. Beat eggs and 2 quarts water; add to dry mixture. Beat until smooth; cook, stirring constantly, over low heat until slightly thickened. Cool; place in freezer container. Add fruit, lime juice and food coloring. Stir in additional water or skim milk to bring level of mixture to fill line. Freeze according to freezer directions. Yield: 1 gallon ice cream.

Ruth Jeffers, Tatum H.S.
Tatum, New Mexico

VANILLA PUDDING ICE CREAM

1 pkg. vanilla pudding mix
1 can sweetened condensed milk
1/4 c. sugar
Milk

Prepare pudding mix according to package directions; heat until warm. Add sweetened condensed milk and sugar; pour into 1/2 gallon freezer container. Fill container with milk; freeze according to freezer directions. Fruits may be added before freezing, if desired. Yield: 1/2 gallon ice cream.

Mrs. Dorothy Simpson, Richardson Sr. H.S.
Richardson, Texas

GINGER PEACHY SUNDAE

1/2 c. finely chopped preserved ginger
1/4 c. syrup from ginger
3/4 c. chopped walnuts
4 fully ripe peaches
1 qt. ice cream

Combine ginger, syrup and walnuts. Peel peaches and slice. Scoop ice cream into 8 dessert dishes. Arrange peach slices over ice cream. Spoon sauce over each serving. Yield: 8 servings.

Photograph for this recipe on page 4.

Desserts

INDIVIDUAL BAKED ALASKAS

3 egg whites
1/4 tsp. cream of tartar
6 tbsp. sugar
4 slices lemon-flavored cake
1 pt. lemon chiffon ice cream
4 sugar cubes
Lemon extract

Beat egg whites and cream of tartar until foamy; add sugar, 2 tablespoons at a time, beating well after each addition. Continue beating until meringue stands in stiff peaks. Place cake slices on bread board or baking sheet covered with heavy paper or aluminum foil. Cut firm ice cream into 4 equal parts; place on cake. Spread meringue over cake and ice cream, covering completely. Bake at 450 degrees until meringue is delicately browned. Saturate sugar cubes with lemon extract; place 1 sugar cube on top of each Baked Alaska. Ignite sugar cubes; serve immediately. Yield: 4 servings.

Mrs. Beverlee Williams, Campbell H.S.
Campbell, California

FROZEN LEMON CUSTARD

3/4 c. graham cracker crumbs
3 tbsp. melted butter
1 egg, separated
1/3 c. sugar
1/4 tsp. grated lemon rind
3 tbsp. lemon juice
Dash of salt
1/3 c. instant nonfat dry milk

Combine crumbs and butter; press half the mixture on bottom of 1-quart freezer tray. Mix egg yolk, sugar, lemon rind, lemon juice and salt. Mix egg white, 1/3 cup water and instant milk; beat at high speed until mixture stands in peaks. Beat in lemon mixture gradually; pour custard into prepared tray. Top with remaining crumbs or cherries. Freeze until firm. Crust may be omitted and 1/4 cup graham cracker crumbs sprinkled over the top, if desired. Yield: 4 servings.

Mrs. Joyce Fortin, Jefferson Jr. H.S.,
Minneapolis, Minnesota

LEMON ICE

2 c. sugar
3/4 c. lemon juice

Combine sugar and 1 quart water; bring to a boil. Boil for 5 minutes; cool. Add lemon juice; place in freezer tray. Freeze. Serve scraped ice in sherbet glasses, topped with pineapple chunks, strawberries, bananas or oranges.

Mrs. Evelyn Peper, Minnewaukan No. 5 School
Minnewaukan, North Dakota

LEMON FREEZE

1/2 c. evaporated milk
1 egg, separated
4 tbsp. lemon juice
1/2 c. sugar
1/2 tsp. lemon rind
Dash of salt
Graham cracker crumbs

Place milk in freezer tray; chill until ice crystals form around edges. Place in mixer bowl; beat at high speed. Add egg white and continue beating; add 2 tablespoons lemon juice. Beat until stiff; add sugar, egg yolk, remaining lemon juice, lemon rind and salt, beating at low speed. Place in pan; sprinkle top with graham cracker crumbs. Freeze until firm. Yield: 6 servings.

Mrs. Evelyn Q. Webb, Columbia H.S.
Columbia, Mississippi

LIME-BUTTEREMILK FREEZE

1 env. unflavored gelatin
Grated rind and juice of 2 lg. limes
3/4 c. (about) sugar
3 c. buttermilk
1 egg white
Few drops of green food coloring

Soften gelatin in 2 tablespoons water; dissolve over hot water. Combine gelatin, lime rind, lime juice, sugar and buttermilk. Beat egg white until stiff but not dry; fold into gelatin mixture, adding more sugar, if needed. Add food coloring. Pour into 1-quart freezer tray; freeze until mixture is firm around edges. Turn into chilled bowl; beat until fluffy. Return to tray. Freeze to desired consistency. Spoon into serving dishes; garnish with lime slices or strawberries. Yield: 6-8 servings.

Mrs. Mable Wallmark, Mead Sr. H.S.
Mead, Washington

NEAPOLITAN MOLD

1 qt. Neapolitan ice cream
3/4 c. chopped pecans
3/4 c. small chocolate bits

Allow ice cream to stand at room temperature until slightly soft. Sprinkle pecans and chocolate bits over top. Stir slightly only until colors of ice cream are swirled and pecans and chocolate are blended in. Place in mold or individual molds; freeze until ready to serve. Yield: 4-6 servings.

Mrs. L. V. Conner, Callaway H.S.
Callaway, Nebraska

PEACHES AND CREAM

1 1/2 c. crushed vanilla wafers
3 tbsp. melted butter
2 tbsp. orange juice
1 tbsp. lemon juice
1/2 lb. marshmallows
1 c. crushed fresh peaches
1 pkg. Dream Whip

Combine vanilla wafers and butter; pat evenly over bottom and around sides of 8-inch square cake pan. Combine fruit juices; heat to boiling. Add marshmallows; stir until dissolved. Cool; add peaches. Prepare Dream Whip according to package directions; fold into peach mixture. Pour into wafer crust; freeze for 3 to 4 hours or until firm. Yield: 8 servings.

Mrs. Ruth Kardos, Marlington H.S.
Alliance, Ohio

KOOL-AID SHERBET

1 c. sugar
1 pkg. Kool-Aid
3 c. milk

Dissolve sugar and Kool-Aid in milk; pour in freezer tray. Freeze until mushy; spoon into cold bowl. Beat until smooth. Return to freezer tray; freeze for at least 2 hours. Yield: 5-6 servings.

Mrs. Patsy Lenz, Windsor H.S.
Windsor, Illinois

LEMON-ORANGE SHERBET

1/2 c. orance juice
1/3 c. lemon juice
3/4 c. sugar
1 c. milk
1 6-oz. can evaporated milk, chilled

Combine orange juice and lemon juice; add sugar. Stir in milk gradually; pour into refrigerator tray. Freeze until firm; break into chunks. Beat until smooth. Whip evaporated milk until stiff; fold into frozen mixture. Return to tray; freeze until firm. Yield: 6 servings.

Catharine A. Smuk, Manchester H.S.
Manchester, Michigan

CARBONATED ORANGE SHERBET

1 can sweetened condensed milk
3 tbsp. milk
6 king size bottles orange carbonated
   beverage
1 No. 2 can crushed pineapple

Combine all ingredients; place in 1-gallon freezer container. Freeze according to freezer instructions. Yield: 10-12 servings.

Mary Ella Porter, Como-Pickton School
Como, Texas

REFRESHING ORANGE SHERBET

6 bottles orange carbonated beverage
2 cans sweetened condensed milk
2 No. 2 cans crushed pineapple

Blend all ingredients thoroughly; place in 1 1/2 gallon freezer container. Freeze according to freezer instructions. Yield: 8-10 servings.

Sister M. Del Rey, St. Mary H.S.
Dell Rapids, South Dakota

PINEAPPLE-BUTTERMILK SHERBET

2 c. buttermilk
1/2 c. sugar
1 c. crushed pineapple
1 egg white, beaten
1 tsp. vanilla extract

Combine buttermilk, sugar and pineapple; pour into freezer tray. Freeze until mushy; mix in egg white and vanilla. Return to freezer tray. Freeze until firm. Yield: 4-6 servings.

Mrs. Ruth Ann Franklin, Del Norte H.S.
Albuquerque, New Mexico

LIGHT PINEAPPLE SHERBET

1 c. sugar
1 No. 2 can crushed pineapple
2 egg whites

Combine sugar and 2 cups water; boil slowly for 5 minutes. Add pineapple. Freeze. Beat egg whites until stiff and dry. Beat pineapple mixture until consistency of fondant; fold in egg whites. Freeze until firm. Yield: 16 servings.

Mrs. Rama G. Steen, Caldwell High
Caldwell, Ohio

Desserts

FRESH ORANGE JUICE SHERBET

2 tsp. unflavored gelatin
3/4 c. sugar
1 1/2 c. orange juice
3 tbsp. lemon juice
1 tbsp. grated orange rind
Dash of salt

Soften gelatin in 1/4 cup cold water. Combine 1/2 cup water and sugar; bring to a boil. Boil for 1 minute. Add softened gelatin; stir until dissolved. Add remaining ingredients. Strain and cool; pour into freezer tray. Freeze until mushy; place in chilled bowl. Beat until smooth; return to tray. Freeze until firm, stirring several times. Yield: 4-6 servings.

Lyvonne Johnson
South Peace Sr. Secondary School
Dawson Creek, British Columbia, Canada

TROPICAL PINEAPPLE SHERBET

1 6-oz. can frozen pineapple juice, thawed
1 qt. buttermilk
1 c. sugar

Combine all ingredients; stir until sugar is dissolved. Pour mixture into 2 freezer trays; freeze until mushy. Turn into chilled bowl; beat until fluffy. Return to trays; freeze until firm. Cover sherbet with waxed paper to prevent formation of ice crystals on surface. Yield: 12 servings.

Mrs. May Schlichtemier Koch, Converse Co. H.S.
Douglas, Wyoming

WINTER APPLE CRISP

1 can sliced apples for pie
1/2 tsp. cinnamon
1/2 tsp. nutmeg
Juice from 1/2 lemon
1 1/4 c. (packed) brown sugar
1/2 c. all-purpose flour
1/2 c. butter or margarine

Drain apple slices, reserving 1/4 cup liquid. Place apple slices in greased 10 x 7 x 2-inch baking dish. Sprinkle apples with cinnamon, nutmeg and lemon juice. Pour reserved liquid over apples. Blend brown sugar, flour and butter together until mixture is crumbly. Sprinkle over apples. Bake at 350 degrees for 30 minutes. Serve hot; top with whipped cream or ice cream.

Loretta Wadkins, Cowden Comm. H.S.
Cowden, Illinois

ALABAMA APPLE BETTY

1 can pie apples
1/2 stick margarine, cut in sm. pieces
1 3/4 c. graham cracker crumbs

Combine all ingredients in casserole. Bake in preheated 400-degree oven for 25 minutes. Serve topped with whipped cream. Yield: 4 servings.

Mrs. Jean Head, Etowah H.S.
Attalla, Alabama

APPLE BROWN BETTY

1/3 c. fine gingersnap crumbs
3 tbsp. brown sugar
2 tbsp. nonfat dry milk powder
2 tbsp. melted butter
1 c. applesauce

Blend first 3 ingredients together well. Add melted butter; mix well. Divide 1/2 cup applesauce into custard cups; cover with crumb mixture. Add remaining applesauce; cover with remaining crumbs. Bake at 350 degrees for about 15 minutes. Serve warm with hard sauce, if desired. Yield: 2 servings.

Judith A. Svoboda, Platteview Jr.-Sr. H.S.
Springfield, Nebraska

EASY APPLE DESSERT

1 can apple pie filling
1/2 box white cake mix
1 stick margarine or butter

Place pie filling in greased 8 x 8-inch baking dish. Sprinkle cake mix evenly over top. Dot with butter. Bake at 350 to 375 degrees for about 40 minutes. May be served plain or warm with ice cream. Yield: 5-6 servings.

Mrs. Wyladine F. Reed, Aberdeen H.S.
Aberdeen, Mississippi

QUICK APPLE CRISP

1 No. 2 1/2 can apple pie filling
1/2 c. (packed) brown sugar
1/2 c. rolled oats
1/2 c. flour
1/3 c. soft butter or margarine
3/4 tsp. cinnamon
3/4 tsp. nutmeg

Pour pie filling into ungreased baking dish. Combine brown sugar, rolled oats, flour, butter, cinnamon and nutmeg; mix until crumbly. Sprinkle over pie filling. Bake at 375 degrees for 35 minutes. Serve warm with whipped cream, if desired. Yield: 6 servings.

Mrs. Jorene Hopkins, Permian H.S.
Odessa, Texas

SPICY FRUIT CRISP

4 c. sliced apples or peaches
Sugar
1 1/4 c. Bisquick
2 tsp. cinnamon
1 egg
1/4 c. oil

Place apples in greased 8 or 9-inch square cake pan; cover with 1/4 to 1/3 cup sugar. Sprinkle with 2 tablespoons water. Mix Bisquick, 1/2 cup sugar, cinnamon and egg until crumbly. Sprinkle evenly over apples in cake pan. Pour oil over top. Bake in preheated 400-degree oven for 20 to 25 minutes or until golden brown. Serve hot or warm with ice cream. Yield: 6 servings.

Nedra O'Brien, Tri City H.S.
Buffalo, Illinois

SPICED APPLE COMPOTE

6 firm cooking apples
3 tbsp. cornstarch
1/2 tsp. cinnamon or 1   3-in.cinnamon stick
1/4 tsp. nutmeg
1/4 tsp. salt
2 c. apple juice or water
2 tsp. liquid non-caloric sweetener

Peel, quarter and core apples; place in custard cups or casserole. Mix cornstarch, cinnamon, nutmeg and salt with 1/2 cup apple juice until smooth. Bring remaining apple juice to a boil; add cornstarch mixture and sweetener. Cook, stirring constantly, until thickened. Pour over apples. Bake at 350 degrees for about 30 minutes or until apples are soft, but not mushy. Serve plain or with whipped topping. Yield: 6 servings.

Mrs. Ruth S. Riale, Central Columbia H.S.
Bloomsburg, Pennsylvania

APPLESAUCE WHIP

1 No. 303 can applesauce
2 tbsp. mint jelly
1 egg white
Cinnamon

Heat applesauce and jelly over a low heat until jelly is completely dissolved. Chill. Beat egg white until stiff peaks form; fold into chilled applesauce. Spoon into dessert dish; sprinkle with cinnamon. Serve immediately. Yield: 4 servings.

Mrs. Ethelyne Wooten, Ruleville Pub. School
Ruleville, Mississippi

SPICED APPLE CRUNCH

1 No. 2 can applesauce
1 box spice apple cake mix
1/4 c. chopped pecans
1 c. melted margarine

Pour applesauce into 2 greased and floured 8 x 8 x 2-inch cake pans. Sprinkle dry cake mix over applesauce. Sprinkle pecans over dry cake mixture. Pour margarine over top. Bake at 350 degrees for 5 minutes. Serve warm with whipped cream. Yield: 5-6 servings.

Janyth Brasher, Keiser H.S.
Keiser, Arkansas

BAKED APRICOT WHIP

3/4 c. cooked dried apricots,
     sieved or pureed
4 egg whites, stiffly beaten
Dash of salt
3 tbsp. honey

Fold apricot puree into egg whites. Add salt and honey, mixing lightly. Pile lightly into 1-quart casserole. Bake in preheated 375-degree oven for 30 minutes or until firm. Yield: 6 servings.

Elizabeth Trennepohl, Angola H.S.
Angola, Indiana

BLACKBERRY COBBLER

2 qt. frozen blackberries or peaches
1/4 c. lemon juice
1/4 tsp. salt
2 c. sugar
1 pkg. white or yellow cake mix
1/2 c. melted butter
1/2 c. chopped nuts

Spread blackberries in well-buttered baking dish. Mix lemon juice, salt and sugar; pour over blackberries. Sprinkle cake mix over top; drizzle with butter. Sprinkle with nuts. Bake at 350 degrees for 30 minutes. Yield: 6 servings.

Louise Hall, Amador Co. H.S.
Sutter Creek, California

Desserts

DEWBERRY COBBLER

1 stick butter or margarine
1 c. flour
1 c. sugar
2 tsp. baking powder
1 c. milk
1 pt. dewberries or blackberries

Melt butter in 12 x 8 x 1 1/2-inch baking pan. Sift dry ingredients together; mix with milk. Pour over butter. Arrange dewberries evenly over all. Bake in 375-degree oven until browned. Yield: 8-10 servings.

Beulah G. Mounger, Morganza H.S.
Morganza, Louisiana

BLUEBERRY CRUMB PUDDING

1 c. graham cracker crumbs
1/4 c. sugar
1/4 tsp. cinnamon
3 tbsp. melted margarine
2 c. blueberries
Whipped cream

Combine crumbs, sugar and cinnamon; add margarine. Mix well. Place 1 cup blueberries in small greased casserole; cover with 1/2 cup crumb mixture. Top with remaining blueberries and crumbs. Press down firmly with spoon. Bake in 350-degree oven for 30 minutes. Top with cream. Yield: 6 servings.

Flora Harmon, Hope H.S.
Hope, Arkansas

ALMONDY CHERRY COBBLER

2 cans cherry pie filling
1/2 tsp. almond flavoring
2 c. biscuit mix
1/4 c. milk
1 tbsp. sugar

Combine cherry pie filling and almond flavoring. Pour into 1 1/2-quart casserole. Combine biscuit mix with milk and sugar; beat vigorously for 20 strokes. Drop by spoonfuls over cherries. Bake in preheated 400-degree oven for about 20 minutes. Yield: 6-8 servings.

Mrs. Mary F. Dunn, Byers H.S.
Byers, Texas

CHERRY SUPREME CRUNCH

1 1-lb. 6-oz. can cherry pie filling
1 tsp. lemon juice
1 pkg. cherry supreme cake mix

1/2 c. chopped nuts
1/2 c. margarine, melted
Ice cream or whipped cream

Spread pie filling in 9-inch square pan. Sprinkle with lemon juice. Blend dry cake mix with nuts and melted margarine; sprinkle over pie filling. Bake in preheated 350-degree oven for 45 to 50 minutes or until brown. Serve with ice cream or whipped cream. Yield: 8-10 servings.

Linda Medlen, Lake Co. H.S.
Tiptonville, Tennessee

COOL CHERRY DELIGHT

16 graham crackers, crushed
1/2 c. melted margarine
1 pkg. vanilla pudding mix
1 can cherry pie filling

Mix graham cracker crumbs and margarine together; pat into 8 x 8 x 2-inch cake pan. Prepare pudding mix according to package directions; pour over graham cracker crust. Top with cherry pie filling. Chill until set. Yield: 12 servings.

Jo Ann Greenman, Herscher H.S.
Herscher, Illinois

CHERRY-CHEESE DELIGHT

1 3-oz. package cream cheese
1 pt. sour cream
1 can cherry pie filling

Soften cream cheese; blend with sour cream. Alternate layers of cream cheese mixture and cherry pie filling in sherbet glasses. Top with a cherry. Refrigerate for at least 1 hour. Yield: 6-8 servings.

Mrs. Roberta Sundberg, Nooksack Valley H.S.
Nooksack, Washington

CHERRY COBBLER DELUXE

1 can cherry pie filling
1 8-oz. can crushed pineapple, drained
1 box yellow or white cake mix
Butter (opt.)

Place cherry pie filling and pineapple in 9 x 13-inch baking dish; stir to mix. Sprinkle dry cake mix over fruit. Sprinkle 1/2 to 1 cup warm water over top; do not stir. Dot with butter. Bake in 350-degree oven for 45 to 50 minutes. Serve warm with ice cream or whipped cream. Yield: 6 servings.

Phyllis L. Barton, Fort Hunt H.S.
Alexandria, Virginia

JIFFY CHERRY COBBLER

1 No. 303 can tart cherries or other
   tart fruit
1/2 tsp. lemon juice
3/4 c. sugar
1 8-oz. package Jiffy yellow cake mix
1 stick margarine

Empty cherries into Pyrex baking dish. Add lemon juice and sugar. Sprinkle cake mix over top; cut margarine over cake mix. Bake at 400 degrees for 20 minutes. Yield: 4-6 servings.

Mrs. Chloe Thorp, Madison Jr. H.S.
Abilene, Texas

CHERRY-ORANGE ROLLS

1 can cherry pie filling
1 pkg. refrigerator orange Danish rolls

Pour pie filling into buttered 9-inch cake pan. Arrange rolls on top. Bake at 350 degrees for 30 minutes or until rolls are done. Frost with orange frosting that comes with rolls. Yield: 8 servings.

Janis Williams, West Rusk H.S.
New London, Texas

JIFFY SURPRISE FRUIT COBBLER

1/2 c. butter or margarine
1 c. flour
1 c. sugar
1 tsp. baking powder
1/4 tsp. salt
1 tsp. cinnamon
1 c. milk
1 qt. cherries, apples or sliced peaches
  with juice

Melt butter in large baking dish. Combine dry ingredients; blend with milk until smooth. Pour into melted butter. Pour cherries and juice over all. Sweeten with additional sugar, if desired. Bake in preheated 350-degree oven for 30 to 40 minutes or until bubbly and top is lightly browned. Yield: 6-8 servings.

Mrs. Katy Jo Powers, Haysi H.S.
Haysi, Virginia

SOUR CHERRY DELIGHT

2 c. frozen sour cherries
2/3 c. sugar
1/8 tsp. cinnamon
1/4 c. Minute tapioca

Combine ingredients and 1 cup water; cook until thick. Pour in individual dishes; cool and serve. Top with whipped cream or vanilla ice cream, if desired. Yield: 4 servings.

Mrs. Adele Logue, Williamsburg H.S.
Williamsburg, Pennsylvania

CHERRY-ORANGE COBBLER

1 can cherry, apple, peach or blueberry
   pie filling
1 tbsp. lemon juice
1 can refrigerator Danish orange rolls

Mix pie filling, lemon juice and 1/4 cup water in bottom of 8-inch cake pan. Bring to a boil. Top with rolls. Bake at 375 degrees for 20 minutes. Remove from oven; top with orange frosting from roll package. Serve warm or cold. Yield: 8 servings.

Janet S. Duckwall, Dekalb H.S.
Waterloo, Indiana

QUICK CHERRY COBBLER

1 1-lb. 6-oz. can cherry pie filling
1 1-lb. 3-oz. package white cake mix
1/2 c. butter or margarine, cut into
   thin slices

Pour pie filling into 9 x 9 x 1 3/4-inch baking pan; spread evenly. Sprinkle dry cake mix evenly over filling. Cover dry cake mix with butter slices. Bake at 350 degrees for 1 hour. Blueberry pie filling may be used instead of cherry. Yield: 8 servings.

Mrs. Cele Olson, Eagle Bend H.S.
Eagle Bend, Minnesota

TEXAS FRUIT PUDDING

1/2 c. margarine
1 c. sugar
1 c. flour
3 tsp. baking powder
1 tsp. vanilla extract
1 c. milk
2 c. fresh or canned fruit

Melt margarine in baking dish. Combine sugar, flour and baking powder; add vanilla and milk. Mix well. Pour batter over butter in baking dish. Spread fruit over the top. Bake at 375 degrees for 30 minutes. Yield: 4 servings.

Judith Ball, Dumas Jr. H.S.
Dumas, Texas

Desserts

LEMON ROYAL

1 No. 303 can Wilderness lemon pie filling
2 bananas, sliced
1 sm. can mandarin oranges, drained
1 sm. can crushed pineapple, drained
1 sm. can grapes, drained
10 maraschino cherries, halved

Combine all ingredients; refrigerate to allow flavors to blend. Garnish with whipped cream and a cherry. May be served as a topping or filling for an angel food cake. Yield: 8 servings.

Barbara Jo Huotari, Kimball H.S.
Kimball, Minnesota

ORANGE MINT

4 med. oranges
1/4 lb. old-fashioned mints
12 marshmallows, cut up

Let oranges stand in boiling water for 5 minutes to remove peeling and membrane easier. Cut each section in several pieces; place in a large bowl. Mix mints with oranges; let stand at room temperature for 2 hours before serving. Add marshmallows just before serving; mix well. Decorate with maraschino cherry. Yield: 8 servings.

Louise Kelsey, Santa Ana H.S.
Santa Ana, California

CINNAMON-PEACH COBBLER

1 1-lb. 5-oz. can peach pie filling
1 can refrigerator cinnamon rolls with icing

Pour pie filling into a 9-inch pie pan. Separate cinnamon rolls; cut each in half or fourths. Place over filling. Bake at 350 degrees for 20 to 25 minutes or until golden brown. Spread icing on rolls. Serve warm. Yield: 6 servings.

Mrs. Shelley Langley, Coppell H.S.
Coppell, Texas

ONE BIG PEACH DUMPLING

1/2 c. butter
3/4 c. flour
3/4 c. sugar
3/4 c. milk
1 tsp. baking powder
4 c. sliced peaches, sweetened to taste

Melt butter in 1 1/2-quart casserole. Combine flour, sugar, milk and baking powder; pour over melted butter. Pour peaches over batter. Bake at 350 degrees for 35 to 45 minutes. Serve warm with vanilla ice cream. Yield: 6 servings.

Mrs. Martha B. Godwin, Windsor H.S.
Windsor, Virginia

QUICK PEACH COBBLER

1 lg. can sliced peaches
1 c. flour
1 c. sugar
3 tsp. baking powder
1/2 c. margarine

Drain peaches, reserving juice. Add enough water to juice to measure 2/3 cup liquid. Combine flour, sugar and baking powder. Add reserved juice; mix well. Melt butter in baking dish. Pour batter into baking dish. Spoon peaches over batter. Bake at 350 degrees for about 45 minutes or until lightly browned. Yield: 6 servings.

Mona Faye Fordham, Sikes H.S.
Sikes, Louisiana

PEACH-BISCUIT COBBLER

1/2 c. margarine
2 c. peaches or other fruit
1 c. sugar
1 can biscuits, baked

Melt margarine in 5 x 9-inch pan. Combine peaches and sugar; add to butter. Cut biscuits in half; place, cut side down, over peaches. Dot biscuits with additional margarine; sprinkle with additional sugar. Bake in 350-degree oven for several minutes or until peaches are bubbly. Do not overbrown biscuits. Yield: 6 servings.

Mrs. Lelias White, Jonesboro H.S.
Jonesboro, Texas

CRAZY PINEAPPLE CAKE

1 lg. can crushed pineapple
1 pkg. yellow cake mix
1 can coconut
1 c. chopped nuts (opt.)
1 c. melted margarine

Spread pineapple into 9 x 14-inch pan. Cover with cake mix. Sprinkle coconut over mix; sprinkle nuts over coconut. Pour margarine over top. Bake at 325 to 350 degrees for 40 minutes to 1 hour. Serve with ice cream or whipped cream. Yield: 12-15 servings.

Mrs. Willa Mae Scroggs, Sylva-Webster H.S.
Sylva, North Carolina

HOLIDAY DUMP CAKE

1 No. 2 can crushed pineapple
1 1-lb. 5-oz. can cherry pie filling
1 box yellow cake mix
1/2 to 1 c. chopped pecans
1 c. melted butter or margarine

Pour pineapple into 13 x 9-inch cake pan; pour cherry filling over pineapple. Sprinkle cake mix directly from box over cherry filling. Spread pecans over cake; cover cake with a thin layer of butter. Bake at 350 degrees for 1 hour. Top with whipped cream or ice cream, if desired. Yield: 12-15 servings.

Mary Ellen Weiss, O. W. Holmes H.S.
San Antonio, Texas

TEN-DOLLAR COBBLER

3/4 stick butter
1 c. flour
1 c. sugar
1 tbsp. baking powder
1 c. milk
1 1-lb can crushed pineapple or peaches

Melt butter in 7 x 12-inch baking dish. Combine flour, sugar, baking powder and milk; mix until smooth. Pour batter over melted butter. Heat but do not boil pineapple; pour over batter. Do not stir. Bake in preheated 350-degree oven for about 40 minutes. Serve hot. May be reheated. Yield: 8 servings.

Mrs. Jo Elam Gates, Midlothian H.S.
Midlothian, Virginia

FRUIT COCKTAIL CRUMBLE

2 1-lb. 13-oz. cans fruit cocktail or
   sliced peaches, drained
1 pkg. white or yellow cake mix
2 sticks butter or margarine

Arrange fruit cocktail in 13 x 9 x 2-inch pan. Sprinkle dry cake mix over fruit. Slice butter into thin pats; cover cake mix completely. Bake in preheated 350-degree oven for 35 to 40 minutes or until top is browned. Serve warm with a scoop of ice cream, sour cream or whipped cream sprinkled with grated nutmeg. Yield: 10-12 servings.

Essie Stanley, Saltillo H.S.
Saltillo, Texas

APPLE-BERRY MERINGUE

1 1-lb. 4-oz. can apple pie filling
1 7-oz. can whole cranberry sauce
1/4 c. (packed) brown sugar
1/8 tsp. cinnamon
1/8 tsp. nutmeg
3 egg whites
2 tbsp. sugar

Combine fruits, brown sugar and spices in 1-quart shallow baking dish. Bake at 400 degrees for 20 minutes. Beat whites until soft peaks form, adding sugar gradually. Beat until stiff peaks form. Spoon over apple mixture. Bake for 5 minutes longer or until meringue is brown. Yield: 6 servings.

Mabel V. Garst, Eaton H.S.
Eaton, Ohio

PINEAPPLE-DATE CRUNCH

1 No. 2 can crushed pineapple
1 8-oz. package chopped dates
1 c. chopped pecans
1 pkg. white cake mix
1 c. melted butter or margarine

Pour pineapple in 9 x 13-inch baking pan. Add dates and pecans. Sprinkle cake mix over top. Pour butter over cake mix. Bake at 350 degrees until browned. Cut into squares. May be topped with whipped cream or ice cream. Yield: 24 servings.

Marjorie M. De Sordi, Homer H.S.
Homer, Louisiana

APPLELESS APPLE PIE

20 soda crackers
2 c. sugar
2 tsp. cream of tartar
2 tsp. cinnamon
1 unbaked pie shell

Crumble crackers; add sugar, cream of tartar, cinnamon and 2 cups water; mix well. Turn into pie shell. Bake in preheated 350-degree oven until browned. Yield: 5 servings.

Mrs. W. B. Wilkerson, Jr., Aldine Sr. H.S.
Houston, Texas

APRICOT NECTAR DELIGHT

1 med. package marshmallows
1 12-oz. can apricot nectar
1 c. cream, whipped
1 baked pie shell

Melt marshmallows in juice. Cool; stir into whipped cream. Pour into pie shell. Place in freezing compartment for about 1 hour and 30 minutes or until set. Other fruit juices may be substituted for the apricot juice. Yield: Two 8-inch pies.

Margaret Tisdale, Treadwell School
Memphis, Tennessee

Desserts

APPLE PIE WITH CRUMB TOPPING

4 to 5 med. tart apples
1 tsp. cinnamon
1/4 c. sugar
1   9-in. unbaked pie shell
3/4 c. (packed) brown sugar
3/4 c. flour
1/3 c. butter or margarine

Peel and chop apples; sprinkle with mixture of cinnamon and sugar. Pour into pie shell. Blend brown sugar, flour and butter together with pastry blender; place over apples. Bake at 350 degrees for 35 to 45 minutes or until apples are tender and crust is browned. Yield: 6-8 servings.

Mrs. Bobbie J. Nix, Memorail Jr. H.S.
Kingsville, Texas

REFRESHING APRICOT PIE

1 can sweetened condensed milk
1/4 c. lemon juice
1 No. 303 can peeled apricot halves,
    drained and crushed
1/2 pt. whipping cream, whipped
Vanilla wafers

Combine milk, lemon juice, apricots and 3 to 4 tablespoons whipped cream. Line 9-inch pie pan with wafers; add filling. Top with remaining whipped cream; chill thoroughly. Yield: 6 servings.

Willie Dean Flowers, Murphy H.S.
Walnut Grove, Mississippi

MAGIC BLUEBERRY PIE

1/3 c. lemon juice
1 c. sweetened condensed milk
1 pkg. Dream Whip, prepared
1 can wild blueberries, drained
1 crumb crust

Add lemon juice to milk. Fold Dream Whip into lemon mixture. Fold in blueberries. Pour into crumb crust; chill thoroughly. Yield: 6-8 servings.

Mrs. Noal Akins, Jr., Pontotoc H.S.
Pontotoc, Mississippi

BLUEBERRY-VANILLA PIE

2 pkg. vanilla pudding mix
1 pt. vanilla ice cream, softened
1 baked graham cracker crust, cooled
1 can prepared blueberry pie filling

Prepare vanilla pudding mix using half the milk required on package directions. Combine with softened ice cream. Place mixture in crust; allow to cool. Chill for 1 hour. Pour pie filling over vanilla mixture; chill until ready to serve. Yield: 6 servings.

Cheryl Grater, Oregon H.S.
Oregon, Illinois

BLUEBERRY WHIP PIE

1/4 c. chopped nuts
1   9-in. unbaked pie shell
1 pkg. Dream Whip
1/2 c. cold milk
1   3-oz. package cream cheese
1 c. powdered sugar
1 tsp. vanilla extract
1 can blueberry pie mix

Add nuts to pie shell; bake and cool. Beat Dream Whip with milk. Blend cream cheese until smooth; add to Dream Whip. Add powdered sugar and vanilla. Pour half the Dream Whip mixture in shell; add blueberries. Top with remaining Dream Whip mixture. Chill and serve. Yield: 6 servings.

Mrs. John L. Hansbrough
Magee Attendance Center
Magee, Mississippi

BLUEBERRY-BANANA PIES

1   8-oz. package cream cheese
1 c. sugar
1 lg. box Dream Whip
4 bananas
2 baked pie shells, cooled
1 can prepared blueberry pie filling

Soften cream cheese; blend with sugar until smooth. Prepare Dream Whip according to package directions. Add cream cheese mixture to prepared Dream Whip. Slice bananas on pie shell; pour whipped mixture over bananas. Top with blueberry pie filling. Yield: 2 pies.

Doris Strauss, Atlanta H.S.
Atlanta, Texas

JIFFY BUTTERSCOTCH PIE

1 pkg. fluffy white frosting mix
1 tsp. vanilla extract
1 c. graham cracker crumbs
1   6-oz. package butterscotch pieces
1/2 c. flaked coconut
1/2 c. chopped pecans
Whipped cream

Prepare frosting mix according to package directions; stir in vanilla. Fold in graham cracker crumbs, butterscotch pieces, coconut and pecans. Turn into a greased 9-inch pie plate. Bake in 350-degree oven for 30 minutes or until lightly browned. Cut in wedges. Serve warm or cool with unsweetened whipped cream. Yield: 8 servings.

Mrs. Irene Struble, Fairview H.S.
Sherwood, Oklahoma

CHERRY CREAM PIE

1/2 pt. whipping cream
1/2 c. powdered sugar
1 tsp. vanilla extract
1 3-oz. package cream cheese
1 9-in. baked pie shell
1 can cherry pie filling

Whip cream until stiff; add powdered sugar, vanilla and softened cream cheese. Spread in bottom of cooled pie shell. Pour cherry filling on top. Chill 6 to 8 hours. Yield: 6 servings.

Anna Mae Strickler, Senior H.S.
Chino, California

CHERRY DELIGHT PIE

1 8-oz. package cream cheese
1/2 c. powdered sugar
1 pkg. Dream Whip
1/2 c. sugar
1 graham cracker crust
1 can cherry pie filling

Beat softened cream cheese until smooth and fluffy; add powdered sugar. Prepare Dream Whip according to package directions; add sugar. Fold into cream cheese; pour into graham cracker crust. Pour cherry pie filling over all. Refrigerate for 24 hours or longer. Yield: 8 servings.

Frances C. Coates, Deep Creek Jr. H.S.
Chesapeake, Virginia

CHERRY-BANANA PIE

2 lg. bananas
1 9-in. baked pastry shell
1 1-lb. 6-oz. can cherry pie filling
1 pkg. Lucky Whip
2 tbsp. sugar
1/3 c. chopped nuts

Slice bananas over pie shell; cover with cherries. Prepare Lucky Whip according to package directions, adding sugar. Sprinkle nuts over top; refrigerate until well chilled. Yield: 6 servings.

Carolyn K. Rankin, Unified School No. 274
Oakley, Kansas

PEGGY'S PIE

1 1/2 c. vanilla wafer crumbs
1/4 c. butter or margarine, softened
1/4 c. sugar
1 can cherry pie filling
1 pkg. instant cherry or vanilla pudding mix

Blend crumbs, butter and sugar together thoroughly. Press firmly into bottom and side of 9-inch pie plate. Pour cherry pie filling into crumb pie shell, reserving 3 cherries for garnish. Prepare pudding according to package directions. Pour over cherries, spreading evenly. Garnish with cherries or mint leaves; chill until ready to serve. Yield: 6 servings.

Emily Minnichsoffer, Turtle Lake H.S.
Turtle Lake, Wisconsin

CHOCOLATE-CHEESE PIE

1 3 3/4-oz. package chocolate fudge whipped dessert mix
1 8-oz. package cream cheese
1 1-oz. envelope no-melt unsweetened chocolate
1 8-in. chocolate cookie crumb or graham cracker crumb crust
1 can whipped cream or whipped topping

Prepare whipped dessert mix according to package directions in medium bowl. Beat cream cheese and chocolate until smooth in a small bowl. Add to whipped dessert, beating until blended. Turn chocolate mixture into crumb crust; chill until ready to serve. Garnish with whipped cream.

Mrs. Marcia Miller, Petoskey Sr. H.S.
Petoskey, Michigan

CHOCOLATE-RUM TARTS

1 recipe 2-crust pie pastry
1 pkg. chocolate Whip 'n Chill
1/4 c. finely chopped nuts
1 tbsp. rum
1 pkg. prepared Dream Whip or whipped cream
Shaved chocolate

Prepare pastry; line 6 tart pans. Bake at 350 degrees until golden brown; cool. Prepare chocolate whip. Chill according to package directions; add nuts and rum. Pour into cooled, baked tart shells. Chill thoroughly in refrigerator. Serve with topping of Dream Whip and garnish with shaved chocolate. Yield: 6 servings.

Virginia O. Savedge, Northampton H.S.
Eastville, Virginia

Desserts

COTTAGE CHEESE PIE

2 tbsp. lemon juice
1 env. unflavored gelatin
1/2 c. boiling milk
2 egg yolks
1/3 c. sugar
2 c. mild creamed cottage cheese
1 graham cracker pie crust
Canned fruit, well drained

Combine 2 tablespoons cold water, lemon juice and gelatin in blender container. Cover; process at low speed to soften gelatin. Remove feeder cap; add boiling milk. Blend until gelatin is dissolved, scraping side with rubber spatula. Add egg yolks, sugar and cottage cheese; process at high speed until smooth and well blended. Pour into crust. Chill for about 2 hours or until set. Top with fruit; garnish with whipped cream, if desired. Yield: 6 servings.

Ruth W. Wingo, Kaufman H.S.
Kaufman, Texas

FEBRUARY PARTY PIES

1 No. 2 can crushed pineapple
1 family-sized box cherry gelatin
1 8-oz. package cream cheese
2 No. 2 cans cherry pie filling
2 prepared graham cracker crusts

Drain pineapple; reserve juice. Add enough water to juice to measure 3 cups liquid. Dissolve gelatin in boiling pineapple juice and water. Add cream cheese; stir until smooth. Let set until almost firm. Whip until light and fluffy. Fold in pineapple and cherry pie filling. Pile into graham cracker crusts; chill until set. Garnish with dessert topping. Yield: 2 pies.

Patricia M. Elsner, Hampton H.S.
Allison Park, Pennsylvania

FIVE-MINUTE BERRY CREAM PIE

1 env. unflavored gelatin
3/4 c. cold orange juice or water
1 pt. strawberry ice cream
1 8-in. baked pie shell or crumb crust

Sprinkle gelatin on juice to soften; stir over moderate heat for about 3 minutes or until gelatin is dissolved. Spoon ice cream into hot mixture; stir until melted and smooth. Turn into prepared pie shell; chill for 5 minutes. Top may be garnished with fresh or frozen berries. Yield: 6 servings.

Mrs. Rebecca Burns Drone, College Grove H.S.
College Grove, Tennessee

HEAVENLY PINEAPPLE PIE

1 1-lb. 4 1/2-oz. can crushed pineapple
1 3-oz. package lemon gelatin
5 tbsp. sugar
1 tbsp. lemon juice
1 tsp. vanilla extract
1/2 c. nonfat dry milk powder
1 prepared graham cracker crust

Drain pineapple, reserving juice. Add enough water to juice to measure 1 1/2 cups liquid. Bring to a boil; pour over gelatin mixed with 2 tablespoons sugar. Stir until sugar and gelatin are dissolved. Refrigerate until slightly thickened. Combine 1/2 cup ice water, lemon juice and vanilla in a bowl. Sprinkle dry milk powder over top. Beat for about 10 minutes or until stiff. Beat in remaining 3 tablespoons sugar; continue beating until stiff. Combine with gelatin mixture. Pour into prepared graham cracker crust. Yield: 6-8 servings.

Mrs. Dorothea Crites, Harry E. Wood H.S.
Indianapolis, Indiana

CRANBERRY-CREAM PIE

2 pt. vanilla ice cream
1 can whole cranberry sauce
1 unbaked graham cracker crust
Toasted buttered pecan halves

Let ice cream stand until soft enough to spread. Spread cranberry sauce into pie crust; spread softened ice cream over cranberry sauce. Top with pecans. Freeze for 12 to 24 hours before serving. Yield: 6-8 servings.

Mrs. Rudene Myer, McEachern Schools
Powder Springs, Georgia

KOOL-AID PIE

1 can evaporated milk
2/3 c. sugar
1 env. Kool-Aid
1 8-in. baked pie shell

Chill milk until partially frozen; whip until fluffy. Add sugar and Kool-Aid; whip until stiff. Place in pie shell; freeze until firm. Yield: 5 servings.

Ruth J. Severson, Huntley H.S.
Huntley, Illinois

LEMONADE-ICE CREAM PIE

1 1/2 c. flaked coconut
1/4 c. margarine

1 qt. hand-packed vanilla ice cream
1 sm. can frozen lemonade

Brown coconut in margarine in heavy pan; line 9-inch pie pan with coconut mixture. Cool. Beat softened ice cream and lemonade together; pour into coconut crust. Freeze until firm. Yield: 6-8 servings.

Grace Dricken, Madison H.S.
Madison, Illinois

LUSH LIME PIE

1 qt. ice milk
1 6-oz. can frozen limeade concentrate
Few drops of green food coloring (opt.)
1 8-in. graham cracker pie crust

Place ice milk in large bowl; beat with electric mixer until softened. Add limeade concentrate gradually, beating until smooth. Add green food coloring. Pour into crust; freeze until firm. Garnish with fresh lime slices, maraschino cherry halves or candy lime slices. Lemonade concentrate may be substituted for limeade. Yield: 8 servings.

Mrs. D. Frances Reed, Anthony Jr. H.S.
Minneapolis, Minnesota

FROZEN STRAWBERRY PIES

1 lg. can evaporated milk, well chilled
1 pkg. strawberry gelatin
1 c. sugar
1 pkg. frozen strawberries
2 8-in. graham cracker pie crusts

Whip milk with electric mixer at high speed until very stiff; reduce speed. Add gelatin and sugar. Fold in strawberries; pour into pie shells. Freeze until firm. Yield: 12 servings.

Mrs. Gilbert Hill, Clay Co. Vocational H. S.
Montpelier, Mississippi

FROZEN PUMPKIN PIE

1 8-in. baked pie shell
1 pt. vanilla ice cream
1 sm. can pumpkin
1 1/4 c. sugar
1/4 tsp. nutmeg
1/2 tsp. ginger
1/2 tsp. salt
1 c. cream, whipped

Line pie shell with ice cream; place in freezer. Combine pumpkin, sugar, nutmeg, ginger and salt; fold into whipped cream. Pour into ice cream-lined pie shell; freeze for 2 hours or until firm. Remove from freezer just before serving. Garnish with additional whipped cream, if desired. Yield: 6 servings.

Mrs. Marjorie Bradley, Cameron H.S.
Cameron, Wisconsin

GRAHAM CRACKER PUDDING PIE

2 pkg. lemon pudding mix
1 8-oz. package cream cheese
1 c. whipped cream
1 9-in. graham cracker crust

Prepare pudding mix according to package directions. Add cream cheese; cool. Fold in whipped cream; pour into graham cracker crust. Sprinkle with additional graham cracker crumbs; chill until set. Yield: 8 servings.

Mrs. Wilma Davis, Sandy Hook H.S.
Sandy Hook, Kentucky

LEMON SPONGE PIE

1 c. sugar
1/4 tsp. salt
1 tbsp. flour
1 c. hot milk
3 eggs, separated
Juice and grated rind of 1 lemon
1 tbsp. melted butter
1 baked pie crust

Combine sugar, salt and flour. Add hot milk and beaten egg yolks; beat thoroughly. Add lemon juice and rind. Add melted butter; cool. Fold in beaten egg whites. Pour into pie crust. Bake in preheated 325-degree oven until firm. Increase temperature to 350 degrees; bake until browned. Yield: 6 servings.

Mrs. Thelma Bishop, Greenville Jr. H.S.
Greenville, West Virginia

OPEN PEACH CREAM PIE

3/4 c. sugar
1/4 c. flour
1/4 tsp. salt
1/4 tsp. nutmeg
3 c. peeled and sliced peaches
1 9-in. unbaked pastry shell
1 c. whipping cream or half and half

Combine sugar, flour, salt and nutmeg; add to peaches. Mix lightly. Turn into pastry shell; pour cream over top. Bake at 400 degrees for 35 to 45 minutes or until firm. Chill well before serving. Yield: 6 servings.

Patricia W. Gould, Valley H.S.
Pine Grove, West Virginia

Desserts

LIME DELIGHT PIE

1 sm. package lime gelatin
1 pkg. vanilla pudding mix
2 c. reconstituted nonfat dry milk
Graham cracker crumbs

Dissolve gelatin in 1 cup hot water; do not use additional cold water. Refrigerate until gelatin begins to thicken. Prepare pudding mix according to package directions using nonfat dry milk; cool. Line greased pie pan with crumbs; set aside. Place bowl of gelatin in bowl of crushed ice. Beat with mixer until foamy and fluffy. Add cooled pudding gradually; beat. Pour into crust. Refrigerate for about 2 hours or overnight. Garnish with whipped cream or Dream Whip and lime slices. Yield: 6 servings.

Karen Jodock, Kellogg Sr. H.S.
St. Paul, Minnesota

OATMEAL PIE

4 eggs, well beaten
1 c. sugar
1/4 c. butter
1 c. milk
2 tbsp. flour
1 tsp. vanilla extract
1 tsp. maple flavoring
1/4 c. dark Karo syrup
1/4 c. oatmeal
1/2 c. chopped pecans
1/2 c. flaked coconut
1 10-in. unbaked pie crust

Combine eggs, sugar, butter, milk, flour, vanilla, maple flavoring and corn syrup; beat well. Blend in oatmeal, pecans and coconut. Pour into pie shell. Bake on lowest rack in oven at 350 degrees for 45 minutes or until knife inserted in center comes out clean. Yield: 8-10 servings.

Mrs. Bernice Hansbore, East Liberty H.S.
Center, Texas

PEACH TARTS

1 1/2 c. sifted all-purpose flour
3/4 tsp. salt
1/2 c. shortening
1 2 3/4-oz. package custard mix, prepared
1 10-oz. package frozen peach slices,
    thawed and drained

Sift flour and salt together. Cut in shortening until pieces are size of small peas. Sprinkle with 3 to 5 tablespoons water, mixing lightly until dough begins to stick together. Turn out on a piece of Saran Wrap that has been pressed on damp counter surface.

Cover with another piece of Saran Wrap. Roll out 1/8 inch thick. Cut 9 or 10 circles; shape over tops and sides of inverted muffin tins or custard cups. Prick bottoms and sides. Bake in a preheated 450-degree oven for 10 to 12 minutes or until lightly browned. Remove from tins to wire racks; cool. Pour prepared custard mix in shells. Chill until set. Cover tops with peach slices. Refrigerate until serving time. Yield: 9-10 servings.

Mrs. Charlotte Schroeder, Goodland H.S.
Goodland, Kansas

EASY PUMPKIN PIE

1 1-lb. can pumpkin
1 can sweetened condensed milk
3/4 tsp. cinnamon
1/2 tsp. ginger
1/2 tsp. nutmeg
1/2 tsp. salt
1 egg
1 unbaked pie shell

Combine all ingredients except pie shell in a small bowl; mix well. Pour into pie shell. Bake at 375 degrees for 50 to 55 minutes or until firm.

Mrs. Frank Joyce, Franklin Co. H.S.
Winchester, Tennessee

PENNSYLVANIA DUTCH MILK PIE

1/4 c. flour
1/4 c. sugar
1/4 c. syrup
1 8-in. unbaked pie crust
1 1/2 c. milk
2 tsp. butter
Dash of cinnamon

Combine flour, sugar and syrup. Distribute evenly over bottom of pie crust. Pour in milk. Swirl milk carefully through flour mixture with back of tablespoon; do not tear crust. Dot with butter; sprinkle with cinnamon. Bake at 400 degrees for 45 minutes. Yield: 6 servings.

Mrs. Gayle C. Johns, Greenwood H.S.
Millerstown, Pennsylvania

QUICK CUSTARD PIE

1/3 c. chopped pecans
1/4 c. margarine
1 can flaked coconut
1 pkg. golden egg custard mix
Nutmeg to taste

Chop pecans in blender. Cut margarine into small pieces; place in skillet with coconut and pecans. Stir constantly over medium heat until coconut is golden brown. Press around side and bottom of 8-inch pie plate. Chill well. Prepare custard mix according to package directions; pour into cooled shell. Sprinkle with nutmeg. Yield: 6-8 servings.

Mrs. Glenda Ballinger, Kirkman Technical H.S.
Chattanooga, Tennessee

RASPBERRY CHIFFON PIE

1 10-oz. package frozen red
   raspberries, thawed
1 3-oz. package raspberry gelatin
2 tbsp. lemon juice
1 2 or 2 1/2-oz. envelope dessert
   topping mix, prepared
Dash of salt
2 egg whites
1/4 c. sugar
1 baked 9-in. pastry shell

Drain raspberries; add enough water to syrup to measure 2/3 cup liquid. Dissolve gelatin in 3/4 cup boiling water; add lemon juice and raspberry syrup. Chill until partially set. Beat until soft peaks form. Fold in raspberries and half the whipped topping mix. Add salt to egg whites; beat until soft peaks form. Add sugar gradually; beat until stiff peaks form. Fold into raspberry mixture. Pile into cooled pastry shell; chill. Pile remaining whipped topping mix into a pastry bag with large decorator tip. Form scrolls over top of chilled pie. May garnish with whole fresh frozen raspberries, if desired. Yield: 7-8 servings.

Mrs. Bev France, St. Paul H.S.
St. Paul, Oregon

STRAWBERRY MINUTE PIE

1 3-oz. package strawberry gelatin
1 pkg. frozen sweetened sliced strawberries
1 8-in. baked pie shell

Dissolve gelatin in 1 cup boiling water. Add unthawed strawberries, breaking up with a fork. Gelatin will thicken as strawberries thaw. Pour into cooled pie shell. Chill until completely set. Serve with whipped cream. Yield: 6 servings.

Mrs. Carole Fisher, Martinsville H.S.
Martinsville, Indiana

STRAWBERRY ICEBOX PIE

1 17-oz. package marshmallows
1 1-lb. box frozen strawberries or
   2 c. sweetened fresh strawberries

1 c. whipping cream, whipped
1 9-in. baked pastry shell

Place marshmallows in a double boiler; add 2 tablespoons strawberry juice. Cook until marshmallows are melted. Add strawberries and mix thoroughly. Chill for about 2 hours. Fold in whipped cream; pour into cold pastry shell. Yield: 8 servings.

Mrs. Esther D. Leed, Wiscasset H.S.
Wiscasset, Maine

STRAWBERRY-PECAN PIE

1/2 c. (or more) chopped pecans
2 9-in. unbaked pie shells
1 8-oz. package cream cheese
1 c. sugar
1 tsp. vanilla extract
1 pt. whipping cream, whipped
Fresh or frozen strawberries

Press pecans into pie shells. Bake at 350 degrees until browned. Combine cream cheese, sugar and vanilla; beat until fluffy. Fold whipped cream into cheese mixture; pour into shells. Top with whole strawberries; chill thoroughly. Yield: 2 pies.

Mrs. Madonna M. Mahurin, Webster Co. H.S.
Dixon, Kentucky

SLIMMER'S STRAWBERRY PIE

1 env. D-Zerta gelatin
1 20-oz. box frozen strawberries, broken
   into chunks
1 graham cracker pie shell
1 c. low-calorie whipped topping

Dissolve D-Zerta gelatin in 1 cup boiling water; add frozen strawberries. Stir until strawberries are separated; spoon into prepared crust. Refrigerate until firm; top with swirls of whipped topping. Yield: 5-6 servings.

Mrs. Daisymae Eckman, Pawnee H.S.
Pawnee City, Nebraska

GRAHAM CRACKER CRUST

1 tbsp. butter or margarine
1/2 c. graham cracker crumbs
1/4 tsp. cinnamon

Grease side and bottom of 9-inch pie plate using most of butter for side. Combine crumbs and cinnamon; press into buttered pie plate, leaving bottom center thin. Bake in 375-degree oven for 5 minutes. Cool and fill.

Mrs. Val C. Manley, Virginia Jr. H.S.
Bristol, Virginia

Desserts

CORN OIL PIE CRUST

1 1/2 c. all-purpose flour
3 tbsp. sugar
1/2 c. Mazola oil
3 tbsp. milk

Mix flour and sugar together in 9-inch pie pan using a fork. Blend oil with milk. Add oil mixture to dry mixture in pie pan; mix with a fork. Press around side and bottom of pan. Bake at 425 degrees for about 10 minutes or until lightly browned. Cool; fill with favorite filling.

Mrs. Betty Lute, Avon Lake H.S.
Avon Lake, Ohio

BAKED HONEY CUSTARD

2 eggs
1/4 c. honey
1/4 tsp. salt
2 c. skim milk
1/2 tsp. vanilla extract
Nutmeg to taste

Combine first 5 ingredients; beat until well blended. Pour into 1 1/2-quart baking dish. Set baking dish in pan of hot water to depth of 1 inch. Sprinkle with nutmeg. Bake at 350 degrees for 1 hour or until knife inserted 1 inch from edge comes out clean. Yield: 6 servings.

Mable Gray, Savanna H.S.
Savanna, Illinois

SOUTHERN-BAKED CUSTARD

3 eggs, slightly beaten
1/4 c. sugar
1/4 tsp. salt
2 c. scalded milk, slightly cooled
1/2 to 1 tsp. vanilla extract

Combine eggs, sugar and salt; stir in milk and vanilla slowly. Pour into six 5-ounce custard cups; set custard cups in shallow pan of hot water to the depth of 1 inch. Bake at 325 degrees for 40 to 45 minutes or until knife inserted in center comes out clean. Serve warm or chilled. Yield: 6-8 servings.

Ruth Cooper Humphrey, Wheeler Co. H.S.
Alamo, Georgia

ANGIE'S BAKED CUSTARD

2 eggs
3 tbsp. sugar

1/8 tsp. salt
2 c. skim milk, scalded
1/2 to 1 tsp. vanilla extract
Dash of nutmeg

Combine eggs, sugar and salt; beat until well blended. Add milk and vanilla. Pour into lightly buttered custard cups; place cups in pan of hot water to the depth of 1 inch. Sprinkle nutmeg over top. Bake in preheated 325-degree oven for 40 minutes or until custard is set. Serve warm or cold. Yield: 5 servings.

Angie T. Miller, James Monroe H.S.
Fredericksburg, Virginia

JIFFY QUICK CUSTARD

4 eggs
1/4 c. sugar
1 tsp. vanilla extract
3 c. milk

Beat eggs slightly; beat in remaining ingredients. Pour into 6 custard cups; place cups in deep frying pan with tightfitting cover. Pour hot water in skillet to level of custard. Bring water to a full boil; cover pan immediately. Turn off heat. Let stand for at least 6 minutes. Remove custard cups; cool and chill. Sprinkle with nutmeg before serving, if desired. Yield: 6 servings.

Mrs. Thyra Davis, Manhattan H.S.
Manhattan, Kansas

SUNNY CUSTARD

4 tsp. honey
2 eggs, slightly beaten
2 c. skim milk
1/2 tsp. vanilla extract
1 tbsp. grated lemon rind

Place 1 teaspoon honey in each of 4 custard cups; brush around sides of cups. Combine remaining ingredients; pour into cups. Place in pan of hot water. Bake at 325 degrees for 50 minutes to 1 hour or until custard is set. Chill. Yield: 4 servings.

Mrs. Effie Gaymon, Leonard School
Saxtons River, Vermont

GOLDEN APPLE PUDDING

1 1-lb. 4-oz. can apple slices
1 12-oz. can apricot nectar
1 tbsp. lemon juice
Dash of salt
1 pkg. tapioca pudding mix

Drain apples, reserving syrup; add enough water to syrup to measure 1/2 cup liquid. Place apples and liquid in saucepan; stir in apricot nectar, lemon juice and salt. Cover; bring to a boil. Reduce heat; cook for 10 to 12 minutes or until apples are almost tender. Stir in pudding mix; cook over medium heat, stirring constantly, for 8 to 10 minutes. Serve warm or cold. Serve with honey sauce, if desired. Yield: 4-6 servings.

Zona Kay Bunger, Woodland H.S.
Woodland, Washington

QUICKIE BANANA PUDDING

1 pkg. vanilla Whip 'n Chill
2 or 3 bananas
1 sm. package vanilla wafers

Prepare Whip 'n Chill according to package directions. Alternate layers of bananas and wafers in dish; pour Whip 'n Chill over top. Chill for 1 hour. Yield: 5 servings.

Mrs. Janie Vandiver, Sulphur Bluff School
Sulphur Bluff, Texas

BUTTERSCOTCH ANGEL PUDDING

1/4 angel food cake
1 pkg. butterscotch pudding
2 c. milk
2 tbsp. toasted coconut or pecans

Cut angel food cake into 1-inch chunks. Line 8-inch square serving dish with cake chunks. Cook pudding with milk according to package directions. Pour hot pudding over cake; top with coconut. Serve warm with whipped topping or whipped cream.

Mrs. Betty Boyd, Roosevelt H.S.
Emporia, Kansas

CHOCOLATE CHIP POTS DE CREME

2/3 c. milk
1 6-oz. package chocolate chips
1 egg
2 tbsp. sugar
1 tsp. vanilla extract
1/8 tsp. salt

Heat milk just to boiling point. Place remaining ingredients in blender container; add hot milk. Blend at low speed for 1 minute. Pour into 6 pots de creme dishes. Chill for several hours. Garnish each dish with teaspoon of whipped topping. Yield: 6 servings.

Martha Jo Albin, Churchill Jr. H.S.
Galesburg, Illinois

TOP HAT CHERRY DESSERT

1 egg, slightly beaten
1/3 c. sugar
1/8 tsp. salt
1 3/4 c. milk
3 tbsp. Minute tapioca
3/4 tsp. vanilla extract
1 can cherry pie filling

Combine all ingredients except vanilla and cherry pie filling in saucepan. Let stand for 5 minutes. Cook over medium heat, stirring constantly, for 6 to 8 minutes or until mixture comes to a full boil. Pudding will thicken when cooled. Remove from heat. Stir in vanilla. Pour in individual serving dishes; cool. Spoon cherry pie filling over each serving. Yield: 6-8 servings.

Mrs. Esther Williams, Pocatello H.S.
Pocatello, Idaho

QUICK DATE PUDDING

1 c. sugar
1 1/2 tsp. flour
1 c. milk
3 egg yolks
2 tbsp. butter
1/2 8-oz. package chopped dates
1/2 c. chopped pecans
1 tsp. vanilla extract

Sift sugar and flour into saucepan; add just enough milk to form paste. Add egg yolks; stir. Add remaining milk, butter and dates; cook, stirring constantly, until thick. Add pecans and vanilla; cool. Serve as pudding or pour into baked pie shell.

Elsie Hadley, Weinert H.S.
Weinert, Texas

SPICY PUMPKIN PUDDING

1 c. cold pumpkin
1 c. cold skim milk
1 pkg. instant vanilla pudding mix
1/2 tsp. cinnamon
1/2 tsp. allspice
1/4 tsp. nutmeg

Combine all ingredients; beat with electric beater until smooth. Pour into dessert dishes; cool for about 15 minutes. May be served with whipped topping. Yield: 6 servings.

Emma Catherine Lawson, Carrizozo H.S.
Carrizozo, New Mexico

Desserts

PUDDING-IN-A-HURRY

1 3-oz. package instant vanilla pudding mix
1 1/2 c. cold milk
1/4 tsp. salt
1tsp. shredded orange rind
1/4 c. Sherry
1/2 c. whipping cream, whipped
1 box fresh strawberries or 2 lg. bananas

Prepare pudding mix according to package directions, using 1 1/2 cups milk. Add salt and orange rind. Stir in Sherry; fold in whipped cream. Serve over fresh fruit or serve plain garnished with additional orange rind. Yield: 4-6 servings.

Mrs. Janet M. Tucker, Franklin Sr. H.S.
Stockton, California

QUICK RAISIN PUDDING

1 c. sifted flour
1 c. sugar
2 tsp. baking powder
Pinch of salt
1 c. seedless raisins
1/2 c. milk
1 c. (packed) brown sugar

Combine first 6 ingredients thoroughly; place in 8 x 12-inch baking pan. Combine brown sugar and 2 cups boiling water; pour over batter. Bake at 350 degrees for 30 minutes. Serve hot or cold. Yield: 6 servings.

Mrs. Vera Troyer, Bennett Co. H.S.
Martin, South Dakota

TIPSY PUDDING

1 pkg. vanilla pudding mix
1/4 c. Sherry
Ladyfingers

Prepare pudding mix according to package directions, adding Sherry; place in serving bowl. Chill. Place ladyfingers vertically around inside edge of bowl; serve.

Mrs. Annie Laurie Clock, Westminster Jr. H.S.
Westminster, Maryland

APRICOT BAVARIAN

1 tbsp. gelatin
2 c. apricot juice
1 c. sieved apricots
1/3 c. nonfat dry milk
1 tsp. lemon juice

Soften gelatin in 2 tablespoons cold water. Dissolve in 1/2 cup hot apricot juice. Blend in apricots; cool until mixture begins to thicken. Sprinkle dry milk over remaining apricot juice; add lemon juice. Beat until thick and fluffy; fold into gelatin mixture. Turn into mold; chill until firm. Unmold; garnish with apricot halves, if desired. Yield: 4 servings.

Carolyn E. Nordlund, Mayville H.S.
Mayville, Wisconsin

BUSY DAY LEMON CHEESECAKE

1 8-oz. package cream cheese
2 c. milk
1 pkg. instant lemon or pineapple pudding mix
1 8 or 9-in. graham cracker pie crust

Soften cream cheese; blend with 1/2 cup milk. Add remaining milk and pudding mix. Beat for about 1 minute with egg beater or until well mixed. Do not overbeat. Pour into graham cracker crust. Sprinkle additional graham cracker crumbs lightly over top. Chill for about 1 hour before serving. Yield: 6 servings.

Mrs. Elizabeth H. Harrell, Oak City School
Oak City, North Carolina

CHERRY REFRIGERATOR DESSERT

2 tbsp. soft butter
2 tbsp. brown sugar
1/2 c. coconut
1/4 c. chopped nuts
3/4 c. Rice Krispies
1/2 lb. marshmallows, cut into sm. pieces
1 c. whipping cream, whipped
1 No. 2 can cherry pie mix

Combine first 5 ingredienst; spread over bottom of 9 x 9-inch pan. Fold marshmallows into whipped cream. Spread over mixture in pan. Cover with cherry pie mix; refrigerate until set. Yield: 9 servings.

Mrs. Carol Ludtke, Morton Public School
Morton, Minnesota

SWISS CHERRY TORTE

1 1/2 c. whipping cream
1 pkg. white frosting mix
1 angel food cake
1 1-lb. 5-oz. can cherry pie filling

Blend whipping cream with frosting mix in small mixer bowl; chill for 1 hour. Beat until stiff. Spread frosting on the angel food cake. Spoon the cherry pie filling on top of frosting; allow to drizzle down side. Chill until ready to serve. Yield: 12 servings.

Carolyn Christian, Central Jr. H.S.
Biloxi, Mississippi

PORT-O-CHERRY DESSERT

1 1-lb. 1-oz. jar dark sweet Bing cherries
1 c. Port
1 3-oz. package cherry gelatin
Softened vanilla ice cream

Drain cherries; remove pits. Return cherries to jar; pour in wine. Cover tightly; place in refrigerator overnight or longer. Add 1 cup boiling water to gelatin; stir until gelatin is dissolved. Cool slightly. Drain Port from cherries; add to gelatin. Pour into shallow dish; refrigerate until mixture begins to set. Stir in cherries. Chill until firm; cut into cubes. Pile in sherbet glasses. Top with spoonfuls of softened ice cream. Yield: 4-6 servings.

Mrs. Eddie Hilou, Cayuga H.S.
Cayuga, Texas

CHOCOLATE MOUSSE

1/2 c. semisweet chocolate chips
3 eggs, separated
1 tsp. vanilla extract
1/2 tsp. salt
2 tbsp. sugar
1/2 c. chopped pecans

Melt chocolate over hot water. Beat egg yolks slightly with fork; add vanilla and salt. Blend into chocolate. Beat egg whites for about 1 minute or until soft peaks form. Beat in sugar for 30 seconds. Fold in chocolate mixture until well blended. Add pecans; spoon into sherbet dishes. Chill until set; garnish with whipped topping and chocolate shavings. Yield: 4 servings.

Mrs. Rebecca Ann Hudson, Clinton H.S.
Clinton, Mississippi

LIME-CHOCOLATE DELICIOUS

1 13-oz. can evaporated milk
1 3-oz. package lime gelatin
1/4 c. lime juice
2 tsp. lemon juice
1 c. sugar
2 c. chocolate wafer crumbs
1/3 c. melted butter

Chill evaporated milk in freezing compartment until icy. Dissolve gelatin in 1 3/4 cups hot water; chill until partially set. Whip until fluffy. Stir in lime juice, lemon juice and sugar. Whip milk; fold into gelatin. Combine crumbs and butter; press into bottom of 13 x 9 x 2-inch pan. Pour gelatin mixture into crumb crust. Chill until firm. Cut into squares; garnish top of each serving with semisweet chocolate curl.

Arlene E. Kendrick, Fort Vancouver H.S.
Vancouver, Washington

COCONUT CREAM DESSERT

1 c. flour
1/4 c. (packed) brown sugar
1/2 c. butter
1/2 c. chopped nuts
2 pkg. instant coconut cream pudding mix
2 2/3 c. milk
1 c. whipped cream or Dream Whip

Combine first 4 ingredients; pat into 9 x 13-inch pan. Bake in a 350-degree oven for 12 minutes. Cool completely; crumble. Pat back into pan. Prepare pudding mix, using 1 1/3 cups milk for each package. Fold in whipped cream; pour over crust. Refrigerate until well chilled. Serve with whipped cream. Garnish with cherry. Yield: 12 servings.

Mrs. Dorothy Soderlund, Milaca H.S.
Milaca, Minnesota

COCONUT CRUMB PIE

4 c. corn flake crumbs
1/2 c. sugar
1 c. soft butter or margarine
2 qt. cold skim milk
1 lb. instant coconut cream pudding mix
Fruit pie filling

Combine crumbs, sugar and butter; mix well. Reserve about 1 1/2 cups crumb mixture for topping. Spread remaining crumb mixture evenly in bottom of 16 x 10 x 1 1/2-inch pan; press firmly to form a crumb crust. Chill until firm. Pour cold milk into mixer bowl; add pudding mix. Whip at low speed just enough to dampen mix. Scrape bottom and side of bowl. Continue whipping at low speed until evenly mixed and pudding is smooth and slightly thickened. Spread pudding over crumb crust; sprinkle with reserve crumb mixture. Refrigerate until thoroughly set. Spread pie filling over top. Yield: 20 servings.

Mrs. D. G. Headley, Glendora H.S.
Glendora, California

Desserts

COFFEE FLUFF

1 env. unflavored gelatin
6 tbsp. sugar
2 tsp. instant coffee
1/4 tsp. salt
2 eggs, separated
1 tsp. vanilla extract
1/4 c. nonfat dry milk solids

Combine gelatin, 2 tablespoons sugar, instant coffee and salt thoroughly in top of double boiler. Beat egg yolks and 1 3/4 cups water together; add to gelatin mixture. Cook over boiling water, stirring constantly, for 8 minutes or until gelatin is dissolved; remove from heat. Add vanilla; chill to unbeaten egg white consistency. Beat egg whites until stiff; beat in remaining 4 tablespoons sugar. Fold in gelatin mixture. Beat 1/4 cup ice water and dry milk solids together until stiff and mixture stands in peaks; fold into gelatin mixture. Turn into 5-cup mold or individual dessert dishes; chill until firm. Yield: 8 servings.

Medline M. Thomas, Appomattox H.S.
Appomattox, Virginia

DATE DELIGHT

1 c. whipping cream
3 tbsp. confectioners' sugar
1 tsp. vanilla extract
1/2 c. chopped dates
1/2 c. broken walnuts
12 crushed graham crackers
Dash of salt
4 maraschino cherries

Whip cream until stiff; fold in sugar, vanilla, dates, nuts, crackers and salt. Place in 4 sherbet glasses. Top with a maraschino cherry; chill and serve. Yield: 4 servings.

Avys McCadden, Wilder H.S.
Wilder, Idaho

INSTANT DATE-NUT ROLL

2 c. vanilla wafer crumbs
1 c. chopped dates
1/2 c. chopped pecans
1/2 c. sweetened condensed milk
2 tsp. lemon juice

Combine crumbs, dates and pecans; add milk mixed with lemon juice. Knead well. Shape into a 3-inch roll. Wrap in waxed paper; store in refrigerator for 12 hours. Serve plain or with whipped cream. Yield: 8 servings.

Mrs. Sue Harrison, Newark H.S.
Newark, Arkansas

FRUIT JUICE SNOW

1/2 c. sugar
1/3 tsp. salt
1 env. unflavored gelatin
1 6-oz. can frozen fruit juice concentrate
2 egg whites

Combine sugar, salt and gelatin; add 1 1/4 cups hot water. Stir until gelatin dissolves. Add fruit juice; stir until melted. Chill until mixture is slightly thicker than consistency of unbeaten egg white; add egg whites. Beat until mixture holds shape; spoon into sherbet glasses or individual molds. Chill until firm. Garnish with a cherry, if desired. Yield: 6 servings.

Mrs. J. Fred Jones, Ridgeroad Jr. H.S.
North Little Rock, Arkansas

GRAPE VELVET

2 c. grape juice
1 env. unflavored gelatin
Juice of 1 lg. lemon
1/4 c. sugar
Pinch of salt
2 egg whites, stiffly beaten

Heat grape juice. Soften gelatin in lemon juice; add to grape juice. Stir in sugar and salt. Cool. Beat egg whites until stiff; fold into gelatin mixture. Chill in refrigerator until set. Yield: 6 servings.

Mrs. Mary McKinney, Thornton Fractional H.S.
Calumet City, Illinois

LEMON FLUFF

1 14 1/2-oz. can evaporated milk
1 3-oz. package lemon gelatin
1/4 c. lemon juice
1 c. sugar
2 1/2 c. vanilla wafer crumbs
Maraschino cherries

Chill evaporated milk until icy. Dissolve gelatin in 1 3/4 cups hot water. Chill until partially set. Whip until light and fluffy. Add lemon juice and sugar; beat well. Whip chilled evaporated milk until stiff; fold into gelatin mixture. Line bottom of 9 x 13-inch pan with 2 cups vanilla wafer crumbs. Pour gelatin mixture over crumbs. Top with remaining crumbs. Chill until firm. Cut into squares; center each square with maraschino cherry. Yield: 12-16 servings.

Grace Lamusga, Hosterman Jr. H.S.
Robbinsdale, Minnesota

LEMONADE FLUFF

1 env. unflavored gelatin
4 eggs, separated
1/8 tsp. salt
1 6-oz. can frozen lemonade concentrate
1/2 c. sugar
1 env. Dream Whip, prepared

Soften gelatin in 1/2 cup cold water. Beat egg yolks slightly; add salt. Combine with gelatin. Cook over medium heat, stirring constantly, for about 2 minutes or until thickened. Remove from heat; stir in lemonade concentrate. Chill until mixture is slightly congealed. Beat egg whites until foamy; add sugar gradually. Beat until soft peaks form. Fold in gelatin mixture and Dream Whip. Chill until firm. Yield: 6 servings.

Margarette C. Weeks, Highland Jr. H.S.
Highland, California

LEMON-FRUIT DESSERT

1 pkg. whipped topping mix
1 can lemon pie filling
1/2 tsp. lemon flavoring
1 No. 2 1/2 can fruit cocktail, drained

Prepare the whipped topping mix according to directions. Combine with pie filling and lemon flavoring. Fold in fruit cocktail. Chill until ready to serve. Marshmallows and other fruit may be added, if desired. Yield: 6-8 servings.

Mardelle Parkinson, Hampton Comm. H.S.
Hampton, Iowa

LEMON BISQUE

1 3-oz. package lemon gelatin
1/3 c. honey or white Karo syrup
Juice of 1 lemon
1 lg. can evaporated skim milk, chilled
1 1/2 c. vanilla wafer crumbs

Combine gelatin, 1 1/2 cups water, honey and lemon juice in a large mixing bowl; stir until gelatin is dissolved. Set aside until mixture begins to thicken. Pour milk into a chilled bowl; whip until very stiff. Fold into gelatin mixture. Sprinkle half the cracker crumbs in bottom of an oblong shallow baking dish. Pour in gelatin mixture. Cover with remaining cracker crumbs. Let stand in refrigerator for 2 to 3 hours or overnight. Cut into squares to serve. Different flavored gelatin and fruits such as crushed pineapple and sliced strawberries may be used, if desired. Yield: 6-8 servings.

Ruth A. Williams, East Mecklenburg H.S.
Charlotte, North Carolina

SNOW PUDDING

1 env. unflavored gelatin
1 1/2 c. sugar
1/4 c. lemon or orange juice
4 eggs, separated
1/8 tsp. salt
2 c. scalded milk
1 tsp. vanilla extract

Soak gelatin in 4 tablespoons cold water; add 1 cup boiling water. Stir until gelatin is dissolved. Add 1 cup sugar and lemon juice; set aside to cool, stirring occasionally, until thick. Beat with electric mixer until fluffy; add stiffly beaten egg whites. Continue beating until mixture holds shape. Turn into individual molds; chill. Beat egg yolks slightly; add remaining 1/2 cup sugar and salt. Stir in hot milk slowly. Cook in double boiler for about 10 minutes or until mixture is of consistency of thin cream. Chill well; add vanilla. Unmold pudding in sauce dish; pour custard sauce over top. Yield: 8-12 servings.

Helen Z. Sullivan, Hillsboro Union H.S.
Hillsboro, Oregon

ORANGE CHARLOTTE

1 tbsp. gelatin
1/2 c. sugar
3/4 c. orange juice
1 tbsp. lemon juice
1/2 c. cream, whipped

Dissolve gelatin in 1/4 cup cold water; add 1/4 cup boiling water. Add sugar and juices; chill until mixture begins to thicken. Fold in whipped cream. Chill until set.

Mrs. Susie Jablonic, Marshall H.S.
Marshall, Wisconsin

ORANGE CHIFFON DELIGHT

2 eggs
1 c. sugar
1 1/2 c. pineapple juice
1 pkg. orange gelatin
1 lg. can evaporated milk
1 graham cracker crust recipe

Combine eggs, sugar and pineapple juice in saucepan; bring to a boil. Add gelatin; cool. Chill milk until icy; beat until stiff. Fold into egg mixture. Press graham cracker crust mixture into rectangular pan; pour in gelatin mixture. Chill until set. Cut into squares to serve. Yield: 12 servings.

Mrs. Linda Perry, South Side H.S.
Memphis, Tennessee

Desserts

PARTY FLUFF

1 pkg. fruit-flavored gelatin
1 c. vanilla ice cream
3 ice cubes

Combine gelatin and 1 cup hot water in container with tightfitting lid; mix well. Add ice cream and ice cubes; shake until ice cubes have melted. Pour into serving dishes; refrigerate for 10 to 15 minutes. Yield: 6 servings.

Sharon George, Alta Vista H.S.
Alta Vista, Kansas

1 1-lb. 4 1/2-oz. can crushed pineapple
1 3-oz. package lime or lemon gelatin
1/2 c. milk
1/4 tsp. almond extract
3/4 c. crushed ice

Drain pineapple, reserving 3/4 cup syrup. Bring syrup to a boil; add gelatin, stirring until dissolved. Combine pineapple and milk in blender container; process until well blended. Add gelatin mixture, almond extract and ice. Mix thoroughly in blender; pour into dessert dishes. Chill for about 1 hour or until set. Yield: 6 servings.

Mrs. Madge Lumsden, Vassar H.S.
Vassar, Michigan

QUICK FRUIT ROYALE

1 pkg. instant vanilla pudding mix, prepared
1 pkg. dessert topping mix, prepared
2 1-lb. cans fruit cocktail, well drained
1 to 1 1/2 c. miniature marshmallows

Combine pudding and dessert topping. Add fruit cocktail and marshmallows. Chill for 45 minutes to 1 hour in refrigerator or in freezer for 15 to 20 minutes. Yield: 4-6 servings.

Judith Hintze, Jackson H.S.
Jackson, Minnesota

PINEAPPLE BAVARIAN

1 3-oz. package lemon gelatin
1/4 c. sugar
1 8 3/4-oz. can pineapple tidbits
1 env. whipped topping mix
1/2 c. cold milk
1/2 tsp. vanilla extract

Dissolve gelatin and sugar in 1 cup boiling water. Drain syrup from pineapple; add enough water to measure 3/4 cup liquid. Add to gelatin; chill until slightly thickened. Prepare topping mix with milk and vanilla as directed on package. Add pineapple to topping mix; blend. Fold into gelatin mixture. Pour into a 1-quart mold; chill or freeze for about 4 hours or until firm. Yield: 6-8 servings.

Sonia M. Cole, Asst. Supvr.
Vocational Home Ec., State Dept of Ed.
Columbus, Ohio

CHILLED PINEAPPLE DESSERT

1 tbsp. unflavored gelatin
1/3 c. sugar
1/8 tsp. salt
1 8-oz. can crushed pineapple
2 tbsp. lemon juice
1 tbsp. fruit punch concentrate
1/2 tsp. pineapple extract
1/2 tsp. lemon extract
1 2-oz. envelope dessert topping mix
1/2 c. cold milk
1 tsp. almond extract

Mix gelatin, sugar and salt in a saucepan; set aside. Drain juice from pineapple into a glass measuring cup; add lemon juice, punch concentrate, pineapple extract, lemon extract and enough water to measure 1 cup liquid. Pour into saucepan; place over low heat until gelatin dissolves. Pour into a cool mixing bowl; add 5 or 6 large ice cubes. Stir for about 3 minutes until gelatin begins to thicken. Remove any unmelted ice. Chill until thick, but not firm. Remove 1/2 cup from bowl; set aside. Fold chilled pineapple into remaining gelatin. Pour into serving dishes. Chill until firm. Prepare topping mix and milk according to package directions. Add almond extract and reserved gelatin; mix well. Spoon whipped mixture over pineapple mixture; swirl to a peak in center. Chill for at least 30 minutes before serving. Yield: 5-6 servings.

Mrs. Nerine Kinsey, Gatesville H.S.
Gatesville, Texas

PINEAPPLE WHIP

1/2 c. whipping cream, whipped
1 to 2 tbsp. confectioners' sugar
1 8-oz. can crushed pineapple, well drained
1 c. miniature marshmallows

Sweeten whipped cream with confectioners' sugar. Fold in pineapple and marshmallows. Place in serving dishes. Garnish with chopped walnuts and a cherry, if desired. Chill well. Yield: 4 servings.

Mary A. Buckley, North Andover H.S.
North Andover, Massachusetts

RASPBERRY CREAM DELIGHT

1 pkg. raspberry gelatin
1 c. vanilla ice cream
3 tbsp. orange juice
1 9-oz. can crushed pineapple
1/2 c. chopped pecans
1 med. banana, sliced

Combine gelatin and 1 cup hot water; add ice cream. Stir until thoroughly dissolved. Add orange juice; chill until partially thickened. Combine pineapple, pecans and bananas; add to gelatin mixture. Pour into 1-quart mold; chill until firm. Yield: 6-8 servings.

Mrs. Peggy O. Munter, Moore Jr. H.S.
Moore, Oklahoma

STRAWBERRY POUND CAKE TORTE

1 frozen butter cake, thawed
1 3-oz. package vanilla pudding mix
1 1/4 c. milk
1 1/2 c. sliced fresh or thawed frozen
   strawberries
1 c. whipping cream
2 tbsp. sugar
1/2 tsp. vanilla extract

Remove cake from foil pan; slice lengthwise into 3 layers. Prepare pudding according to package directions, using 1 1/4 cups milk; cool completely. Spread half the pudding on bottom layer of cake; arrange 1/2 cup strawberries on pudding. Top with middle cake layer, repeat pudding and strawberry layers. Add top cake layer. Whip cream with sugar and vanilla; fold in remaining 1/2 cup strawberries. Spread on top and sides of cake. Refrigerate for at least 1 hour before serving. Yield: 8 servings.

Mrs. Carol Porter, Marion H.S.
Marion, Michigan

STRAWBERRIES BRULEE

1 8-oz. package cream cheese, softened
1 1/2 c. sour cream
6 tbsp. sugar
2 pt. fresh California strawberries, hulled
1 c. (packed) brown sugar

Beat cream cheese in bowl until fluffy. Add sour cream and sugar; blend thoroughly. Slice strawberries; sweeten to taste. Arrange strawberries in shallow ovenproof serving dish. Spoon cream cheese mixture over strawberries. Sprinkle with brown sugar. Place on lowest broiler rack. Broil until sugar bubbles and browns lightly. Serve at once. Yield: 6-8 servings.

Photograph for this recipe on page 135.

STRAWBERRIES OVER DEVONSHIRE CREAM

1 env. unflavored gelatin
1 c. sour cream
1 c. whipping cream
1/2 c. sugar
1 tsp. vanilla extract
2 pt. fresh California strawberries, sliced

Sprinkle gelatin over 3/4 cup water in saucepan. Dissolve over low heat. Stir into sour cream. Set aside. Beat cream in mixing bowl, gradually adding sugar until soft peaks form. Stir in vanilla and sour cream mixture. Pour into 1-quart mold, rinsed with cold water. Chill until firm. Unmold on serving plate. Surround with sliced strawberries, sweetened to taste. Slice mold to serve. Top each serving with strawberries. Yield: 8 servings.

Photograph for this recipe on page 135.

RING AROUND THE STRAWBERRIES

2 pkg. dietetic gelatin
1 pt. strawberries, halved
1 3-oz. package cream cheese
1 tsp. vanilla extract

Dissolve gelatin in 2 cups boiling water. Add 1 1/2 cups cold water. Chill 2 1/2 cups gelatin until thickened, leaving remaining gelatin at room temperature. Add strawberries to thickened gelatin; pour into a 6-cup ring mold. Chill until set but not firm. Beat cream cheese until smooth; add reserved gelatin and vanilla gradually, beating until well blended. Spoon over gelatin in the mold. Chill for about 3 hours or until firm. Unmold. Yield: 10-12 servings.

Mrs. Jean Bauer, Hilda School
Hilda, Alberta, Canada

CREAMY STRAWBERRY DELIGHT

1 3-oz. package strawberry gelatin
1 pkg. frozen strawberries
1 pkg. Dream Whip or Lucky Whip
1 3-oz. package cream cheese, softened
1 c. miniature marshmallows

Dissolve gelatin in 1 cup boiling water. Add frozen strawberries. Stir until strawberries are thawed. Refrigerate until set. Prepare Dream Whip according to package directions, omitting vanilla. Add cream cheese and marshmallows; beat until well blended and smooth. Spread over gelatin mixture. Yield: 8 servings.

Mrs. Mildred Jarding, Alexandria H.S.
Alexandria, South Dakota

Desserts

FRUIT NOG

1 6-oz. can frozen orange juice concentrate
1 c. instant nonfat dry milk
Cinnamon or nutmeg to taste

Combine orange juice concentrate, nonfat dry milk and 3 cups water; beat until thoroughly blended. Chill before serving. Sprinkle cinnamon over each serving. Yield: 4-6 servings.

Mrs. Barbara Knawlton, Wellman H.S.
Wellman, Texas

GRAPEFRUIT AND APPLE MIST

1 18-oz. can grapefruit juice
1 1/2 c. apple juice
1/4 c. lime juice
2 tbsp. sugar or to taste
1 12-oz. bottle ginger ale

Combine all ingredients except ginger ale in a pitcher. Add ginger ale; pour over ice cubes in six 12-ounce glasses. Stir before serving. Yield: 6 servings.

Mrs. Magdaline Dhuey, Luxemburg-Casco H.S.
Casco, Wisconsin

AMBER FRUIT PUNCH

1 6-oz. can frozen lemon juice concentrate
1 No. 3 can grapefruit and orange juice
1 No. 3 can orange juice
1 No. 3 can pineapple juice
1 lg. bottle ginger ale

Dilute frozen juice with water according to can directions. Add remaining fruit juices. Add crushed ice and ginger ale just before serving. Yield: 25 servings.

Mrs. Sara Edge, LaFayette H.S.
LaFayette, Alabama

BANANA COCOA

3 tbsp. unsweetened cocoa
2 tbsp. sugar
3 c. milk
1 c. mashed ripe bananas

Mix cocoa and sugar in small saucepan. Stir in milk and bananas. Place over medium heat. Stir constantly until mixture comes to a boil. Serve garnished with sliced bananas. Yield: 4 servings.

Photograph for this recipe on page 136.

HOT CINNAMON COCOA

3 tbsp. sugar
3 tbsp. cocoa
1 c. nonfat dry milk
1/4 tsp. cinnamon
Pinch of salt
1/4 tsp. vanilla extract

Combine sugar, cocoa, milk, cinnamon and salt in 2-quart saucepan. Stir in 3 cups water gradually. Heat quickly to boiling; reduce heat. Cook for 3 minutes, stirring constantly. Stir in vanilla; serve hot. Yield: 4 servings.

Mrs. Margaret L. Egolf, Armstrong Twp. H.S.
Armstrong, Illinois

HOT CHOCOLATE MIX

1 c. instant cocoa
1/2 c. powdered sugar
1/4 tsp. salt
1/2 c. powdered cream
4 c. powdered skim milk

Combine all ingredients thoroughly. Store in airtight container. Stir 6 tablespoons mix into 3/4 cup hot water. This mix gives a much richer flavor than the instant cocoa on the market and is very convenient to keep on hand and use as needed. Yield: 15 servings.

Mrs. Mary Jo Clapp, Jamaica Consolidated H.S.
Sidell, Illinois

PARTY RUSSIAN TEA

3 c. sugar
Grated rind of 1 lemon
Grated rind of 1 orange
10 tsp. instant tea
Juice of 3 oranges
Juice of 8 lemons
1/2 tsp. ground cloves
1/2 tsp. ground cinnamon

Combine sugar and rinds in 2 quarts water in saucepan; bring to a boil. Add tea. Blend with juices and spices. Store in refrigerator. Serve hot as needed. Yield: 32 servings.

Mrs. Nonie Lee Hardage, Carthage School
Carthage, Mississippi

INSTANT RUSSIAN TEA

1/2 c. instant tea
2 1/2 c. sugar

2 c. (about) Tang
2 sm. packages Twist lemonade mix
1 tsp. cloves
2 tsp. ground cinnamon

Combine all ingredients; mix well. Store in jar. Add 2 teaspoons mixture to 1 cup hot water when ready to serve. Yield: 1 quart.

Mrs. Evelyn Wagner, Clinch H.S.
Eidson, Tennessee

STRAWBERRY BREAKFAST SHAKE

1/2 c. cooked oatmeal, chilled
1/2 c. fresh or frozen strawberries
2 to 4 tbsp. sugar
2 c. milk
1/2 tsp. vanilla extract

Place all ingredients in blender container; blend for 1 minute. Serve cold. Yield: 3 servings.

Mrs. Susan Thompson, Ogden H.S.
Ogden, Iowa

GRAPE ALE

1 sm. can grape juice
1 12-oz. bottle diet ginger ale

Fill glasses with ice. Pour glasses half full of grape juice. Add ginger ale to fill glasses; stir. Serve immediately. Yield: 2 servings.

Patricia G. Green, Johns Creek H.S.
Pikeville, Kentucky

SOUTHERN PINEAPPLE ADE

2 pkg. presweetened lemon-lime Kool-Aid
1 1-qt. 14-oz. can pineapple juice
2 tall bottles Sprite

Combine Kool-Aid and 3 quarts water; add juice. Pour over ice in large punch bowl. Add Sprite just before serving. Yield: 50 servings.

Mrs. Gwendolyn Mote, Lookeba-Sickles School
Lookeba, Oklahoma

SWEDISH GLUG

4 tsp. tea
1 qt. boiling water

2 sticks cinnamon
1 46-oz. can grapefruit-pineapple juice
1 pt. apple juice

Steep tea and 1 quart boiling water with cinnamon for 3 minutes; strain. Add juices; bring to a boil. Serve hot. Store in refrigerator. Yield: 20 servings.

Catherine D. Hildebolt, Eaton H.S.
Eaton, Ohio

SPICED APPLE CIDER

2 qt. apple cider
2 tsp. whole allspice
3 2-in. sticks cinnamon
10 whole cloves
1/8 tsp. salt
1/4 tsp. Sweeta

Pour cider into large saucepan; add spices and salt. Cover; bring slowly to boiling point. Reduce heat; simmer for 10 minutes. Stir in Sweeta; remove from heat. Serve at once in mugs; garnish with additional cinnamon sticks. Yield: 12 servings.

Mrs. Warren Webb, Columbia Jr. H.S.
Columbia, Kentucky

TOMATO JUICE COCKTAIL

1 sprig parsley, chopped (opt.)
1 tsp. Worcestershire sauce
1 tsp. salt
2 c. tomato juice
1 tbsp. lemon juice

Add seasonings to tomato juice; cover. Refrigerate for several hours or overnight. Strain. Add lemon juice before servings. Yield: 4 servings.

Marybelle McAfee Duff, Hazard H.S.
Hazard, Kentucky

VEGETABLE COCKTAIL

2 c. tomato juice
1 c. carrot juice
1 tsp. grated onion
1 tsp. grated celery
1 tsp. grated green pepper

Combine all ingredients; chill until ready to serve. Yield: 6 servings.

Fernette G. Honaker, Menaul Presbyterian H.S.
Albuquerque, New Mexico

Quick Breads

Even the busiest homemaker enjoys the timeless art of making bread in her own kitchen. She, and her family and friends, all love the homey and appetizing aroma that fills the house as the bread bakes; and, of course, the delicious results have a lot to do with the popularity of homemade breads. But, not every homemaker can always spare the many hours required for baking yeast breads and rolls. Instead, she depends on recipes for quick, yeastless breads, muffins, and coffee cakes, as well as the traditional recipes for biscuits, waffles, and sweet loaves. In creating quick breads, homemakers use everything from corn meal and whole wheat flour to self-rising flour, refrigerator biscuits, and prepared mixes. Still, there is almost no end to the many varieties of breads she serves — popovers, bran muffins, hush puppies, bread sticks and spoon bread are just a few!

The imaginative use of any number of herbs, spices, seasonings, and other flavorful additions is the key to variety in serving quick breads. Plain waffles become even more scrumptious with the addition of fresh berries, Cheddar cheese or devilled ham. Ordinary corn muffins become something special in a matter of minutes with the addition of chopped onions, herbs, or jalapeno cheese. Breadsticks can be seasoned to fit the dish they will accompany. To accomplish this, add to taste the herbs, spices, or seasonings of your choice to melted butter or margarine. Lightly brush this seasoned butter over the breadsticks and serve. Garlic breadsticks are great with spaghetti, while breadsticks garnished with poppy seed are the perfect accompaniment with a chilled fruit cup. Sesame seed breadsticks are a great appetizer. The same imaginative use of flavorful additions works equally as well with pancakes, waffles, muffins, biscuits, coffee cakes, and doughnuts. And, don't overlook the use of pancakes and waffles as the base for a creamed meat entree. Sweet breads make an excellent and elegant addition to breakfast and brunch; and during Holiday seasons, they make memorable gifts. Remember, quick breads store perfectly in the freezer, so keep a wide selection there, and you will always have a delicious bread right on hand.

Home Economics teachers believe that every homemaker has time to experience the culinary excitement of baking breads that delight everyone. With the quick and easy recipes featured in this section, perfect breads can be a part of any mealtime in your house, no matter how hectic the schedule.

Breads

BACON BARS

1/2 c. shredded sharp process American cheese
6 slices crisp-cooked bacon,
    coarsely crumbled
2 c. packaged biscuit mix
3 tbsp. bacon drippings

Stir cheese and bacon into dry mix. Prepare dough according to package directions for rich biscuits, substituting bacon drippings for salad oil. Knead as directed for rolled biscuits; roll out to 10 x 6-inch rectangle. Cut in six 10-inch strips, 1 inch wide; cut each in thirds crosswise to make 18 bars. Place 1 inch apart on ungreased baking sheet. Bake at 450 degrees for 10 minutes. Yield: 18 bars.

Sande J. Speck, Watertown Sr. H.S.
Watertown, Minnesota

BUTTERY BREADSTICKS

6 tbsp. butter or margarine
2 c. biscuit mix
1 tbsp. sugar
1/2 c. milk

Melt butter in 13 x 9 x 2-inch baking pan in oven. Combine biscuit mix, sugar and milk in mixing bowl; stir with a fork until a soft dough is formed. Beat vigorously for 20 strokes or until stiff but still sticky. Turn out on board lightly dusted with biscuit mix. Knead gently for about 20 times. Roll to 12 x 8-inch rectangle. Cut dough in half lengthwise with floured knife; cut each half crosswise into 16 strips. Dip each strip in melted butter in pan, turning to coat both sides. Arrange strips in 2 rows. Bake in 400-degree oven for about 12 minutes or until golden brown. Serve warm. Yield: 32 breadsticks.

Mrs. Floyd Craig, Divide H.S.
Nolan, Texas

BUTTER DIPS

1/4 c. margarine
1 can baking powder biscuits
Poppy seed, sesame seed, Parmesan cheese
    or garlic salt (opt.)

Place margarine in 9 x 13-inch pan. Place pan in preheated 425-degree oven for 3 to 4 minutes or until margarine is melted. Form biscuits into 3 1/2 x 1-inch oblongs; dip each biscuit in margarine. Place in pan with sides barely touching. Sprinkle with poppy seed. Bake at 425 degrees for 8 to 10 minutes or until golden brown. Yield: 6 servings.

Mrs. Patricia Webb, Forestville Central School
Forestville, New York

QUICK BREADSTICKS

1 pkg. refrigerator biscuits
1/4 c. butter, melted
Sesame seed or poppy seed

Shape biscuits into 6 to 8-inch long sticks. Twist sticks, if desired. Pour half the butter into 9 x 12-inch pan; place sticks in butter. Pour remaining butter over sticks; sprinkle with sesame seed. Bake in 400-degree oven for 10 minutes or until done.

Mrs. Catharine M. Moore, Martin Jr. H.S.
Natchez, Mississippi

BUTTER STICKS

1/2 c. margarine
2 c. self-rising flour
2 tsp. sugar
2/3 c. plus 1 tbsp. milk
Poppy seed

Melt margarine in an oblong pan. Combine flour, sugar and milk; stir with fork until mixture clings together as for biscuit dough. Place on floured board; knead until dough holds togehter. Roll into oblong shape. Cut down center with knife; cut into 1 1/2-inch strips. Place in pan of melted margarine. Sprinkle with poppy seed. Bake in preheated 425-degree oven for about 15 minutes or until brown.

Mrs. Cecile Poling, North Shore Jr. H.S.
Houston, Texas

CHEESE-PECAN BISCUITS

1/2 c. margarine, softened
1/2 lb. grated sharp cheese, softened
1 tbsp. Worcestershire sauce
2 c. flour
1/2 tsp. salt
1/2 tsp. cayenne pepper
1 c. finely chopped pecans

Blend margarine and cheese together well using hands. Add remaining ingredients; mix well. Shape into balls the size of large marbles; place on cookie sheet. Bake at 350 degrees for about 20 minutes or until done. Sprinkle biscuits with paprika, if desired. Yield: 75 servings.

Mary E. Roddam, Barbour County H.S.
Clio, Alabama

EASY DROP BISCUITS

2 c. self-rising flour
1/2 c. mayonnaise
1/2 c. milk

Mix all ingredients together well; drop by table-spoonfuls into greased muffin cups. Bake at 375 degrees for 12 to 15 minutes or until done. Yield: 1 dozen.

Mrs. Nancy D. Stubblefield
McMinnville City H.S.
McMinnville, Tennessee

MAGIC BISCUITS

5 c. flour
1 tsp. soda
1 to 3 tsp. baking powder
1 tsp. salt
1/4 c. sugar
3/4 to 1 c. shortening
1 to 1 1/2 pkg. dry yeast
2 c. buttermilk

Combine first 5 ingredients; cut in shortening. Dissolve yeast in 3 to 4 tablespoons lukewarm water. Stir buttermilk and yeast mixture into flour mixture; mix well. Place in oiled bowl; refrigerate until ready to use. Shape into biscuits; place on baking sheet. Bake at 400 to 450 degrees for 10 minutes or until done. It is not necessary to let biscuits rise before baking.

Mrs. Mildred Wagoner, Gainesville H.S.
Gainesville, Texas

MAGIC FORMULA BISCUIT MIX

4 c. all-purpose presifted flour
8 tsp. baking powder
1 tsp. salt
1/2 c. vegetable shortening
2/3 c. milk

Place flour in large mixing bowl; stir in baking powder and salt. Cut in shortening to make fine crumbs, using pastry blender. Store in airtight container until ready to use. Combine 2 cups biscuit mix with milk. Knead lightly on floured board. Cut out biscuits; place on baking sheet. Bake at 450 degrees for 8 to 10 minutes or until done. Yield: 1 quart mix.

Mrs. Stirling Welker, Scottsdale H.S.
Scottsdale, Arizona

CRUNCHY CHEESE BISCUITS

1/2 c. margarine, softened
2 c. all-purpose flour
2 c. grated cheese
2 c. rice cereal

Combine margarine, flour, cheese and cereal; mix well. Shape into small balls, using hands. Flatten biscuits; place on greased cookie sheet. Bake in pre-

heated 375-degree oven for 8 to 10 minutes or until done. Yield: 40 biscuits.

Mrs. Nancy Harveil, Greenville Jr. H.S.
Greenville, South Carolina

SOUTHERN BISCUITS

1 can refrigerator biscuits
Cornmeal

Dredge biscuits with cornmeal; place on baking sheet. Bake at 475 degrees for 8 to 10 minutes or until done.

Mrs. Charles Woolf, North Central School
Morrowville, Kansas

SHORT BISCUITS

2 c. unsifted self-rising flour
1/2 c. shortening
3/4 c. milk

Place flour in bowl; cut in shortening with pastry blender or meat fork. Add milk, all at one time; mix lightly. Turn out dough onto floured surface; knead lightly. Pat out about 1/2 inch thick or to desired thickness. Cut out biscuits; place on baking sheet. Bake at 400 degrees for 12 to 15 minutes or until done. Butter and serve. May be reheated by sprinkling with water and baking at 350 degrees for 5 minutes. Yield: 15-20 servings.

Zane Wells, Pelahatchie H.S.
Pelahatchie, Mississippi

CHEESE WAFFLES

3 eggs, separated
2 c. milk
1/2 c. butter, melted
3 c. sifted flour
3 tbsp. sugar
1 1/2 tbsp. baking powder
Salt and pepper to taste
1 1/4 c. grated cheese

Beat egg yolks; stir into milk. Add melted butter; mix well. Stir in next 3 ingredients; blend well. Season with salt and pepper. Add cheese, stirring just enough to mix. Fold in stiffly beaten egg whites. Bake in hot waffle iron until golden brown. Serve hot. Yield: 10-12 servings.

Mrs. Annie Fred Wright, Blacksburg H.S.
Blacksburg, Virginia

Breads

CORN BREAD DELUXE

1 6 or 8-oz. package corn bread mix
1 c. drained whole kernel corn
3 tbsp. shortening

Prepare corn bread according to package directions. Add corn; mix well. Melt shortening in pan; pour corn bread mixture into shortening. Bake at 450 degrees for 40 minutes or until brown. Cut into squares and serve hot. Yield: 4-6 servings.

Rosalind M. Clark, Oliver H.S.
Pittsburgh, Pennsylvania

HUSH PUPPIES

1 1/2 c. white or yellow cornmeal
1/2 c. sifted flour
2 tsp. baking powder
1 tbsp. sugar
1/2 tsp. salt
1 sm. onion, finely chopped
1 egg, beaten
3/4 c. milk

Sift dry ingredients together; add onion. Add egg and milk, stirring lightly. Drop 1 teaspoon batter for each hush puppy into hot fat. Fry several at a time until golden brown. Drain on absorbent paper. Serve hot. Yield: 2 dozen.

Mrs. Carolyn G. Chance, Goochland H.S.
Goochland, Virginia

SPOON BREAD

1 c. cornmeal
1/2 tsp. salt
2 tbsp. margarine
4 eggs, beaten
1 c. cold milk

Stir cornmeal and salt into 2 cups boiling water. Stir for 1 minute; remove from heat. Add margarine; beat well. Add eggs and cold milk; beat again. Pour into buttered baking dish. Bake in preheated 450-degree oven for 25 minutes or until done. Serve in baking dish. Yield: 8 servings.

Janice Hamblin, Combs Memorial H.S.
Jeff, Kentucky

CRISPY CORN STICKS

1/2 c. finely chopped onion
2 tbsp. butter or margarine, melted
1 14-oz. package corn muffin mix

1 12-oz. can golden whole kernel corn, drained
Corn syrup

Saute onion in butter. Prepare muffin mix according to package directions, stirring in sauted onion and corn with dry ingredients. Do not overmix. Brush corn stick pans liberally with oil. Fill pans so batter is level with top. Refrigerate batter until baked. Bake at 400 degrees for about 20 minutes. Remove sticks from pan. Brush tops with corn syrup. Yield: 21 corn sticks.

Photograph for this recipe on page 178.

TOPPER CORN BREAD

1/4 c. chopped onion
1 tbsp. butter or margarine
1 pkg. corn muffin or corn bread mix
1 c. shredded sharp process American cheese
1 tsp. celery seed

Cook onion in butter until tender but not brown. Prepare mix according to package directions. Spread batter in greased 10 x 6 x 1/2-inch baking dish; sprinkle cheese evenly over batter. Dot onion mixture over all; sprinkle with celery seed. Bake at 375 degrees for 20 minutes or until done. Serve immediately. Yield: 8 servings.

Virginia T. Bond, Scott H.S.
Madison, West Virginia

FLAT BREAD

1/2 c. sugar
1/2 c. shortening or vegetable oil
1 qt. buttermilk
1 tsp. salt
3 c. whole wheat flour
3 c. all-purpose flour
2 tsp. baking powder
2 tsp. soda

Cream sugar and shortening together. Add buttermilk gradually; mix well. Mix in salt and whole wheat flour. Sift remaining dry ingredients together. Add, all at one time; mix well. Roll out on pastry cloth until almost paper thin. Place on cookie sheets. Bake in 375-degree oven for 12 minutes or until brown and crisp.

Ruth Radcliffe, Riverside Jr. H.S.
Billings, Montana

COMPANY HERB BREAD

1/4 c. margarine, melted
2 tsp. parsley flakes
2 tbsp. lemon juice

1/4 tsp. dill seed
2 cans refrigerator biscuits

Combine margarine, parsley flakes, lemon juice and dill seed. Dip biscuits into margarine mixture; stand on end in greased 1-quart ring mold. Bake in 425-degree oven for 15 minutes or until golden brown. Yield: 10-12 servings.

Mrs. Imogene Spring, Seymour H.S.
Seymour, Texas

FRENCH ONION BREAD

1 loaf French bread
5 to 7 scallions or 1/4 pkg. dry onion
    soup mix
1/2 c. butter or margarine, softened

Cut loaf lengthwise. Chop scallions; mix with butter and spread on loaf. Wrap loaf in aluminum foil. Bake in 400-degree oven for 20 minutes or until heated through.

Joanne Zahorik, Campbellsport H.S.
Campbellsport, Wisconsin

MAGIC FRENCH BREAD

2 cans refrigerator plain or
    buttermilk biscuits
1 egg white, slightly beaten
Sesame seed

Open biscuits according to package directions, but do not separate. Place rolls of biscuits, end to end to form long loaf. Brush with egg white; sprinkle with sesame seed. Bake in preheated 350-degree oven for 30 minutes or until golden brown. Serve hot.

Marilyn Berousek, Maysville H.S.
Maysville, Oklahoma

MASTER MIX

1/3 c. baking powder
1 tbsp. salt
2 tsp. cream of tartar
1/4 c. sugar
9 c. sifted all-purpose flour
2 c. vegetable shortening

Stir baking powder, salt, cream of tartar and sugar into flour. Sift together 3 times into large mixing bowl. Cut in shortening with pastry blender until mixture is consistency of cornmeal. Store in covered containers at room temperature.

Master Mix Muffins

2 tbsp. sugar
3 c. Master Mix
1 c. milk
1 egg, beaten

Combine sugar and mix. Combine milk and egg. Add to mix; stir about 15 strokes or until flour is just moistened. Spoon batter into greased muffin pans. Bake at 425 degrees for about 20 minutes or until done. Yield: 12 muffins.

Master Mix Biscuits

2/3 to 1 c. milk
3 c. Master Mix

Add milk to mix, all at one time; stir for 25 strokes. Knead on lightly floured board for 15 to 18 times. Roll out 1/2 inch thick; cut biscuits. Place on baking sheet. Bake at 450 degrees for 10 to 12 minutes or until done. Yield: Eighteen 2-inch biscuits.

Mrs. C. L. Hillis, Pine Tree H.S.
Longview, Texas

MAKE-AHEAD BRAN MUFFINS

6 c. All-Bran
3 c. sugar
1 c. Crisco
3 c. ground raisins
1 qt. buttermilk
4 eggs, beaten
5 c. sifted flour
1 tsp. salt
5 tsp. soda

Pour 2 cups boiling water over 2 cups All-Bran; set aside. Cream sugar, Crisco, raisins, buttermilk and eggs together. Fold flour, salt, soda and remaining All-Bran into creamed mixture. Add All-Bran mixture; mix only until dry ingredients are moistened. Store in refrigerator. Do not stir when ready to use. Spoon into greased muffin tins, filling cups 2/3 full. Bake at 400 degrees for 20 minutes or until done. Will keep in refrigerator for 4 to 6 weeks.

Mrs. C. B. Haas, Elgin H.S.
Elgin, North Dakota

Breads

COTTAGE CHEESE-CHIVE MUFFINS

2 c. all-purpose flour
3 tsp. baking powder
2 tbsp. sugar
2 tbsp. chopped chives
2 eggs, beaten
3/4 c. milk
3 tbsp. melted butter
1 c. small curd creamed cottage cheese

Sift flour, baking powder and sugar together; stir in chives. Blend eggs, milk and butter together; stir in cottage cheese. Add to flour mixture, stirring until moist. Fill greased muffin cups half full. Bake in preheated 425-degree oven for 15 to 20 minutes. Let cool in pan or on wire rack for several minutes before removing muffins. Yield: 1 1/2 dozen.

Jessie K. Lannan, Sherrard H.S.
Sherrard, West Virginia

MILO MUFFINS

1/2 c. milo flour
1 1/4 c. all-purpose flour
2 1/2 tsp. baking powder
2 tbsp. sugar
3/4 tsp. salt
1 egg, well beaten
1/2 c. plus 1 tbsp. skim milk
1/3 c. liquid shortening

Sift dry ingredients into mixing bowl; make a well in center. Combine egg, milk and liquid shortening; add all at one time to dry ingredients. Stir quickly only until dry ingredients are moistened. Drop batter from tablespoon into greased muffin tins, filling 2/3 full. Bake at 400 degrees for 25 minutes or until done. Milo flour, if unavailable, may be prepared by grinding milo in a meat or coffee grinder 4 or 5 times. Sift flour from cracked milo. Yield: 1 dozen.

Mrs. Ray R. Robertson, Madison H.S.
Madison, Nebraska

MUFFINS IN A HURRY

2 c. sifted self-rising flour
1 c. milk
1/4 c. salad dressing

Place flour in a mixing bowl. Add milk and salad dressing; stir quickly until flour is just moistened and batter has lumpy appearance. Fill oiled muffin pans 2/3 full. Bake in preheated 400-degree oven for 20 minutes or until done. Serve hot. Yield: 12 servings.

Elizabeth McClure, Greencastle H.S.
Greencastle, Indiana

LIGHT POPOVERS

1 c. flour
Pinch of salt
3 eggs
1 c. milk
1 tsp. shortening

Combine flour and salt. Beat eggs until light; add milk and shortening. Add egg mixture slowly to flour, stirring until well blended. Beat mixture vigorously for 1 to 2 minutes. Pour batter into hot buttered muffin tins or custard cups, filling 1/3 full. Bake at 450 degrees for 30 minutes or until done. Remove popovers from tins immediately. Yield: 8 servings.

Mrs. Virginia McCarthy, Berryville School
Berryville, Arkansas

SUSAN'S ONION-CHEESE BREAD

1/2 c. chopped onion
1 egg, beaten
1/2 c. milk
1 1/2 c. biscuit mix
1 c. shredded sharp process American cheese
2 tbsp. snipped parsley
2 tbsp. melted butter

Cook onion in small amount of hot fat until tender but not brown. Combine egg and milk. Add to biscuit mix; stir until just moistened. Add onion, half the cheese and parsley. Spread dough in greased 8 x 1 1/2-inch round cake pan. Sprinkle with remaining cheese; drizzle melted butter over top. Bake at 400 degrees for 20 minutes or until toothpick inserted in center comes out clean. Yield: 6-8 servings.

Mrs. Susan T. Campana, Perry Jr. H.S.
W. Hollywood, Florida

ONION-CHEESE SQUARES

Margarine
1 c. chopped onion
2 c. self-rising flour
2 tbsp. parsley flakes
1 egg, beaten
1 c. milk
1/2 c. grated sharp Cheddar cheese

Heat 3 tablespoons margarine in small skillet. Add onion; cook over low heat, stirring occasionally, for 10 minutes or until tender. Combine flour, parsley and 2 tablespoons onion in mixing bowl. Cut in 1/3 cup margarine until mixture resembles cornmeal. Make a well in center; add egg and milk. Stir until just moistened. Do not overmix. Grease 9-inch square pan with margarine; spread batter in pan. Spoon remaining onion over top; sprinkle with cheese. Bake at 425 degrees for 20 minutes or until top is golden brown. Cut into squares; serve hot. Yield: 9-12 servings.

Mrs. Loretta Fowler Bennett
Thomas Jefferson H.S.
Alexandria, Virginia

ONION CRESCENT ROLLS

1/4 c. butter
2 med. onions, sliced
1/4 c. sugar
2 tbsp. poppy seed
1 pkg. refrigerator crescent rolls

Melt butter in frypan. Separate onion slices into rings; saute until almost tender. Add sugar and poppy seed; cook until onions are tender. Place a spoonful of onions on each piece of roll dough; roll up into crescent shapes. Bake according to package directions.

Delores Kluckman, Central Jr. H.S.
Monterideo, Minnesota

PICALILLY HOT BREAD

2 c. biscuit mix
2/3 c. milk
1 egg, slightly beaten
2 tbsp. instant minced onion
1 tbsp. oil
1/3 c. drained sweet pickle relish
1/4 c. grated Parmesan or American cheese

Place biscuit mix in large bowl. Combine milk, egg, onion, oil and relish; add, all at one time, to mix. Stir until just moistened. Turn into greased 8-inch pan; sprinkle with cheese. Bake in 400-degree oven for 17 to 20 minutes or until bread is done and cheese is golden. Serve hot. Yield: 6-8 servings.

Sister Mary Gustava, Notre Dame H.S.
Quincy, Illinois

PARSLEY ROLL-UPS

1 10-count pkg. refrigerator biscuits
10 2 x 1/4 x 1/2-in. strips cheese
Dehydrated onions or dry onion soup mix
Parsley flakes

Roll each biscuit into 4 x 3-inch rectangle. Place 1 cheese strip in each center; sprinkle with onions. Roll up lengthwise; roll in parsley flakes. Bake according to package directions.

Mrs. Phil Fulkerson, Belleville H.S.
Belleville, Wisconsin

GARLIC BREADSTICKS

1 11-in. loaf unsliced sandwich bread
1/2 c. butter, melted
2 cloves of garlic, minced
1/4 c. sesame seed, toasted

Trim crusts from bread. Cut loaf in half crosswise, then in half lengthwise. Cut each piece crosswise into 4 sticks, 1 1/4 inches thick. Combine butter and garlic; brush on all sides of breadsticks. Sprinkle with sesame seed. Arrange in baking dish, not touching. Bake at 400 degrees for about 10 minutes or until golden. Yield: 16 sticks.

Janet McGhee, Hayden H.S.
Winkelman, Arizona

BEST BUTTERMILK ROLLS

2 pkg. yeast
3 tbsp. sugar
4 1/2 c. flour
1 tsp. salt
1/2 tsp. soda
1 1/2 c. buttermilk
1/2 c. corn oil
3 tbsp. margarine, melted

Combine yeast, 1/4 cup lukewarm water and 1 tablespoon sugar in large bowl; stir until yeast is dissolved. Set aside. Sift flour, salt and soda together. Heat buttermilk over low heat until lukewarm; combine with yeast mixture. Add remaining sugar and corn oil; mix well. Add flour mixture, 2 cups at a time; mix well. Let stand for 10 minutes; knead for 5 minutes. Shape into rolls; place on greased pans. Brush tops with melted margarine. Let rise for 30 minutes. Bake in preheated 400-degree oven for 8 to 10 minutes or until done. Yield: 2-3 dozen.

Mrs. Vera High, Mer Rouge H.S.
Mer Rouge, Louisiana

QUICKIE TOAST

6 tbsp. butter
1 1/8 c. (packed) light brown sugar
1/4 c. evaporated milk
3/4 c. chopped pecans
10 slices day-old bread

Melt butter in saucepan over low heat; stir in brown sugar, evaporated milk and pecans. Toast bread on one side under broiler. Turn bread; spread pecan mixture on untoasted side. Return to broiler for 1 to 2 minutes or broil until bubbly.

Sophia Campbell, Berne Union School
Sugar Grove, Ohio

Breads

SUNDAY NIGHT WAFFLES

2 eggs
3/4 c. Wesson oil
2 1/2 c. milk
2 1/2 c. flour
1 1/2 tbsp. sugar
3/4 tsp. salt
4 tsp. baking powder

Combine eggs, Wesson oil and milk in electric mixer bowl; mix well. Combine dry ingredients; add to egg mixture, beating at medium speed. Beat for about 2 minutes. Pour batter into hot waffle iron; bake until done. Serve with favorite topping. Yield: 6 servings.

Marthanne Limehouse, St. Paul's H.S.
Yonges Island, South Carolina

BANANA WAFFLES

2 c. unsifted all-purpose flour
3 tsp. baking powder
1/4 tsp. salt
1/2 tsp. grated lemon rind (opt.)
3 eggs, separated
1 1/4 c. milk
3 tbsp. butter or margarine, melted
1 c. mashed ripe bananas
Apricot-Banana Sauce

Mix flour, baking powder, salt and lemon rind in large bowl. Beat egg yolks, milk, melted butter and mashed bananas together in a bowl. Add all at once to dry mixture; stir just enough to moisten. Beat egg whites until stiff but not dry; fold into batter. Let batter stand for 5 to 10 minutes to develop banana flavor. Bake in waffle iron according to manufacturer's directions. Serve with Apricot-Banana Sauce. Yield: 4 large waffles.

Apricot-Banana Sauce

1 tbsp. cornstarch
1/4 tsp. salt
1 1/2 c. apricot nectar
2 tbsp. honey
1 tbsp. lemon juice
2 tbsp. butter or margarine
3 bananas, sliced

Mix cornstarch and salt with a small amount of apricot nectar in medium saucepan. Stir in remaining apricot nectar and honey gradually. Cook over low heat, stirring constantly, until mixture thickens and comes to a boil. Remove from heat; add lemon juice and butter. Add banana slices to sauce. Serve over waffles, French toast or pancakes. Yield: 2 1/2 cups.

Photograph for this recipe on page 136.

SLICED APPLE ROLL

2 c. Bisquick
3/4 c. milk
1 c. chopped apples
1/2 tsp. cinnamon
1/2 c. sugar
2 tbsp. butter
Few drops of red food coloring

Combine Bisquick and milk; roll out dough to 1/4-inch thickness. Spread dough with apples; roll as for jelly roll. Cut in slices 1 inch thick; place slices, cut side down, in greased pan. Add cinnamon, sugar, butter and food coloring to 1/2 cup boiling water; pour over rolls in pan. Bake at 375 degrees for 35 to 40 minutes. Serve with light cream or top milk. Yield: 4-5 servings.

Jeanne C. Jackson, Lehi H.S.
Lehi, Utah

CINNAMON-NUT COFFEE CAKE

2 cans refrigerator biscuits
1/4 c. butter, melted
3/4 c. sugar
1 tbsp. cinnamon
1/4 c. chopped nuts

Separate biscuits. Dip biscuits in melted butter; coat with mixture of sugar and cinnamon. Overlap 15 biscuits around outer edge of greased 9-inch round layer pan; overlap remaining 5 biscuits around inner circle to fill pan. Pour remaining butter over top; sprinkle with chopped nuts. Bake in preheated 375-degree oven for 24 to 30 minutes or until done. Let stand for 5 minutes. Turn out coffee cake on rack; invert onto serving plate. Yield: 10 servings.

Mrs. Betty Jones, Cedarville H.S.
Cedarville, Michigan

SUNDAY MORNING COFFEE CAKE

1 egg, beaten
1/2 c. milk
1/2 c. sugar
2 tbsp. shortening, melted
Flour
1/2 tsp. salt
2 tsp. baking powder
1/4 c. (packed) brown sugar
1 tsp. cinnamon
1 tbsp. melted butter
1/2 c. chopped nuts

Combine egg, milk, sugar and melted shortening. Sift 1 cup flour, salt and baking powder together; add to egg mixture. Mix well. Pour into greased and floured 8-inch square pan. Combine brown sugar, cinnamon, 1 tablespoon flour, melted butter and nuts; sprinkle over top of batter. Bake in 375-degree oven for 25 minutes or until done. Yield: 9 servings.

Mrs. R. A. Moore, Breckenridge H.S.
Breckenridge, Texas

HONEY DOME COFFEE CAKE

1 can refrigerator Parker House dinner rolls
1/4 c. butter
1/4 c. honey
1/2 c. chopped nuts
1/2 c. flaked coconut
2 tbsp. grated orange rind
2 tbsp. maraschino cherry halves

Line 1 1/2-quart ovenproof mixing bowl or casserole with aluminum foil. Separate dough into 12 rolls. Melt butter in saucepan; stir in honey. Dip each roll into honey mixture, then into mixture of nuts, coconut, orange rind and cherries. Place in foil-lined bowl. Bake at 350 degrees for 40 to 45 minutes or until deep golden brown. Invert onto serving plate immediately; serve warm. Yield: 12 servings.

Mrs. Shirley Bonomo, Spring Valley H.S.
Spring Valley, Wisconsin

GOLDEN COFFEE CAKE

2 tsp. baking powder
1 tbsp. butter, softened
1 egg, beaten
1 c. sugar
3/4 c. milk
2 c. flour
Brown sugar
Cinnamon

Mix first 6 ingredients together in order listed. Place in 9-inch pan. Sprinkle brown sugar and cinnamon over top. Dot with additional butter. Bake in 350-degree oven for about 45 minutes or until golden brown. Yield: 6-8 servings.

Rosalind Smither, Rutland H.S.
Rutland, Vermont

APPLE COFFEE CAKE

Sugar
1/2 tsp. salt
2 tbsp. soft butter
1 egg, beaten
3/4 c. milk
Cake flour

2 tsp. baking powder
1 tsp. vanilla extract
5 or 6 baking apples

Combine 2 tablespoons sugar, salt and 1 tablespoon butter; add egg and milk. Blend in 2 cups cake flour, baking powder and vanilla; mix well. Spread in greased 6 x 10 x 2-inch cake pan. Pare and cut apples into wedges; place in rows over dough. Combine 1/2 cup sugar, 2 tablespoons flour and remaining 1 tablespoon butter; sprinkle over apple wedges. Bake at 350 degrees for 30 minutes or until apple slices are tender and golden brown. Yield: 8-10 servings.

Mrs. Helen Goska, West Bend H.S.
West Bend, Wisconsin

PEACHY COFFEE CAKE

2 pkg. flaky refrigerator biscuits
1 12-oz. jar peach or apricot
preserves, heated
1/2 c. chopped nuts
Maraschino cherries

Separate each biscuit into 3 layers. Overlap 1 package of layered biscuits to form a 9-inch circle on ungreased baking sheet. Brush with preserves; sprinkle with 1/4 cup nuts. Dip remaining layered biscuits into preserves and overlap on top. Bake at 400 degrees for 18 minutes. Brush with remaining preserves; sprinkle with remaining 1/4 cup nuts. Garnish with cherries. Yield: 6-8 servings.

Gerry Fanning, East Jr. H.S.
Tullahoma, Tennessee

TEXAS COFFEE CAKE

2 c. sugar
1 c. margarine, softened
2 eggs
1 lg. can evaporated milk
1 tsp. vanilla extract
3 c. flour
2 tsp. baking powder
1/2 tsp. salt
1 c. chopped pecans
1/2 c. drained cut cherries

Cream sugar and margarine together. Add eggs, one at a time, beating well after each addition. Stir in milk and vanilla. Sift flour, baking powder and salt together. Combine flour mixture with sugar mixture; fold in pecans and cherries. Pour into lightly greased 9-inch tube pan. Bake at 350 degrees for 1 hour and 30 minutes or until done. Cool on rack.

Mrs. Patricia Pause, Marcellus Cen. School
Marcellus, New York

187

TWENTY-MINUTE COFFEE CAKE

2 eggs
3/4 c. sugar
2 c. sifted flour
3 tsp. baking powder
1/4 tsp. salt
1 c. milk
2 tbsp. melted butter
Cinnamon

Combine eggs and sugar; mix well. Sift flour, baking powder and salt together. Add dry ingredients alternately with milk to egg mixture; stir well. Pour into greased 8 x 12-inch pan. Pour melted butter over batter; sprinkle with additional sugar and cinnamon. Bake at 375 degrees for 20 minutes. Yield: 6 servings.

Sharyn Ann Pfrehm, Canute H.S.
Canute, Oklahoma

SPICY COFFEE RING

Pecan halves
1 pkg. refrigerator biscuits
Melted butter or margarine
1/3 c. (packed) brown sugar
1 tsp. cinnamon
2 tbsp. seedless raisins

Place ring of pecan halves in greased 5 1/2-cup ring mold. Dip biscuits into melted butter, then in mixture of brown sugar and cinnamon. Place in mold, overlapping slightly. Tuck raisins between biscuits. Bake at 425 degrees for 13 to 15 minutes or until done. Yield: 8 servings.

Kathleen Burchett, Flatwood H.S.
Jonesville, Virginia

APPLE DOUGHNUTS

4 c. biscuit mix
1/2 c. sugar
2 c. canned apple slices, chopped
1/4 c. milk
2 tsp. vanilla extract
3 eggs
1/2 tsp. cinnamon
1/4 tsp. ginger
1/2 tsp. nutmeg
1/2 c. apple juice
1 1/2 tsp. lemon juice
4 c. confectioners' sugar
1/2 c. coconut, toasted or tinted

Combine biscuit mix and sugar; add apples, milk, vanilla, eggs and spices. Stir until well blended. Knead dough on heavily floured board until smooth.

Roll out dough about 1/2 inch thick. Cut out doughnuts with a floured 3-inch doughnut cutter. Drop doughnuts, a few at a time, into 2-inch deep 400-degree oil. Cook for about 1 minute on each side or until evenly browned. Drain on paper toweling. Bring apple juice and lemon juice to a boil. Stir in confectioners' sugar; beat until smooth. Spoon about 2 tablespoons glaze over each warm doughnut; roll half the glazed doughnuts in coconut. Yield: 2 dozen.

Joyce Antley, Southwest Jr. H.S.
Melbourne, Florida

BUTTERMILK DOUGHNUTS

4 1/2 c. sifted flour
1 tbsp. baking powder
1 tsp. salt
1 tsp. cinnamon
1/2 tsp. soda
1/2 tsp. nutmeg
2 eggs
1 c. sugar
2 tbsp. melted shortening
1 c. buttermilk
Cooking oil

Sift 4 cups flour, baking powder, salt, cinnamon, soda and nutmeg together; set aside. Beat eggs with rotary beater until thick. Add sugar gradually, beating thoroughly after each addition. Mix in melted shortening. Blend in dry ingredients alternately with buttermilk; stir lightly until well blended. Dough will be soft. If mixture seems too sticky, add enough of the remaining flour to make a soft dough. Chill in refrigerator for 1 hour. Fill a deep saucepan 1/2 to 2/3 full of cooking oil; heat slowly to 365 degrees. Turn dough onto lightly floured surface; roll out 1/2 inch thick. Cut with lightly floured doughnut cutter. Deep fry in hot fat. Turn with fork when doughnuts rise to surface; do not pierce. Turn doughnuts often. Deep fry for 2 to 3 minutes or until lightly browned. Drain on absorbent paper. Serve plain or roll warm doughnuts in confectioners' sugar. Yield: 24 doughnuts.

Linda J. McCraw, Gaffney Sr. H.S.
Gaffney, South Carolina

DOUGHNUT DAISIES

Vegetable cooking oil
1 can refrigerator buttermilk biscuits
Sugar
Jelly

Fill electric skillet 1/3 full with cooking oil; set control at 375 degrees. Cut each refrigerator biscuit almost to center in 5 equal sections; pinch centers. Drop cut biscuits, 4 at a time, into oil. Brown on both sides. Remove doughnuts; drain on absorbent paper. Place in a plastic bag with sugar; shake to coat. Spoon a small amount of jelly into center of each doughnut.

Kay Porters, Northmor H.S.
Galion, Ohio

LOOPY LOOPS

2 1/2 c. deluxe pancake mix
Sugar
3 tbsp. brown sugar
1 tsp. nutmeg
1 egg, well beaten
1/2 c. milk
3 tbsp. melted butter
1 tsp. cinnamon

Combine pancake mix, 3 tablespoons sugar, brown sugar and 3/4 teaspoon nutmeg. Add egg, milk and butter; mix thoroughly. Turn out on a lightly floured surface; knead gently for several seconds. Roll out to 1/3-inch thickness; cut into 6 x 1/2-inch stirps. Gently lift each strip; shape to form loop. Press together lightly to join ends. Fry in deep fat at 375 degrees for 1 minute on each side; drain. Combine 1/2 cup sugar, cinnamon and remaining nutmeg; roll warm loops in sugar mixture. Yield: 2 1/2 dozen.

Janice Svingen, Round Lake H.S.
Round Lake, Minnesota

DOUGHNUTS IN A JIFFY

Fat or oil
1 pkg. refrigerator buttermilk or
 country-style biscuits
Sugar or cinnamon

Heat fat to 375 degrees. Make a hole in center of each biscuit with thumb; stretch into doughnut shape. Fry in fat for about 2 minutes or until golden brown. Remove from fat; place on paper towels to drain. Roll in sugar; serve warm.

Donna Knutson, Dos Palos H.S.
Dos Palos, California

NUTTY HONEY BUNS

2/3 c. butter
1/3 c. honey
1/2 c. sugar
1/2 c. chopped nuts
2 pkg. refrigerator biscuits

Melt butter in 9 x 13-inch flameproof pan. Stir in honey and sugar; bring to boiling point over medium heat. Boil for 1 minute, stirring constantly. Sprinkle in nuts; place biscuits over honey mixture. Bake at 425 degrees for 12 minutes or until done. Invert onto serving plate to serve. Yield: 20 servings.

Pearl T. Aitken, Custer H.S.
Custer, South Dakota

BANANA CAKE BREAD

Banana cake mix
1 ripe banana, mashed
1/2 c. flour
1/2 c. chopped nuts

Prepare cake mix according to package directions; add banana, flour and nuts. Mix together; pour into 2 loaf pans. Bake at 400 degrees for 50 minutes to 1 hour or until done. Yield: 12 servings.

Phyllis A. Stephens, Cody H.S.
Cody, Wyoming

DELICIOUS BANANA BREAD

1 c. butter
1 c. sugar
2 eggs, separated
2 c. flour
1/4 tsp. salt
1 tsp. soda
3 to 4 lg. bananas, mashed
1 c. chopped nuts

Cream butter. Add sugar and egg yolks; mix well. Sift flour, salt and soda together; add to butter mixture alternately with bananas. Mix well. Add nuts; fold in stiffly beaten egg whites. Line greased loaf pan with waxed paper. Spoon batter into loaf pan; smooth top. Bake at 350 degrees for 1 hour and 20 minutes or until done.

Mrs. Helen Harvy, Bluefield H. S.
Bluefield, West Virginia

BUSY DAY BANANA-NUT BREAD

1 box banana-nut bread mix
1 ripe banana, mashed

Prepare batter according to package directions; stir in banana. Pour batter into pan. Bake according to package directions.

Mrs. Iola Kirby, Kermit H.S.
Kermit, Texas

Breads

APPLESAUCE-NUT BREAD

1 egg, beaten
1 c. applesauce
2 tbsp. melted butter
2 c. flour
3/4 c. sugar
1 tsp. cinnamon
3 tsp. baking powder
1/2 tsp. soda
1 tsp. salt
3/4 c. chopped nuts

Combine egg, applesauce and butter. Sift flour, sugar, cinnamon, baking powder, soda and salt together; add to egg mixture. Mix well. Add nuts. Pour into well-greased loaf pan. Bake at 350 degrees for 45 minutes or until done.

Mrs. Rosetta Haire, Crescent-Iroquois H.S.
Crescent City, Illinois

CHEERY CHERRY BREAD

2 eggs
1 c. sugar
1   6-oz. jar maraschino cherries
3/4 c. chopped nuts
1 1/4 tsp. salt
1 1/2 c. all-purpose flour
1 1/2 tsp. baking powder

Beat eggs and sugar together. Drain cherries, reserving juice. Add nuts and cherries; mix well. Add dry ingredients alternately with reserved cherry juice; mix well. Pour into greased loaf pan. Bake at 350 degrees for 45 minutes or until done. Yield: 12 servings.

Mrs. Louise H. Griner, Baker H.S.
Columbus, Georgia

CRANBERRY-ORANGE-NUT BREAD

1 box orange muffin mix
1 c. whole cranberry sauce
1 c. chopped pecans

Prepare muffin mix according to package directions. Break up cranberry sauce with fork; add to muffin mix. Add pecans; mix gently. Pour into greased loaf pans. Bake at 350 degrees for 30 minutes or until golden brown. Let cool; remove from pans. May bake in well-greased tall juice cans, if desired. Fill 2/3 full; place on cookie sheet. Bake as directed for loaf. Yield: 36 servings.

Mrs. Edith Pollock, Kerens H.S.
Kerens, Texas

GINGER HEALTH BREAD

1/2 c. shortening
1/2 c. (packed) brown sugar
1/2 c. honey
2 eggs
1 c. cottage cheese
1/4 c. unsweetened apple butter
1/2 tsp. ginger
1/4 tsp. cinnamon
1/4 tsp. salt
3/4 tsp. soda
2 c. flour
2 tsp. baking powder
1/2 c. raisins

Melt shortening slightly; place in large bowl. Add brown sugar; mix well. Add honey in a fine stream, beating constantly. Beat until creamy. Add eggs; beat until fluffy. Mix in cottage cheese, apple butter, spices and salt. Stir in soda. Sift flour and baking powder together; add to batter. Stir until batter is smooth. Add raisins. Pour into deep baking dish. Bake at 375 degrees for 45 minutes or until done. This bread will stay fresh and moist for several days without refrigeration. Yield: 12 servings.

Maryetta Bowyer, Miller City H.S.
Miller City, Ohio

LEMON-NUT BREAD

2 tbsp. shortening
1 c. sugar
2 eggs
1 tbsp. ground lemon rind
1 1/2 c. flour
1 1/2 tsp. baking powder
1/2 tsp. salt
1/2 c. milk
1/2 c. chopped nuts

Mix all ingredients together in large bowl; beat until well mixed. Pour into well-greased and floured 9 x 5 x 3-inch loaf pan. Bake at 325 degrees for 1 hour or until done. Romove from oven; cool for 5 minutes.

Lemon Topping

3 tbsp. lemon juice
1/2 c. sugar

Combine lemon juice and sugar; spread over bread.

Mrs. Margaret Redman, Graveraet Jr. H.S.
Marquette, Michigan

OATEN BREAD

2 c. sifted all-purpose flour
2 1/2 tsp. baking powder

1/2 tsp. soda
1 1/4 tsp. salt
1/2 c. sugar
1 c. rolled oats
2 tbsp. melted shortening
1 1/4 c. buttermilk
1 c. drained cooked prunes
1/2 c. chopped nuts
Nut halves

Sift flour with baking powder, soda, salt and sugar. Add oats. Stir shortening into buttermilk; blend into dry ingredients just enough to moisten. Cut 3 prunes in half; dice remaining prunes. Add diced prunes and chopped nuts to batter; pour into greased loaf pan. Arrange nut halves and prune halves on top. Bake in preheated 350-degree oven for 50 minutes or until done.

Pollyanna Rogers, Howe H.S.
Howe, Oklahoma

MONKEY BREAD

2 pkg. refrigerator rolls
1/2 c. melted margarine or butter
3/4 c. sugar
1 tsp. cinnamon

Separate rolls. Dip each into margarine, then into sugar and cinnamon mixture. Stack unevenly in casserole or ring pan. Bake at 425 degrees for 20 to 25 minutes. Turn out onto plate. Drizzle powdered sugar icing over top, if desired.

Mrs. Ella Adair, Bryce Valley H.S.
Tropic, Utah

POPPY SEED PINWHEEL

3/4 c. poppy seed
1/3 c. seedless raisins
2/3 c. sugar
1/2 c. milk
1 1/2 tsp. chopped candied lemon peel (opt.)
3 pkg. refrigerator crescent dinner rolls
Melted butter
Confectioners' sugar

Combine poppy seed, raisins, sugar, milk and lemon peel in small saucepan; bring slowly to boiling point, stirring constantly. Cook for 5 minutes. Remove from heat. Separate rolls into 12 rectangles. Spread each with poppy seed filling; roll up as for jelly roll. Place rolls lengthwise in greased loaf pan, making 2 layers of 6 each. Bake at 350 degrees for 50 minutes or until golden. Cool in pan on wire rack for 5 minutes; remove from pan. Brush top with melted butter and sprinkle with sifted confectioners' sugar while still hot.

Mrs. Trudy Polanovich, Haltom H.S.
Ft. Worth, Texas

APPLE MUFFINS WITH TOPPING

2 1/4 c. sifted cake flour
3 1/2 tsp. baking powder
1/2 tsp. salt
1/2 tsp. cinnamon
1/2 tsp. nutmeg
1/4 c. shortening
Sugar
1 egg, beaten
1 c. milk
1 c. finely chopped apples

Sift flour with baking powder, salt, 1/4 teaspoon cinnamon and 1/4 teaspoon nutmeg. Cream shortening with 1/2 cup sugar. Stir in egg; add flour mixture alternately with milk. Fold in apples. Fill greased muffin pans almost full; sprinkle with a mixture of 2 tablespoons sugar, remaining cinnamon and nutmeg. Bake in 425-degree oven for 20 to 25 minutes or until done.

Carolyn Stevens, Delaplaine H.S.
Delaplaine, Arkansas

CREAMY BLUEBERRY MUFFINS

1 1/2 c. self-rising flour
2 c. vanilla ice cream, melted
1 1/2 c. fresh blueberries or 1 No. 303
    can blueberries

Stir flour into ice cream until all flour is dissolved. Add blueberries; fold in gently. Pour into greased muffin tins. Bake at 350 degrees for 15 minutes. Yield: 12 muffins.

Mrs. Martha A. Stewart, Mercer Jr. H.S.
Garden City, Georgia

BUSY DAY BRAN MUFFINS

2 c. All-Bran
1/2 c. molasses
1 1/4 c. milk
1 c. sifted flour
1 tsp. soda
1/2 tsp. salt
1 egg
1/2 c. raisins

Combine bran, molasses and milk in bowl; let stand. Sift next 3 ingredients together. Beat egg into bran mixture; add raisins. Sift in dry ingredients; stir just until mixed. Pour into Teflon muffin tin. Bake at 350 degrees for 20 minutes or until done. Yield: 12 servings.

Mrs. Sharon Crain
Sherburne-Earlville Central School
Earlville, New York

191

Breads

CRANBERRY CORN MUFFINS

1 7-oz. can jellied cranberry sauce
1 8-oz. package corn muffin mix

Cut cranberry sauce into 1/4-inch cubes. Prepare muffin mix according to package directions. Fold in cranberry sauce. Fill paper-lined muffin cups 1/2 full. Bake according to package directions. Serve hot with butter. Yield: 12 muffins.

Dianne Fynboh, Onamia H.S.
Onamia, Minnesota

SUGAR-COATED BUNS

2 c. Bisquick
Sugar
1 tsp. nutmeg
1/8 tsp. cinnamon
2/3 c. cream or 1/2 c. milk
1 egg
1/4 c. butter, melted

Combine Bisquick, 2 tablespoons sugar and spices. Add cream and egg; mix thoroughly. Drop dough into greased muffin cups filling cups 1/2 full. Bake in preheated 400-degree oven for about 15 minutes or until done. Dip warm buns in melted butter then into 1/2 cup sugar, coating all sides. Serve warm. Yield: 10-12 buns.

Mrs. Jo Anne Tuttle, Spencer Jr. H.S.
Spencer, Iowa

SUNDAY MORNING FRENCH BREAKFAST PUFFS

1/3 c. shortening
1 c. sugar
1 egg
1 1/2 c. sifted flour
1 1/2 tsp. baking powder
1/2 tsp. salt
1/4 tsp. nutmeg
1/2 c. milk
6 tbsp. melted butter
1 tsp. cinnamon

Mix shortening, 1/2 cup sugar and egg together thoroughly. Sift flour, baking powder, salt and nutmeg together; stir into egg mixture alternately with milk. Fill greased muffin tins 2/3 full. Bake at 350 degrees for 20 to 25 minutes or until golden brown. Roll in butter immediately, then in mixture of cinnamon and remaining sugar. Yield: 12 servings.

Mrs. Margaret Egolf, Armstrong Township H.S.
Armstrong, Illinois

NANCY'S REFRIGERATOR BRAN MUFFINS

1 c. 100% bran
1/2 c. plus 1 tbsp. shortening
1 1/2 c. sugar
2 eggs, beaten
2 c. buttermilk
2 1/2 c. flour
2 1/2 tsp. soda
1/2 tsp. salt
2 c. All-Bran
1 c. raisins (opt.)

Pour 1 cup boiling water over 100% bran. Cream shortening and sugar; add eggs and buttermilk. Sift flour, soda and salt together. Add All-Bran and flour mixture; fold into soaked bran. Stir in raisins; pour into muffin tins. Bake at 400 degrees for 15 to 18 minutes. Batter stored in tightly covered container in refrigerator will keep for 6 to 7 weeks. Yield: 6 dozen.

Nancy M. Riley, Waterford H.S.
Waterford, Ohio

MAKE-AHEAD REFRIGERATOR BRAN MUFFINS

2 c. All-Bran
1 1/4 c. shortening
2 1/2 c. sugar
4 eggs
1 qt. buttermilk
4 c. Bran Buds
6 c. flour
5 tsp. soda

Pour 2 cups boiling water over All-Bran; let stand. Cream shortening and sugar. Add eggs; mix well. Add buttermilk, bran mixture and Bran Buds; beat in dry ingredients. Store in refrigerator until ready to use. Bake muffins at 400 degrees for 15 to 20 minutes or until done. Dough will keep for 4 weeks. Yield: 3 dozen muffins.

Mrs. Nadene Lyles, Canyon Jr. H.S.
Canyon, Texas

SASSY CINNAMON MUFFINS

1 1/2 c. flour
1/4 c. sugar
1/4 c. (packed) brown sugar
2 tsp. baking powder
1/2 tsp. salt
1/2 tsp. cinnamon
1 egg, beaten
1/2 c. vegetable oil
1/2 c. milk
1/2 c. chopped pecans

Sift flour, sugars, baking powder, salt and cinnamon together. Combine egg, vegetable oil and milk. Add to dry ingredients; stir just enough to moisten. Fold in pecans. Fill greased muffin pans 2/3 full. Bake at 400 degrees for 20 to 25 minutes or until done. Yield: 12 muffins.

Shari Bolander, Del Norte H.S.
Del Norte, Colorado
Mrs. Betty Glasgow, Bokoshe H.S.
Bokoshe, Oklahoma

APPLE BISCUITS

1 c. crushed Wheat Chex
1/2 c. grated unpeeled apples
1/2 c. apple juice
2 c. biscuit mix
1/8 tsp. nutmeg
1/8 tsp. cinnamon

Combine cereal crumbs and apples; pour juice over apple mixture. Mix dry ingredients; stir into apple mixture. Mix thoroughly. Drop by spoonfuls onto buttered baking sheet. Bake in preheated 450-degree oven for 10 minutes. Yield: 16-18 servings.

Alice P. Lynum, Jerusalem Avenue Jr. H.S.
North Bellmore, New York

BROWN SUGAR ROLLS

1 pkg. brown and serve rolls
Melted butter
Brown sugar

Dip each roll into melted butter then into brown sugar. Place on cookie sheet. Bake according to package directions. Yield: 6 servings.

Frances M. Watson, Lake H.S.
Millbury, Ohio

NUTTY CARAMEL ROLLS

1/3 c. margarine
1/4 c. (packed) brown sugar
1/3 c. blue label syrup
1/4 c. halved or chopped nuts
12 brown and serve rolls

Bring margarine, brown sugar and syrup to a boil in saucepan, stirring constantly. Boil for 1 minute, stirring constantly. Divide mixture into 12 medium-sized muffin cups; sprinkle nuts into syrup. Press rolls into cups. Bake at 375 degrees for 15 minutes or until browned. Remove from oven. Let cool for about 30 seconds. Turn upside down onto waxed

paper; shake pan gently to remove rolls. Yield: 12 servings.

Iva Lea Schupp, Arkansas City Jr. H.S.
Arkansas City, Kansas

INSTANT CARAMEL ROLLS

Margarine
3/4 c. (packed) brown sugar
1 tsp. cinnamon
3 tbsp. chopped or ground pecans (opt.)
1 pkg. refrigerator biscuits, halved

Melt 1/4 cup margarine in aluminum pie pan or similar metal pan over low heat. Add brown sugar, cinnamon and pecans; mix well. Remove from heat. Place biscuits over brown sugar mixture; place small piece of margarine on top of each piece of biscuit. Bake in preheated 425-degree oven for 12 minutes or until done.

Barbara Sue Bersche, Champaign Central H.S.
Champaign, Illinois

DELICATE PECAN ROLLS

2 tbsp. melted butter
3 tbsp. corn syrup
1/2 c. (packed) brown sugar
1/2 c. pecan halves
1 pkg. refrigerator biscuits

Brush muffin pans generously with melted butter. Pour small amount of corn syrup over butter in each muffin pan; sprinkle with sugar. Place several pecans in each muffin cup; top with a biscuit. Brush biscuits with remaining butter. Bake at 425 degrees for 10 minutes or until done. Yield: 8 servings.

Helen Keller Foster, Quaker Valley Jr. H.S.
Sewickley, Pennsylvania

PINEAPPLE BREAKFAST ROLLS

1/2 c. (packed) brown sugar
1/2 c. soft butter
3/4 c. drained crushed pineapple
1 tsp. cinnamon
1 can biscuits

Melt brown sugar and butter in 8 or 9-inch square cake pan. Add pineapple and cinnamon; mix well. Place biscuits on top. Bake at 425 degrees for 10 minutes or until done. Yield: 6 servings.

Mrs. Carolyn Saxe, Edwards Sr. H.S.
Albion, Illinois

Cereals, Pastas, Eggs & Cheese

Mealtime can be as uncomplicated or as out-of-the-ordinary as you want it to be, and you can count on cereal, pasta, eggs, and cheese to make meals as interesting and trouble-free as possible. They are most often considered the staple ingredients in side dishes, but each one plays a big part in family-favorite entrees, as well. All four are also the biggest help in stretching the flavor and nutrition of meats, poultry, seafood, and vegetables — especially in main dish casseroles. But, there are so many other ways to use each one — cheese for dips, sauces, and spreads of every flavor; eggs for omelets, quiches, and souffles; as well as dumplings, devilled eggs, cheese fondue, and all the side dishes that traditionally complement a wide-ranging array of entree selections.

Pastas and cereals are not only the basic ingredients in many of the most popular entrees and side dishes, but they are also one of the best ways to use up leftovers. For example, meat loaf can be cut into bite-sized pieces, warmed in a rich tomato sauce to create an almost instant spaghetti sauce; bits of pork or poultry can be baked in a dish of seasoned rice; leftover ham can be diced and added to macaroni and cheese, or shredded into a recipe of cheese grits. Eggs and cheese are too often overlooked by time-conscious cooks, except as breakfast or snack foods. Actually, both are extremely protein-rich, flavorful, and filling, and are ideal for quick and easy meals, anytime. Best of all, the dishes you create with cereal, pastas, eggs, and cheese can be made to taste exactly as you want them to. Everything from green peppers, tomatoes and onions to raisins, nuts, mushrooms, and bacon can be combined with these four foods for any of varied, exciting dishes that can be proudly served on any occasion.

Home Economics teachers recommend using all of these foods often, especially when you have to prepare a meal in a hurry — but even when you don't. You will find that everyone appreciates the hearty, taste-tempting qualities of the recipes in this section, so you should plan on serving seconds!

CHEESE-GRITS CASSEROLE

1 c. grits
1 tsp. salt
1/2 c. margarine
1/2 lb. Cheddar cheese, grated
3 eggs
Milk

Cook grits in 1 cup boiling water with salt until slightly thickened; beat in margarine and cheese. Beat eggs slightly; add enough milk to eggs to measure 1 cup liquid. Add egg mixture to grits; pour into greased 1-quart baking dish. Bake at 325 degrees for 45 minutes. Yield: 8 servings.

Mrs. Josephine P. Clark, Fairview H.S.
Fairview, Tennessee

GARDEN SKILLET

2 sm. zucchini, sliced
1/2 c. chopped onion
1/2 tsp. basil leaves, crushed
2 tbsp. butter or margarine
1 11-oz. can condensed Cheddar cheese soup
3 c. cooked elbow macaroni
2 c. shredded sharp Cheddar cheese
1 16-oz. can tomatoes, chopped and
    well drained
1/2 tsp. prepared mustard

Cook zucchini and onion with basil in butter in a skillet until tender. Add remaining ingredients. Heat until cheese melts; stir occasionally. Yield: 4-6 servings.

Photograph for this recipe on cover.

CRUMB-TOPPED MACARONI CASSEROLE

1 pkg. macaroni
1 sm. onion, finely chopped
1/4 c. butter
1 can cream of mushroom soup
1 soup can milk
1 c. grated cheese
1/2 c. buttered bread crumbs

Cook macaroni according to package directions. Saute onion in butter until tender; add soup, milk and cheese. Combine macaroni and soup mixture. Place in buttered casserole; sprinkle top with buttered crumbs. Bake at 350 degrees until brown. Yield: 6 servings.

Pauline K. Brown, Lone Wolf H.S.
Lone Wolf, Oklahoma

MACARONI AND CHEESE IN A SKILLET

1 tbsp. margarine
1/4 c. chopped onion
1 11-oz. can cheese soup
1/2 c. milk
3 c. cooked elbow macaroni

Melt margarine in skillet over medium heat; add onion. Cook until tender. Blend in soup and milk gradually; mix in macaroni. Cover; cook over low heat for 5 minutes. Yield: 4 servings.

Mrs. Ned R. Mitchell, Charleston H.S.
Charleston, South Carolina

MACARONI SAUTE

2 c. macaroni
1/2 c. chopped onion
1/2 c. chopped green pepper
1 clove of garlic, minced (opt.)
1/2 c. salad oil
1 tsp. salt
3 c. undrained canned tomatoes or
    tomato juice
1/4 tsp. pepper
2 tsp. Worcestershire sauce

Saute macaroni, onion, green pepper and garlic in oil until macaroni turns yellow. Add remaining ingredients; bring to a boil. Simmer, covered, for 20 minutes or until macaroni is tender. Yield: 6 servings.

Mrs. Betty Otteson, Pearl City H.S.
Pearl City, Illinois

QUICK-RONI-BAKE

2 tsp. salt
1 8-oz. package small macaroni
1 tbsp. dry pepper flakes
1 tsp. dry onion flakes
2 tbsp. butter or margarine
Dash of pepper
1 can cream of cheese soup
Dash of paprika

Add salt to 6 cups boiling water; add macaroni slowly. Boil for about 10 minutes; drain all but 1/2 cup water from macaroni. Soak pepper flakes and onion flakes in 1/4 cup water for 5 minutes; add to macaroni. Spread butter evenly over bottom and sides of 2-quart casserole. Combine macaroni mixture, pepper and soup; toss lightly. Turn into casserole; sprinkle with paprika. Bake at 350 degrees for 15 minutes.

Neva Z. Pickett, Wellston School
Wellston, Ohio

MACARONI SUPPER CASSEROLE

4 c. cooked macaroni
1/2 c. mayonnaise
1/4 c. diced green pepper
1 sm. onion, chopped
1/2 tsp. salt
1 can cream of mushroom soup
1/2 c. milk
1 c. grated cheese

Combine first 5 ingredients. Blend soup and milk together; add to macaroni mixture with 1/2 cup cheese. Pour into greased 1 1/2-quart casserole; sprinkle with remaining cheese. Bake at 400 degrees for 20 minutes. Yield: 6 servings.

Mrs. Helen Watson, Lakeview H.S.
Winter Garden, Florida

SOUPER MACARONI AND CHEESE

2 c. cooked macaroni
1 tbsp. butter
1 10 1/2-oz. can cream of mushroom soup
1 c. shredded Cheddar cheese
1 tbsp. finely minced onion

Blend hot macaroni with butter in 1 1/2-quart casserole; stir in soup, 1/3 cup water, 3/4 cup cheese and onion. Sprinkle remaining cheese on top. Bake at 350 degrees for 30 minutes or until browned and bubbly. Yield: 4 servings.

Mina F. Robinson, Perry H.S.
Perry, Kansas

TOMATO-CHEESE MACARONI

2 c. macaroni
1 can tomato soup
1/2 c. milk
2 c. shredded Cheddar cheese
1/4 c. chopped parsley
2 tbsp. buttered bread crumbs

Cook macaroni according to package directions. Heat soup, milk and 1 1/2 cups cheese over low heat until cheese melts; add parsley. Blend soup mixture and macaroni together; pour into greased 2-quart casserole. Top with remaining cheese and bread crumbs. Bake at 400 degrees for 20 minutes or until hot. Yield: 6 servings.

Mrs. C. William Franks, Southeast H.S.
Ravenna, Ohio

NOODLES IN CREAM

1 lb. wide noodles
1 pt. whipping cream
1/2 c. butter
Salt and pepper to taste

Cook noodles according to package directions; drain. Add cream, butter, salt and pepper; toss gently. Serve. Yield: 8 servings.

Mrs. Marilyn Bushnell, Avonworth School
Pittsburgh, Pennsylvania

PARMESAN-RICE SQUARES

2 c. Rice Chex cereal
3 tbsp. melted butter
1/4 c. grated Parmesan cheese

Toss cereal in butter until coated in shallow pan. Sprinkle with Parmesan cheese. Bake in 300-degree oven for about 15 minutes, stirring occasionally; cool.

Ginger Clarke, Dake Middle School
Rochester, New York

BEEFY RICE

2/3 c. long grain rice
2 beef bouillon cubes
Dash of garlic powder
2 tbsp. slivered almonds

Bring 1 2/3 cups water to a boil; add rice, bouillon cubes and garlic powder. Cover. Cook for 25 minutes, stirring once. Fluff lightly with fork; stir in almonds. Serve immediately. Yield: 4 servings.

Mrs. Edward K. Waitz, Lyons H.S.
Lyons, Colorado

BROWN RICE CASSEROLE

1 c. rice
2 cans beef consomme
1 sm. onion, chopped
1/2 c. margarine

Combine all ingredients in greased 1 1/2-quart casserole. Cover. Bake at 350 degrees for 1 hour. Yield: 4-6 servings.

Charlene Olsen, Sidney H.S.
Sidney, Ohio

CHEESE-RICE RING

2 tbsp. chopped onion
1 green pepper, chopped
2 tbsp. butter
1 1/2 c. cooked tomatoes
3 1/2 c. cooked rice
1/4 tsp. salt
Dash of pepper
1/2 c. grated cheese

Cook onion and green pepper in butter until tender; add tomatoes and rice. Cook slowly until rice has absorbed liquid; add seasonings and cheese. Pack into buttered ring mold; unmold immediately onto serving plate. Fill with scrambled eggs or green vegetable. Yield: 6-8 servings.

Mrs. Mary Lou Thurman, Monterey H.S.
Lubbock, Texas

CHINESE-FRIED RICE

2 eggs
Dash of pepper
1 to 2 tbsp. chopped green onion
4 c. cooked rice
2 tbsp. soy sauce
1/2 tsp. sugar
1 c. cooked chopped shrimp

Beat eggs slightly; add pepper. Turn into hot Teflon pan. Cook until eggs begin to set. Add remaining ingredients quickly, blending well. Cook, stirring gently, until heated through. Yield: 4 servings.

Mrs. Elaine Skurdal, Fisher School
Fisher, Minnesota

SPECIAL FRIED RICE

1 c. rice
1/4 c. peanut oil
1 egg, slightly beaten
1/4 c. ground cooked meat or chopped shrimp
1 tsp. salt
1/4 tsp. pepper
1/4 c. chopped green onion
1 1/2 tsp. soy sauce

Cook rice in 1 1/2 cups water until done; let stand, covered, for 15 minutes. Heat oil in skillet; add egg. Cook for 2 minutes, stirring to break into small pieces. Add meat, rice, salt, pepper, onion and soy sauce; blend and cook over moderate heat for 7 minutes. Yield: 4 servings.

Mrs. Dorothy Arch, Nappanee H.S.
Nappanee, Indiana

HERBED FRIED RICE

2/3 c. chopped onion
3 tbsp. butter or margarine
1 c. rice
1 tsp. marjoram
1 tsp. rosemary
1/2 tsp. savory
3 c. chicken broth

Saute onion in butter until soft; add rice, marjoram, rosemary and savory. Cook, stirring constantly, until rice is lightly browned; add broth. Simmer for 20 mintues or until rice is tender. Serve as a main dish or with chicken chow mein. Yield: 6 servings.

Mrs. Juno Brooke Mulder, French H.S.
Beaumont, Texas

GREEN RICE

2 c. rice
1 1/2 c. milk
1/2 c. salad oil
1 c. chopped fresh parsley
1 c. chopped green onions
1 c. chopped green pepper
2 cloves of garlic, minced
1 lb. grated sharp cheese
Salt and pepper to taste

Cook rice according to package directions; mix with remaining ingredients. Place in oiled casserole. Bake, uncovered, at 350 degrees for 1 hour. Yield: 12 servings.

Mrs. Robert D. Marstiller, Valley Mills H.S.
Valley Mills, Texas

RANCH RICE

1 c. rice
1 can consomme
1 can onion soup
1   2 1/2-oz. can mushroom pieces
1/2 c. margarine

Combine all ingredients in 1 1/2-quart casserole. Bake at 350 degrees for 45 minutes to 1 hour, stirring at least once. Yield: 4-6 servings.

Mrs. Elaine Buston Booker, Lee Jr. H.S.
Ft. Myers, Florida

INSTANT SPANISH RICE

10 slices bacon, cut up
1 med. onion, diced
2 1/2 c. tomato juice
1 tsp. salt

1/2 tsp. pepper
2 1/2 c. Minute rice

Fry bacon in frypan with onion until bacon is crisp and onion is tender. Drain off half the drippings. Add tomato juice, salt and pepper to pan; bring to a boil. Add rice; cover. Remove from heat; let stand for 5 minutes. Fluff rice; serve. Yield: 4-6 servings.

Donna E. Johnson, Buena Vista H.S.
Saginaw, Michigan

RICE AND BACON DISH

1 c. rice
1/2 c. dehydrated minced onion
1 tsp. salt
1/2 tsp. pepper
1 c. crumbled cooked bacon
1/2 c. finely chopped green pepper (opt.)
1 can golden mushroom soup

Place all ingredients and 2 cups water in heavy saucepan; bring to a full boil. Stir; reduce heat. Simmer, covered, for 20 minutes; remove from heat. Let stand for 5 to 10 minutes. Yield: 4-6 servings.

Mrs. Virginia F. Darling, Olivet H.S.
Olivet, Michigan

CREAMY RICE CASSEROLE

2 c. cooked rice
1 carton sour cream
1 sm. can chili peppers, chopped
Grated Cheddar cheese

Combine rice, sour cream and chopped chilies in casserole; top with cheese. Bake, covered, at 350 degrees for 20 to 30 minutes. Yield: 6 servings.

Mrs. Sammie Stone, Avinger H.S.
Avinger, Texas

RICE AND ONION CASSEROLE

1 onion, sliced
1/2 c. margarine
1 can mushrooms
1 c. rice
2 cans bouillon
Salt and pepper to taste

Place onion and margarine in casserole; heat until margarine melts. Add remaining ingredients. Bake, covered, at 375 degrees for 45 minutes. Yield: 8 servings.

Mrs. Jo Marler, Forest H.S.
Forest, Mississippi

RICE-PECAN CASSEROLE

1 c. rice
1/2 c. butter
1 can cream of mushroom soup
1 c. chopped pecans

Cook rice according to package directions; add butter to hot rice. Add soup and pecans; place in greased casserole. Bake at 350 degrees for 20 minutes. Yield: 6 servings.

Mrs. Virginia C. Taylor, Springville H.S.
Springville, Alabama

BUSY DAY RICE CASSEROLE

1 c. rice
1 can beef bouillon
1 can onion soup
2 tbsp. butter

Combine rice, bouillon, soup and butter in 1 1/2-quart buttered casserole. Bake, covered, at 375 degrees for 1 hour or until moisture is absorbed. Yield: 6 servings.

Carolyn Wilkins, Winter Park H.S.
Winter Park, Florida

RICE-MUSHROOM MEDLEY

1 6-oz. package long grain and wild
  rice mix
1 can beef broth
1/2 c. chopped onion
1/2 c. chopped celery
1/4 c. margarine
1 3-oz. can broiled mushrooms, drained

Prepare rice according to package directions, substituting beef broth and 1 1/4 cups water for liquid required. Cook onion and celery in margarine until tender, but not brown; add with mushrooms to rice 5 minutes before rice is done. Continue cooking until all liquid is absorbed. Yield: 6 servings.

Mrs. Pauline Moxley, McAllen H.S.
McAllen, Texas

RICE IN ONION SOUP

1 c. rice
1 pkg. dry onion soup mix

Combine rice, soup mix and 3 cups water in electric skillet; cover. Cook at 300 to 350 degrees for 25 minutes. Yield: 6 servings.

Mrs. June Patchett, Young America H.S.
Metcalf, Illinois

Cereals, Pastas, Eggs & Cheese

BACON-CHEESE OMELET

8 slices bacon
6 slices American cheese, quartered
4 eggs
1/2 c. milk
1/2 c. chopped pimento
1/4 tsp. salt

Bake bacon at 350 degrees for 15 minutes. Arrange cheese on bottom of lightly greased 9-inch pie pan. Beat eggs; add milk, pimento and salt. Pour egg mixture over cheese; arrange bacon strips pinwheel fashion over top. Bake at 350 degrees for 25 minutes or until knife inserted in center comes out clean. Yield: 3-4 servings.

Mrs. Jean Hall, Frackville H.S.
Frackville, Pennsylvania

BACON AND EGG PIE

8 slices bacon, cut in half
3 eggs
1/2 tsp. salt
1/4 tsp. pepper
1 c. heavy cream
1 tsp. A-1 sauce
1 baked 9-in. pastry shell
1/4 lb. American cheese, sliced

Fry bacon until well done. Beat eggs lightly; add salt, pepper, cream and A-1 sauce. Beat well. Place bacon in pastry shell; cover with cheese. Pour egg mixture over cheese. Bake at 275 degrees for 20 to 25 minutes or until eggs are set. Yield: 4 servings.

Mrs. Kathryn J. Lumpkin, Randolph County H.S.
Wedowee, Alabama

BREAD AND CHEESE PUFF

8 slices buttered bread
8 slices American cheese
Salt and pepper to taste
4 eggs, beaten
1 qt. milk
1 tsp. Worcestershire sauce
Dash of Tabasco sauce

Place 4 slices bread in shallow baking dish, cutting to fit. Cover bread with 4 slices cheese; sprinkle with salt and pepper. Repeat layers. Combine remaining ingredients; pour over bread and cheese. Bake at 350 degrees for 40 minutes or until top is puffed and golden brown. Yield: 6 servings.

Marilee J. Wirkkala
Naselle-Grays River Valley H.S.
Naselle, Washington

BAKED SWISS CHEESE SANDWICH

6 slices white bread
3/4 c. dry white wine
2 eggs, well beaten
2 c. grated Gruyere or Swiss cheese
3 tbsp. butter

Place bread in greased shallow 13 x 9-inch baking pan; spoon wine over bread, allowing wine to soak into bread. Add eggs to cheese, blending well. Pour cheese mixture over bread; dot with butter. Bake at 350 degrees until golden brown. Yield: 4-6 servings.

Mrs. Lillian P. Dunbar, Abington H.S.
North Abington, Massachusetts

BROILER EGG-CHEESE SANDWICH

2 hard-cooked eggs, chopped
1 1/2 tbsp. mayonnaise
1/8 tsp. salt
Dash of pepper
1/4 to 1/2 tsp. dry mustard
1/8 tsp. Worcestershire sauce
6 slices bread
3 slices American cheese
3 tbsp. melted butter or margarine

Combine eggs, mayonnaise, salt, pepper, mustard and Worcestershire sauce; spread mixture evenly over 3 slices bread. Top with cheese slices; cover with remaining bread. Brush melted butter over outside surfaces of each sandwich; place on broiler rack. Broil 4 inches from heat for 3 to 4 minutes or until golden brown; turn and broil until brown. Serve hot. Yield: 3 servings.

Mrs. C. Dean Schmid, North Platte Sr. H.S.
North Platte, Nebraska

CANADIAN CHEESE SOUP

1/2 c. chopped carrots
1/2 c. chopped celery
2 tbsp. chopped onion
Butter or margarine
1 can Cheddar cheese soup
1/2 soup can milk
Chopped parsley to taste

Saute carrots, celery and onion in small amount of butter until tender. Blend soup, milk and 1/2 soup can water together. Add vegetables; bring just to a boil. Add parsley; serve. Yield: 4 servings.

Augusta Jannett, Yoakum H.S.
Yoakum, Texas

CHEESE AND BACON OPEN-FACED SANDWICHES

2 c. grated sharp cheese
1 tbsp. minced onion
1 egg
1/2 tsp. baking powder
1 tbsp. soft butter
1 tbsp. milk
Bread slices
2 slices bacon, cut up

Combine first 6 ingredients in order listed; spread generously on bread. Top with bacon. Broil until cheese bubbles and bacon is crisp. Yield: 4 servings.

Glenda Gehrig, Randolph H.S.
Randolph, Massachusetts

CHEESE BARBECUE

3 tbsp. chopped green pepper
1/3 to 1/2 c. chopped onion
2 hard-cooked eggs, chopped
3 tbsp. chopped stuffed olives or pickles
3 tbsp. catsup or tomato sauce
1 tbsp. melted butter
1 1/2 c. grated Cheddar cheese
1 tbsp. mustard (opt.)
1/2 tsp. Worcestershire sauce (opt.)
Hot sauce to taste (opt.)
6 hamburger buns

Combine all ingredients except buns. Split buns; place 1/2 cup cheese mixture on each bun. Place on cookie sheet. Broil for about 5 minutes or until heated through. Serve at once. Yield: 6 servings.

Frances L. Rice, Litton Sr. H.S.
Nashville, Tennessee

COTTAGE CHEESE DIP

1 pt. cream-style cottage cheese
1/2 pkg. dry onion soup mix
1/3 c. milk

Place all ingredients in blender container; blend until creamy. Serve with chips or pretzels. Yield: 20 servings.

Mrs. Elizabeth Skaggs, Cerro Gordo H.S.
Cerro Gordo, Illinois

CHEESE RAREBIT CASSEROLE

1/4 c. milk
1/4 tsp. salt
2 eggs, well beaten
2 slices day-old bread
1/2 c. grated sharp cheese
1 can shrimp (opt.)

Add milk and salt to eggs; beat well. Break bread into pieces; mix into egg mixture. Toss in cheese; mix well. Spoon into well-greased casserole; garnish with shrimp. Bake at 350 degrees for 20 minutes or until cheese is browned. Yield: 2 servings.

Elizabeth L. Hudson, Fairfield Jr. H.S.
Richmond, Virginia

CHEESE GOODIES

2 c. grated sharp cheese
1 c. margarine, softened
2 c. sifted flour
1/2 tsp. salt
1/2 tsp. red pepper
2 c. Rice Krispies

Combine cheese and margarine. Add flour, salt and pepper; mix until well blended. Add Rice Krispies; mix well. Roll into marble-sized balls. Place on baking sheet; press gently with tines of fork. Bake at 350 degrees for 10 minutes. Yield: 10-12 servings.

Dorothy S. Barrick, West End H.S.
Nashville, Tennessee

CHEESE PUDDING

10 slices bread
Butter
1/2 lb. cheese, grated
2 c. milk
1 tsp. salt
3 eggs, beaten

Remove crusts from bread and discard; spread bread with butter. Cut into cubes; place in baking dish alternately with cheese. Combine milk, salt and eggs; pour over bread and cheese mixture. Refrigerate for several hours. Bake at 300 degrees for 35 to 45 minutes. Yield: 8 servings.

Mrs. Miriam B. Templeton, Hickory Tavern H.S.
Gray Court, South Carolina

CREAMED COTTAGE CHEESE

1 pt. cream-style cottage cheese
2 tbsp. fresh or dried chopped chives
2 tbsp. salad dressing

Blend cottage cheese in blender or with fork until fairly smooth. Add chives and salad dressing; mix well. Serve on baked potatoes. Yield: 6-8 servings.

Ramona K. DeSilva, Fresno H.S.
Fresno, California

Cereals, Pastas, Eggs & Cheese

DEVILED EGGS IN TOMATO SAUCE

6 deviled eggs
1/4 c. minced onion
1/2 c. diced celery
1/4 c. margarine
3 tbsp. flour
1   10 1/2-oz. can tomato soup
Seasoning to taste

Place eggs in casserole. Saute onion and celery in margarine until golden brown; remove celery and onion from pan. Blend flour into margarine in pan; add soup and 1/2 soup can water. Cook until thickened, stirring constantly. Add onion, celery and seasoning; pour over eggs. Bake at 350 degrees for 20 minutes. Serve over rice. Yield: 6 servings.

Sister M. John Vianney, SS.C.M., Andrean H.S.
Gary, Indiana

EGGS A LA KING ON TOAST

1/4 c. butter
6 tbsp. flour
2 c. milk
1 tsp. salt
1/4 tsp. pepper
2 tbsp. catsup
1/4 c. cooked peas
1 sm. can chopped pimentos
6 hard-cooked eggs, chopped

Melt butter in saucepan; blend in flour. Stir in milk, salt and pepper. Cook, stirring constantly, until thick. Blend in catsup. Add peas, pimentos and eggs; heat thoroughly. Serve on buttered toast.

Mrs. Nancy J. Slezak, Seneca Valley H.S.
Harmony, Pennsylvania

ORIENTAL OMELET

4 eggs, separated
Dash of white pepper
1/4 tsp. salt
1/4 tsp. cream of tartar
Butter
1/4 c. soy sauce
1/4 c. (packed) brown sugar
2 tbsp. vinegar
2 tbsp. cornstarch
1/2 tsp. dry mustard
1/2 c. green pea pods, thawed and drained
1/4 c. water chestnuts, cut in strips
1/4 c. green pepper strips
1/4 c. red pepper strips
1 1/4 c. shredded Cheddar cheese

Beat egg yolks and pepper in a small mixing bowl until thick and lemon colored. Beat egg whites, 1/4 cup water, salt and cream of tartar in a small mixing bowl until stiff but not dry. Fold beaten yolks into beaten whites. Melt 2 teaspoons butter in a 10-inch skillet with heatproof handle until just hot enough to sizzle a drop of water. Turn egg mixture into skillet. Cook over low heat until puffy and browned on bottom, about 5 minutes. Transfer to preheated 325-degree oven. Bake for 12 to 15 minutes or until knife inserted near center comes out clean. Heat 1 cup water, soy sauce, brown sugar, vinegar, cornstarch and dry mustard in a 1-quart saucepan. Cook over medium heat, stirring constantly, until thickened. Cook 2 minutes longer. Remove from heat. Stir in 2 tablespoons butter until melted. Add pea pods, water chestnuts and pepper strips. Keep warm. Remove omelet to heated platter. Score omelet down the center with a sharp knife. Spread 1 cup cheese on bottom half of omelet. Fold in half. Top with remaining cheese. Spoon 1/2 cup sauce over omelet. Serve remaining sauce with omelet. Yield: 4 servings.

Photograph for this recipe on page 194.

OVERNIGHT EGG AND CHEESE CASSEROLE

6 slices bread
Butter
1 c. grated American cheese
4 eggs
2 c. milk
Dash of salt and pepper
1/2 tsp. dry mustard

Spread bread with butter; cut into cubes. Place in baking dish; sprinkle with cheese. Beat eggs, milk, salt, pepper and mustard together; pour over bread and cheese. Refrigerate overnight. Bake at 350 degrees for 40 minutes. Yield: 4 servings.

Kathleen Brown, Elk Creek H.S.
Elk Creek, California

HUEVOS RANCHEROS CON QUESO

4 tbsp. cooking oil
1 med. onion, chopped
1 lg. tomato, chopped
6 eggs, beaten
1 c. shredded Cheddar cheese
Salt and pepper to taste

Heat oil in heavy saucepan; add onion and tomato. Cook until tender; add eggs. Cook, stirring constantly, until eggs are almost set; add cheese, salt and pepper. Cook until eggs are set; serve. Yield: 6 servings.

Mrs. Silma Vidaurri, H. M. King H.S.
Kingsville, Texas

NUTTY CHEESE SPREAD

1 8-oz. package cream cheese
1 5-oz. jar sharp cheese spread
2 5-oz. jars Roquefort cheese spread
1 sm. onion, minced
1 clove of garlic, minced
1/2 c. finely chopped pecans or walnuts

Let cheeses warm to room temperature; beat together until fluffy and well blended. Beat in onion and garlic; chill until firm. Shape into ball. Roll in pecans; refrigerate until ready to serve.

Mrs. Janet Prentice, Chico Sr. H.S.
Chico, California

QUICK CHEESE PUFF

3/4 c. milk
2 slices bread, crumbled fine
2 tbsp. Wesson oil
6 tbsp. grated sharp cheese
3 eggs, separated
Salt and pepper to taste

Scald milk; add bread. Stir until smooth; add oil. Add cheese; cook for 5 minutes, stirring constantly. Remove from heat; cool slightly. Stir in beaten egg yolks. Fold in stiffly beaten egg whites; season with salt and pepper. Turn into greased casserole. Bake at 425 degrees for 15 minutes or until puffed and browned. Serve immediately. Yield: 4 servings.

Mrs. Martha McDaniel, Gray Court-Owings School
Gray Court, South Carolina

QUICK CHEESE STRAWS

1 box pie crust mix
1 jar Old English sharp cheese spread
Paprika (opt.)
Red pepper (opt.)
Onion salt (opt.)

Mix first 2 ingredients, working dough with hands until thoroughly blended. Do not add any liquid. Season. Press dough through cookie press, using design for cheese straws, in long strips on ungreased cookie sheet. Score at intervals with knife. Bake at

450 degrees until lightly browned. Break at scored places.

Mrs. Betty J. Houston, Early Co. H.S.
Blakely, Georgia

SAVORY DIP

1/2 sm. onion
1 stalk celery
1 pt. cottage cheese
1/4 c. skim milk
1/2 tsp. salt

Chop onion and celery in blender; add cottage cheese, skim milk and salt. Blend until smooth. Serve in bowl with carrot sticks or other vegetables. Yield: 6 servings.

Dorothy R. Trodahl, Algoma H.S.
Algoma, Wisconsin

SPANISH DELIGHT

4 strips bacon, cut up
1/4 c. flour
4 c. stewed tomatoes
2 c. cubed sharp Cheddar cheese
Salt and pepper to taste
4 slices toast

Fry bacon until crisp; blend in flour. Add tomatoes and cheese; cook, stirring constantly, until thickened. Season with salt and pepper; serve over toast. Yield: 4 servings.

Mrs. Linda Cerini, Healdsburg H.S.
Healdsburg, California

TANGY CHEESE ROLL

1 lb. sharp New York or Cheddar cheese
1 8-oz. package cream cheese
Dash of Tabasco sauce
1/4 c. Durkees dressing
2 tbsp. Worcestershire sauce
3/4 c. pecans
2 cloves of garlic (opt.)
Pinch of salt
Paprika

Dice cheeses; place in blender container with Tabasco sauce, Durkees dressing, Worcestershire sauce, pecans, garlic and salt. Process until well blended, scraping sides with spatula frequently. Shape into roll; roll in paprika. Refrigerate until ready to serve.

Mrs. Lee Thames, Lee H.S.
Baton Rouge, Louisiana

Low-Calorie Dishes

Many cooks feel that incorporating low-calorie recipes into their meal plans is too time-consuming for a busy schedule — especially when only one or two family members are consciously counting their calories. The truth of the matter is that every family member can benefit from calorie-reduced foods — whether it be a salad or a dessert. Our land of plenty is a blessing, but we have become more urban and less active in recent years — so more and more people of every age group weigh more than they should for health and longevity. Weight control, which is basically a matter of balanced eating habits, is a practice followed even by persons of normal weight, whether they know it or not. So, if they can eat and enjoy it, it becomes obvious that calorie-conscious meals don't have to be tasteless, boring and insubstantial.

Sensible, well-planned eating habits and regular exercise are the only successful ways to reach and maintain a proper weight. If you are overweight, it is because you are taking in more calories than you use up in a normally active day. So, meals should be designed to exclude as many needless calories as possible. Sugar intake can be greatly reduced, or even replaced by artificial, non-caloric sweeteners. To eliminate other hidden calories that you will never miss, switch to imitation (low-calorie) mayonnaise., margarine, and cheese; start using water-packed tuna and salmon; serve fruit canned in its own juice rather than in heavy syrup; use yogurt in place of sour cream. Also, begin using the recipes in this section in place of the ones you normally use, because they have had calories cut from them wherever possible. Many also have the calories per serving noted in the recipe, to aid you in counting daily calories. You will find that you can enjoy reasonable amounts of all the foods you love, and still be able to control your weight if you make a conscious effort at knowing what you eat. You will gear your eating habits to maintain your proper weight, and it will become an almost-effortless practice.

Well-planned meals, healthy exercise, and sensible eating habits are the key to keeping slim and trim. Home Economics teachers want to share these low-calorie recipes with you so you can include them in your quick and easy cooking. You will be convinced that low-calorie eating can be appetizing, fulfilling, and healthful — and trouble-free, too!

Low-Calorie

DIETER'S CHIP DIP

1 lb. creamed cottage cheese
1/4 c. mayonnaise
1/4 tsp. garlic salt
1/4 tsp. Worcestershire sauce

Blend all ingredients together with mixer or blender. Serve with chips or fresh vegetables.

Georgia Geiger, Frost Jr. H.S.
Livonia, Michigan

DUTCH DIET DIP

1 c. cream-style cottage cheese
1 tbsp. lemon juice
Dash of salt
1 tsp. dillweed
Carrot slices

Place cottage cheese, lemon juice and salt in blender container; cover. Blend at low speed for 4 minutes or until smooth, scraping sides of container occasionally. Pour into serving dish; sprinkle with dillweed. Top with carrot slices. Serve as a dip with celery sticks, carrot sticks or potato chips. Yield: 4 servings.

Myrtle Knutson, Fairview Jr. H.S.
St. Paul, Minnesota

COTTAGE CHEESE-ONION DIP

1 pt. cottage cheese
1 pkg. dry onion soup mix
2 tbsp. lemon juice

Blend cottage cheese in blender until smooth; add soup mix and lemon juice. Mix well; serve as dip for crackers or fresh vegetables. Yield: 1 pint.

Mrs. Laurena Ward, Ashford H.S.
Ashford, Alabama

SPICY LOW-CALORIE DIP

1 12-oz. carton cream-style cottage cheese
1 tbsp. salad dressing
1 tsp. salad spice-and-herb mix
Minced parsley

Place cottage cheese, salad dressing and dry salad mix in blender container or mixer; blend until almost smooth. Chill. Sprinkle with parsley. Yield: 6 servings.

Mrs. Judy Ramm, Fremont Jr. H.S.
Fremont, Michigan

APRICOT-COTTAGE CHEESE SALAD

1 pkg. apricot gelatin
1 8 1/2-oz. can diet crushed pineapple
1 c. fine curd cottage cheese
1 c. evaporated skim milk

Dissolve gelatin in 2/3 cup hot water; stir in remaining ingredients. Chill until firm. May be served on lettuce leaf with low-calorie dressing. Yield: 6-8 servings.

Mrs. Violet Moseley, Avon Park H.S.
Avon Park, Florida

APRICOT-PINEAPPLE SALAD

1 env. unflavored gelatin
1 No. 303 can low-calorie crushed pineapple
1 No. 303 can low-calorie apricots
1 c. small curd cottage cheese

Soften gelatin in 1/2 cup cold water. Drain pineapple and apricots, reserving juice. Add enough water to reserved juice, if needed, to measure 1 1/2 cups liquid. Heat juice; add gelatin. Stir until dissolved. Chill until thickened. Dice apricots; add pineapple and cottage cheese. Stir into gelatin. Chill until set. Serve on lettuce with low-calorie dressing, if desired. Yield: 6-8 servings.

Mrs. Murray Applegate, Knoxville Sr. H.S.
Knoxville, Iowa

LOW-CALORIE APRICOT BAVARIAN

1 No. 2 can water-packed apricots
1 pkg. lemon or apple gelatin
1/3 c. nonfat dry milk
1 tbsp. lemon juice

Drain apricots, reserving juice. Press apricots through sieve. Add enough water to reserved apricot juice to measure 1 1/2 cups liquid. Heat half the liquid; pour over gelatin. Stir until dissolved. Add remaining liquid and apricot pulp. Chill until thickened. Sprinkle dry milk over 1/4 cup cold water and lemon juice; beat until stiff. Fold into apricot mixture. Pour into mold; chill until firm. Serve on lettuce. Yield: 6 servings.

Mrs. Laquita B. Neill, J. Z. George School
North Carrollton, Mississippi

APRICOT-COTTAGE CHEESE SALAD

1 tbsp. unflavored gelatin
1 c. apricot liquid
12 dried apricot halves, cooked without sugar

2 tbsp. lemon juice
6 tbsp. cottage cheese

Soften gelatin in 1/4 cup water for 5 minutes. Add hot apricot liquid; stir until gelatin is dissolved. Place in pan of ice water; stir until mixture begins to thicken. Chop apricots; blend into gelatin mixture. Pour lemon juice over cheese; mix thoroughly. Add to apricot mixture. Rinse mold in cold water; pour in apricot mixture. Chill until firm. Yield: 6 servings.

F. Pauline Foster, Carstairs H.S.
Carstairs, Alberta, Canada

COOKED CRANBERRY SALAD

1 lb. cranberries
Artificial sweetener to equal 1/3 c. sugar
2 env. cherry D-Zerta
1 No. 2 can dietetic pineapple
1 c. finely cut celery
1 c. Tokay grape halves

Place cranberries and 1 cup water in saucepan; cook until cranberries pop. Add sweetener and D-Zerta; stir until dissolved. Add remaining ingredients; pour into 6 x 9-inch dish. Chill until set.

Mrs. Mary Margaret Moyer, Monroe-Winamac H.S.
Winamac, Indiana

CRANBERRY RELISH

6 non-caloric sweetener tablets
1 lb. cranberries
1 orange
1 apple

Crush sweetener tablets. Grind fruits together; add sweetener. Mix thoroughly. Serve on crisp lettuce or watercress. Yield: 8 1/3 cups.

Mrs. Lucille Murray, Power H.S.
Power, Montana

TROPICAL FRUIT SALAD SUPREME

1 orange
1 pink grapefruit
1 No. 2 can unsweetened crushed pineapple
2 tbsp. honey
1/2 tsp. grated ginger
2 tbsp. lemon juice

Peel and section orange and grapefruit, reserving as much of the juice as possible. Add pineapple; stir well. Mix honey, ginger and lemon juice in a small dish. Add to fruit; stir well. Chill thoroughly. Serve on crisp lettuce leaf; garnish with cherry. Yield: 4 servings.

Justine C. Irwin, Meeker H.S.
Meeker, Colorado

CRANBERRY-ORANGE SALAD

2 c. fresh cranberries
1 orange
2 tbsp. Sucaryl liquid or 48 Sucaryl
tablets, crushed

Wash and sort cranberries; remove seeds from orange. Put cranberries and orange through the fine blade of food chopper; blend in Sucaryl. Chill. Serve as salad or as relish with roast turkey or chicken. Yield: 8 servings/22 calories per serving.

Mrs. George A. Miller, Milan H.S.
Milan, Ohio

ALWAYS READY FROZEN FRUIT SALAD

1 tbsp. unflavored gelatin
2 egg yolks
1/4 c. sugar
1/4 c. lemon juice
1/2 c. pineapple juice
1/2 c. nonfat dry milk
2 c. fresh or diet pack fruit

Soak gelatin in 2 tablespoons water. Combine yolks, sugar, lemon juice and pineapple juice in double boiler. Cook, stirring, until slightly thickened. Add gelatin; cool. Beat dry milk and 1/2 cup ice water together until stiff; fold into cooled mixture with fruit. Pour into freezer tray; freeze until firm, Yield: 6-8 servings.

Mrs. Kathleen Boeckstiegel, Detroit H.S.
Detroit, Oregon

FRESH FRUIT SALAD

2 bananas, sliced
3 apples, diced
3 oranges, sectioned
1 c. sliced grapes
4   1/2-grain saccharin tablets
Salad dressing
Juice of 1 lemon

Combine fruits. Dissolve saccharin in 1 teaspoon water; sprinkle over fruits. Stir in enough salad dressing to moisten mixture. Sprinkle with lemon juice; serve in lettuce cups. Yield: 4 servings.

Mrs. Warren Webb, Columbia Jr. H.S.
Columbia, Kentucky

Low-Calorie

LOW-CALORIE FRUIT SALAD AND DRESSING

Lettuce
1 fresh pear, halved and cored
Lemon juice
3 maraschino cherries, halved
1 c. cottage cheese
16 grapefruit sections
6 cooked prunes
2 lemon slices
Low-Calorie Fruit Salad Dressing

Arrange lettuce leaves on luncheon plates. Dip pear halves in lemon juice to retain color; drain. Place 1 pear half at one side of plate with point toward center. Fill cavity with 3 maraschino cherry halves. Heap half the cottage cheese in a mound on lettuce on opposite side of plate. Fan out grapefruit sections in each of the two remaining areas. Garnish center with 3 whole prunes and 1 lemon slice. Repeat with remaining ingredients. Serve with salad dressing. Yield: 2 servings/249 calories per serving.

Low-Calorie Fruit Salad Dressing

1 clove of garlic, minced
1/4 c. vinegar
1/2 c. orange juice
1/4 tsp. paprika
1 tsp. sugar
1/2 tsp. salt
1/8 tsp. pepper

Let garlic stand in vinegar for 1 hour; strain. Add remaining ingredients to vinegar; shake or beat well. Refrigerate. Shake before serving. 10 calories per tablespoon.

Louise Wilcox, Fairview H.S.
Ashland, Kentucky

GOLDEN GLOW SALAD

2 3-oz. packages orange gelatin
2 c. orange diet pop
1 sm. can diet evaporated milk
2 c. cottage cheese
2 c. low-calorie crushed pineapple, drained
2 tbsp. cornstarch
2 tbsp. sugar
1 c. pineapple juice
1 1/2 tsp. liquid sweetener
1 pkg. whipped topping mix

Dissolve gelatin in 1 cup boiling water; add diet pop and evaporated milk. Chill until thickened. Whip until light; fold in cottage cheese and pineapple.

Place in 9 x 13-inch baking dish; refrigerate until firm. Combine cornstarch and sugar in a saucepan. Add pineapple juice gradually and sweetener. Cook, stirring, until thick. Cool. Prepare whipped topping according to package directions; fold into cooked mixture. Spread over gelatin mixture. Yield: 15 servings.

Mrs. Lola M. Rogers, Winchester H.S.
Winchester, Kansas

GRAPEFRUIT-GINGER SALAD

1 env. unflavored gelatin
6 saccharin tablets
1/8 tsp. salt
1 1-lb. can unsweetened grapefruit sections
2 tbsp. lemon juice
1/4 c. diced celery
1/4 c. diced apples
1 tsp. chopped crystalline ginger

Combine gelatin, sacharin and salt. Drain syrup from grapefruit; add enough water to juice to measure 1 1/4 cups liquid. Add 1/2 cup juice to gelatin mixture. Place over low heat; cook, stirring constantly, until gelatin is dissolved. Remove from heat; add remaining liquid and lemon juice. Chill until thickened. Fold in celery, apples, ginger and grapefruit. Turn into 3-cup mold; chill until firm. Yield: 6 servings.

Florence T. Shaffer, Berwick Area Sr. H.S.
Berwick, Pennsylvania

SLIM JANE SALAD

Iceberg lettuce
1 pt. low-calorie cottage cheese
1 c. red grapes, seeded
1 1-lb. can cling peach slices, drained

Arrange lettuce on 4 plates. Arrange 1/2 cup cottage cheese, 1/4 cup grapes and 5 to 6 peach slices on each plate. Serve with dressing. Yield: 4 servings.

Low-Calorie Dressing

1 c. low-fat yogurt
1 tbsp. orange juice
2 1/2 tsp. grated orange rind
1/4 tsp. salt
1/2 tsp. prepared horseradish

Combine all ingredients; mix well.

Mrs. Joseph S. Klimczak, Jr., Bogalusa H.S.
Bogalusa, Louisiana

SPRING STRAWBERRY SALAD

1 sm. can dietetic pack crushed pineapple
2 boxes dietetic strawberry gelatin
1 lb. strawberries, sliced
3 bananas, mashed

Drain juice from pineapple; add enough water to juice to measure 2 cups liquid. Bring to a boil; dissolve gelatin in liquid. Add 1 cup cold water. Cool until thickened. Add strawberries, bananas and pineapple. Pour into 9 x 13-inch pan; chill until set. Yield: 15 servings.

Mrs. Weldon Russell, Howard H.S.
Howard, Kansas

SPARKLING CITRUS SALAD

1 9-oz. can unsweetened crushed pineapple
1 1-lb. can unsweetened grapefruit sections
2 env. unflavored gelatin
Dash of salt
Dash of paprika
2 c. low-calorie pop

Drain pineapple and grapefruit, reserving juices. Sprinkle gelatin over reserved juice in saucepan to soften. Heat and stir to dissolve. Remove from heat; stir in salt and paprika. Cool slightly. Stir in pineapple and grapefruit. Chill until thickened; stir in pop. Chill until set. Unmold and serve. Yield: 8 servings.

Mrs. Lynda Harriman, Montezuma-Cortez H.S.
Cortez, Colorado

MOLDED WALDORF SALAD

3 env. unflavored gelatin
3 cans banana Sego
2 tsp. lemon flavoring
1/4 tsp. yellow food coloring
1 1/2 c. diced apples
1 c. finely cut celery

Soften gelatin in 1/2 cup water in 1-quart saucepan; stir in 1 can Sego. Stir over medium heat until gelatin is dissolved. Add remaining Sego, flavoring and food coloring. Chill until thick, but not set. Stir in apples and celery. Pour into 5 1/2-cup mold; chill until firm. Yield: 6-8 servings.

Mrs. Aleta B. Nelson, Tidehaven H.S.
Blessing, Texas

CHEESE AND FRUIT SALAD

1 env. unflavored gelatin
2 tbsp. lemon juice
1/8 tsp. salt
Artificial sweetener to equal 1/4 cup sugar
2 oz. low-calorie cream cheese
1/2 c. small curd cottage cheese
1/2 c. drained crushed pineapple
1/2 c. grapes or desired fruit
2 tbsp. low-calorie salad dressing

Prepare gelatin according to package directions; chill until thickened. Combine remaining ingredients; fold into gelatin. Turn into mold; chill until firm. Serve on lettuce. Yield: 6 servings.

Mrs. Gladyce Davis, Poteau H.S.
Poteau, Oklahoma

LIMEY COTTAGE CHEESE SALAD

2 env. diet lime gelatin
2 tsp. vinegar
1/8 tsp. salt
1/2 c. cottage cheese
2 tsp. chopped pimento
1 tsp. grated onion

Dissolve gelatin in 2 cups hot water; stir in vinegar and salt. Pour 1 cup into 3-cup mold; chill until almost firm. Chill remaining gelatin mixture until slightly thickened; fold in cheese, pimento and onion. Pour over firm layer in mold; chill until firm. Unmold on lettuce. Yield: 4 servings/40 calories per serving.

Iris Hendershot, Southern Fulton Jr.-Sr. H.S.
Warfordsburg, Pennsylvania

CHICKEN-PINEAPPLE MOLD

1 env. unflavored gelatin
1 3/4 c. chicken stock
2 drops of Sweeta
1 tsp. salt
2 tbsp. lemon juice
1/2 c. diced canned unsweetened pineapple
1 1/2 c. cooked diced chicken

Sprinkle gelatin over 1/2 cup of chicken stock to soften. Add sweetener; place over low heat. Stir until gelatin is dissolved. Remove from heat; add remaining chicken stock, salt and lemon juice. Chill to unbeaten egg white consistency. Fold in pineapple and chicken. Turn into a 3-cup mold; chill until firm. Serve on lettuce. Yield: 6 servings.

Mrs. B. E. Waggoner, Hickory Attendance Center
Hickory, Mississippi

Low-Calorie

TUNA LUNCHEON SALAD

1 tbsp. unflavored gelatin
1/2 tsp. salt
1 drop of Sucaryl
3 tbsp. vinegar
1 8-oz. can dietetic tuna, flaked
2 tbsp. sweet minced pickle or pepper relish
1/4 green pepper, minced
1/2 sm. onion, minced
1 c. minced celery

Soften gelatin in 1/4 cup cold water. Add 1 1/2 cups boiling water, salt and Sucaryl; stir until gelatin is dissolved. Add vinegar; chill until partially set. Stir in tuna, pickle and minced vegetables. Pour into mold; chill until firm. Unmold; garnish with salad greens. Serve with low-calorie dressing. One cup canned shellfish or diced cooked meat or chicken may be substituted for tuna, if desired. Yield: 4 servings.

Mrs. Ruth S. Riale
Central Columbia School Dist.
Bloomsburg, Pennsylvania

APPLE-TUNA SALAD

Juice of 1/2 lemon
1 1/2 c. chopped tart apples
1 sm. can tuna

Sprinkle lemon juice over apples; add tuna. Mix well. Top with diet dressing just before serving, if desired. Yield: 4-6 servings.

Mrs. Mary Frances Wilson, Cherokee Co. H.S.
Centre, Alabama

FANTASTIC TUNA MOLD

1 env. unflavored gelatin
2 egg yolks
1 1/4 c. skim milk
1 tsp. salt
Dash of pepper
1 6-oz. can tuna, drained
1 tsp. prepared mustard
2 tbsp. lemon juice
1/2 c. chopped celery
2 tbsp. finely chopped pimento
1 tbsp. chopped olives (opt.)

Sprinkle gelatin into 1/2 cup water to soften. Beat egg yolks and skim milk together; add salt and pepper. Cook over low heat for about 8 minutes or until thickened, stirring constantly. Remove from heat; add softened gelatin. Stir until dissolved. Chill to unbeaten egg white consistency. Combine tuna with mustard, lemon juice, celery, pimento and olives. Fold into gelatin mixture; turn into a 3-cup mold or

individual molds. Chill until firm. Unmold on salad greens; serve with salad dressing, if desired. Yield: 4 servings/160 calories per serving.

Mrs. Annie R. Gonzales, Prescott Jr. H.S.
Baton Rouge, Louisiana

LEMONY SEAFOOD SALAD

2 env. low-calorie lemon gelatin
1 tsp. salt
2 tsp. vinegar
1 c. crab meat or diced shrimp
2 tbsp. chopped celery
2 tbsp. chopped green pepper
2 tsp. chopped onion

Dissolve gelatin and salt in 2 cups hot water. Add vinegar; chill until slightly thickened. Add crab meat, celery, green pepper and onion. Pour into individual molds; chill until firm. Unmold onto crisp salad greens. Yield: 4 servings/50 calories per serving.

Mr. A. J. Kennedy, Vonore H.S.
Vonore, Tennessee

ESCABECH OF SHRIMP

2 lb. fresh med. shrimp, peeled and deveined
Lime or lemon juice
Salt
3 tbsp. salad oil
1 med. onion, sliced
2 cloves of garlic, halved
1/4 tsp. pepper

Sprinkle shrimp with juice of 1 lime and 1 teaspoon salt. Heat 1 tablespoon oil in a large skillet. Saute onion and garlic just until onion is trasparent. Discard garlic; remove onion to plate. Braise shrimp in flavored oil for about 5 minutes or until pink, stirring occasionally. Combine remaining oil, 3 tablespoons lime juice, pepper and dash of salt to make dressing. Arrange shrimp and onion in layers in deep bowl, pouring a small amount of dressing over each layer. Chill for several hours before serving. Yield: 6 servings/175 calories per serving.

Mrs. Anna D. Keeley, Bay Ridge H.S.
Brooklyn, New York

FRUITED SHRIMP SALAD

2 c. cooked cleaned shrimp
1 1/2 c. drained pineapple chunks
1 c. drained orange sections
1/2 c. thinly sliced celery
1/4 c. mild low-calorie French dressing
1 bunch endive

Combine shrimp, pineapple chunks, orange sections and celery; add French dressing. Mix lightly; chill. Serve on endive. Yield: 6 servings/115 calories per serving.

Alta Mae Kemp, George W. Carver H.S.
DeRidder, Louisiana

WEIGHT WATCHER'S SHRIMP SALAD

1 6-oz. can shrimp
1 sm. head lettuce, chopped
1 sm. onion, chopped
3 hard-cooked eggs, chopped
1/4 c. chopped green pepper
2 tomatoes, chopped
Salt and pepper to taste
Low-calorie French dressing

Drain and rinse shrimp; combine all ingredients except dressing. Toss to mix. Serve with dressing. Yield: 4 servings.

Mrs. Janice Feil, Gonvick H.S.
Gonvick, Minnesota

ASPIC BEAN MOLDS

1 env. unflavored gelatin
2 c. tomato juice
2 tbsp. lemon juice
Few drops of red pepper seasoning
1/2 tsp. salt
1 c. crisply cooked cut green beans
Iceberg lettuce
1 1/2 tsp. low-calorie mayonnaise

Soften gelatin in 1/2 cup tomato juice in saucepan; heat slowly, stirring constantly, until gelatin dissolves. Remove from heat; stir in remaining tomato juice, lemon juice, red pepper seasoning and salt. Chill until thickened. Fold in green beans. Spoon into 6 individual molds or custard cups; chill for several hours or until firm. Unmold onto lettuce-lined plates; top each mold with 1/4 teaspoon mayonnaise. Yield: 6 servings/31 calories per serving.

Mrs. Gayle Meacham, Gordon H. Garrett H.S.
Charleston Heights, South Carolina

GREEN BEAN AND CARROT SALAD

1 lg. can whole green beans
4 carrots, cut in julienne strips
2 tbsp. oil
1 tbsp. wine vinegar
1/2 red onion, thinly sliced

Salt and pepper to taste
1 tsp. capers

Drain beans thoroughly; pat dry and chill. Cook carrots in small amount of water until crisp tender; drain. Chill thoroughly. Comine oil and vinegar. Toss beans, carrots and onion together with salt and pepper. Pour oil and vinegar over all; toss lightly. Sprinkle capers on top. Yield: 6 servings/55 calories per serving.

Vera High, Mer Rouge H.S.
Mer Rouge, Louisiana

CONGEALED GREEN BEAN SALAD

1 No. 303 can French-style green beans
1 3-oz. package lemon gelatin
1 sm. onion, grated
1/4 c. chopped pecans
2 drops of green food coloring
1/2 c. mayonnaise
2 tbsp. half and half
1 tsp. lemon juice

Drain beans, reserving 1 cup liquid; bring liquid to a boil. Add gelatin; stir until dissolved. Chill until thickened. Add beans, onion, pecans and food coloring; pour into greased 1-quart tube mold. Chill until set. Mix remaining ingredients for dressing; serve with salad. Unmold on bed of lettuce greens on serving tray. Garnish with tomato wedges. Yield: 6 small servings/143 calories per serving.

Mrs. Lindell Stanton, Butte Valley H.S.
Dorris, California

CARROT-ORANGE SALAD

1 env. unflavored gelatin
1/2 c. orange juice
Artificial sweetener to equal 9 tsp. sugar
3 tbsp. lemon juice or vinegar
1/4 tsp. salt
1/2 c. shredded carrots
1/2 c. well-drained unsweetened crushed
    pineapple
1/2 c. drained orange sections, cut
    in pieces

Sprinkle gelatin on orange juice to soften. Add sweetener; place over low heat and stir until gelatin is dissolved. Remove from heat; add 1 cup water, lemon juice and salt. Chill to unbeaten egg white consistency. Fold in carrots, pineapple and orange. Turn into a 3-cup mold or individual molds. Chill until firm. Yield: 6 servings.

Mrs. Elizabeth Myers Culbreth, Chapman H.S.
Inman, South Carolina

Low-Calorie

SOUTHERN SUNSHINE SALAD

6 carrots, shredded
1   8 1/2-oz. can crushed pineapple, drained
1   11-oz. can mandarin oranges, drained
1 tbsp. lemon juice
1 tsp. sugar or Sweeta to taste
1/4 c. low-calorie salad dressing or mayonnaise

Combine carrots, crushed pineapple, orange sections, lemon juice and sugar. Serve with salad dressing. Yield: 4-6 servings.

Mrs. Rosemary M. Pace, Fort Campbell H.S.
Fort Campbell, Kentucky

CARROT AND PINEAPPLE CONGEALED SALAD

1   6-oz. box dietetic lemon gelatin
1   6-oz. box dietetic orange gelatin
1 No. 2 can dietetic crushed pineapple
1 1/2 c. grated carrots

Dissolve gelatins in 2 cups hot water; add pineapple with juice and carrots. Chill until set.

Mrs. Elizabeth Harrison, Murfreesboro Cen. H.S.
Murfreesboro, Tennessee

FIESTA COLESLAW

1 lg. head green cabbage, shredded
1 Spanish onion, thinly sliced
1 sm. carrot, shredded
1 c. white vinegar
2 tbsp. oil
1/2 c. diced sweet red peppers
4 or 5 drops of liquid sugar substitute
    or 1/3 c. sugar
1/2 tsp. salt
1/2 tsp. pepper

Toss cabbage, onion and carrot together. Combine vinegar, 2 tablespoons water, oil, red peppers, sugar substitute, salt and pepper; add to cabbage mixture. Toss well; chill for 6 hours before serving. Yield: 8 servings.

Mrs. Adele Charlson, Campbell Union Dist. H.S.
Campbell, California

ITALIAN-STYLE COLESLAW

4 c. finely sliced cabbage
1 1/2 c. finely sliced celery
1 1/2 c. cherry tomatoes, halved
1/2 c. low-calorie Italian salad dressing

2 tbsp. chopped fresh chives
    or 2 tsp. dried chives

Toss cabbage, celery and tomatoes together; chill until serving time. Combine salad dressing and chives; chill. Add dressing to cabbage mixture just before serving; toss. Yield: 6 servings/35 calories per serving.

Mrs. Eleonora Free, Oswego H.S.
Oswego, Kansas

COLESLAW PARFAIT SALAD

2 env. unflavored gelatin
1/3 c. lemon juice
2 tbsp. vinegar
2/3 c. diet sugar
1/4 tsp. salt
1/3 c. mayonnaise
1 1/2 c. shredded cabbage
1/2 c. diced celery
1/4 c. chopped green pepper
2 tbsp. minced onion

Soften gelatin in 1/2 cup cold water; add 1 1/2 cups boiling water, stirring to dissolve. Add lemon juice, vinegar, diet sugar and salt; blend well. Chill until mixture begins to thicken; fold in remaining ingredients. Pour into lightly oiled 4-cup mold; chill until set. Yield: 6 servings.

Mrs. Wilda Carr, Savior H.S.
Holdredge, Nebraska

NORWEGIAN SLAW

1 med. head cabbage, shredded
1 tbsp. salt
2 1/3 tbsp. Sucaryl
1 c. white vinegar
1 tsp. mustard seed
1 tsp. celery seed
2 c. diced celery
1 green pepper, diced
1 sm. onion, diced

Sprinkle cabbage with salt; let stand for 2 hours. Boil sucaryl and vinegar together. Add mustard seed, celery seed, celery, green pepper and onion to cabbage; pour vinegar syrup over cabbage. Refrigerate for at least 24 hours.

Pearl Robinson, Ahrens Trade H.S.
Louisville, Kentucky

BASIC PERFECTION SALAD

1 env. unflavored gelatin
1/4 c. vinegar

1 tbsp. lemon juice
2 tsp. liquid sweetener
1/2 tsp. salt
1 c. finely chopped celery
1/2 c. finely shredded cabbage
1 pimento, finely chopped

Soften gelatin in 1/4 cup cold water; stir in 1 cup hot water, vinegar, lemon juice, sweetener and salt. Chill until thickened; fold in celery, cabbage and pimento. Spoon into individual molds; chill until firm. Serve on salad greens. Yield: 6 servings.

Bernetha Gillette, Byron H.S.
Byron, Nebraska

PERFECTION RING

2 env. unflavored gelatin
8 drops of Sucaryl
1 tsp. salt
1/2 c. vinegar
2 tbsp. lemon juice
2 c. finely shredded cabbage
1 c. chopped celery
1/2 c. chopped green pepper
1/4 c. chopped pimento

Combine gelatin, Sucaryl, salt and 1/2 cup cold water; let stand for 5 minutes. Add 1 cup boiling water; stir until dissolved. Add 1 1/2 cups cold water, vinegar and lemon juice; chill until partially set. Add vegetables; pour into 6 1/2-cup ring mold. Chill until firm. Unmold on greens; serve with low-calorie dressing. Garnish with cucumber and tomato slices, if desired. Yield: 8-10 servings.

Virginia H. Culbertson, Mid-Carolina H.S.
Prosperity, South Carolina

CUCUMBER-PINEAPPLE SALAD

1 env. unflavored gelatin
2 8 1/2-oz. cans dietetic pack
   pineapple tidbits
1/4 c. lemon juice
1 tbsp. liquid sweetener
1 c. finely chopped cucumber

Soften gelatin in 3/4 cup cold water. Drain pineapple, reserving juice. Bring pineapple juice to a boil; add softened gelatin. Stir until dissolved. Add lemon juice and sweetener. Chill until partially set; fold in pineapple and cucumber. Turn into 1-quart mold; chill until firm. Yield: 6 servings.

Mrs. Garry C. Pittman, Darien H.S.
Darien, Georgia

CREAMY CUCUMBER SALAD

3 pkg. low-calorie lime gelatin
Salt to taste
1/4 c. vinegar
2 tsp. grated onion
2 c. low-calorie sour cream
2 med. cucumbers, peeled and coarsely grated

Dissolve gelatin in 2 cups boiling water; stir until dissolved. Chill until partially congealed; add remaining ingredients. Mix well; place in oiled 8-inch ring mold. Refrigerate until set; serve on a bed of lettuce. Yield: 6-8 servings.

Mrs. Esther Wasson, Bridgeton H.S.
Bridgeton, New Jersey

GOLDEN SUNSET SALAD

1 env. unflavored gelatin
3/4 tsp. Sucaryl
1/4 tsp. salt
1/2 c. orange juice
2 tbsp. vinegar
1/2 c. canned crushed pineapple, drained
1/2 c. drained orange sections
1/2 c. grated carrots

Soften gelatin with Sucaryl and salt in 1/4 cup cold water; add 3/4 cup boiling water. Stir until gelatin is thoroughly dissolved. Add orange juice and vinegar. Chill to unbeaten egg white consistency; fold in pineapple, orange sections and carrots. Turn into a 3-cup mold or individual molds; chill until firm. Unmold on salad greens; serve with salad dressing. Yield: 6 servings.

Dorothy Carson, Willamette H.S.
Eugene, Oregon

TEXAS SUNSHINE SALAD

1 8-oz. can dietetic pineapple chunks
Orange juice
1 env. unflavored gelatin
1/8 tsp. salt
Artificial sweetener to equal 1/4 c. sugar
3 tbsp. lemon juice
1 c. coarsely grated carrot

Drain liquid from pineapple; add enough orange juice to measure 1 1/2 cups liquid. Pour 1/2 cup liquid into saucepan; sprinkle gelatin over liquid. Place over low heat; stir constantly for 2 to 3 minutes or until gelatin dissolves. Remove from heat. Stir in remaining liquid, salt, sweetener and lemon juice; add pineapple and carrot. Turn into 3-cup mold; chill until firm. Unmold; garnish with salad greens. Yield: 4 servings/89 calories per serving.

Elizabeth Higgs, Sanger H.S.
Sanger, Texas

Low-Calorie

UNUSUAL GREEN SALAD MOLD

1 env. unflavored gelatin
1 tbsp. sugar
1 tsp. salt
1/8 tsp. pepper
1/4 c. vinegar
1 tbsp. lemon juice
1/4 c. chopped scallions
1 c. shredded fresh spinach
1 c. chopped celery
1/4 c. shredded carrots

Combine gelatin, sugar, salt and pepper thoroughly in saucepan; add 1/2 cup water. Place over low heat, stirring constantly, until gelatin is dissolved; remove from heat. Stir in 1 1/4 cups cold water, vinegar and lemon juice; chill until mixture is consistency of unbeaten egg white. Fold in scallions, spinach, celery and carrots; turn into 3-cup mold or individual molds. Chill until firm; unmold and garnish with tomatoes and olives. Yield: 6 servings.

Jean C. Boychuk, Motley Sr. H.S.
Motley, Minnesota

JELLIED SPRING VEGETABLE SALAD

1 tbsp. unflavored gelatin
1/2 tsp. salt
1/4 c. lime juice
2 tsp. Sucaryl
Few drops of green food coloring
1 c. diced peeled cucumber
1 c. sliced radishes
1/4 c. sliced scallions

Soften gelatin in 1/4 cup cold water; dissolve in 2 cups boiling water. Add salt, lime juice, Sucaryl and food coloring; chill until mixture begins to thicken. Fold in remaining ingredients; pour into 5-cup mold. Chill until set. Yield: 8 servings/17 calories per serving.

Mrs. Muriel F. Richards, Battle Creek H.S.
Battle Creek, Nebraska

CREAMY LIME VEGETABLE SALAD

1 pkg. low-calorie lime gelatin
1/2 c. low-calorie whipped topping
3 tbsp. salad dressing
1 1/2 tbsp. grated onion
3 tbsp. grated carrots
3 tbsp. finely chopped celery
3 tbsp. (or more) cottage cheese

Dissolve gelatin in 2 cups hot water; chill until thickened. Add whipped topping and salad dressing; fold

in vegetables and cottage cheese. Chill until set. Yield: 4 servings.

Eileen Brenden, Central H.S.
Glenwood, Minnesota

GREENS AND HERBS SALAD

1 1/2 qt. salad greens
1 tbsp. olive oil
2 tbsp. garlic vinegar
1 tsp. grated lemon rind
1 tsp. parsley flakes
1 bay leaf, crumbled
1 tsp. celery salt
1/2 tps. chervil leaves
1/4 tsp. fennel seed
1/4 tsp. basil
1/4 tsp. oregano
1/8 tsp. pepper

Place salad greens in bowl; add oil. Toss until all greens are thoroughly coated. Add remaining ingredients and 1 tablespoon water; toss and serve. Yield: 6-8 servings.

Claudine Bettencourt, Lemoore Union H.S.
Lemoore, California

TANGY SAUERKRAUT SALAD

2 3-oz. packages lemon gelatin
1 No. 2 can sauerkraut, drained
2 tbsp. chopped pickles
1 tbsp. chopped stuffed olives

Dissolve gelatin in 1 1/2 cups boiling water; add 2 1/2 cups ice water. Chill until thickened; add remaining ingredients. Chill until firm. Yield: 8-10 servings.

Mrs. Kenneth Bartholomew, Woodston H.S.
Woodston, Kansas

FRESH SPINACH SALAD

1/2 lb. spinach, torn into bite-sized pieces
1 sm. onion, sliced
1/4 c. diced celery
4 hard-cooked eggs, sliced
Low-calorie French dressing

Combine all ingredients except dressing; toss together lightly. Chill. Toss lightly with dressing. Yield: 8 servings.

Mrs. Myrtle Lois Hardin, Brock H.S.
Weatherford, Texas

SLIMMING SPRING SALAD

2 env. low-calorie lime gelatin
1 tsp. salt
1 tbsp. vinegar
2/3 c. finely diced cucumber
1/2 c. finely diced celery
1/4 c. finely cut scallions

Dissolve gelatin and salt in 2 cups hot water. Add vinegar; chill until slightly thickened. Add cucumber, celery and scallions. Pour into individual molds. Chill until firm. Unmold on crisp lettuce. Yield: 4 servings/20 calories per serving.

Mrs. Rosetta Haire, Crescent-Iroquois H.S.
Crescent City, Illinois

SUMMER VEGETABLE ROUNDUP

1 3-oz. package lemon gelatin
1/2 c. diet mayonnaise
1 c. chopped celery
1 c. grated cucumber
1/3 c. grated carrot
1 tsp. onion salt
2 tbsp. lemon juice
3/4 c. evaporated skim milk

Combine gelatin and 3/4 cup hot water; stir until dissolved. Add mayonnaise, celery, cucumber, carrot and onion salt; chill for 45 minutes or until thickened. Stir lemon juice gradually into milk; add to gelatin mixture. Blend well; spoon into 1-quart mold. Chill until set; unmold and garnish with parsley. Yield: 4-6 servings.

Mary Hetrick, Cardinal Stritch School
Oregon, Ohio

DIETER'S TOMATO ASPIC

2 env. unflavored gelatin
2 c. hot tomato juice
1 tsp. grated onion
Salt to taste
1/4 tsp. pepper
2 tbsp. vinegar
Few drops of Sucaryl

Soften gelatin in 1/4 cup cold water; dissolve in hot tomato juice. Add remaining ingredients; blend well. Pour into cold water-rinsed ring mold. Chill until firm. Yield: 6 servings/20 calories per serving.

Mrs. Madge G. Young, Annapolis Sr. H.S.
Annapolis, Maryland

SLIMMER'S VEGETABLE ASPIC

1 env. unflavored gelatin
1 3/4 c. tomato juice
2 tbsp. lemon juice
1/2 tsp. Worcestershire sauce
1/4 tsp. salt
3 drops of liquid sweetener
1 drop of Tabasco sauce
1 c. shredded cabbage
1/2 c. chopped celery
1/4 c. chopped green pepper

Sprinkle gelatin over 1/2 cup tomato juice; cook over low heat, stirring constantly, until gelatin is dissolved. Remove from heat; add remaining tomato juice, lemon juice, Worcestershire sauce, salt, sweetener and Tabasco sauce. Chill until thickened but not set; stir in cabbage, celery and green pepper. Turn into 3-cup mold or 6 individual molds; chill until firm. Yield: 6 servings/15 calories per serving.

Mrs. Faye Jean Dean, Valley Heights H.S.
Blue Rapids, Kansas

OLD-FASHIONED COOKED SALAD DRESSING

1 tbsp. flour
2 tbsp. sugar
1 1/4 tsp. salt
Dash of red pepper
1 tsp. prepared mustard
1 tbsp. salad oil
2 eggs
1/4 c. vinegar
1 tbsp. catsup
1/2 tsp. horseradish
1/2 tsp. Worcestershire sauce
2 tbsp. chili sauce
2 tbsp. chopped green pepper
1/2 hard-cooked egg

Combine flour, sugar, salt, red pepper, prepared mustard, salad oil and 1 cup water in top of double boiler; cook over hot water, stirring constantly, until slightly thickened. Beat eggs slightly; add vinegar gradually. Add half the hot sauce to egg mixture, stirring constantly. Return to hot mixture; stir and cook over hot, not boiling, water until mixture coats a spoon. Overcooking after eggs have been added will cause dressing to curdle. Remove from heat at once; pour into a jar. Let cool; cover and refrigerate. Add catsup to 1/4 cup dressing for Russian dressing. Add horseradish and Worcestershire sauce to 1/4 cup dressing for a gourmet dressing. Add chili sauce, chopped green pepper and hard-cooked egg to 1/4 cup dressing for Thousand Island dressing.

Mrs. Laura Russell, Freelandville H.S.
Freelandville, Indiana

Low-Calorie

EASY COOKED SALAD DRESSING

1/2 tsp. salt
1/4 tsp. dry mustard
1/4 tsp. paprika
Dash of cayenne pepper
2 tbsp. vinegar
1/4 c. nonfat milk
1 egg, beaten
1/4 tsp. liquid sweetener

Place all ingredients in top of double boiler; mix well. Cook over hot water, stirring constantly, until thickened. Cool and chill. Yield: 1/2 cup dressing/13 calories per tablespoon.

Mrs. Dorothy Campbell, Deer Park H.S.
Deer Park, Washington

CREAMY COOKED SALAD DRESSING

1 tsp. unflavored gelatin
2 c. skim milk or buttermilk
2 egg yolks
3 tbsp. vinegar
1/8 tsp. white pepper
3/4 tsp. salt
1/2 tsp. dry mustard
1/8 tsp. hot pepper sauce

Soften gelatin in 1/2 cup milk for 5 minutes. Mix remaining milk, egg yolks, vinegar, white pepper, salt, mustard and pepper sauce in saucepan; add softened gelatin. Bring to a boil, stirring constantly; remove from heat. Chill. Yield: 2 cups dressing.

Mrs. Effie Gaynon, Leonard School
Saxton's River, Vermont

SMOOTH COOKED SALAD DRESSING

1 tbsp. dry mustard
2 tbsp. flour
1/2 tsp. seasoned salt
Dash of cayenne pepper
2 eggs, separated
1/2 tsp. artificial sweetener
1/3 c. vinegar

Combine mustard, flour, salt and pepper in small saucepan; blend well. Beat egg yolks well; add enough water to make 1/2 cup liquid. Stir into flour mixture; stir in sweetener and vinegar. Cook until mixture comes to a boil. Cook, stirring, for 1 minute. Remove from heat. Pour hot mixture slowly into stiffly beaten egg whites; mix until thoroughly blended. Chill before adding to salad.

Serola Fulgham, Safford H.S.
Safford, Arizona

CALORIE-RESTRICTED COOKED SALAD DRESSING

1 env. unflavored gelatin
2 tsp. dry mustard
2 tsp. salt
1/4 tsp. paprika
2 eggs
2 tbsp. butter
4 artificial sweetener tablets
1/2 c. vinegar

Mix gelatin, mustard, salt and paprika thoroughly in top of double boiler. Beat eggs and 2 cups water together; add to gelatin mixture. Add butter and sweetener; cook over boiling water, stirring constantly, until gelatin is dissolved. Remove from heat; stir in vinegar slowly. Chill until slightly thickened; beat with beater until well blended. Store, covered, in refrigerator. Beat lightly with fork before serving. Yield: 2 1/2 cups.

Mrs. Katherine E. Heiderich
John Peterson Jr. Secondary School
Kamloops, British Columbia, Canada

FRUIT JUICE GLAZE SALAD DRESSING

Juice from 1 can pineapple
3 tbsp. lemon juice
Orange juice
2 tsp. artificial sweetener
1 tbsp. cornstarch

Combine pineapple juice and lemon juice; add enough orange juice to make 1 cup liquid. Add sweetener. Dissolve cornstarch in 2 tablespoons cold water; add to juices in saucepan. Boil, stirring constantly, until slightly thickened; cool. Store in refrigerator. Serve with fruit salad. Yield: 1 cup dressing.

Mrs. Edith Larson, Parkrose Sr. H.S.
Portland, Oregon

BLENDER BLEU CHEESE DRESSING

1 pt. cottage cheese
1/2 c. skim milk
1/4 c. bleu cheese
1/4 tsp. garlic salt
1/4 tsp. sweet basil, crushed
1/2 tsp. Worcestershire sauce

Place all ingredients in blender container; blend at high speed until smooth. Store in covered container in refrigerator for several hours before serving.

Mrs. June Schellin, Sante Fe H.S.
Sante Fe Springs, California

BLEU CHEESE-OLIVE DRESSING

3/4 c. crumbled bleu cheese
1 c. buttermilk
1 c. cottage cheese
1 c. mayonnaise
1/2 c. chopped green olives

Combine bleu cheese, buttermilk and cottage cheese; blend until mixture is well mixed. Add mayonnaise and olives; mix well. Chill. Serve on green salad. Yield: 1 quart.

Mrs. Mallie Venn Steger, Montgomery H.S.
Montgomery, Texas

BLENDER COTTAGE CHEESE DRESSING

1/2 c. cottage cheese
1/2 c. buttermilk
1/4 c. lemon juice
1 tsp. salt
1/2 tsp. paprika

Place all ingredients in blender container; blend until smooth. Yield: 1 cup dressing.

Mrs. F. L. Moseley, Valdosta Jr. High
Valdosta, Georgia

DANISH DRESSING

1 c. cream-style cottage cheese
2 tbsp. crumbled bleu cheese
2 tbsp. skim milk

Combine cottage cheese, bleu cheese and skim milk in blender container; cover. Process until smooth; chill. 24 calories per tablespoon.

Mrs. Glenda Campbell, Gates-Chili Jr. H.S.
Rochester, New York

CALORIE-WATCHER'S ALL-PURPOSE SALAD DRESSING

1 can tomato soup
1/4 tsp. garlic salt or garlic powder
1 tbsp. pickle relish
1/8 tsp. pepper
1/4 tsp. onion salt
2 or 3 tbsp. wine vinegar

Place ingredients in order listed in jar with tightfitting lid. Cover; shake vigorously. Chill overnight. Yield: 1 1/2 cups dressing.

Brenda K. Jensen, Chaffey H.S.
Ontario, California

3 tbsp. lemon juice
3 tbsp. soy sauce
1 tbsp. sugar
1 tsp. finely chopped candied ginger

Combine all ingredients; blend well. Serve on sliced cucumber and tomato. Yield: 1/2 cup dressing.

Patricia C. Mott, Clarkstown H.S.
New City, New York

DIETER'S DELIGHT DRESSING FOR GREEN SALADS

1   10 1/2-oz. can beef broth
2 tbsp. chili sauce or catsup
2 tbsp. vinegar
1 tbsp. grated onion
1 oz. crumbled bleu cheese (opt.)

Combine all ingredients; shake well. Serve over green salads. Yield: 6 servings.

Mallie Venn Steger, Montgomery H.S.
Montgomery, Texas

EASY FRENCH DRESSING

1 can tomato soup
2 tbsp. Sucaryl
1/2 c. soy bean oil
1/2 c. vinegar
1 tsp. salt
1 tsp. minced garlic
1 lg. onion, sliced thin
1/4 c. prepared mustard
1/2 tsp. paprika

Combine all ingredients; mix well. Store in covered jar in refrigerator. Yield: 3 cups dressing.

Emma A. Podoll, Phoenix Indian H.S.
Phoenix, Arizona

FANTASTIC FRENCH DRESSING

1   6-oz. can frozen grapefruit concentrate
1/2 c. catsup
1/4 c. salad oil

Shake all ingredients until blended; store in refrigerator. Shake before using.

Mrs. Audrey Buhl, Milaca H.S.
Milaca, Minnesota

Low-Calorie

MR. MOSER'S FRENCH DRESSING

1 c. tomato juice
2 tbsp. grated onion
3 or 4 tbsp. catsup
Juice of 1 1/2 lemons
2 tsp. sugar
1 cut clove of garlic

Combine first 5 ingredients; shake well. Store in covered jar in refrigerator. Rub bowl with garlic clove when ready to prepare salad; discard garlic clove. Yield: 25-30 servings/5 calories per tablespoon.

Mrs. G. T. Lilly, Murray H.S.
Murray, Kentucky

COOKED FRENCH DRESSING

1 tbsp. cornstarch
1/4 c. lemon juice
2 tbsp. corn oil
1 tbsp. Worcestershire sauce
2 egg yolks

Mix cornstarch with lemon juice in saucepan; add 3/4 cup water. Cook over low heat, stirring constantly, until smooth and slightly thickened. Beat in oil and Worcestershire sauce. Beat egg yolks; beat hot mixture gradually into egg yolks. Chill; store in refrigerator. Shake well before serving. Yield: 1 1/2 cups dressing.

Mrs. Bonnie Shaw, Clarkfield Public School
Clarkfield, Minnesota

DOUBLE FRENCH DRESSING

1 can tomato soup
3 tbsp. herb and garlic French dressing
1/4 tsp. onion salt
Dash of garlic salt
Dash of pepper
1 tsp. (or more) artificial sweetener

Blend all ingredients well; store in refrigerator. Yield: 2 cups dressing.

Marsha Faye Smith, Quinter H.S.
Quinter, Kansas

TOMATO FRENCH DRESSING

1/2 c. tomato juice
2 tbsp. cider vinegar
1 tbsp. finely chopped onion
1 tbsp. finely chopped green pepper
1 tsp. Worcestershire sauce
1/4 tsp. garlic salt

1/2 tsp. salt
1/2 tsp. dry mustard
1/4 tsp. liquid sugar substitute

Combine all ingredients in blender container; blend well. Store in refrigerator. Dressing thickens and improves in flavor as it stands. Serve on tossed green salads.

Mrs. Esther Williams, Pocatello H.S.
Pocatello, Idaho

GOURMET HERB DRESSING

1 pt. low-fat cottage cheese
1 c. low-fat yogurt
Dash of garlic powder
1 tsp. salt
1/4 tsp. parsley
1/4 tsp. lemon juice
1/4 tsp. oregano
1/4 tsp. savory
3 tsp. tarragon

Place all ingredients in blender container; blend thoroughly. Yield: 3 cups dressing.

Barsha Elzey, Terra Linda H.S.
San Rafael, California

TANGY GOURMET DRESSING

3 tbsp. vinegar
1 env. French salad dressing mix
2 tbsp. salad oil
2/3 c. tomato juice

Pour vinegar into cruet; add salad dressing mix. Shake well. Add oil and tomato juice; shake to blend. Serve over fruit or green salad. Yield: 1 cup dressing/20 calories per tablespoon.

Hazel C. Tassis, Imperial H.S.
Imperial, California

HONEY AND FRUIT SALAD DRESSING

1/4 c. pineapple juice
2 tbsp. frozen orange juice concentrate
2 tbsp. lemon juice
2 tbsp. honey
1/8 tsp. salt
1 egg, well beaten
1/3 c. instant nonfat dry milk
1/4 c. sieved cottage cheese

Blend fruit juices, honey, salt and egg in saucepan; cook over low heat until mixture coats a spoon. Let cool. Place 1/4 cup water and dry milk in electric mixer; whip until very stiff. Fold in cottage cheese and fruit juice mixture; chill. Serve on fruit salads.

Phyllis Nichiporik, Two Hills H.S.
Tow Hills, Alberta, Canada

SPECIAL DRESSING FOR GREENS

1 c. yogurt
2 tbsp. tarragon vinegar or lemon juice
1/2 tsp. minced fresh basil
1/2 tsp. salt
1/4 tsp. freshly ground pepper
1 clove of garlic, crushed or 1 sm. white
   onion, minced
1 tbsp. minced parsley
Pinch of dry mustard
Dash of Worcestershire sauce

Combine all ingredients; mix well. Refrigerate for 15 to 30 minutes before using. Pour over head lettuce or watercress and fresh spinach salad. Yield: 4-6 servings.

Marie M. Mullins, Saddle Rock School
Great Neck, New York

AMY'S SALAD DRESSING

1 garlic clove, minced
1/4 c. vinegar
1/2 c. orange juice
1/4 tsp. paprika
5 drops of Sweeta
1/2 tsp. salt
1/8 tsp. pepper

Add garlic to vinegar; let stand for 1 hour. Strain. Add remaining ingredients to vinegar; shake well. Chill. Shake again before using. Yield: 3/4 cup.

Amy H. Redfearn, Cheraw H.S.
Cheraw, South Carolina

SIMPLE SALAD DRESSING

1/2 c. tomato juice
2 tbsp. lemon juice or cider vinegar
1 tbsp. minced onion
1/4 tsp. salt
1/8 tsp. pepper

Combine all ingredients; mix well. Chill. Yield: 1/2 cup dressing.

Mildred Sanderson, Central H.S.
West Allis, Wisconsin

COTTAGE CHEESE TOPPING FOR BAKED POTATOES

1/2 c. dry cottage cheese
1/4 c. sour cream
1 tbsp. snipped chives
1/4 tsp. salt
Dash of pepper

Combine all ingredients in blender container; cover. Blend at high speed for 1 minute or until mixture is creamy. Serve on baked potatoes.

Mrs. Leola Becker, Hustisford H.S.
Hustisford, Wisconsin

QUICK SOUR CREAM

1 c. cottage cheese
1 tbsp. lemon juice

Place cottage cheese, lemon juice and 1/4 cup water in blender container; blend for 10 seconds or until smooth. Remove cover and scrape down sides of container lightly with a rubber spatula, if necessary. Yield: 1 cup.

Linda Kautzmann, Montour H.S.
McKees Rocks, Pennsylvania

SLIM-TRIM SOUR CREAM

1/4 to 1/2 c. buttermilk
1 c. large curd cottage cheese
1/4 tsp. lemon juice
Pinch of salt

Combine all ingredients in blender container; blend until smooth. Store in refrigerator. Serve as low-calorie substitute for sour cream. Mixture does not tolerate heat as does regular sour cream. Yield: 1 cup.

Mrs. R. Gale Manley, Virginia Jr. H.S.
Bristol, Virginia

BLENDER MOCK SOUR CREAM

8 oz. large curd cottage cheese
1/2 tsp. salt
1/4 c. (about) skim milk
1/4 tsp. lemon juice

Place all ingredients in blender container; cover. Blend until smooth, scraping sides of container occasionally. Yield: 1 1/4 cups.

Sister Clotilda, S.N.D., Juliene H.S.
Dayton, Ohio

SOUR CREAM SUBSTITUTE

12 oz. cottage cheese
2 tbsp. lemon juice

Place cottage cheese and lemon juice in blender container; blend until mixture is consistency of sour cream. Yield: 1 pint.

Mrs. Louise W. Winslow, Orange H.S.
Hillsborough, North Carolina

LEMONY MOCK SOUR CREAM

1/4 c. skim milk
2 tbsp. lemon juice
1/2 tsp. salt
1 c. cottage cheese
2 tbsp. chopped chives or 1/4 c. chopped
    celery (opt.)

Pour milk and lemon juice into blender container; add salt and cottage cheese. Blend at high speed until mixture is smooth. Serve plain as a dip or add chives and serve on baked potatoes. Yield: 1 1/2-2 cups.

Laura Anderson, Sutherlin H.S.
Sutherlin, Oregon

YOGURT MOCK SOUR CREAM

3 tbsp. lemon juice
1 tsp. salt
1/4 tsp. prepared mustard
1 c. yogurt

Mix lemon juice and salt; blend in mustard. Stir slowly into yogurt; blend well. Chill for at least 30 minutes before serving. Yield: 20 tablespoons.

Margaret Ide, George Rogers Clarke School
Whiting, Indiana

ORANGE SAUCE FOR CHICKEN

1/4 c. lemon juice
1 c. orange juice
2 tsp. Sucaryl
1 tbsp. grated orange peel
1/2 tsp. caraway seed
1/4 tsp. marjoram
1/4 tsp. rosemary
1 tbsp. cornstarch

Combine juices and Sucaryl; set aside. Combine remaining ingredients in a small saucepan. Add a small amount of juice mixture to make smooth paste; add remaining juice mixture. Cook over low heat, stirring constantly, until slightly thick. Serve with chicken. Yield: 1 1/4 cups.

Betty Herbel, TMCS
Belcourt, North Dakota

TOMATO SAUCE FOR MEATBALLS

1 tbsp. instant minced onion
2 6-oz. cans tomato paste
1 1-lb. can tomatoes
1 1/2 tsp. salt
1 tsp. oregano
1 tsp. liquid Sweet-10
1/2 tsp. garlic salt
1/2 tsp. crushed basil
1/4 tsp. pepper

Combine all ingredients and 1 1/2 cups water in 10-inch skillet; cover. Simmer for 20 minutes. Serve over meatballs and spaghetti. Yield: 5 cups.

Mrs. Winnie Carter, Karnack H.S.
Karnack, Texas

CREOLE COD FILLETS

2 lb. cod fillets
2 tbsp. flour
1 sm. onion, sliced
1 1-lb. can tomatoes
1 pimento, chopped
1 bay leaf
1/4 tsp. monosodium glutamate
1 tsp. salt
Dash of pepper
1/4 tsp. oregano

Cut fish into serving pieces; place in shallow 2-quart baking dish. Combine remaining ingredients; pour over fish. Bake at 350 degrees for about 1 hour. Yield: 6 servings/133 calories per serving.

Mrs. Sherri Day, West H.S.
Anchorage, Alaska

BAKED FLOUNDER FILLET LUNCHEON

4 3-oz. flounder fillets
Seasoned salt
4 slices Swiss cheese
1/4 tsp. dehydrated onion
1/2 c. sliced fresh mushrooms
2 tsp. minced parsley (opt.)
1/4 c. skim milk
1/4 c. tomato sauce

Sprinkle fillets lightly on both sides with seasoned salt; roll up. Fold cheese in half. Arrange flounder rolls and cheese slices alternately down center of baking dish. Soak onion flakes in several tablespoons water until soft; add mushrooms, 3/4 teaspoon seasoned salt, parsley and 1/4 cup water. Add skim milk and tomato sauce. Bring to a boil; pour over fish. Bake in preheated 400-degree oven for 12 minutes or until fillets are golden and easily flaked with fork. Serve hot from baking dish. Yield: 4 servings.

Georgia A. Potterton, Eastern Jr. H.S.
Riverside, Connecticut

SALMON LOAF WITH MUSHROOM SAUCE

2 c. canned salmon
1 c. dry bread crumbs
1/4 c. chopped pitted ripe olives
1 egg, beaten
1 tbsp. lemon juice
1/2 tsp. salt
1/8 tsp. pepper

Drain salmon; reserve liquid. Add enough water to reserved liquid to measure 2/3 cup. Place salmon in bowl; flake with fork. Add liquid and remaining ingredients; mix until well blended. Turn into greased 9 x 5 x 3-inch loaf pan. Bake at 375 degrees for about 45 minutes or until done. Let stand for several minutes. Loosen edge with spatula; unmold onto serving platter. Yield: 4 servings/340 calories per serving.

Mushroom Sauce

1 c. mushroom liquid and water
1/3 c. nonfat dry milk
2 tbsp. flour
1/2 tsp. salt
Pinch of pepper
3/4 c. drained canned sliced mushrooms

Combine mushroom liquid and water with dry milk, flour, salt and pepper. Beat with rotary beater until well blended. Cook over medium heat, stirring constantly, until sauce thickens and comes to a boil. Remove from heat. Stir in mushrooms. Serve over salmon loaf.

Mrs. Nadine Martin, Vernon H.S.
Vernon, Texas

POACHED FILLET OF SOLE

1/2 med. onion
1 bay leaf
1 tbsp. lemon juice
1 tbsp. vinegar
3 peppercorns
1 tsp. salt
1 lb. fillet of sole
Chopped parsley

Place 1 1/2 cups water, onion, bay leaf, lemon juice, vinegar, peppercorns and salt in saucepan; heat for 5 minutes. Cut fish into serving-sized pieces; add to

water mixture. Cook over low heat for 5 to 10 minutes or until fish flakes easily with a fork. Sprinkle with chopped parsley before serving. Yield: 4 servings/153 calories per serving.

Mrs. Lee Britton, Buhler H.S.
Buhler, Kansas

SWEET-SOUR TUNA

1 8 3/4-oz. can low-calorie
   pineapple tidbits
1 c. green pepper strips
1 vegetable bouillon cube
1 tbsp. cornstarch
1 tsp. artificial sweetener
1 6 1/2-oz. to 7-oz. can tuna, drained
1 tbsp. low-calorie margarine
Rice, melba toast or chow mein noodles (opt.)

Drain pineapple tidbits, reserving juice. Combine reserved 1/3 cup pineapple juice, green pepper strips, bouillon cube and 1/2 cup water in saucepan; bring to a boil. Simmer for 5 minutes. Mix cornstarch, remaining pineapple juice and sweetener; stir into pineapple mixture. Cook, stir constantly, until thickened and bubbling. Stir in tuna and margarine. Serve over rice. Yield: 4 servings.

Mrs. Diane Caviezel, Enumclaw Jr. H.S.
Enumclaw, Washington

CRAB-STUFFED MUSHROOMS

1 lb. mushroom caps
1 tsp. salt
1/8 tsp. pepper
1 tbsp. minced onion
2 tbsp. chopped celery
1 tbsp. diet margarine
2 slices white gluten diet bread
2 7 1/2-oz. cans crab meat
1/8 tsp. thyme
2 tbsp. chopped parsley

Wash outside of mushrooms gently with damp paper towel; remove stems. Place mushrooms, cap side down, in lightly oiled shallow baking dish. Season with half the salt and pepper. Saute onion and celery in margarine. Chop bread in blender; mix with crab meat. Add remaining salt and pepper, thyme and parsley. Combine onion and crab meat mixtures; adjust seasonings. Fill caps with stuffing mixture. Add 1 tablespoon water to pan; cover with foil. Bake in 350-degree oven about 15 minutes. Spoon broth over mushrooms when serving. Yield: 4 servings/75 calories per serving.

Janet W. Mann, Rice Ave. Union H.S.
Girard, Pennsylvania

Low-Calorie

STUFFED TOMATO WITH TUNA

2 hard-cooked eggs, chopped
1 tsp. chopped onion
1/4 c. chopped celery
Salt to taste
4 tomatoes
1 can tuna, drained

Combine all ingredients except tomatoes and tuna. Place tuna in a large strainer; pour hot or lukewarm water over tuna until most of oil disappears. Drain. Add to egg mixture. Scoop centers out of tomatoes; add pulp to tuna. Season to taste. Fill each tomato with tuna mixture; serve on lettuce leaves. Yield: 4 servings.

Jacqueline Matz, Cherry Hill H.S.
Inkster, Michigan

LAST MINUTE SHRIMP CREOLE

2 med. onions, sliced
1/4 c. chopped green pepper
6 mushrooms, sliced
1/2 tsp. salt
1/4 tsp. paprika
1/4 tsp. sage
1/8 tsp. pepper
1/4 tsp. liquid sweetener
1/4 c. tomato sauce
1 1/2 c. drained canned tomatoes
2   5-oz. cans shrimp, drained
1/4 tsp. curry powder

Combine onions, green pepper, mushrooms, salt paprika, sage, pepper, sweetener and tomato sauce in saucepan; simmer until tender. Add tomatoes, shrimp and curry powder; heat until bubbly. Yield: 4 servings/100 calories per serving.

Mary Bety Stine, Flora Twp. H.S.
Flora, Illinois

SHRIMP-EGGPLANT CASSEROLE

1/2 c. chopped onion
1/4 c. diced celery
2 tbsp. consomme
1 green pepper, chopped
1 clove of garlic, minced
1 c. stewed tomatoes
1/4 tsp. oregano
Salt and pepper to taste
1   1-lb. eggplant
1/2 c. cleaned sm. shrimp

Combine onion, celery and consomme in saucepan. Cover tightly; simmer for 10 minutes. Add green pepper, garlic, tomatoes, oregano and seasonings.

Peel eggplant; cut into 1 1/2-inch cubes. Arrange layer of eggplant in bottom of casserole; cover with half the tomato mixture. Add remaining eggplant then remaining sauce. Top with shrimp. Bake at 350 degrees for 30 minutes or until bubbly. Yield: 4 servings/60 calories per serving.

Mrs. Beverly McGlamery, Carey H.S.
Carey, Ohio

SHRIMP WITH SAUCE

1 lb. shrimp
2 onions, sliced
2 tbsp. butter or margarine
1/2 c. instant nonfat dry milk
2 tbsp. flour
1   1-lb. 3-oz. can tomatoes
1/2 tsp. salt
1/4 tsp. pepper

Clean and cook shrimp for about 5 minutes or until pink. Cook onions in butter until soft. Combine dry milk and flour; stir in tomatoes, salt and pepper, blending thoroughly. Add to onions. Cook, stirring, until mixture thickens. Add shrimp; cook until shrimp are heated through. Serve with a border of toast or low-calorie wafers. Yield: 4 servings.

Mrs. F. L. Moseley, Valdosta Jr. H.S.
Valdosta, Georgia

BAKED CHICKEN AND MACARONI

1 c. macaroni
2 c. skim milk
1/4 c. flour
2 chicken bouillon cubes
1/4 tsp. marjoram
1/4 c. snipped parsley
1/4 c. chopped onion
1 c. drained mushroom pieces
2 tbsp. minced green pepper
1 tbsp. chopped pimento
2 c. diced cooked chicken
Salt to taste

Cook macaroni according to package directions; drain. Add milk slowly to flour in a 2-quart flame-proof casserole to form a smooth paste. Add bouillon cubes; cook, stirring constantly, until bouillon dissolves and sauce is thickened and smooth. Stir in macaroni and remaining ingredients. Bake in preheated 350-degree oven for 25 to 30 minutes or until bubbly. Yield: 5 servings/250 calories per serving.

Mrs. Herman Voxland, McIntosh Pub. School
McIntosh, Minnesota

OVEN-BARBECUED CHICKEN

2 1 1/4-lb. broilers, quartered
1/4 c. vinegar
2 tbsp. chili sauce
1 tsp. salt
1/4 tsp. pepper
1 tsp. paprika
1 tsp. Worcestershire sauce
1/4 tsp. dry mustard
1/2 tsp. liquid sweetener
2 tbsp. grated onion
1 clove of garlic, minced

Place quartered chickens in baking dish. Combine 1/4 cup water and remaining ingredients in a saucepan; bring to a boil. Pour over chicken. Bake in preheated 375-degree oven for about 1 hour or until chicken is tender. Yield: 4 servings/125 calories per serving.

Mrs. Emma M. Meyer, Florence H.S.
Florence, Wisconsin

BROILED BARBECUED CHICKEN

1 c. tomato juice
1/4 c. vinegar
2 tbsp. Worcestershire sauce
2 tsp. prepared light mustard
1 tsp. sugar
1 clove of garlic, crushed
2 tbsp. soup stock or water
3 med. broilers, cut in half
1/2 lemon

Heat tomato juice; blend in next 5 ingredients. Simmer for 5 minutes. Remove from heat; add soup stock. Stir before using. Place chicken, skin side down, on broiler rack. Rub well with cut lemon; brush with 3/4 cup sauce. Broil in preheated broiler 7 to 9 inches from source of heat for 30 minutes; turn chicken pieces. Rub again with cut lemon; brush with remaining sauce. Broil for 15 to 30 minutes longer or until fork tender and well browned. Garnish with parsley. Yield: 6 servings/345 calories per serving.

Mrs. Leon Davis, Lumpkin County H.S.
Dahlonega, Georgia

CHICKEN CURRY IN A HURRY

2 whole chicken breasts
1 c. long grain rice
1/2 lb. fresh mushrooms, thinly sliced
1/3 c. chopped onion
1 tbsp. butter or margarine
3 tbsp. flour
1 chicken bouillon cube

1 tsp. salt
1 1/2 tsp. curry powder
1 c. finely chopped apple
1/4 c. snipped parsley
3/4 c. skim milk

Split, skin and bone chicken breasts; cut into bite-sized pieces. Cook rice according to package directions, omitting butter. Fluff with fork; keep warm. Saute chicken pieces, mushrooms and onion in butter in large skillet for about 10 minutes or until lightly browned on all sides and tender. Stir in flour, bouillon cube, salt and curry powder. Add apple and parsley; stir in milk and 1 cup water. Simmer, stirring constantly, for 3 minutes or until apple is tender. Serve sauce over rice. Yield: 6 servings/260 calories per serving.

Gwladys Jeanneret, Kettle Falls H.S.
Kettle Falls, Washington

EASY CHICKEN LOAF

2 lg. eggs
3 c. chopped cooked chicken
1/2 c. finely chopped green pepper and celery
1 tbsp. minced onion
1 c. coarse soft bread crumbs
1 1/2 tsp. salt
1/2 tsp. paprika
1 tsp. Worcestershire sauce
Juice of 1/2 lemon
1 1/2 c. milk

Beat eggs slightly in bowl. Add remaining ingredients; mix well. Pack mixture into greased 9 x 5 x 3-inch loaf pan. Bake at 350 degrees for about 40 minutes. Unmold onto hot platter. Garnish with parsley and hard-cooked egg segments. Yield: 8-10 servings/191 calories per serving.

Mrs. C. Dean Schmid, North Platte Sr. H.S.
North Platte, Nebraska

CHICKEN LOW-CAL

4 or 5 chicken breasts
1 med. onion, quartered
2 tbsp. cooking wine
1/4 tsp. nutmeg
Salt and pepper to taste

Place 1 1/2 cups water in pressure pan; arrange chicken and onion in pan. Sprinkle with remaining ingredients. Cook for 25 to 30 minutes. Yield: 4-5 servings.

Mrs. Lucille Clowdis, Gordon H.S.
Decatur, Georgia

Low-Calorie

CRISP-BAKED CHICKEN

1 3-lb. chicken, disjointed
1/2 tsp. salt
Instant garlic powder to taste
Pepper and paprika to taste

Place chicken pieces, skin side up, in shallow baking dish. Sprinkle with salt, garlic powder, pepper and paprika. Bake at 375 degrees for 1 hour or until golden brown. Yield: 6 servings/175 calories per serving.

Mrs. Raymond M. Akin, Highland Park H.S.
Dallas, Texas

CURRIED PEACH CHICKEN

1 2 1/2-lb. chicken, disjointed
1 tsp. salt
5 peppercorns
2 bay leaves
Parsley
1 med. onion, quartered
2 tbsp. flour
2 tsp. curry powder
1/4 c. lemon juice
Salt and pepper to taste
1 1-lb. can low-calorie sliced
   peaches, drained

Cover chicken with water; add salt, peppercorns, bay leaves, 2 sprigs of parsley and onion. Bring to a boil; simmer for 30 minutes. Remove chicken from broth; keep warm. Reduce broth to 1 1/2 cups liquid. Chill broth in freezer; remove excess fat. Remove skin from chicken; arrange on hot platter. Combine flour, curry powder and broth in saucepan; bring to a boil, stirring constantly. Simmer for 5 minutes. Add lemon juice; season with salt and pepper. Pour over chicken; garnish with peaches and parsley. Yield: 4 servings.

Mrs. Betty C. Mullins, Forest Park Sr. H.S.
Forest Park, Georgia

MARVELOUS OVEN-FRIED CHICKEN

1 tsp. paprika
1 tsp. salt
1/8 tsp. garlic powder
1/2 tsp. onion salt
1 egg
2 lg. fryers, cut up
1 c. crushed corn flakes
1/4 c. chicken stock or bouillon

Combine seasonings and egg. Dip chicken pieces into egg mixture; coat with corn flakes. Place in baking dish. Add stock; cover tightly. Bake in preheated 375-degree oven for 30 minutes. Uncover; bake for 30 minutes longer. Garnish with paper-thin orange slices. Yield: 6 servings.

Bernice Dukerschein, Flambeau H.S.
Tony, Wisconsin

COMPANY CHINESE PEPPER STEAK

1 1/2 lb. beef sirloin steak, trimmed
1/4 c. (or less) vegetable oil
2 cloves of garlic, crushed
Dash of salt
1 tsp. ground ginger
1/2 tsp. pepper
3 green peppers, sliced
2 lg. onions, sliced
1 tbsp. cornstarch
1/4 c. soy sauce
1/2 tsp. sugar or sweetener
1 can beef bouillon
1 can water chestnuts, sliced
4 green onions, sliced

Freeze steak for 1 hour to make cutting easier. Cut steak into 1/4-inch strips. Heat oil in skillet. Add garlic, salt, ginger and pepper; saute until garlic is golden. Add steak strips; brown lightly. Remove beef. Add green peppers and onions; cook for 3 to 5 minutes. Dissolve cornstarch in 1/2 to 1 cup water. Return beef to pan; add soy sauce, sugar, bouillon, water chestnuts, cornstarch and green onions. Simmer for about 15 to 20 minutes. Serve over hot rice. Yield: 6-8 servings.

Mrs. Theresa H. Smith, Northside H.S.
Warner Robins, Georgia

DIETER'S CHINESE PEPPER STEAK

1 lb. beef top sirloin, sliced thin
1 tbsp. salad oil
1 c. diagonally sliced celery
1/4 c. chopped onion
2 cloves of garlic, crushed
3 green peppers, cut in thin strips
1 c. canned consomme or bouillon
1 tbsp. cornstarch
2 tbsp. soy sauce

Cut beef slices into thin strips. Heat salad oil in skillet. Add beef. Sear strips quickly; remove from pan while still rare. Add celery, onion, garlic, green peppers and consomme; simmer for about 5 minutes or until vegetables are tender crisp. Thicken with cornstarch blended with 1/4 cup water and soy sauce; simmer for 5 minutes. Add beef; reheat for several minutes. Serve with rice. Yield: 4 servings/281 calories per serving.

Mrs. Ronald Haney, Wallace Co. H.S.
Sharon Springs, Kansas

BEEF ORIENTAL

1 lb. sirloin steak
2 tbsp. salad oil
1/3 c. soy sauce
Dash of Sucaryl
1 tsp. monosodium glutamate
2 c. diagonally sliced celery
2 c. diagonally sliced green onions
1 green pepper, cut in 1/4-in. strips
2 5-oz. cans water chestnuts, sliced
1 6-oz. can sliced mushrooms, drained

Slice beef into 1/4-inch strips across the grain. Heat 12-inch electric skillet. Add salad oil and beef. Cook briskly, turning beef until well browned. Pour soy sauce and 1/3 cup water over beef; stir in Sucaryl and monosodium glutamate. Bring to a boil. Add celery, onions and green pepper. Cook and stir over high heat for about 3 minutes or until vegetables are tender crisp. Add water chestnuts and mushrooms; cook for 2 minutes longer or until heated through. Thicken pan juices with 1 tablespoon cornstarch blended with 2 tablespoons cold water, if desired. Serve with dry Melba toast or hot steamed rice. Yield: 6 servings/295 calories per serving.

Mrs. Layne Storment, Kahlotus H.S.
Kahlotus, Washington

DIETER'S BEEF STROGANOFF

1 lb. beef tenderloin
2 tbsp. margarine
1/2 lb. sliced fresh mushrooms
1/2 c. chopped onion
1 10 1/2-oz. can beef bouillon
1/2 c. buttermilk
2 tbsp. flour
Salt and pepper to taste

Trim beef tenderloin; slice 1/4 inch thick. Cut into strips 1/4 inch wide. Brown quickly in margarine in skillet. Push to one side; add mushrooms and onion. Cook until tender, but not brown. Add bouillon; heat just to boiling. Blend buttermilk with flour; stir into beef mixture. Cook, stirring constantly, until thickened. Sauce will be thin. Season with salt and pepper. May be served over hot rice. Yield: 5 servings/240 calories per serving.

Estella Hottel, Dimmitt H.S.
Dimmitt, Texas

STEAK DIETER

1 steak
1 lg. onion, chopped
2 beef bouillon cubes

Brown steak in small amount of cooking oil with chopped onion. Dissolve bouillon cubes in 1 to 2 cups hot water. Pour over steak. Simmer until tender. Yield: 4 servings.

Mrs. Etna Gaskin, Wewahitchka H.S.
Wewahitchka, Florida

SIRLOIN SUKIYAKI

2 lb. sirloin steak
1/2 c. soy sauce
1/2 c. beef broth
1/4 c. beer
Sugar substitute to equal 3 tbsp. sugar
1/4 tsp. pepper
3/4 tsp. monosodium glutamate
2 tbsp. oil
2 c. sliced onions
1 c. sliced celery
1 c. sliced bamboo shoots
1 c. sliced mushrooms
1 c. sliced scallions

Cut steak across grain in paper-thin slices. May be slightly frozen for easier slicing. Combine soy sauce, beef broth, beer, sugar substitute, pepper and monosodium glutamate; set aside. Heat oil in skillet; brown steak. Push to one side of pan; pour half the soy sauce mixture over steak. Add onions, celery, bamboo shoots and mushrooms; saute for 3 minutes. Pour remaining soy sauce mixture over vegetables; add scallions. Cook, stirring, for 3 minutes. May be served over 1/2 cup cooked rice. Four pounds chicken or boneless pork may be substituted for beef. Yield: 6 servings/350 calories per serving.

Mrs. Eve Kuehn, Edgar H.S.
Edgar, Wisconsin

LOW-CALORIE BEEF STEW

1 c. cubed cooked beef roast
1 onion, chopped
1 med. potato, cubed
1 green pepper, chopped
1 stalk celery, chopped
1 lg. carrot, diced
1/2 tsp. oregano
1/4 tsp. pepper
1 tbsp. dried parsley leaves
1/2 tsp. paprika
Salt to taste
1/8 tsp. garlic salt
3/4 c. tomato juice or water

Place beef in 1-quart pan; add remaining ingredients. Cook over low heat until vegetables are tender, stirring occasionally. Yield: 3 servings.

Marinda Craiger, Rock Hill H.S.
Ironton, Ohio

Low-Calorie

ROMAN-STYLE BEEF STEW

2 lb. round of beef
2 tbsp. corn oil
1 c. thinly sliced onions
1 clove of garlic, minced
1 1/2 tsp. salt
1/2 tsp. pepper
1/4 tsp. oregano
1 c. Burgundy
1 tbsp. tomato paste

Slice beef 1/2 inch thick. Heat oil in a heavy sauce-pan; add onions and garlic. Saute for 5 minutes. Add beef; brown on all sides. Add salt, pepper, oregano, Burgundy, tomato paste and 1/2 cup boiling water; bring to a boil. Simmer for 1 hour and 30 minutes or until tender. Skim off any fat. Yield: 8 servings/205 calories per serving.

Mrs. Beatrice Birchard, Hackettstown H.S.
Hackettstown, New Jersey

SWISS LIVER

2 lb. calves liver
Flour
Salt and pepper to taste
Corn oil
1 onion, chopped or sliced
1 green pepper, chopped
1 c. catsup

Dredge liver with flour; season with salt and pepper. Brown in small amount of oil. Saute onion and green pepper until limp. Place liver in electric skillet; top with onion, green pepper and catsup. Cover. Simmer for 20 to 30 minutes. Yield: 6 servings.

Fernette G. Honaker, Menaul Presby. H.S.
Albuquerque, New Mexico

QUICK CHOP SUEY

1 lb. lean ground beef
Seasonings to taste
1 c. bean sprouts
1 lg. onion, thinly sliced
1/2 c. sliced water chestnuts
1/2 green pepper, finely chopped
1 tbsp. chopped pimento
2 tbsp. soy sauce

Mix beef with seasonings. Brown quickly in skillet over low heat. Add bean sprouts, onion, water chest-nuts, green pepper, pimento and soy sauce. Cover; cook until onion is tender but not soft. Yield: 4 servings/250 calories per serving.

Rita Klodt, Ottumwa H.S.
Ottumwa, Iowa

LOW-CALORIE CHOW MEIN

1 lb. ground beef chuck
1 onion, finely chopped
2 c. chopped celery
1 can bean sprouts, drained
1/2 c. sliced mushrooms
1/3 c. soy sauce

Brown beef and onion; add remaining ingredients. Cook over low heat, covered, for 30 minutes.

Mrs. Dean Iverson, Interstate 35 Comm. School
New Virginia, Iowa

SKILLET MEAT LOAF

1 1/2 lb. lean ground beef
2 eggs, slightly beaten
3/4 c. fine bread crumbs
1/2 c. nonfat dry milk
1/4 c. chopped green pepper
1/4 c. chopped onion
Seasonings to taste

Combine all ingredients; mix lightly. Pour mixture into lightly greased ovenproof skillet. Bake in 350-degree oven for 1 hour. Yield: 6 servings/225 calories per serving.

Mrs. Charlotte Callihan, Greene Central H.S.
Snow Hill, North Carolina

SARAH'S MEAT LOAF

1 1/2 lb. lean ground beef
1 egg, beaten
1/4 c. crushed corn flakes
1/4 med. onion, chopped
2 tbsp. grated carrot
1/2 tsp. monosodium glutamate
1/2 c. dietetic tomato juice
1/2 tsp. baking powder
1 tsp. dry mustard
1 tbsp. seasoned pepper

Combine all ingredients with 1/2 cup ice water; shape lightly into a loaf. Place in shallow pan. Bake at 350 degrees for 45 minutes. Yield: 6 servings.

Martha R. Phillips, Kennett H.S.
Conway, New Hampshire

MEAT LOAF WITH SAUCE

2 eggs
1 1/2 lb. fat-free ground top round
1 med. onion, chopped

1/2 c. finely chopped celery
1/2 c. chopped gherkins or dill pickle
1/4 c. chopped parsley
1 1/4 tsp. salt
1/4 tsp. pepper
1 tsp. Worcestershire sauce
1 8-oz. can tomato sauce
3/4 tsp. prepared mustard
2 tbsp. vinegar
1 tbsp. honey

Beat eggs slightly with a fork in a large mixing bowl. Add ground beef and next 7 ingredients with half the tomato sauce. Toss lightly to blend; shape into an oval loaf. Do not overmix. Place in a shallow foil-lined baking pan. Combine remaining tomato sauce, mustard, vinegar and honey; pour over loaf. Bake in a preheated 350-degree oven for 1 hour. Yield: 6 servings/100 calories per serving.

Mrs. Kathryn Leischner, Deland-Weldon H.S.
Deland, Illinois

PATTY CAKE MEAT LOAF

1 1/2 lb. ground beef
1 5-oz. jar baby food carrots
1/2 c. tomato juice
1/4 c. chopped parsley
1/4 c. chopped onion
1 1/2 tsp. salt
1/2 tsp. Italian seasoning

Combine all ingredients; mix until blended in a large bowl. Form into a thick round patty about 8 inches in diameter; place on rack in broiler pan. Bake at 375 degrees for 35 minutes or until brown. Slice patty into 6 wedges. Yield: 6 servings/260 calories per serving.

Mrs. Florence Boots, Arsenal Tech. H.S.
Indianapolis, Indiana

PINEAPPLE MEAT LOAF

3 pineapple slices
1 lb. ground beef
1/2 lb. ground veal
1 c. soft bread crumbs
3/4 c. skim milk
1/2 c. chopped onion
1 egg, beaten
1 tsp. salt
1/2 tsp. monosodium glutamate
1/4 tsp. paprika
1/4 tsp. marjoram
1/8 tsp. thyme
1/8 tsp. pepper

Cut 2 slices of pineapple into halves. Arrange halves and slice in an attractive pattern in bottom of greased 9 1/2 x 5 1/4 x 2 3/4-inch pan. Combine beef, veal, bread crumbs, milk, onion and egg; mix in salt, monosodium glutamate, paprika, marjoram, thyme and pepper. Pack lightly into loaf pan. Bake at 350 degrees for about 1 hour and 30 minutes. Loosen loaf gently from sides of pan with a spatula; pour off excess juice. Invert onto platter. Yield: 8 servings/184 calories per serving.

Alma C. McGimsey, Nebo H.S.
Nebo, North Carolina

LOW-CALORIE MEATBALLS

1 lb. ground beef
3/4 c. finely chopped onion
2/3 c. powdered milk
1 c. drained whole tomatoes
2 slices bread, crumbled
1 tsp. salt
1/8 tsp. pepper
1/8 tsp. dry mustard
1/4 tsp. celery salt
1/4 tsp. garlic salt
3 tbsp. Worcestershire sauce
Flour
Shortening
1 can cream of mushroom soup
1/2 tsp. beef extract
1/2 c. tomato juice

Combine first 10 ingredients with 2 teaspoons Worcestershire sauce; mix until well blended. Form into balls. Roll in flour; brown in small amount of shortening. Place meatballs in baking dish. Combine remaining Worcestershire sauce and remaining ingredients in saucepan; heat through. Pour over meatballs. Bake at 350 degrees for 30 minutes. Yield: 6 servings.

Corrine Myhra, New Town H.S.
New Town, North Dakota

LOW-CALORIE SPAGHETTI

1 lb. ground round beef
1 tsp. oil
1 env. spaghetti sauce mix
1 6-oz. can tomato puree
8 oz. destarched spaghetti, cooked

Brown beef lightly in oil. Sprinkle sauce mix over beef; add tomato puree and 2 puree cans water. Simmer for 10 minutes. Serve sauce with spaghetti. Yield: 4 servings.

Ruby Sewright, Franklin H.S.
Portland, Oregon

Low-Calorie

SKINNYBURGERS

1 1/2 lb. ground beef
1 can consomme
1 tbsp. chopped onion
1 tsp. salt
1/8 tsp. pepper
2 tbsp. meat sauce
1/4 c. shredded carrot

Combine all ingredients; mix well. Shape into thin patties. Broil patties to desired doneness. Serve on open-faced toasted English muffin with green pepper ring for garnish. Yield: 6 servings.

Mrs. Linda Hair, Pearce Jr. H.S.
Austin, Texas

TASTY BROILED BURGER

3 lb. ground beef
2 tbsp. Worcestershire sauce
1 tbsp. dry onion flakes
1 tsp. garlic salt

Combine all ingredients; form into 4-inch patties. Place patties on broiler rack in a preheated broiler, 3 to 5 inches from heat. Broil for 4 minutes; turn. Broil for 2 minutes on second side. Do not overcook. Serve immediately with relish plate and cottage cheese. Yield: 6 servings.

Mrs. Pat Bloomer, Sterling H.S.
Sterling, Oklahoma

LAMB AND BEAN CASSEROLE

1/4 c. corn oil
2 c. chopped onions
2 c. cubed cooked lamb
2 10-oz. packages frozen French-style beans
2 c. canned tomatoes
1 tbsp. Worcestershire sauce
1/2 tsp. salt

Heat oil in a skillet. Saute onions until golden brown. Add lamb; saute for 2 minutes longer. Thaw green beans; drain. Place over lamb mixture. Combine tomatoes, Worcestershire sauce and salt; pour over green beans. Cover tightly; cook over low heat for 15 minutes or until beans are tender. Yield: 6 servings/275 calories per serving.

Mrs. Marion Tover, Mellen Pub. School
Mellen, Wisconsin

VEAL LOAF

1 lb. lean ground veal
1 c. cream-style cottage cheese

3 med. carrots, shredded
1 sm. onion, chopped
1 egg
1 tsp. salt
1/4 tsp. pepper
1/2 tsp. basil
1 tsp. monosodium glutamate

Combine all ingredients in large bowl; mix well. Shape into loaf; place in ungreased shallow baking pan. Bake at 350 degrees for 50 minutes or until brown. Yield: 6 servings.

Mrs. Colleen Randel, Wainwright H.S.
Lafayette, Indiana

MEAT AND VEGETABLE CASSEROLE

2 c. chopped cooked lean meat
1 c. cooked carrots
1 c. drained green or yellow beans
1 c. cooked celery
1 c. diced boiled potatoes
1 med. onion, diced
1 c. boiled rice
1 c. drained canned mushrooms
1 c. drained canned peas
1 c. meat or chicken broth

Combine all ingredients; place in a large casserole or roaster. Bake in a 325-degree oven for 1 hour and 30 minutes.

Mrs. Norine E. Sipe, Goffstown H.S.
Goffstown, New Hampshire

LOW-FAT CHEESE SOUFFLE

6 tbsp. flour
1/8 tsp. celery salt
1 tsp. paprika
1/2 tsp. salt
1 tbsp. grated onion
Dash of Tabasco sauce
1 tsp. Worcestershire sauce
2/3 c. nonfat dry milk crystals
2 c. grated Cheddar cheese
5 eggs, separated

Blend first 7 ingredients with 1/2 cup water in saucepan until smooth. Add dry milk and 1 1/2 cups water; blend well. Cook until thickened. Stir cheese into hot sauce; cook until smooth, stirring constantly. Beat egg whites until moist peaks form. Beat egg yolks slightly. Stir a small amount of hot sauce into egg yolks; stir egg yolks into hot mixture. Fold hot mixture into egg whites. Pour into ungreased 1 1/2-quart baking dish. Bake at 375 degrees until golden brown. Yield: 4 servings.

Agnes Smith, McKinney H.S.
McKinney, Kentucky

CREAMY CORN SOUP

1 can chicken-rice soup
1 soup can reconstituted nonfat dry milk
1 8-oz. can cream-style corn
2 tbsp. snipped parsley
1/4 tsp. salt
Dash of thyme

Combine all ingredients in saucepan; simmer for 5 minutes. Serve immediately. Yield: 4 servings/100 calories per serving.

H. M. Olszewski, St. Mary's Jr. H.S.
Medicine Hat, Alberta, Canada

ASPARAGUS WITH WATER CHESTNUTS

4 servings fresh asparagus
1 tbsp. butter
1/4 c. sliced water chestnuts
Juice of 1/2 lemon
Salt and pepper to taste

Cook asparagus until tender. Melt butter in saucepan; brown slightly. Stir in water chestnuts; saute lightly. Add lemon juice, salt and pepper; pour over hot drained asparagus.

Mrs. Frances Siemens, Phillipsburg H.S.
Phillipsburg, Kansas

PICADILLO-STYLE BEANS

1 sm. onion, thinly sliced
1/4 c. chopped green pepper
1 tbsp. seedless raisins
Pinch of cumin seed (opt.)
Dash of thyme, crushed
Butter
1 1-lb. can beans and ground beef in
   barbecue sauce
2 ripe olives, sliced
Dash of Tabasco

Cook onion, green pepper, raisins, cumin and thyme in butter until vegetables are tender. Add remaining ingredients; heat through, stirring frequently. Yield: 2-3 servings.

Pauline Reeves, Emma Sansom H.S.
Gadsden, Alabama

TASTY GREEN BEANS

1 qt. fresh or home-canned green beans
1/2 c. concentrated beef stock
1/2 tsp. celery salt
1/2 tsp. dried onion flakes

Place beans in small amount of water in saucepan. Cover; bring to a boil. Add beef stock, salt and onion flakes; cook until tender. This dish will have a delicious flavor without fat flavoring and extra salt. Yield: 6-8 servings.

Jeanne K. Ross, Clendenin Jr. H.S.
Clendenin, West Virginia

CLASSIC HARVARD BEETS

2 tsp. Sucaryl
1 tbsp. cornstarch
1/2 tsp. salt
1/2 tsp. beet liquid
1/2 c. cider vinegar
3 c. sliced cooked beets

Mix Sucaryl, cornstarch, salt, beet liquid and vinegar in saucepan; bring slowly to a boil, stirring constantly. Cook over low heat until thickened. Add beets; simmer for 15 minutes. Serve hot or cold. Yield: 6 servings.

Kathleen L. Zehr, Carthege Jr.-Sr. H.S.
Carthege, New York

MAKE-AHEAD HARVARD BEETS

2 tsp. Sucaryl
1/2 tbsp. cornstarch
1/4 c. beet juice or water
1/4 c. vinegar
2 c. cooked sliced or diced beets
1 tbsp. margarine or butter

Combine Sucaryl, cornstarch, beet juice and vinegar in saucepan; cook until clear and thickened. Add beets; let stand for at least 30 minutes. Bring to boiling point just before serving; add butter. Yield: 6 servings/57 calories per serving.

Elizabeth Hays, Campbellsville School
Pulaski, Tennessee

CHEESE-STUFFED CELERY

8 inner stalks celery
1/3 c. low-fat cottage cheese
Marjoram and garlic powder to taste

Place celery stalks in ice water; let stand for several minutes. Drain and dry stalks. Season cottage cheese with marjoram and garlic powder; blend well. Stuff celery with cheese; serve. Yield: 8 servings/19 calories per serving.

Mrs. Etta Belle Landers, Polk-Clark H.S.
Milan, Tennessee

229

Low-Calorie

CARROT-CELERY SANDWICH SPREAD

4 med. carrots
1/2 green pepper
3 stalks celery
2 tbsp. chopped nuts
2 tbsp. wheat germ
1 tbsp. horseradish
3 tbsp. low-calorie mayonnaise
1 tsp. lemon juice
Salt to taste

Grind carrots, green pepper, celery, nuts and wheat germ together. Add remaining ingredients; blend well. Serve on Melba toast or Rye Krisp as open-faced sandwiches. Yield: 2 cups/9 calories per tablespoon.

Jean Passino, Keewatin-Nashwauk Jr. H.S.
Keewatin, Minnesota

SWEET-SOUR GERMAN CABBAGE

2 tbsp. butter or low-calorie margarine
6 c. shredded red cabbage
1 med. onion, sliced in rings
1/2 c. vinegar
1 tsp. Sucaryl

Melt butter in large saucepan. Add cabbage. Cook, covered, over low heat until tender, stirring occasionally to prevent sticking. Add onion rings, 1/4 cup water, vinegar and Sucaryl. Cover; cook for about 10 minutes longer. Yield: 6 servings/68 calories per serving.

Mrs. James R. Baker, Sycamore H.S.
Sycamore, Illinois

BRAISED FRESH CUCUMBERS

4 cucumbers, pared and thinly sliced
2 tsp. salt
3 slices bacon, diced
1 tsp. sugar
1/4 tsp. artificial sweetener
1/8 tsp. pepper
1 tbsp. cider vinegar

Arrange cucumbers in layers in small bowl; sprinkle with salt. Refrigerate, covered, for 30 minutes. Saute bacon in large skillet until crisp; drain well. Add drained cucumbers and remaining ingredients; stir to mix well. Cook, covered, over low heat for 10 to 12 minutes. Yield: 6 servings.

Chris Wallgren, Central H.S.
Red Wing, Minnesota

CAULIFLOWER CAPRI

1 lg. head cauliflower
1   8-oz. can tomato sauce
1 tsp. Spice Islands chicken stock base
1 tsp. instant toasted onions
1/2 tsp. sweet basil

Cook cauliflower in boiling salted water until crisp tender. Drain well. Place in ungreased glass pie plate. Combine tomato sauce, chicken stock base, instant onions and basil until blended. Spoon over cauliflower, covering head completely. Bake in 350-degree oven for 15 to 20 minutes or until tender. Serve immediately. Yield: 6 servings/44 calories per serving.

Darlene Heilmann, McFarland H.S.
McFarland, California

CUCUMBER PICKLES

Cucumbers
Salt
Vinegar
8 whole-grain saccharin tablets

Wash and prepare cucumbers; sprinkle generously with salt. Let cucumbers stand for 1 hour. Pack cucumbers tightly into sterilized 1-quart jar. Pour vinegar over cucumbers to fill jar; pour cucumbers and vinegar from jar into saucepan. Add saccharin. Bring to a boil. Return cucumbers to jar. Bring vinegar to second boil; pour over cucumbers and seal. Process in water bath for 10 minutes to complete seal.

Mrs. Chris Smith, Westminster H.S.
Westminster, South Carolina

EGGPLANT FRESNO

1 med. onion, thinly sliced
1 med. green pepper, coarsely chopped
1 1/2 tsp. butter or margarine
1 med. eggplant, peeled and cut into
    3/4-in. cubes
1   1-lb. can tomatoes
1/2 tsp. salt
1 tsp. sugar

Saute onion and green pepper in butter until onion is golden. Add eggplant cubes, tomatoes, salt and sugar. Cover; simmer for 10 minutes or until eggplant is just tender. Yield: 6 servings/40 calories per serving.

Charmiane W. Freeman, Halls H.S.
Halls, Tennessee

BAKED SUMMER SQUASH

1 1/2 to 2 lb. yellow summer squash
1/2 tsp. (or more) salt
2 tbsp. brown sugar
1 tbsp. butter

Cut squash in half lengthwise. Place cut side down in baking pan; sprinkle with salt and sugar. Dot with butter; sprinkle with 2 tablespoons water. Bake in preheated 375 to 400-degree oven for about 30 minutes or until tender. Yield: 4-6 servings.

Mrs. Martha Berryhill, Corner H.S.
Warrior, Alabama

ORANGE ZUCCHINI

1 1/2 lb. small zucchini
1 tbsp. butter
1/2 tsp. salt
1/8 tsp. pepper
2 tbsp. undiluted frozen orange concentrate

Cut zucchini in 1/2-inch slices. Saute in butter until crisp tender, turning once. Season with salt and pepper. Add juice; heat through, stirring gently. Garnish with orange rind, if desired. Yield: 6 servings.

Mrs. Rose Pyle, Pateros H.S.
Pateros, Washington

RICE AND SPROUTS

1/2 c. rice
1 bouillon cube
1 1-lb. can bean sprouts, drained
Salt, pepper and Worcestershire sauce
   to taste

Cook rice according to package directions using bouillon cube to replace salt. Toss with bean sprouts; heat through. Season with salt, pepper and Worcestershire sauce. Yield: 4 servings.

Mrs. Joy Isley, Paradise Valley H.S.
Phoenix, Arizona

PARSLEY EGG DROPS

1 egg
3 tbsp. flour
1/4 tsp. salt
1 tbsp. chopped parsley

Beat egg and 3 tablespoons water until fluffy; blend in flour and salt. Add parsley; drop mixture by half teaspoonfuls into boiling beef or chicken soup. Cover; cook over medium heat for 10 minutes. Serve at once.

Mrs. J. Sigurdson, Hasting Jr. H.S.
Winnipeg, Manitoba, Canada

DIETER'S VEGETABLE SOUP

2 c. clear broth
1/2 med. tomato
1/2 lg. celery stalk, chopped
3 tbsp. shredded cabbage
1/2 sm. onion, chopped
1 carrot, sliced
Salt and pepper to taste

Combine broth and vegetables; cook for 15 to 20 minutes or until vegetables are tender. Season with salt and pepper. Yield: 2 servings/16 calories per serving.

Mrs. Joe Maxson, Bokchito School
Bokchito, Oklahoma

APPLESAUCE TEA BREAD

2 c. sifted flour
3/4 c. Sweetness and Light
3 tsp. baking powder
1/2 tsp. soda
1/2 tsp. cinnamon
1/2 tsp. salt
1 c. unsweetened applesauce
1 egg, beaten
2 tbsp. melted butter
1/2 tsp. almond extract

Combine flour, Sweetness and Light, baking powder, soda, cinnamon and salt. Combine remaining ingredients; mix well. Add flour mixture all at once, stirring just until flour is dampened; spoon into lightly greased 7 3/8 x 3 5/8 x 2 1/4-inch loaf pan. Bake at 350 degrees for 1 hour or until done. Yield: 12 servings/109 calories per serving.

Mrs. Ruth Torpey, Sewanhaka H.S.
Floral Park, New York

GETTYSBURG BANANA NUT BREAD

1 tbsp. sugar substitute
3 or 4 bananas, mashed
2 eggs, well beaten
1 3/4 c. cake flour
3 tsp. baking powder
1/4 tsp. salt
1/4 c. chopped walnuts

Sprinkle sugar substitute over bananas; stir until dissolved. Blend in eggs. Sift flour, baking powder and salt together; add walnuts. Blend thoroughly into banana mixture, but do not overmix. Pour batter into greased 4 x 7-inch loaf pan. Bake in preheated 350-degree oven for 25 minutes. Reduce temperature to 300 degrees; bake for 35 to 40 minutes longer. Yield: 20 slices/59 calories per slice.

Eva Jane Schwartz, Gettysburg Sr. H.S.
Gettysburg, Pennsylvania

Low-Calorie

BANANA TEA BREAD

1 3/4 c. sifted flour
2 tsp. baking powder
1/4 tsp. soda
1/2 tsp. salt
1/4 c. melted shortening
2 eggs, well beaten
4 tsp. Sucaryl solution
1 tsp. vanilla extract
2 med. bananas, mashed

Sift flour, baking powder, soda and salt togther. Combine shortening, eggs, Sucaryl and vanilla; add to flour mixture, stirring only until flour is moistened. Fold in bananas; turn into greased 8 x 4 x 3-inch loaf pan. Bake at 350 degrees for 1 hour and 10 minutes. Yield: 15 servings/98 calories per serving.

Lula Smith, Sand Springs Jr. H.S.
Sand Springs, Oklahoma

MOLASSES BROWN BREAD

3 c. sour milk
1 tbsp. soda
1 egg
1/2 c. molasses
1 tsp. salt
3 c. graham flour
2 c. all-purpose flour

Combine all ingredients; mix until well blended. Place in loaf pan. Bake at 350 degrees for 30 minutes or until done. Yield: 1 loaf.

Judith A. Svoboda, Platteview Jr.-Sr. H.S.
Springfield, Nebraska

BUTTERMILK COFFEE CAKE

6 tbsp. soft margarine
Sugar
1 tbsp. Sucaryl
2 eggs
2 c. (scant) flour
1/8 tsp. salt
1 tsp. soda
1 tsp. baking powder
1 c. (scant) buttermilk
2 tbsp. cinnamon

Beat margarine, 1/2 cup sugar and Sucaryl until light; add eggs, one at a time, beating constantly. Mix flour, salt, soda and baking powder; add to creamed mixture alternately with buttermilk. Pour half the batter into greased pan. Mix 2 tablespoons sugar and cinnamon; sprinkle half the sugar mixture over batter in pan. Add remaining batter; sprinkle remaining sugar mixture over top. Bake at 350 de-

grees for 40 minutes. Yield: 16 servings/94 calories per serving.

Mrs. Jo Anne Tuttle, Spencer Jr. H.S.
Spencer, Iowa

FRESH CRANBERRY BREAD

2 c. sifted flour
2 tsp. baking powder
1 tsp. salt
1/2 tsp. soda
2 eggs, slightly beaten
3/4 c. unsweetened orange juice
1/4 c. cooking oil
4 tsp. liquid Sweet-10
1 c. cranberries

Sift flour with baking powder, salt and soda. Combine eggs, orange juice, oil and Sweet-10; blend well. Add orange juice mixture to dry ingredients; mix until moistened. Stir in cranberries; pour into greased 8 x 4-inch pan. Bake at 375 degrees for 55 to 60 minutes or until golden brown. Remove from pan; cool. Yield: 18 servings.

Sister Mary Carmelita, Regis H.S.
Cedar Rapids, Iowa

SPECIAL HEALTH BREAD

1 c. raisins
1 c. oatmeal
1 c. graham flour
1 c. Bran Buds or All-Bran
1 tsp. salt
3/4 c. sugar
1 tsp. soda
1 c. sour milk

Combine raisins and 1 cup water in saucepan; boil for 5 minutes. Cool. Mix remaining ingredients; add raisins. Turn into 4 x 11 x 2 1/2-inch loaf pan. Bake at 350 degrees for 1 hour.

Mrs. Carl Ruff, Oak Harbor H.S.
Oak Harbor, Ohio

ORANGE MARMALADE-WALNUT BREAD

2 c. sifted flour
1 1/2 tsp. baking powder
1/2 tsp. soda
1/4 to 1/2 tsp. salt
1/3 c. skim milk
1 egg
2 tbsp. melted butter
1 tbsp. Sucaryl
1/2 c. dietetic orange marmalade
1/4 c. chopped walnuts

Combine flour, baking powder, soda and salt. Combine milk, egg, butter and Sucaryl; add to flour mixture. Stir just until flour is dampened; fold in marmalade and walnuts, mixing as little as possible. Spoon batter into lightly greased 9 x 5 x 3-inch loaf pan. Bake at 350 degrees for 1 hour and 40 minutes. Cool before slicing. Yield: 12 servings/110 calories per serving.

Mrs. Thomas Kestel, Long Island Luth. H.S.
Glen Head, New York

DIETER'S MUFFINS

1 c. flour
3 tsp. baking powder
1/2 tsp. salt
1 tsp. cinnamon
5 egg whites
3 tbsp. sugar
1 tsp. cream of tartar
1 tsp. grated orange peel
1/4 tsp. almond flavoring

Sift flour, baking powder, salt and cinnamon together; set aside. Add 5 tablespoons water to egg whites; beat until just stiff. Beat in sugar. Fold dry ingredients lightly into egg whites; beat in cream of tartar. Add orange peel and flavoring. Fill greased muffin tins full. Bake at 375 degrees until golden brown. Yield: 16 servings/36 calories per serving.

Grace M. Shepard, Palmetto H.S.
Williamston, South Carolina

DESSERT PANCAKES

3 eggs, separated
1/4 tsp. salt
3/4 c. cottage cheese, drained
1/4 c. sifted flour
1 tbsp. butter or margarine

Beat egg whites until stiff but not dry. Beat egg yolks with salt until thick; add cottage cheese and flour, mixing lightly. Fold in egg whites. Melt half the butter in skillet or on griddle. Drop batter by spoonfuls onto skillet; brown lightly on both sides. Add remaining butter as needed. Serve with maple or fruit sauce. Yield: 6 servings/115 calories per serving.

Mrs. Judith Sudheimer Payne, Central Linn H.S.
Halsey, Oregon

FRENCH TOAST DELUXE

4 eggs
1/2 c. skim milk
Dash of salt
6 slices slightly dry diet bread
2 tbsp. butter or margarine
4 tbsp. honey

Beat eggs slightly with milk and salt in pie plate or shallow bowl. Dip bread slices, one at a time, into egg mixture, turning to coat both sides well. Saute slowly in half the butter, turning once and adding remaining butter as needed. Cut in half diagonally; drizzle with honey. Yield: 4 servings/275 calories per serving.

Virginia R. Garber, Grundy Sr. H.S.
Grundy, Virginia

BANANA MILK SHAKE

1 lg. ripe banana
1 tbsp. sugar
1/2 c. crushed ice
1/2 tsp. vanilla extract
1/3 c. nonfat dry milk

Slice banana into blender container; add sugar. Beat until smooth. Pour in 1/2 cup cold water; add ice, vanilla and dry milk. Beat until smooth and fluffy. Pour into 2 chilled glasses. Yield: 2 servings.

Mrs. Virginia Carlson, Port Allegany School
Port Allegany, Pennsylvania

COFFEE MILK SHAKE

2/3 c. powdered skimmed milk
2 tbsp. instant coffee
5 grains sweetener

Combine all ingredients in shaker or blender; add 1 cup water. Mix well. Store in refrigerator.

Caroline Einstein, Southwestern H.S.
Detroit, Michigan

MAKE YOUR OWN BUTTERMILK

1 c. nonfat dry milk
3 3/4 c. water
1/2 c. buttermilk
Pinch of salt

Mix dry milk with 3 3/4 cups water; add buttermilk and salt. Mix well; cover. Let stand at room temperature overnight or until clabbered. Stir until smooth; refrigerate until ready to serve. Yield: 4-5 servings.

Ida Mae Gray, Asst. Supvr., Home Ec. Ed.
State Dept. of Ed.
Jackson, Mississippi

Low-Calorie

COCOA FOR ONE

1 tsp. sugar or 1/8 tsp. Sucaryl
Dash of salt
2 tsp. cocoa
3/4 c. skim milk

Combine sugar, salt, cocoa and 1/4 cup water in top of small double boiler; cook over direct heat for 2 to 4 minutes. Add milk; place over hot water until thoroughly heated. Beat with rotary beater to prevent formation of film on surface of cocoa. Serve. Yield: 1 serving/106 calories per serving.

Catharine I. Moyer, Wilson Sr. H.S.
West Lawn, Pennsylvania

SKIM MILK HOT COCOA

1/4 c. cocoa
6   1/2-grain saccharin tablets
3 c. skim milk
4 marshmallows (opt.)

Place cocoa in saucepan; combine with crushed saccharin tablets and 1/4 cup milk. Stir until dissolved. Add remaining milk gradually; heat thoroughly over medium heat, stirring constantly. Place marshmallow in each cup; pour hot cocoa over marshmallows. Serve hot. Yield: 4 servings.

Mrs. Dale Kiser, Erie Comm. H.S.
Erie, Illinois

CHOCOLATE DRINK

2 2/3 c. instant nonfat dry milk
7 1/2 c. water
1/2 c. sugar
1/2 c. (or more) P.D.Q. Swiss-style
   chocolate-flavored beads

Place dry milk and 7 1/2 cups water in saucepan; mix well. Add sugar and chocolate; mix. Heat thoroughly. Serve hot or cold. Yield: 6 servings.

Esta Newman, Bluffs H.S.
Bluffs, Illinois

CRANBERRY MILK PUNCH

1/2 c. instant nonfat dry milk
2 tbsp. lemon juice
1/4 c. sugar
1 tbsp. maraschino cherry juice
1 qt. cranberry juice cocktail, chilled
Whole red maraschino cherries with stems

Mix dry milk with 1/2 cup ice water; whip for 3 to 4 minutes or until soft peaks form. Add lemon juice; continue whipping for 3 to 4 minutes or until stiff peaks form. Add sugar and cherry juice gradually; fold into cranberry juice. Garnish with maraschino cherries. Yield: 6 servings.

Linda Lang, Spring Grove H.S.
Spring Grove, Minnesota

BREAKFAST DIET DRINK

2 1/2 c. nonfat dry milk
1/2 c. Vitamin A and C Mineral fortified
   malted milk powder
1/4 c. corn oil

Mix dry milk and malted milk. Add corn oil; work together until well mixed. Add 4 cups ice water. Process in blender until smooth. Refrigerate. Shake well before using.

Mrs. Louise Kregel, Peru State College
Peru, Nebraska

DIETER'S FRUIT DELIGHT

1 c. chilled pineapple juice
1/8 tsp. liquid non-calorie sweetener
1/3 c. instant dry milk solids
1 c. cracked ice
1/3 10-oz. package frozen strawberries

Place all ingredients in blender container; blend at high speed for 30 seconds or until thick and foamy. Pour into small glasses. Other fruits may be substituted for strawberries, if desired. Yield: 6 servings/ 34 calories per serving.

Margaret Tisdale, Treadwell School
Memphis, Tennessee

MINTED LIME MIST

1/2 c. fresh lime juice
1/8 tsp. mint extract
4 drops of green food coloring
1 1/2 tsp. liquid sweetener or
   12 tablets, crushed
1 pt. non-caloric lime carbonated beverage

Combine 2 cups warm water, lime juice, mint extract, green food coloring and sweetener; mix well. Chill for several hours; add carbonated beverage. Fill glasses with crushed ice; pour lime mist over ice. Garnish each glass with a maraschino cherry, wedge of lime and fresh mint. Yield: 6 servings.

Carol J. Henderson, Shelby Public School
Shelby, Nebraska

COCONUT-MARSHMALLOW SQUARES

2 env. unflavored gelatin
2 egg whites
4 tsp. Sucaryl
1/4 tsp. vanilla extract
1/4 c. toasted shredded coconut

Soften gelatin in 1/2 cup cold water; dissolve over hot water. Beat egg whites until soft peaks form. Add hot gelatin slowly while beating. Add Sucaryl and vanilla. Continue beating at high speed for 1 minute. Pour into 8-inch square pan; chill until set. Unmold onto board; cut into squares with wet knife. Toss lightly in toasted coconut. Yield: 36-40 pieces.

Ann Penny Bowman, Halbrook H.S.
Halbrook, Arizona

ORANGE GELATIN CANDY

3 env. unflavored gelatin
1 3/4 c. orange juice
1/4 c. Sucaryl
1 tsp. vanilla extract
1/2 c. nonfat dry milk
2 tbsp. lemon juice
1/2 c. shredded coconut

Soften gelatin in 1/2 cup orange juice. Combine Sucaryl and 3/4 cup orange juice in saucepan; bring to a boil. Add to softened gelatin; stir until dissolved. Add vanilla. Let stand at room temperature for about 45 minutes or until thick. Combine remaining orange juice and dry milk; beat until well mixed. Add lemon juice; beat until very stiff. Fold into gelatin mixture. Pour into lightly oiled 9-inch square pan; chill until set. Cut into pieces; roll in coconut. Yield: 49 pieces/14 calories per piece.

Sara Snyder, Pleasantville Elem. School
Carlisle, Indiana

SPICY APPLESAUCE CUPCAKES

1 c. sifted flour
1/2 tsp. soda
1/4 tsp. salt
1 1/2 tsp. cinnamon
1/4 tsp. nutmeg (opt.)
1/4 tsp. ginger (opt.)
1/4 tsp. cloves
1/8 tsp. allspice
1/2 c. raisins (opt.)
1/2 c. unsweetened applesauce
1/4 c. oil or melted shortening
1 egg
1 tsp. vanilla extract
2 tsp. Sweet-10

Sift flour, soda, salt, cinnamon, nutmeg, ginger, cloves and allspice together; stir in raisins. Combine applesauce, oil, egg, vanilla and Sweet-10; blend well. Add to dry ingredients all at once; stir only until moistened. Fill lined muffin cups half full. Bake at 350 degrees for 20 to 25 minutes. Yield: 12 servings/120 calories per serving.

Mrs. Georgia Watson, Blossom H.S.
Blossom, Texas

OATMEAL-RAISIN CUPCAKES

1 c. sifted flour
1/2 tsp. salt
1 tsp. soda
1/2 tsp. nutmeg
1 tsp. cinnamon
1/3 c. (firmly packed) brown sugar
3 tbsp. soft margarine
2 eggs
3/4 c. buttermilk
1 c. rolled oats
1/4 c. raisins

Sift flour, salt, soda and spices together; add sugar, margarine, eggs and half the buttermilk. Beat for 2 minutes or until smooth; fold in remaining buttermilk, oats and raisins. Fill small paper baking cups or small greased muffin cups half full. Bake at 375 degrees for 12 to 15 minutes. Yield: 20 servings/82 calories per serving.

Mrs. Mary M. Radford, Waverly H.S.
Waverly, Ohio

DIETER'S LEMON SPONGE CAKE

7 eggs, separated
3 tbsp. liquid artificial sweetener or
    1 1/2 c. granulated artificial sweetener
1/2 tsp. vanilla extract
1 to 2 tbsp. lemon juice
3/4 tsp. cream of tartar
1 1/2 c. sifted cake flour
1/4 tsp. salt
2 tbsp. grated lemon rind (opt.)

Beat egg yolks until thick and lemon colored. Combine 1/2 cup cold water, sweetener, vanilla and lemon juice; add to egg yolks. Beat until mixture is thick and fluffy. Beat egg whites until foamy; add cream of tartar. Beat until stiff peaks form; fold into egg yolk mixture carefully. Sift flour and salt together; add slowly to mixture, folding in very gently. Add grated rind; pour into ungreased 9 or 10-inch tube pan. Bake at 325 degrees for 1 hour and 5 minutes to 1 hour and 15 minutes. Invert and let cool before removing from pan. Yield: 12 servings.

Mercedes Hoskins, Lynn Jr. H.S.
Las Cruces, New Mexico

Low-Calorie

D-ZERTA CAKE

1 box white cake mix
1 box strawberry D-Zerta
1 box strawberry Whip 'n Chill

Prepare and bake cake according to package directions; cool. Punch holes in top of cake with fork. Prepare D-Zerta according to plackage directions; pour over top of cake slowly, allowing D-Zerta to soak into cake. Prepare Whip 'n Chill according to package directions; spread over top of cake. Refrigerate until firm; cut and serve. Yield: 12-15 servings.

Janice M. Howard, Webster Pub. H.S.
Webster, South Dakota

SPICY PRUNE CAKE

1 c. Wesson oil
2 tbsp. liquid sweetener
3 eggs
1 c. cooked mashed prunes
2 c. sifted flour
1 tsp. salt
1 tsp. soda
1 tsp. cloves
1 tsp. cinnamon
1 tsp. nutmeg
1 tsp. allspice
1 c. buttermilk
1 c. chopped walnuts

Combine oil, sweetener, eggs and prunes. Combine flour, salt, soda and spices; add alternately with buttermilk to prune mixture. Blend well; add walnuts. Turn into greased and floured tube pan. Bake at 350 degrees for 1 hour and 10 minutes. Yield: 12 servings.

Clara W. Grimes, Payson H.S.
Payson, Arizona

ONE-EGG CHOCOLATE CAKE

1/3 c. shortening
1/3 c. sugar
1 egg
2 c. sifted flour
1/2 tsp. salt
2 1/2 tsp. baking powder
2 tbsp. Nestle's Quick
2 tsp. liquid Sucaryl
3/4 c. skim milk
1 tsp. vanilla extract

Grease bottom of 8-inch square pan; dust lightly with flour. Cream shortening; beat in sugar. Add egg; beat until very light and fluffy. Sift dry ingredients together. Combine liquid ingredients. Add dry ingredients alternately with liquid ingredients to creamed mixture, beating just until smooth. Turn mixture into prepared pan. Bake in preheated 350-degree oven for 40 minutes or until cake tests done. Yield: 12 servings/165 calories per serving.

Yvonne M. Stubbs, Monroe Union H.S.
Monroe, Oregon

SUGARLESS CARROT-PECAN CAKE

1 c. salad oil
Artificial sweetener to equal 3/4 c. sugar
2 c. sifted flour
1 tsp. soda
1 tsp. salt
2 tsp. cinnamon
4 eggs
3 c. finely grated carrots
1/2 c. finely chopped pecans

Combine oil and sweetener; mix well. Sift flour, soda, salt and cinnamon together; add half the flour mixture to oil mixture. Blend; add remaining flour mixture alternately with eggs, one at a time, mixing well after each addition. Add carrots and pecans alternately, mixing well to blend. Pour into lightly oiled loaf pan. Bake at 325 degrees for about 1 hour; cool in pan. Yield: 15 servings.

Mrs. Sharron Altmaier, Pleasanton Pub. School
Pleasanton, Nebraska

CHERRY CHEESECAKE

1/2 c. graham cracker crumbs
1 tbsp. softened butter
Sucaryl
3 eggs, separated
1 lb. farmer cheese
1 tbsp. sugar
1/2 tsp. vanilla extract
1/4 tsp. cinnamon

Mix crumbs, butter and Sucaryl to taste; press against side of small springform pan. Place egg yolks, cheese, 6 teaspoons Sucaryl, sugar, vanilla and cinnamon in electric blender; blend until smooth and creamy. Scrape mixture into a bowl; fold in stiffly beaten egg whites. Pour into springform pan. Bake in a preheated 325-degree oven for 15 minutes. Increase temperature to 450 degrees; bake for 5 minutes more. Remove cake from oven; cool.

Cherry Glaze

1 lg. can water-pack black Bing
    pitted cherries
1 tbsp. cornstarch
1 tsp. Sucaryl
Few drops of red food coloring

Drain cherries, reserving juice. Add water to juice, if needed, to equal 1 cup liquid. Add cornstarch to juice; mix until blended. Cook over medium heat, stirring constantly, until slightly thickened. Add Sucaryl and food coloring. Remove from heat; mix thoroughly. Arrange cherries on top of the cheesecake; spoon glaze over top. Refrigerate cake in pan for several hours before unmolding. Yield: 8 servings/145 calories per serving.

Mrs. Olga Butts, Chino H.S.
Chino, California

PRETEND PEACH CHEESECAKE

2 env. unflavored gelatin
Sugar
1/4 tsp. salt
2 eggs, separated
1 c. liquified nonfat dry milk
1 tsp. grated lemon peel
1 pkg. frozen sliced peaches, thawed
1/4 tsp. almond extract

Combine gelatin, 3/4 cup sugar and salt in double boiler. Beat egg yolks with milk; add to gelatin mixture. Cook over boiling water, stirring constantly, until gelatin is dissolved. Remove from heat. Add lemon peel, peaches and almond extract. Chill until slightly thicker than unbeaten egg whites. Beat with rotary beater until light and peaches are blended. Beat egg whites until stiff, adding 2 tablespoons sugar. Fold into gelatin mixture. Turn into mold; chill until firm.

Mrs. Nelle McLellan, Smithville H.S.
Smithville, Texas

NO-BAKE CHEESECAKE

2 env. unflavored gelatin
12 tbsp. sugar
1/4 tsp. salt
3 eggs, separated
1 1/2 c. skimmed milk
1 tsp. grated lemon rind
3 c. creamed cottage cheese
1 tbsp. lemon juice
1 tsp. vanilla extract
1/3 c. graham cracker crumbs

Mix gelatin, 6 tablespoons sugar and salt in top of double boiler. Beat egg yolks and skimmed milk together; add to gelatin mixture. Place over boiling water; cook, stirring constantly, for about 6 minutes or until gelatin is dissolved and mixture thickens slightly. Remove from heat; stir in lemon rind. Chill to unbeaten egg white consistency. Beat cottage cheese with electric mixer at high speed for 3 minutes; stir in lemon juice and vanilla and fold into gelatin mixture. Beat egg whites until stiff peaks form, adding remaining 6 tablespoons sugar gradually. Fold into cottage cheese mixture. Pour into 8-inch springform pan; sprinkle with crumbs. Chill until firm. Yield: 12 servings/125 calories per serving.

Naomi M. Vaught, Manatee H.S.
Bradenton, Florida

CHEESECAKE PIE

3 c. creamed cottage cheese
1/4 tsp. grated orange rind
3 eggs
1/4 tsp. salt
Liquid sweetener to equal 1 c. sugar
1/4 c. flour
1/2 c. sour cream
2 tbsp. lemon juice
1 tsp. vanilla extract
6 zwieback
1 tsp. cinnamon

Beat cottage cheese and orange rind together until almost smooth. Add eggs, salt and liquid sweetener; beat until blended. Add flour, sour cream, lemon juice and vanilla; mix well. Crush zwieback finely; mix in cinnamon. Spread crumbs evenly over bottom of deep 9-inch pie pan. Spoon cheese mixture carefully over crumbs. Bake at 300 degrees for 1 hour. Chill thoroughly. Yield: 8 servings/190 calories per serving.

Mrs. Rebecca Burns Drone, College Grove H.S.
College Grove, Tennessee

APPLESAUCE-RAISIN COOKIES

1 1/2 c. sifted flour
2 tsp. cinnamon
3/4 tsp. soda
1/4 tsp. salt
1/4 tsp. nutmeg
1/4 tsp. cloves
1/4 tsp. allspice
1/4 c. butter or margarine
1/3 c. raisins
1/2 c. dietetic applesauce
1/4 c. buttermilk
1 egg, slightly beaten
1 1/2 tsp. liquid Sweet-10

Sift flour with cinnamon, soda, salt and spices into mixing bowl. Cut in butter until particles are fine. Stir in raisins. Combine remaining ingredients; blend well. Add to dry ingredients all at once; mix well. Drop by rounded teaspoonfuls onto greased cookie sheets. Bake at 375 degrees for 12 to 15 minutes. Yield: 30 cookies/41 calories per cookie.

Mrs. Erma E. Goehring
Harbor Creek Jr.-Sr. H.S.
Harbor Creek, Pennsylvania

Low-Calorie

APPLESAUCE BRAN COOKIES

1 3/4 c. cake flour
1/2 tsp. salt
1 tsp. cinnamon
1/2 tsp. nutmeg
1/2 tsp. cloves
1 tsp. soda
1/2 c. butter
1 tbsp. Sucaryl
1 egg
1 c. dietetic applesauce
1/3 c. raisins
1 c. All-Bran

Sift flour, salt, cinnamon, nutmeg, cloves and soda together. Cream butter, Sucaryl and egg until light and fluffy. Add flour mixture and applesauce alternately, mixing well after each addition. Fold in raisins and All-Bran. Drop by level tablespoonfuls onto greased cookie sheet, about 1 inch apart. Bake at 375 degrees for 10 minutes or until golden brown. Yield: 4 dozen/39 calories per cookie.

Mrs. Geraldine Marrs, Homer Comm. School
Homer, Illinois

LOW-CALORIE BROWNIES

2/3 c. all-purpose flour
3/4 tsp. soda
1/4 tsp. salt
1/3 c. butter
1 sq. unsweetened chocolate
2 eggs
1 c. sugar replacement
3 tbsp. milk
1 tsp. vanilla extract
1/2 c. chopped nuts

Mix flour, soda and salt. Melt butter and chocolate over hot water. Beat eggs well; add sugar replacement gradually, beating well. Blend chocolate mixture, milk and vanilla together. Mix in flour mixture, then nuts. Spread in greased 8-inch square pan. Bake at 350 degrees for 15 minutes. Cool. Cut into squares. Yield: 25 brownies.

Mrs. Buddy Fallin, Stamps H.S.
Stamps, Arkansas

CHOCOLATE-NUT BROWNIES

1 sq. unsweetened chocolate
1/3 c. margarine
1 tbsp. Sucaryl
2 tsp. vanilla extract
2 eggs, beaten
1 c. sifted cake flour
1/2 tsp. salt

1/2 tsp. soda
1/2 c. chopped walnuts

Melt chocolate and margarine in saucepan over low heat. Remove from heat. Cool slightly. Add Sucaryl, vanilla and eggs; stir until well blended. Add flour, salt and soda; mix until blended. Stir in walnuts. Pour into well-greased 8-inch square pan. Smooth out batter. Bake in a 325-degree oven for 20 to 25 minutes. Yield: 32 pieces/54 calories per serving.

Emma A. Podoll, Phoenix Indian H.S.
Phoenix, Arizona

CHOCOLATE FUDGE SQUARES

1/4 c. margarine or shortening
2 sq. unsweetened chocolate
1/4 c. Sucaryl
2 lg. eggs, beaten
1 tsp. vanilla extract
1 1/2 c. Bisquick
1/2 c. chopped walnuts

Melt margarine and chocolate together. Cool. Combine Sucaryl, eggs and vanilla; add Bisquick. Blend thoroughly with chocolate mixture. Stir in walnuts. Spread in a greased 8 x 8 x 2-inch pan. Bake at 325 degrees for 25 minutes. Do not overbake. Cool. Cut in 2-inch squares. Yield: 16 squares.

Mrs. Ruth H. Lamoreau, Presque Isle H.S.
Presque Isle, Maine

BASIC DIET DROP COOKIES

1 c. shortening
1/4 c. Sucaryl
2 eggs
1 c. sour milk
2 1/2 to 3 c. flour
1 tsp. soda
1 tsp. salt
1 tsp. vanilla extract

Cream shortening, Sucaryl and eggs until light; add milk and sifted dry ingredients alternately, mixing well. Stir in vanilla. Drop by teaspoonfuls onto greased cookie sheet. Bake at 400 degrees for about 10 minutes. May add 1 cup raisins and 1/2 cup quick-cooking oats or 1 cup drained diet crushed pineapple, if desired. Yield: 3 dozen cookies.

Mrs. Carr Dee Racop, Jr., Portland H.S.
Portland, Arkansas

BRAN FLAKE DROP COOKIES

3/4 c. sifted flour
1/2 tsp. salt

1 1/2 tsp. baking powder
1/2 tsp. cinnamon
3/4 c. bran flakes
2 tbsp. chopped peanuts
1/4 c. finely chopped raisins
1 egg
1 tbsp. sweetener
1/4 c. water
1 tbsp. salad oil
1/2 tsp. vanilla extract

Sift flour, salt, baking powder and cinnamon together; add bran flakes, peanuts and raisins. Beat egg; add remaining ingredients. Stir into dry mixture. Do not overmix. Drop by teaspoonfuls onto very lightly greased cookie sheet. Bake at 350 degrees for 10 minutes. May freeze after cooling. Yield: 30 cookies/27 calories per cookie.

Ruth Cronbeck, Hope H.S.
Hope, North Dakota

CINNAMON PIXIE COOKIES

5 tbsp. butter
1 c. sifted flour
1/4 tsp. baking powder
2 tsp. Sucaryl or other sweetener
2 tsp. vanilla flavoring
1 tbsp. milk, fruit juice or coffee
1 tsp. cinnamon

Cream butter until light and fluffy. Blend in flour and baking powder. Combine sweetener, vanilla and milk; stir into flour mixture. Mix thoroughly. Sprinkle cinnamon over dough; knead lightly to leave streaked appearance. Shape dough into balls about 1/2 inch in diameter; arrange on cookie sheet. Flatten balls with fork dipped in cold water. Bake at 375 degrees for 15 minutes or until edges are browned. Yield: 30 cookies.

Medline M. Thomas, Appomattox H.S.
Appomattox, Virginia

FRUIT COOKIES FOR DIABETICS

1/3 c. salad oil
2 c. seedless raisins
2 tsp. cinnamon
1/2 tsp. nutmeg
1/2 tsp. salt
1 tsp. soda
2 tsp. liquid sweetener
2 eggs, beaten
2 c. flour
1 tsp. baking powder
1/3 c. chopped nuts

Combine 1 cup water, oil, raisins, cinnamon and nutmeg in saucepan; boil for 3 minutes. Let cool. Combine salt, soda, sweetener and 2 tablespoons water; stir until dissolved. Add to eggs. Stir into cooled mixture. Add sifted flour and baking powder; mix well. Blend in nuts. Drop by teaspoonfuls onto greased cookie sheet. Bake at 375 degrees until lightly brown. Yield: 3 dozen cookies.

Jeannette Reynolds, Crowville H.S.
Crowville, Louisiana

LEMON SNAP COOKIES

3/4 c. sugar
1/2 c. butter or margarine
1 egg
2 tbsp. lemon juice
1 1/2 tsp. finely grated lemon peel
2 1/4 c. sifted flour
1/2 tsp. baking powder
1/4 tsp. salt

Cream sugar and butter until light and fluffy. Beat in egg, lemon juice and peel. Sift dry ingredients together; add to butter mixture gradually. Mix until smooth. Refrigerate for 1 to 2 hours or until well chilled. Roll out thin on well-floured pastry cloth or board. Cut with 2-inch cutter. Place on lightly greased cookie sheet. Bake at 400 degrees for 6 to 8 minutes or until edges are golden brown. Yield: 6-7 dozen cookies.

Mrs. Mary Sanders, Spring Woods Sr. H.S.
Houston, Texas

LEMON WAFERS

1 1/2 c. sifted flour
1/2 tsp. salt
1/2 tsp. soda
1/2 c. shortening
1 1/2 tbsp. lemon juice
1 1/2 tsp. grated lemon peel
1 c. (firmly packed) brown sugar
1 egg

Sift flour, salt and soda together; set aside. Cream shortening, lemon juice and peel together until smooth and light, adding sugar gradually. Cream until fluffy after each addition. Add egg; beat well. Add dry ingredients, 1/4 at a time, blending thoroughly after each addition. Shape into rolls 1 inch in diameter; roll in waxed paper. Chill for several hours or overnight. Cut into thin slices; place on cookie sheet. Bake at 400 degrees for 8 to 10 minutes. Remove immediately onto cooling racks. Yield: 4 dozen/49 calories per cookie.

Mrs. Barbara Goedicke
Lindsay Thurber Composite H.S.
Red Deer, Alberta, Canada

Low-Calorie

SPICY LOW-CALORIE COOKIES

1 1/3 c. sifted flour
1/2 tsp. salt
1/3 c. salad oil
1/4 tsp. cinnamon
1/4 c. sugar
1/8 tsp. nutmeg

Combine all ingredients; form into ball. Roll between 2 sheets of waxed paper. Remove top sheet. Cut with 2-inch cookie cutter; move with spatula onto cookie sheet. Bake at 450 degrees for about 15 minutes or until brown. Yield: 4 dozen cookies/30 calories per cookie.

Mabel Moorhouse, Belen H.S.
Belen, New Mexico

APPLESAUCE-OATMEAL COOKIES

1/2 c. butter
1 egg
1 1/2 tbsp. sugar substitute
1 1/2 c. all-purpose flour
1/2 tsp. soda
1/4 tsp. salt
1/2 tsp. ground cloves
1 1/2 tsp. ground cinnamon
2 c. quick-cooking oats
1/2 c. skim milk
2 tsp. vanilla extract
1/4 c. unsweetened applesauce
1/2 c. raisins

Cream butter until soft and creamy. Beat in egg and sugar substitute. Sift flour, soda, salt, cloves and cinnamon together; add oats. Add dry mixture alternately with milk to butter mixture, beginning and ending with dry mixture. Stir in vanilla, applesauce and raisins. Drop by spoonfuls onto greased cookie sheet. Bake in preheated 375-degree oven for 12 to 15 minutes or until golden.

Mrs. Glenda Luke Mitchell, Azle H.S.
Azle, Texas

AFTER SCHOOL OATMEAL COOKIES

1 1/2 c. quick-cooking oatmeal
2/3 c. melted margarine
2 eggs, beaten
1 tbsp. artificial sweetener
1 1/2 c. sifted flour
1/2 tsp. salt
2 tsp. baking powder
1/2 c. skim milk
1 tsp. vanilla extract
1/4 c. raisins

Place oatmeal into mixing bowl; stir in melted shortening, mixing well. Blend in eggs and sweetener. Add sifted dry ingredients alternately with combined milk and vanilla. Mix in raisins. Drop by level teaspoonfuls onto baking sheet. Bake at 400 degrees for 10 to 15 minutes or until goden brown. Yield: 6 dozen cookies.

Mrs. Frances Eldridge, Central Sr. H.S.
Clifton, Illinois

CANADIAN ORANGE COOKIES

1 1/2 c. flour
Pinch of cream of tartar
Pinch of soda
1/2 c. margarine
1 c. Mazola oil
1 c. sugar
1 egg, beaten
Juice of 1 orange
1 tsp. lemon juice
Grated rind of 1 orange

Sift flour, cream of tartar and soda together; set aside. Cream margarine; add oil. Beat until well blended. Add sugar gradually, beating until sugar is dissolved. Blend in egg, juices and rind. Add dry ingredients; mix well. Drop by teaspoonfuls onto buttered baking sheet, 1 inch apart. Press flat with a fork. Bake at 350 degrees for 10 to 12 minutes. Yield: 2 dozen cookies.

Sr. Angeline Tetreault, Academie Assumption
Edmonton, Alberta, Canada

BANANA FREEZE

1/2 c. sugar
Dash of salt
1 lg. ripe banana, mashed
1/4 c. orange juice
1/4 c. lemon juice
1 egg white
1/3 c. nonfat dry milk

Combine sugar and 1 cup water in saucepan; cook until sugar dissolves. Remove from heat; stir in salt, banana, orange juice and lemon juice. Pour mixture into 2 refrigerator trays; freeze for 1 hour or until mushy. Beat egg white, dry milk and 1/3 cup water until stiff; fold into partially frozen mixture. Return to refrigerator trays; freeze until firm. Yield: 10 servings/71 calories per serving.

Mrs. Sandra Faber, North Chicago H.S.
North Chicago, Illinois

FROZEN CRANBERRY WHIP

1 lb. cranberries
3 peeled apples
20 marshmallows
1 c. nuts (opt.)
2 tbsp. artificial sweetener
1 env. Dream Whip

Grind cranberries, apples, marshmallows and nuts; add sweetener. Prepare Dream Whip according to package directions; add to cranberry mixture. Pour into rectangular pan; cover. Freeze until firm. Yield: 9-12 servings.

Mrs. Irma Dixon, Georgetown H.S.
Georgetown, Illinois

FROZEN CHOCOLATE MOUSSE

1 tsp. unflavored gelatin
1 oz. unsweetened chocolate
1/4 tsp. salt
1 tbsp. liquid artificial sweetener
1 tsp. vanilla extract
1/8 tsp. cream of tartar
2/3 c. nonfat dry milk

Soften gelatin in 2 tablespoons water; set aside. Melt chocolate in top of double boiler; add 1/4 cup hot water. Stir until smooth; remove from heat. Stir in softened gelatin until dissolved; add salt, sweetener and vanilla. Chill until slightly thickened. Combine 2/3 cup ice water and cream of tartar; add dry milk. Beat at high speed for 5 minutes or until stiff peaks form; fold in chocolate mixture gently. Pour into 1-quart mold; freeze for at least 6 hours. Yield: 4 servings/110 calories per serving.

Mrs. Sophia S. Boan, Pierce Jr. H.S.
Grosse Pointe, Michigan

FIGURE-WATCHING FRUIT FROST

1/4 c. jam, jelly or preserves
1/4 c. marshmallow whip
1/2 c. ice water or lemon-lime carbonated
  diet beverage
1/2 c. nonfat dry milk
2 tbsp. lemon juice
3 drops of food coloring (opt.)

Blend jam and marshmallow whip together. Pour ice water into small deep mixing bowl; add dry milk. Beat for 3 to 4 minutes or until soft peaks form; add lemon juice. Beat for 3 to 4 minutes longer or until stiff; fold in jam mixture and food coloring. Spoon into refrigerator tray; freeze for 5 hours or until firm

or spoon into sherbet glasses and serve immediately. Yield: 4 servings/75 calories per serving.

Mrs. Clarice Hubbard, Mitchell Jr. H.S.
Mitchell, South Dakota

FROZEN FRUIT COCKTAIL

1 qt. ginger ale
1 c. fruit cocktail, drained

Freeze ginger ale until mushy; spoon into 5 sherbet glasses. Top with well chilled fruit cocktail. Garnish with a cherry and mint leaf. Yield: 5 servings/86 calories per serving.

Mrs. Daniel B. Snead, Glenn Voc. H.S.
Birmingham, Alabama

LO-CAL LEMON FROST

1 egg, separated
1/3 c. nonfat dry milk
1/3 c. sugar
1/4 tsp. grated lemon peel
2 to 3 tbsp. lemon juice
Dash of salt
3 tbsp. graham cracker crumbs

Combine egg white, 1/3 cup water and dry milk; beat until stiff peaks form. Combine slightly beaten egg yolk, sugar, lemon peel, lemon juice and salt; beat into egg mixture gradually. Sprinkle 2 tablespoonfuls crumbs on bottom of refrigerator tray; spoon in lemon mixture. Dust with remaining crumbs; freeze until firm. Cut in wedges to serve. Yield: 6 servings/80 calories per serving.

Betty R. Fitchner, Hoquiam Sr. H.S.
Hoquiam, Washington

SLIMMER'S FROZEN LEMON CUSTARD

1 eggs, separated
2 tsp. Sucaryl
1/4 tsp. grated lemon rind
3 tbsp. lemon juice
1/2 c. nonfat dry milk

Combine egg yolk, Sucaryl, lemon rind and 2 tablespoons lemon juice; set aside. Beat remaining lemon juice, 1/3 cup water, egg white and dry milk solids with electric beater at high speed until stiff; beat in egg yolk mixture gradually. Spoon into refrigerator tray; freeze until firm without stirring. Yield: 4 servings.

Mrs. Paul Penton, Harry L. Johnson School
Johnson City, New York

Low-Calorie

FAR OUT FROZEN LEMON CUSTARD

1 egg, separated
1/3 c. sugar
1/4 tsp. grated lemon rind
3 tbsp. lemon juice
Dash of salt
1/3 c. nonfat dry milk
2 to 4 tbsp. graham cracker crumbs

Combine egg yolk, sugar, lemon rind, lemon juice and salt; mix well. Combine egg white, 1/3 cup water and dry milk; beat until stiff. Beat in lemon mixture gradually. Pour into 1-quart refrigerator tray; sprinkle graham cracker crumbs over top. Freeze until firm without stirring. Yield: 6 servings/78 calories per serving.

Mrs. Elizabeth Hayton, Huntington Jr. H.S.
Kelso, Washington

FROZEN ORANGE PUDDING

2 eggs
1/3 c. cold water
1/3 c. nonfat dry milk
Dash of salt
1/4 c. sugar
1 6-oz. can frozen orange juice
   concentrate, thawed

Combine eggs, 1/3 cup water, dry milk and salt; beat until light and fluffy. Add sugar and orange juice concentrate gradually, beating until thick and lemon colored; turn into refrigerator tray. Freeze until firm. Yield: 8 servings.

Ruth Blevins, Albion H.S.
Albion, Indiana

STRAWBERRIES IN NESTS

1 2-oz. package Dream Whip
1/2 c. cold milk
1/2 tsp. vanilla extract
1 tsp. grated orange peel
1/2 c. chopped pecans (opt.)
Fresh strawberries, raspberries or peaches

Prepare Dream Whip with milk and vanilla according to package directions; fold in orange peel and pecans, blending thoroughly. Spoon heaping table-spoonfuls of mixture to form 6 mounds on waxed paper-lined baking sheet; shape center of each mound into a shell with back of spoon. Freeze until firm; fill centers of each shell with strawberries.

Mrs. Sandra Miller, Lakewood H.S.
Hebron, Ohio

PINEAPPLE-CHERRY SHERBET

9 sm. bottles diet orange carbonated beverage
1 lg. can unsweetened crushed pineapple
1 14-oz. can sweetened condensed milk
1 c. chopped maraschino cherries

Combine all ingredients; turn into gallon freezer container. Freeze according to freezer directions. Yield: 1 gallon.

Mrs. Billie Jeane Garner, L. D. Bell H.S.
Hurst, Texas

HAWAIIAN SHERBET

1 6-oz. can frozen orange-pineapple
   juice concentrate
3/4 c. unsweetened apple juice
1 1/2 tsp. granulated sugar substitute
1/4 c. nonfat dry milk

Combine orange-pineapple juice, apple juice and 3/4 cup cold water; add sugar substitute, stirring until dissolved. Add dry milk, blending well. Pour into chilled refrigerator tray; place tray on bottom shelf of freezer compartment for 45 minutes to 1 hour or until sherbet has begun to freeze. Turn sherbet into chilled bowl; beat with chilled beaters until fluffy. Return to refrigerator tray; freeze until almost set. Repeat beating process. Return to freezer until firm. Yield: 8 servings.

Mary Ann Lea, Oak Grove H.S.
North Little Rock, Arkansas

ORANGE BEVERAGE SHERBET

1 can sweetened condensed milk
2 qt. low-calorie carbonated orange beverage
1 can crushed pineapple

Combine all ingredients; place in 1/2 gallon freezer container. Freeze according to freezer directions. Yield: 8 servings.

Mrs. Ann Edwards, Drane Jr. H.S.
Corsicana, Texas

PEACH AND ORANGE SHERBET

2 c. canned dietetic sliced peaches, drained
1 1/3 tsp. Sweet 'N Low
1 3-oz. can frozen lemonade concentrate
1 3-oz. can frozen orange juice concentrate

1 1/2 tsp. lemon juice
2 egg whites, stiffly beaten

Place peaches, Sweet 'N Low, lemonade concentrate, orange juice concentrate and lemon juice in blender container; blend until smooth. Turn into refrigerator tray; freeze for 30 minutes or until partially frozen. Turn into blender container; blend until smooth. Fold in stiffly beaten egg whites; return to tray. Freeze until firm. Yield: 6 servings.

Mrs. Lester Ewy, Pretty Prairie H.S.
Pretty Prairie, Kansas

DELICIOUS ORANGE-PINEAPPLE SHERBET

1 6-oz. can frozen unsweetened orange juice concentrate
1 6-oz. can frozen unsweetened pineapple juice concentrate
2 tbsp. Sucaryl
1 c. nonfat dry milk

Place all ingredients in 2-quart mixing bowl; add 3 1/2 cups cold water. Beat just enough to blend. Pour into freezer trays; freeze for 1 to 2 hours or until partially frozen. Remove to large chilled mixer bowl; beat at low speed until mixture is softened. Beat at high speed for 3 to 5 minutes or until creamy. Return to freezer trays. Freeze until firm. Yield: 10 servings.

Mrs. Jan King, Sheffield Jr. H.S.
Sheffield, Alabama

LIGHT PINEAPPLE SHERBET

1 1/2 tsp. unflavored gelatin
2 c. buttermilk
4 to 4 1/2 tsp. liquid sweetener
1 c. dietetic crushed pineapple
1 tsp. vanilla extract
1 egg white

Soften gelatin in 2 tablespoons cold water; dissolve over hot water. Combine buttermilk, 3 to 3 1/2 teaspoons sweetener, pineapple, vanilla and gelatin; mix well. Freeze until firm; break mixture into chunks. Turn into chilled bowl; beat until smooth. Beat egg white until soft peaks form; add remaining sweetener gradually, beating until stiff peaks form. Fold into pineapple mixture; return to freezer. Freeze until firm. Yield: 6 servings/48 calories per 1/2 cup serving.

Mrs. Lucy Dennison, Caneyville H.S.
Caneyville, Kentucky

TASTY PINEAPPLE SHERBET

1/2 env. unflavored gelatin
2 c. buttermilk
1 c. sugar
1 9-oz. can crushed pineapple
1 tsp. vanilla extract
1 egg white, stiffly beaten

Soften gelatin in 2 tablespoons cold water; dissolve over hot water. Combine buttermilk, sugar, pineapple and vanilla; add gelatin. Fold in egg white; turn into refrigerator tray. Freeze until firm, stirring once. Yield: 6-8 servings.

Sister Mary St. Clara, B.V.M., Clarke College
Dubuque, Iowa

PEPPERMINT ICED MILK

12 to 18 peppermint candy discs
1 c. reconstituted nonfat dry milk
1/2 tsp. unflavored gelatin
1/2 tsp. Sucaryl
Few drops of red food coloring (opt.)
1 c. ice water
1 c. nonfat dry milk crystals

Chop candy discs in blender; remove from blender. Set aside. Place 1/2 cup cold reconstituted milk and gelatin into blender; let stand for several minutes. Heat remaining reconstituted milk; add to blender. Cover; process until gelatin is dissolved. Add peppermint candy, Sucaryl and food coloring; process until candy is dissolved. Combine 1 cup ice water and dry milk crystals; whip until soft peaks form. Fold in peppermint mixture. Pour into large freezer tray; freeze until mixture is partially frozen. Remove to cold mixing bowl; beat until light and fluffy. Pour into 2-quart container; cover. Return to freezer; freeze for at least 3 hours before serving. Yield: 2 quarts.

Emma Catherine Lawson, Carrizozo H.S.
Carrizozo, New Mexico

KOOL-AID POPSICLES

1 pkg. flavored gelatin
1 pkg. presweetened Kool-Aid

Dissolve gelatin and Kool-Aid in 2 cups boiling water; add 2 cups cold water. Pour into Popsicle forms; freeze until firm. Yield: 18 servings.

Mrs. Barbara Behnke, Port Washington H.S.
Port Washington, Wisconsin

Low-Calorie

SPUMONE CRUSH

1 10-oz. can French vanilla liquid
   diet food
Few drops of red food coloring
1 8-oz. can diet-pack fruit cocktail,
   well drained

Combine diet food and food coloring; freeze until almost firm in center. Place in blender container; process to frappe. Fold in half the fruit cocktail. Garnish with remaining fruit cocktail. Yield: 2 servings/268 calories per serving.

Mrs. Yvonne Lindrum, Montebello Jr. H.S.
Montebello, California

SUMMER VANILLA ICE CREAM

1 tsp. unflavored gelatin
1/2 c. milk
1 tbsp. flour
Pinch of salt
4 tsp. Sucaryl
1 egg, well beaten
2 tsp. vanilla extract
1 1/2 c. chilled evaporated skim milk

Soften gelatin in 2 tablespoons cold water. Combine 1/2 cup water and milk in top of double boiler; scald. Make a paste of flour, salt and 3 teaspoons Sucaryl; stir into scalded milk. Cook for 10 minutes, stirring frequently. Stir small amount into beaten egg; return to hot mixture gradually, stirring constantly. Cook over hot water until mixture coats spoon. Stir in softened gelatin to dissolve; remove from heat. Add vanilla; cool. Whip icy skim milk and remaining Sucaryl in chilled bowl with chilled beaters until consistency of whipped cream; fold into cooked mixture. Pour into freezer tray. Remove from freezer tray 4 times at 30 minute intervals and beat well. Freeze until firm. Yield: 6 servings/61 calories per serving.

Mrs. Esther Sigmund, Christen Jr. H.S.
Laredo, Texas

FROSTED AMBROSIA

1 env. whipped topping mix
1/2 c. cold skim milk
1 tsp. orange extract
1 16-oz. can diet-pack pineapple
   chunks, drained
1 8-oz. can mandarin oranges, drained
1/4 c. angel flake coconut, toasted

Whip topping mix with skim milk according to package directions. Add orange extract. Fold in pineapple and oranges. Arrange fruits in sherbets; garnish with coconut. Chill in refrigerator until serving time. Yield: 6 servings.

Mrs. Violet N. Tabler, Moon Sr. H.S.
Coraopolis, Pennsylvania

PLAIN APPLES

2 lg. baking apples
1/2 tsp. cinnamon
Artificial sweetener to taste (opt.)

Core apples. Rub cinnamon and sweetener in cavities. Place in pan; pour in 1/2 cup water. Bake at 350 degrees for about 30 minutes. Yield: 2 servings/100 calories per serving.

Mrs. Maurice E. Eskridge, Tyron H.S.
Bessemer City, North Carolina

FAVORITE APPLE BETTY

2 tsp. liquid sugar substitute
1/4 c. lemon juice
1 tsp. butter flavoring
3 c. soft coarse bread crumbs
2 tsp. cinnamon
1/2 tsp. salt
4 med. apples, sliced thin

Combine sugar substitute, 1 cup water, lemon juice and butter flavoring. Toss bread crumbs, cinnamon and salt until well mixed. Spread about 1/3 of crumbs in greased 1 1/2-quart casserole; cover with half the apple slices. Add half the remaining crumbs; add remaining apple slices. Top with layer of remaining crumbs. Spoon sugar substitute mixture over top layer; cover. Bake at 375 degrees for 30 minutes. Uncover; bake for 25 to 30 minutes longer. May serve warm or cold. Yield: 6 servings.

Mrs. Francis Reeves, Wilmer-Hutchins H.S.
Hutchins, Texas

LEMON APPLE BETTY

1 1/4 tsp. artificial sweetener
2 tbsp. lemon juice
2 c. soft coarse bread crumbs
1/2 tsp. cinnamon
1/2 tsp. salt
4 med. apples, sliced thin

Mix artificial sweetener with 1/4 cup water and lemon juice. Toss bread crumbs, cinnamon and salt together until well mixed. Spread about 1/3 of the crumbs in greased 1 1/2-quart casserole; cover with half the apple slices. Add a layer of half the remaining crumbs; add remaining apple slices. Top with layer of remaining crumbs. Spoon sweetener mixture over top layer; cover. Bake at 375 degrees for 20 minutes. Remove cover; bake for 30 to 35 minutes longer. May serve warm or cold. Yield: 5 servings/90 calories per serving.

Mrs. Jane Steiner, Waveland H.S.
Waveland, Indiana

APPLE SLICE CAKE

1 1/2 c. sifted flour
1/2 tsp. salt
3 tsp. baking powder
2 tbsp. shortening
1/4 c. skim milk
1 tbsp. liquid sweetener
4 sm. apples, pared and sliced
1 tsp. cinnamon

Sift flour, salt and baking powder together; cut in shortening to make fine crumbs. Add milk and sweetener; place dough on floured board. Roll out to 1/2-inch thickness; place in greased shallow pan. Press apple slices into dough; sprinkle with cinnamon. Bake at 350 degrees for 30 minutes or until done. Yield: 7 servings.

Meroe E. Stanley, Northville H.S.
Northville, Michigan

BAKED TART APPLES

4 med. tart apples
1/4 c. bread crumbs
1 tsp. liquid sweetener
1/4 c. margarine
1/2 tsp. cinnamon
1/4 c. orange juice

Pare and core apples; place in baking pan. Combine crumbs, sweetener, margarine and cinnamon; toss until mixture resembles buttered crumbs. Fill cavities of apples with crumb mixture. Add 1/4 cup water and orange juice; sprinkle any remaining crumbs over tops of apples. Bake in 375-degree oven for 1 hour to 1 hour and 15 minutes or until apples are tender. Yield: 4 servings.

Mrs. Paul Cooley, Lyman H.S.
Lyman, Wyoming

RAISIN-STUFFED APPLES

4 med. apples
Raisins
1 12-oz. can low-calorie black cherry soda

Cinnamon to taste
Nutmeg to taste

Core apples; do not peel. Place in baking dish. Fill each cavity with raisins. Pour black cherry soda over apples; sprinkle each with cinnamon and nutmeg. Bake, uncovered, in 375 to 400-degree oven for 30 or 40 minutes or until apples are soft, basting occasionally with pan juices. Yield: 4 servings.

Mary B. Konefal, New York Ave. Jr. H.S.
Smithtown, New York

DAPPLE APPLE BAKE

4 med. apples, pared and sliced
Artificial sweetener
1 tbsp. lemon juice
1/4 tsp. cinnamon
1/2 c. graham cracker crumbs
1/2 c. zwieback crumbs
1 tbsp. melted butter or margarine

Place apples in 6-cup shallow baking dish; add sweetener equivalent to 1/2 cup sugar. Sprinkle with lemon juice and cinnamon; toss to mix. Toss graham cracker and zwieback crumbs with melted butter in small bowl; sprinkle over apple mixture. Pour in 3/4 cup hot water; cover. Bake in 400-degree oven for 15 minutes. Uncover; bake for 15 minutes longer or until apples are tender. Serve warm. Yield: 8 servings/112 calories per serving.

Sister Jamesine Marie, IHM
Cardinal Dougherty H.S.
Philadelphia, Pennsylvania

TASTY APPLE CRISP

4 c. pared sliced apples
Liquid Sweet-10
1 tbsp. lemon juice
Cinnamon to taste
2 tbsp. melted butter
1/2 c. crushed graham crackers
1/2 c. toasted bread crumbs

Place apples in 1 1/2-quart casserole. Sprinkle with 1 tablespoon Sweet-10, lemon juice and cinnamon. Combine butter, crushed graham crackers, bread crumbs and 1 teaspoon Sweet-10; toss with fork until well combined. Sprinkle over apples. Pour 3/4 cup hot water carefully over top; cover. Bake at 400 degrees for 15 minutes. Uncover; bake for 15 to 20 minutes longer. Serve warm, plain or with whipped instant nonfat dry milk. Yield: 6 servings.

Mrs. George Sanders, Hoffman Pub. School
Hoffman, Minnesota

Low-Calorie

BLUSHING-PINK APPLES

8 med. apples
1 12-oz. can low-calorie red pop

Core apples; peel skin from the top third of each apple. Arrange in 9 x 12 1/2-inch glass baking dish; pour pop over apples. Bake at 400 degrees for about 30 minutes or until apples are soft. Yield: 8 servings.

Mrs. Rebecca Orrin, Wilkinson Jr. H.S.
Madison Heights, Michigan

APPLE CRISP WITH WHIPPED CREAM

4 c. sliced peeled apples
1 tbsp. lemon juice
Dash of cinnamon
Artificial sweetener
2 tbsp. melted margarine
1/2 c. graham cracker crumbs
1/2 c. toasted bread crumbs
Mock Whipped Cream

Arrange apples in shallow 1 1/2-quart baking dish. Sprinkle with lemon juice, cinnamon and sweetener to equal 3/4 cup sugar. Combine margarine, crumbs and sweetener to equal 2 tablespoons sugar, tossing with fork until blended. Sprinkle crumb mixture over apples. Pour 3/4 cup hot water over crumbs; cover. Bake at 400 degrees for 15 minutes. Uncover; bake for 10 minutes longer or until apples are tender. Serve warm with Mock Whipped Cream. Yield: 8 servings/105 calories per serving.

Mock Whipped Cream

1/2 c. dry milk crystals
2 tbsp. lemon juice
Non-nutritive sweetener

Combine milk crystals, 1/2 cup ice water, lemon juice and sweetener to equal 1 1/2 cups sugar; beat until stiff.

Mrs. L.A. Boyd, Lockett H.S.
Vernon, Texas

FLUFFY APPLE SNOW

1 1/2 lb. apples
1 strip of lemon rind
3 or 5 saccharin tablets
2 egg whites, stiffly beaten

Peel and slice apples; cook to a pulp with lemon rind and a small amount of water. Add saccharin; let cool. Remove lemon rind. Fold egg whites into apple mixture; place in serving dish. Decorate as desired with lemon slices, chopped apple, crystallized ginger or sponge fingers. Yield: 4 servings.

Mrs. Mitzi Funk, Del Norte H.S.
Crescent City, California

COLD APPLESAUCE WHIP

1 tbsp. lemon juice
1/2 c. skim milk powder
Sucaryl to taste
1/4 tsp. vanilla extract
2 1/2 c. cold thick applesauce

Combine 2/3 cup water and lemon juice in bowl. Sprinkle with skim milk powder; whip until very stiff. Add Sucaryl and vanilla. Fold in applesauce. Pile into serving dishes; serve immediately. Yield: 6 servings.

Vesta M. Wicke, Augusta H.S.
Augusta, Kansas

CHERRIES FLAMBE

1 1-lb. can water-pack sour cherries
1 tbsp. cornstarch
1 tbsp. Sucaryl
1/4 tsp. salt
1/4 tsp. red food coloring
1 tsp. orange extract
Vanilla ice milk

Combine liquid from cherries with cornstarch in chafing dish to make a smooth paste. Add 1/2 cup water and remaining ingredients except cherries, orange extract and ice milk; cook until mixture thickens, stirring constantly. Add cherries. Pour orange extract into teaspoon; ignite. Spoon flame over cherries; serve over ice milk. Yield: 6 servings.

Mrs. Lucille Mosher, Fergus Falls Jr. H.S.
Fergus Falls, Minnesota

FIGURE CONTROL CHERRY COBBLER

1 1-lb. 7 1/2-oz. jar Figure Control
       Cherries in dessert sauce
1 c. biscuit mix
2 tbsp. nonfat dry milk
3/4 tsp. artificial sweetener
Cinnamon

Place cherries in skillet; heat to boiling point. Combine biscuit mix, dry milk, 6 tablespoons water and sweetener; drop by spoonfuls onto hot cherries. Sprinkle with cinnamon; cover. Simmer for about 20 minutes. Yield: 8 servings/141 calories per serving.

Mrs. Opal Alexander, Sundown H.S.
Sundown, Texas

BANANAS WITH STRAWBERRIES

2 med. bananas
1/2 c. strawberries
Juice of 1 orange
1 tbsp. raisins

Peel and slice bananas. Combine bananas and strawberries in small bowl; moisten with orange juice. Garnish with raisins; chill in refrigerator until ready to serve. Yield: 2 servings/150 calories per serving.

Mrs. Mary Jo Lyle, Putnam Co. H.S.
Eatonton, Georgia

FROSTED BLUEBERRY DESSERT

1 c. vanilla wafer crumbs
1/4 c. margarine, softened
4 oz. low-calorie cream cheese
2 sm. eggs, beaten
1 1/2 tsp. vanilla extract
1/4 c. plus 2 tbsp. sugar
Low-calorie blueberry pie filling
Dream Whip topping

Combine crumbs and margarine; press in 8-inch square cake pan to form crust. Mix cream cheese with next 3 ingredients until smooth; pour into crumb crust. Bake at 350 degrees for 20 minutes. Cool; add pie filling. Spread Dream Whip over top. Yield: 9 servings.

Mrs. Gwen Whitehead, Green Valley H.S.
Green Valley, Illinois

DANISH CRANBERRY FRUIT SOUP

1/4 c. quick-cooking tapioca
2 tsp. Sweet-10
1/8 tsp. salt
2 c. dietetic cranberry juice

Combine tapioca, Sweet-10, salt, cranberry juice and 1/2 cup water in saucepan; mix well. Let stand for 15 minutes. Cook, stirring constantly, over medium heat until mixture comes to a boil. Remove from heat. Let cool, stirring once after 20 minutes. Cover; chill thoroughly. Serve in soup cups or dessert dishes. Yield: 6 servings/47 calories per serving.

Mrs. Sara Webster, Logansport H.S.
Logansport, Indiana

FRESH FRUIT COMPOTE

1 apple, cut into sm. pieces
1 banana, cut into sm. pieces
1 orange, cut into sm. pieces
1/4 lb. seedless green grapes
Fresca or low-calorie beverage
Low-calorie sherbet

Mix fruits together lightly; place in serving dishes. Pour a small amount of the Fresca over each serving; top with 1 teaspoon sherbet. Yield: 6-8 servings.

Elsie Clements, Corbett H.S.
Corbett, Oregon

GELATIN FRUIT JELLY

1 tsp. unflavored gelatin
2 tbsp. Certo
1 c. fruit juice or fruit
2 tsp. artificial sweetener
1 tsp. sugar

Soak gelatin in 1 tablespoon cold water. Add Certo to juice; boil for 1 minute. Add gelatin mixture, sweetener and sugar; stir until well mixed. Let cool. Freeze in small containers. Remove only the amount of jelly that can be used in 3 or 4 days.

Mrs. Lois E. Boy
Unified School District No. 494
Syracuse, Kansas

LOW-CALORIE GRAPE JELLY

1 tbsp. unflavored gelatin
3 c. unsweetened grape juice
2 tbsp. liquid Sweet-10
2 tbsp. lemon juice

Soften gelatin in 1/4 cup grape juice. Heat remaining grape juice with Sweet-10 and lemon juice; stir in softened gelatin. Bring to a rolling boil. Pour into sterilized jars; cover tightly. Store in refrigerator. Yield: 2 pints/7 calories per tablespoon.

Marion A. Winn, Millbrook Central School
Millbrook, New York

CHOCO-CHERRY MOLD

1 8-oz. can artificially sweetened cherries
1 env. low-calorie cherry gelatin
1 10-oz. can chocolate fudge Sego

Drain cherries, reserving 1/2 cup juice. Bring juice to a boil in a saucepan. Add gelatin; stir until dissolved. Stir in Sego. Chill until thick, but not firm. Stir in cherries. Pour into a 2-cup mold. Chill until firm. Unmold. Yield: 4 servings/79 calories per serving.

Photograph for this recipe on page 204.

CAN SIZE CHART

8 oz. can or jar ....1 c.
10 1/2 oz. can (picnic can) ....1 1/4 c.
12 oz. can (vacuum) ....1 1/2 c.
14-16 oz. or No. 300 can ....1 1/4 c.
16-17 oz. can or jar
  or No. 303 can or jar ....2 c.
1 lb. 4 oz. or 1 pt. 2 fl. oz.
  or No. 2 can or jar ....2 1/2 c.

1 lb. 13 oz. can or jar
  or No. 2 1/2 can or jar ....3 1/2 c.
1 qt. 14 fl. oz. or 3 lb. 3 oz.
  or 46 oz. can ....5 3/4 c.
6 1/2 to 7 1/2 lb.
  or No. 10 can .... 12-13 c.

EQUIVALENT CHART

3 tsp. .... 1 tbsp.
2 tbsp. .... 1/8 c.
4 tbsp. .... 1/4 c.
8 tbsp. .... 1/2 c.
16 tbsp. ....1 c.
5 tbsp. + 1 tsp. .... 1/3 c.
12 tbsp. .... 3/4 c.
4 oz. .... 1/2 c.
8 oz. ....1 c.
16 oz. ....1 lb.
1 oz. .... 2 tbsp. fat or liquid
2 c. ....1 pt.

2 pt. ....1 qt.
1 qt. ....4 c.
5/8 c. ....1/2 c. + 2 tbsp.
7/8 c. ....3/4 c. + 2 tbsp.
1 jigger ....1 1/2 fl. oz.(3 tbsp.)
2 c. fat ....1 lb.
1 lb. butter .... 2 c. or 4 sticks
2 c. sugar ....1 lb.
2 2/3 c. powdered sugar ....1 lb.
2 2/3 c. brown sugar ....1 lb.
4 c. sifted flour ....1 lb.
4 1/2 c. cake flour ....1 lb.

3 1/2 c. unsifted whole wheat flour ....1 lb.
8 to 10 egg whites ....1 c.
12 to 14 egg yolks ....1 c.
1 c. unwhipped cream ....2 c. whipped
1 lb. shredded American cheese ....4 c.
1/4 lb. crumbled blue cheese ....1 c.
1 chopped med. onion ....1/2 c. pieces
1 lemon .... 3 tbsp. juice
1 lemon .... 1 tsp. grated peel
1 orange ....1/3 c. juice
1 orange .... about 2 tsp. grated peel
1 lb. unshelled walnuts ....1 1/2 to 1 3/4 c. shelled
1 lb. unshelled almonds ....3/4 to 1 c. shelled
4 oz. (1 to 1 1/4 c.) uncooked macaroni .... 2 1/4 c. cooked
7 oz. spaghetti ....4 c. cooked
4 oz. (1 1/2 to 2 c.) uncooked noodles ....2 c. cooked
28 saltine crackers ....1 c. crumbs
4 slices bread ....1 c. crumbs
14 square graham crackers ....1 c. crumbs
22 vanilla wafers ....1 c. crumbs

SUBSTITUTIONS FOR A MISSING INGREDIENT

1 square *chocolate* (1 ounce) = 3 or 4 tablespoons cocoa plus 1/2 tablespoon fat.
1 tablespoon *cornstarch* (for thickening) = 2 tablespoons flour.
1 cup sifted *all-purpose flour* = 1 cup plus 2 tablespoons sifted cake flour.
1 cup sifted *cake flour* = 1 cup minus 2 tablespoons sifted all-purpose flour.
1 teaspoon *baking powder* = 1/4 teaspoon baking soda plus 1/2 teaspoon cream of tartar.
1 cup *sour milk* — 1 cup sweet milk into which 1 tablespoon vinegar or lemon juice has been stirred; or
        1 cup buttermilk (let stand for 5 minutes).

SUBSTITUTIONS FOR A MISSING INGREDIENT

1 cup *sweet milk* = 1 cup sour milk or buttermilk plus 1/2 teaspoon baking soda.

1 cup *canned tomatoes* = about 1 1/3 cups cut-up fresh tomatoes, simmered 10 minutes.

3/4 cup *cracker crumbs* = 1 cup bread crumbs.

1 cup *cream, sour, heavy* = 1/3 cup butter and 2/3 cups milk in any sour milk recipe.

1 cup *cream, sour, thin* = 3 tablespoons butter and 3/4 cup milk in sour milk recipe.

1 cup *molasses* = 1 cup honey.

1 teaspoon *dried herbs* = 1 tablespoon fresh herbs.

1 *whole egg* = 2 egg yolks for custards.

1/2 cup *evaporated milk* and 1/2 cup *water* or 1 cup *reconstituted nonfat dry milk* and 1 tablespoon *butter* = 1 cup whole milk.

1 package *active dry yeast* = 1 cake compressed yeast.

1 tablespoon *instant minced onion, rehydrated* = 1 small fresh onion.

1 tablespoon *prepared mustard* = 1 teaspoon dry mustard.

1/8 teaspoon *garlic powder* = 1 small pressed clove of garlic

METRIC CONVERSION CHARTS FOR THE KITCHEN

VOLUME

1 tsp.	4.9 cc	2 c.	473.4 cc
1 tbsp.	14.7 cc	1 fl. oz.	29.5 cc
1/3 c.	28.9 cc	4 oz.	118.3 cc
1/8 c.	29.5 cc	8 oz.	236.7 cc
1/4 c.	59.1 cc	1 pt.	473.4 cc
1/2 c.	118.3 cc	1 qt.	.946 liters
3/4 c.	177.5 cc	1 gal.	3.7 liters
1 c.	236.7 cc		

CONVERSION FACTORS:

Liters	X	1.056	=	Liquid Quarts
Quarts	X	0.946	=	Liters
Liters	X	0.264	=	Gallons
Gallons	X	3.785	=	Liters
Fluid Ounces	X	29.563	=	Cubic Centimeters
Cubic Centimeters	X	0.034	=	Fluid Ounces
Cups	X	236.575	=	Cubic Centimeters
Tablespoons	X	14.797	=	Cubic Centimeters
Teaspoons	X	4.932	=	Cubic Centimeters
Bushels	X	0.352	=	Hectoliters
Hectoliters	X	2.837	=	Bushels
Ounces (Avoir.)	X	28.349	=	Grams
Grams	X	0.035	=	Ounces
Pounds	X	0.454	=	Kilograms
Kilograms	X	2.205	=	Pounds

WEIGHT

1 dry oz.	28.3 Grams
1 lb.	.454 Kilograms

LIQUID MEASURE AND METRIC EQUIVALENT

(NEAREST CONVENIENT EQUIVALENTS)

CUPS SPOONS	QUARTS OUNCES	METRIC EQUIVALENTS
1 teaspoon	1/6 ounce	.5 milliliters
		5 grams
2 teaspoons	1/3 ounce	10 milliliters
		10 grams
1 tablespoon	1/2 ounce	15 milliliters
		15 grams
3 1/3 tablespoons	1 3/4 ounces	50 milliliters
1/4 cup (4 tablespoons)	2 ounces	60 milliliters
1/3 cup (5 1/3 tablespoons)	2 2/3 ounces	79 milliliters
1/3 cup plus 1 tablespoon	3 1/2 ounces	100 milliliters
1/2 cup (8 tablespoons)	4 ounces	118 milliliters
1 cup (16 tablespoons)	8 ounces	1/4 liter 236 milliliters
2 cups	1 pint 16 ounces	1/2 liter less 1 1/2 tablespoons 473 milliliters
2 cups plus 2 1/2 tablespoons	17 ounces	1/2 liter
4 cups	1 quart 32 ounces	946 milliliters
4 1/3 cups	1 quart, 2 ounces	1 liter 1000 milliliters

CONVERSION FORMULAS:

To convert Centigrade to Fahrenheit: multiply by 9, divide by 5, add 32.

To convert Fahrenheit to Centigrade: subtract 32, multiply by 5, divide by 9.

DRY MEASURE AND METRIC EQUIVALENT

(MOST CONVENIENT APPROXIMATION)

POUNDS AND OUNCES	METRIC	POUNDS AND OUNCES	METRIC
1/6 ounce	.5 grams	1/4 pound (4 ounces)	114 grams
1/3 ounce	10 grams	4 1/8 ounces	125 grams
1/2 ounce	15 grams	1/2 pound (8 ounces)	227 grams
1 ounce	30 grams (28.35)	3/4 pound (12 ounces)	250 grams
		1 pound (16 ounces)	454 grams
1 3/4 ounces	50 grams	1.1 pounds	500 grams
2 2/3 ounces	75 grams	2.2 pounds	1 kilogram 1000 grams
3 1/2 ounces	100 grams		

NUTRITION LABELING

Modern Americans have become very diet and nutrition conscious, and in response, commercial food producers have begun to include nutrition information on the labels of their products. Nutrition Labeling is an invaluable service in many ways. There are many persons on special diets (diabetic, low-sodium, low-cholesterol) who must know the specifics of the foods they eat. However, whether the homemaker cooks for a special diet or not, Nutrition Labeling on the foods she buys helps her to know the part they play in her overall nutrition and menu planning.

The United States Food and Drug Administration has determined how much of every important nutrient is needed by the average healthy person in the United States, well known as the Recommended Daily Dietary Allowance (RDA). The United States RDA reflects the highest amounts of nutritives for all ages and sexes. Pregnant and nursing women, as well as persons with special dietary needs, should consult their doctors for any recommended increases or decreases in their daily diet.

UNITED STATES RECOMMENDED DAILY ALLOWANCE CHART

Protein	45-65 Grams
Carbohydrates	125 Grams
Vitamin A	5,000 International Units
Thiamine (Vitamin B_1)	1.5 Milligrams
Riboflavin (Vitamin B_2)	1.7 Milligrams
Vitamin B_6	2 Milligrams
Vitamin B_{12}	6 Micrograms
Folic Acid (B Vitamin)	0.4 Milligrams
Pantothenic Acid (B Vitamin)	10 Milligrams
Vitamin C (Ascorbic Acid)	55-60 Milligrams
Vitamin D	400 International Units
Vitamin E	30 International Units
Iron	18 Milligrams
Calcium	1 Gram
Niacin (Nicotinic Acid)	13-20 Milligrams
Magnesium	400 Milligrams
Zinc	15 Milligrams
Copper	2 Milligrams
Phosphorus	1 Gram
Iodine	150 Micrograms
Biotin (Vitamin H)	0.3 Milligrams

IMPORTANT NUTRIENTS YOUR DIET REQUIRES

PROTEIN

Why? Absolutely essential in building, repairing and renewing of all body tissue. Helps body resist infection. Builds enzymes and hormones, helps form and maintain body fluids.

Where? Milk, eggs, lean meats, poultry, fish, soybeans, peanuts, dried peas and beans, grains and cereals.

CARBOHYDRATES

Why? Provide needed energy for bodily functions, provide warmth, as well as fuel for brain and nerve tissues. Lack of carbohydrates will cause body to use protein for energy rather than for repair and building.

Where? Sugars: sugar, table syrups, jellies and jams, etc., as well as dried and fresh fruits. Starches: cereals, pasta, rice, corn, dried beans and peas, potatoes, stem and leafy vegetables, and milk.

FATS

Why? Essential in the use of fat soluble vitamins (A, D, E, K), and fatty acids. Have more than twice the concentrated energy than equal amount of carbohydrate for body energy and warmth.

Where? Margarine, butter, cooking oil, mayonnaise, vegetable shortening, milk, cream, ice cream, cheese, meat, fish, eggs, poultry, chocolate, coconut, nuts.

VITAMIN A

Why? Needed for healthy skin and hair, as well as for healthy, infection-resistant mucous membranes.

Where? Dark green, leafy and yellow vegetables, liver. Deep yellow fruits, such as apricots and cantaloupe. Milk, cheese, eggs, as well as fortified margarine and butter.

THIAMINE (VITAMIN B_1)

Why? Aids in the release of energy of foods, as well as in normal appetite and digestion. Promotes healthy nervous system.

Where? Pork, liver, kidney. Dried peas and beans. Whole grain and enriched breads and cereals.

RIBOFLAVIN (VITAMIN B_2)

Why? Helps to oxidize foods. Promotes healthy eyes and skin, especially around mouth and eyes. Prevents pellagra.

Where? Meat, especially liver and kidney, as well as milk, cheese, eggs. Dark green leafy vegetables. Enriched bread and cereal products. Almonds, dried peas and beans.

VITAMIN B_6

Why? Helps protein in building body tissues. Needed for healthy nerves, skin and digestion. Also helps body to use fats and carbohydrates for energy.

Where? Milk, wheat germ, whole grain and fortified cereals. Liver and kidney, pork and beef.

VITAMIN B_{12}

Why? Aids body in formation of red blood cells, as well as in regular work of all body cells.

Where? Lean meats, milk, eggs, fish, cheese, as well as liver and kidney.

FOLIC ACID

Why? Aids in healthy blood system, as well as intestinal tract. Helps to prevent anemia.

Where? Green leaves of vegetables and herbs, as well as liver and milk. Wheat germ and soybeans.

PANTOTHENIC ACID

Why? Aids in proper function of digestive system.

Where? Liver, kidney and eggs. Peanuts and molasses. Broccoli and other vegetables.

VITAMIN C (ASCORBIC ACID)

Why? Promotes proper bone and tooth formation. Helps body utilize iron and resist infection. Strengthens blood vessels. Lack of it causes bones to heal slowly, failure of wounds to heal and fragile vessels to bleed easily.

Where?   Citrus fruits, cantaloupe and strawberries. Broccoli, kale, green peppers, raw cabbage, sweet potatoes, cauliflower, tomatoes.

VITAMIN D
Why?   Builds strong bones and teeth by aiding utilization of calcium and phosphorus.
Where? Fortified milk, fish liver oils, as well as salmon, tuna and sardines. Also eggs.

VITAMIN E
Why?   Needed in maintaining red blood cells.
Where? Whole grain cereals, wheat germ, and beans and peas, lettuce and eggs.

IRON
Why?   Used with protein for hemoglobin production. Forms nucleus of each cell, and helps them to use oxygen.
Where? Kidney and liver, as well as shellfish, lean meats, and eggs. Deep yellow and dark green leafy vegetables. Dried peas, beans, fruits. Potatoes, whole grain cereals and bread. Enriched flour and bread. Dark molasses.

CALCIUM
Why?   Builds and renews bones, teeth, other tissues, as well as aiding in the proper function of muscles, nerves and heart. Controls normal blood clotting. With protein, aids in oxidation of foods.
Where? Milk and milk products, excluding butter. Dark green vegetables, oysters, clams and sardines.

NIACIN
Why?   Helps body to oxidize food. Aids in digestion, and helps to keep nervous system and skin healthy.
Where? Peanuts, liver, tuna, as well as fish, poultry and lean meats. Enriched breads, cereals and peas.

MAGNESIUM
Why?   Aids nervous system and sleep.
Where? Almonds, peanuts, raisins and prunes. Vegetables, fruits, milk, fish and meats.

ZINC
Why?   Needed for cell formation.
Where? Nuts and leafy green vegetables. Shellfish.

COPPER
Why?   Helps body to utilize iron.
Where? Vegetables and meats.

PHOSPHORUS
Why?   Maintains normal blood clotting function, as well as builds bones, teeth and nerve tissue. Aids in utilization of sugar and fats.
Where? Oatmeal and whole wheat products. Eggs and cheese, dried beans and peas. Nuts, lean meats, and fish and poultry.

IODINE
Why?   Enables thyroid gland to maintain proper body metabolism.
Where? Iodized salt. Saltwater fish and seafood. Milk and vegetables.

BIOTIN (VITAMIN H)
Why?   Helps to maintain body cells.
Where? Eggs and liver. Any foods rich in Vitamin B.

Index

Index

Index

Index

Index

BLACK AND WHITE PHOTOGRAPH RECIPES

COLOR PHOTOGRAPH RECIPES

PHOTOGRAPHY CREDITS

Campbell Soup Company; J. M. Smucker Company; Sunkist Growers, Inc.; Western Iceberg Lettuce, Inc.; The Banana Bunch; The Idaho Potato Commission; The United Fresh Fruit and Vegetable Association; California Strawberry Advisory Board; American Home Foods; National Dairy Council; Department of Interior, Fish and Wildlife Service; Green Giant Company; and Pet, Inc.

Favorite Recipes®
of Home Economics Teachers
COOKBOOKS

Add to
Your Cookbook Collection
Select from These ALL-TIME
Favorites

BOOK TITLE	ITEM NUMBER
Dieting To Stay Fit (1978) 200 Pages	01449
Desserts — Revised Edition (1962) 304 Pages	01422
Our Favorite Meats (1966) 384 Pages	70114
Our Favorite Salads (1968) 384 Pages	01791
Quick and Easy Dishes — Revised Edition (1968) 256 Pages	00043
Money-Saving Cookbook (1971) 256 Pages	70092
Americana Cooking (1972) 192 Pages	70351
Poultry Cookbook (1973) 192 Pages	70319
New Holiday (1974) 200 Pages	70343
Canning, Preserving and Freezing (1975) 200 Pages	70084
Life-Saver Cookbook (1976) 200 Pages	70335
Foods From Foreign Nations (1977) 200 Pages	01279

FOR ORDERING INFORMATION
Write to:
Favorite Recipes Press
P. O. Box 77
Nashville, Tennessee 37202

BOOKS OFFERED SUBJECT TO AVAILABILITY.